ALSO BY VICTOR BOCKRIS

Keith Richards: The Biography
The Life and Death of Andy Warhol
Uptight: The Velvet Underground Story
Making Tracks: The Rise of Blondie
With William Burroughs: A Report from the Bunker
Ali: Fighter, Poet, Prophet

Transformer

The Lou Reed Story

Victor Bockris

Simon & Schuster

New York
London
Toronto
Sydney
Tokyo
Singapore

SIMON & SCHUSTER
Rockefeller Center
1230 Avenue of the Americas
New York, NY 10020

Copyright © 1994 by Victor Bockris
First published in Great Britain by Hutchinson

SIMON & SCHUSTER and colophon are registered trademarks
of Simon & Schuster Inc.

Designed by Hyun Joo Kim

Manufactured in the United States of America

10   9   8   7   6   5   4   3   2   1

Library of Congress Cataloging-in-Publication Data
Brockris, Victor
 Transformer: the Lou Reed story/Victor Bockris.
  p. cm.
 Includes bibliographical references (p.) and index.
  1. Reed, Lou. 2. Rock musicians—United States—Biogra-
phy.
 I. Title.
 ML420.R299B6 1995
 782.42166'092—dc20
 [B]   95-13587
              CIP
              MN

ISBN 0-684-80366-6

This book is dedicated to

STELLAN HOLM,

GERARD MALANGA, BOB GRUEN, AND

LEGS MCNEIL.

CONTENTS

ACKNOWLEDGMENTS

Thanks for input and enlightenment to Andy Warhol, Lisa Krug, Andrew Wylie, Albert Goldman, Robert Dowling, Gerard Malanga, Syracuse University Rare Book Room, the staff of Creedmore Mental Hospital, Paul Sidey, Ingrid von Essen, Dawn Fozard, Stellan Holm, Marianne Erdos, Barbara Wilkinson, Jessica Berens, Chantal Rosset, Elvira Peake, Anita Pallenberg, Marianne Faithfull, Allen Ginsberg, David Dalton, Miles, Jeff Goldberg, Ira Cohen, Rosemary Bailey, Phillip Booth, Allen Hyman, Andy Hyman, Richard Mishkin, Bob Quine, Raymond Foye, Diego Cortez, Clinton Heylin, Jan van Willegen, John Holmstrom, Legs McNeil, Bobbie Bristol, Ann Patty, Carol Wood, John Shebar, Charles Shaar Murray, Mick Farren, Michael Watts, Ernie Thormahlen, Gisella Freisinger, William Burroughs, John Giorno, Stewart Meyer, Terrence Sellers, Chris Stein, Bob Gruen, David Bourdon, Jonathan Cott, Ed and Laura DeGrazia, Bobby Grossman, Art and Kym Garfunkel, Patti Giordano, Stephen Gaines, Lee Hill, Marcia Resnick, Michelle Loud, Terry Noel, Glenn O'Brien, Robert Palmer, Rosebud, Geraldine Smith, Walter Stedding, David Schmidlapp, Lynn Tillman, Hope Ruff, James Carpenter, Tei Carpenter, Toshiko Mori, Gus Van Sant, Mary Woronov, Matt Snow, Roger Ely, Paul Katz, Gayle Sherman, Cassie Jones, Dominick Anfuso, J. P. Jones, James Grauerholz, Terry and Gail Southern, Heiner Bastian, Danny Fields, Dr. J. Gross, Steve Bloom, Bridget Love, Mary Harron, Jeff Butler, Solveig Wilder, Rick Blume, Lenny Kaye, Tony Zanetta, Doug Yule, Tony Conrad, Richard Meltzer, Nick Kent, Richard Witts, Nick Tosches, Kurt Loder, Julie Burchill, and John Wilcock.

When I think of Lou, I remember what a romantic he was. And fun. And then when he had you hooked with that sweetness, he had to destroy you in order to survive. He couldn't help himself, like any predator. He always warned his prey, partly as a challenge and partly to cover his ass for any later moral responsibility. What made the process interesting was the fact that it was an ongoing intellectual and artistic work—a performance piece.

—An acquaintance

Chapter One

KILL YOUR SON

ELECTROSHOCK: 1959—60

I don't have a personality.

—Lou Reed

NINETEEN FIFTY-NINE WAS A BAD YEAR FOR LOU, SEVENTEEN, WHO HAD been studying his bad-boy role ever since he'd worn a black armband to school when the No. 1 R&B singer Johnny Ace shot himself back in 1954. Now, five years later, the bad Lou grabbed the chance to drive everyone in his family crazy. Tyrannically presiding over their middle-class home, he slashed screeching chords on his electric guitar, practiced an effeminate way of walking, drew his sister aside in conspiratorial conferences, and threatened to throw the mother of all moodies if everyone didn't pay complete attention to him.

That spring, Lou's conservative parents, Sidney and Toby Reed, sent their son to a psychiatrist, requesting that he cure Lou of homosexual feelings and alarming mood swings. The doctor prescribed a then popular course of treatment recently undergone by, among many others, the British writer Malcolm Lowry and the famous American poet Delmore Schwartz. He explained that Lou would benefit from a series of visits to Creedmore State Psychiatric Hospital. There, he would be given an electroshock treatment three times a week for eight weeks. After that, he would need intensive postshock therapy for some time.

In 1959 you did not question your doctor. "His parents didn't want to make him suffer," explained a family friend. "They wanted him to be healthy. They were just trying to be parents, so they wanted him to behave." The Reeds nervously accepted the diagnosis.

Creedmore State Psychiatric Hospital was located in a hideous stretch of Long Island wasteland. The large state-run facility was equipped to handle some six thousand patients. Its Building 60, a majestically spooky edifice that stood eighteen stories high and spanned some five hundred feet, loomed over the landscape like a monstrous pterodactyl. Hundreds of corridors led to padlocked wards, offices, and operating theaters, all painted a bland, spaced-out cream. Bars and wire mesh covered the windows inside and out. Among the creepiest of these cells was the Electro Shock Treatment Center.

Into this unit one early summer day walked the cocky, troubled Lou. He was escorted through a labyrinth of corridors, unaware, he later claimed, that his first psychiatric treatment session at the hospital would consist of volts of electricity pulsing through his brain. Each door he passed through would be unlocked by a guard, then locked again behind him. Finally he was locked into the electroshock unit and made to change into a scanty hospital robe. As he sat uncomfortably in the waiting room with a group of people who looked to him like vegetables, Lou caught his first glimpse of the operating room. A thick, milky white metal door studded with rivets swung open revealing an unconscious victim who looked dead. The body was wheeled out on a stretcher and into a recovery room by a stone-faced nurse. Lou suddenly found himself next in line for shock treatment.

He was wheeled into the small, bare operating room, furnished with a table next to a hunk of metal from which two thick wires dangled. He was strapped onto the table. Lou stared at the overhead fluorescent light bars as the sedative started to take effect. The nurse applied a salve to his temples and stuck a clamp into his mouth so that he would not swallow his tongue. Seconds later, conductors at the end of the thick wires were attached to his head. The last thing that filled his vision before he lapsed into unconsciousness was a blinding white light.

In the 1950s, the voltage administered to each patient was not adjusted, as it is today, for size or mental condition. Everybody got the same dose. Thus, the vulnerable seventeen-year-old received the same degree of electricity as would have been given to a heavyweight ax-murderer. The current searing through Lou's body altered the firing pattern of his central nervous system, producing a minor seizure, which, although horrid to watch, in fact caused no pain since he was unconscious. When Lou revived several minutes later, however, a deathly pallor clung to his mouth, he was spitting, and his eyes were tearing and red. Like a character in a story by one of his favorite writers, Edgar Allan Poe, the alarmed patient now found himself prostrate in a dim waiting room under the gaze of a stern nurse.

"Relax, please!" she instructed the terrified boy. "We're only trying to help you. Will someone get another pillow and prop him up. One, two, three, four. Relax." As his body stopped twitching, the clamp was removed, and Lou regained full consciousness. Over the next half hour, as he struggled to return, he was panicked to discover his memory had gone. According to experts, memory loss was an unfortunate side effect of shock therapy, although whatever brain changes occurred were considered reversible, and persisting brain damage was rare. As Reed left the hospital, he recalled, he thought that he had "become a vegetable."

"You can't read a book because you get to page seventeen and you have to go right back to page one again. Or if you put the book down for an hour and went back to pick up where you started, you didn't remember the pages you read. You had to start all over. If you walked around the block, you forgot where you were." For a man with plans to become, among other things, a writer, this was a terrible threat.

The aftereffects of shock therapy put Lou, as Ken Kesey wrote in *One Flew Over the Cuckoo's Nest,* "in that foggy, jumbled blur which is a whole lot like the ragged edge of sleep, the grey zone between light and dark, or between sleeping and waking or living and dying." Lou's nightmares were dominated by the sad, off-white color of hospitals. As he put it in a poem, "How does one fall asleep / When movies of the night await, / And me eternally done in." Now he was afraid to go to sleep. Insomnia would become a lifelong habit.

Lou suffered through the eight weeks of shock treatments haunted by the fear that in an attempt to obliterate the abnormal from his personality, his parents had destroyed him. The death of the great jazz vocalist Billie Holiday in July, and the haunting refrain of Paul Anka's no. 1 teen-angst ballad, "Lonely Boy," heightened his sense of distance and loss.

According to Lou, the shock treatments helped eradicate any feeling of compassion he might have had and handed him a fragmented approach. "I think everybody has a number of personalities," he told a friend, to whom he showed a small notebook in which he had written, " 'From Lou #3 to Lou #8—Hi!' You wake up in the morning and say, 'Wonder which of them is around today?' You find out which one and send him out. Fifteen minutes later, someone else shows up. That's why if there's no one left to talk to, I can always listen to a couple of them talking in my head. I can talk to myself."

At the end of the eight-week treatment, Lou was put on strong tran-quilizing medication. "I HATE PSYCHIATRISTS. I HATE PSYCHI-ATRISTS. I HATE PSYCHIATRISTS," he would later write in one of his best poems, "People Must Have to Die for the Music." But in his heart he felt betrayed. If his parents had really loved him, they would never have allowed the shock treatments.

LEWIS ALAN REED WAS BORN ON MARCH 2, 1942, AT BETH EL HOSPITAL in Brooklyn, New York. His father, Sidney George Reed, a diminutive, black-haired man who had changed his name from Rabinowitz, was a tax accountant. His mother, Toby Futterman Reed, seven years younger than her husband, a former beauty queen, was a housewife. Both parents were native New Yorkers who in a decade would move to the upper-middle class of Freeport, Long Island. Lewis developed into a small, thin child with kinky black hair, buck teeth, and a sensitive, nervous disposition. By that time, his mother, the model of a Jewish mother, had shaped her beauty-queen personality into an extremely nice, polite, formal persona that Lou later criticized in "Standing On Ceremony" ("a song I wrote for my mother"). She wanted her son to have the best opportunities in life and dreamed that one day he would become a doctor or a lawyer.

The emotional milieu that dominated Lewis's life throughout his child-hood was a kind of suffocating love. "Gentiles don't understand about Jewish love," wrote Albert Goldman in his biography of one of Lewis's role models, Lenny Bruce. "They can't grasp a positive, affectionate emotion that is so crossed with negative impulses, so qualified with an-tagonistic feelings that it teeters at every second on a fulcrum of ambiv-alence. Jewish love is love, all right, but it's mingled with such a big slug of pity, cut with so much condescension, embittered with so much tacit disapproval, disapprobation, even disgust, that when you are the object of this love, you might as well be an object of hate. Jewish love made Kafka feel like a cockroach. . . ."

In the opinion of one family friend, "Lou's mother had the Jewish-mother syndrome with her first child. They overwatch their first child. The kid says watch me, watch me, watch me. You can't watch them enough, and they're never happy, because they've spent so much time being watched that's what they expect. His mother was not off to work every morning, the mothers of this era were full-time mothers. Full-time watchers. They set up a scenario that could never be equaled in later life."

When Lewis was five, the Reeds had a second child, Elizabeth, affectionately known as Bunny. While Lou doted on his little sister, her arrival was also cause for alarm. His mother's love had become a trap built around emotional blackmail: First, since the mother's happiness depends upon the son's happiness, it becomes a responsibility for the son to be happy. Second, since the mother's love is all-powerful, it is impossible for the son to return an equal amount of love, therefore he is perennially guilty. Then, with the arrival of the sister, the mother's love can no longer be total. All three elements combine to put the son in an impossible-to-fulfill situation, making him feel impotent, confused, and angry. The trap is sealed by an inability to talk about such matters so that all the bitter hostility boiling below the surface is carefully contained until the son marries a woman who replaces his mother. Then it explodes in her face.

Goldman could have been describing Reed as much as Bruce when he concluded, "The sons develop into twisted personalities, loving where they should hate and hating where they should love. They attach themselves to women who hurt them and treat with contempt the women who offer them simple love. They often display great talents in their work, but as men they have curiously ineffective characters."

The Reeds moved from an apartment in Brooklyn to their house in Freeport back in 1953—the year before rock began. Freeport, a town of just under thirty thousand inhabitants at the time, lay on the Atlantic coast, on the Freeport and Middle Bays—protected from the ocean by the thin expanse of Long Beach. The town, one of a thousand spanning the length of Long Island, was designed and operated around the requirements of middle-class families. Though just forty-five minutes from Manhattan by car or train, it could have been a lifetime away from Brooklyn, the city the family had just deserted. In fact, with well-funded parks, beaches, social centers, and schools, Freeport was suburban utopia. Thirty-five Oakfield Avenue, on the corner of Oakfield and Maxon, was a modern single-story house in a middle-class subsection of Freeport called the Village. Most of the houses in the neighborhood were built in colonial or ranch style, but Lewis's parents owned a house that, in the 1950s, friends referred to as "the chicken coop" because of its modern, angular,

single-floor design. Though squat and odd from the outside, it was beautifully laid out and comfortable, furnished in a 1950s modern style. It also
had a two-car garage and surrounding lawn perfect for children to play on.
In fact, the wide, quiet streets doubled as baseball diamonds and football
fields when the local kids got together for a pickup game. Their neighborhood was for the most part upper-middle class and Jewish. The idea of
urban Jewish ghettos had become as abhorrent to an increasingly powerful
American Jewish population as it was to the continuing wave of European
Jewish immigrants. Many Jewish families who had prospered in postwar
New York had moved out of the city to similar suburban towns to get
away from the last vestiges of the ghetto, and to create for themselves a
middle-class life that would Americanize and integrate them. The resulting migration from New York to Long Island created a suburban middle
class in which money was equated with stability, and wealth with status
and power.

After graduating from Carolyn G. Atkinson Elementary and Freeport
Junior High, in the fall of 1956, Lewis and his friends began attending
Freeport High School (now replaced by a bunkerlike junior high). A
large, stone structure, on the corner of Pine and South Grove, with a
carved facade and expanse of lawn, the school resembled a medieval
English boarding school like Eton or Rugby. It was a ten-minute walk
from Oakfield and Maxon through the tree-lined neighborhood of Freeport Village and just over the busy Sunrise Highway. "I started out in the
Brooklyn Public School System," Lou said, "and have hated all forms of
school and authority ever since."

Lewis was surrounded by children who came from the same social and
economic background. His closest friend, Allen Hyman, who used to eat
at the Reeds' all the time and lived only a block and a half away, remembered, "The inside of their house was fifties modern, living room and
den. At least from sixth grade on my view of his upbringing was very, very
suburban middle class."

The area has a history of fostering comedians and a particular type of
humor. Freeport in the twenties was a clam-digging town with an active
Ku Klux Klan and German-American bund in nearby Lindenhurst. In the
thirties and forties, it attracted a segment of the East Coast entertainment
world, including many vaudeville talents. The vaudevillians brought with
them not only their eccentric lifestyles and corny attitudes, but the town's
first blacks, who initially worked as their servants. By the time the Reeds

got there, the show people were adding their own artistic bent to the town's musical heritage. Their immediate neighbors included Leo Carrillo, who played Pancho on the popular TV show the *Cisco Kid,* as well as Xavier Cugat's head marimba player and *Lassie's* television mother, June Lockhart. Guylanders (Long Islanders) refuse to be impressed by celebrities, dignitaries, and the airs so dear to Manhattanites. "My main memory of Lou was that he had a tremendous sense of satire," recalled high school friend John Shebar. "He had a certain irreverence that was a little out of the ordinary. Mostly he would be making fun of the teacher or doing an impersonation of some ridiculous situation in school."

Much Jewish humor took on a playfully cutting edge, intending to humble a victim in the eyes of God. Despite his modest temperament, Sidney Reed possessed a potent vein of Jewish humor, which he passed on to his son. As a child Lewis mastered the nuances of Yiddish humor, in which one is never allowed to laugh at a joke without being aware of the underlying sadness deriving from the evil inherent in human life. A family friend, recalling a visit to the Reed household, commented, "Lou's father is a wonderful wit, very dry. He's a match for Lou's wit. That's a Yiddish sense of humor, it's very much a put-down humor. A Yiddish compliment is a smack, a backhand. It's always got a little touch of mean. Like, you should never be too smart in front of God. Only God is perfect, and you should remember as pretty as you are that your head shouldn't grow like an onion if you put it in the ground. You can either take it personally, like I think Lou unfortunately did, or not."

During Lou's childhood, Sidney Reed's sense of humor had curious repercussions in the household. His well-aimed barbs often made his son feel put-down and his wife look stupid. Far from being resentful, Toby admired her husband for his obvious wit, Lou, however, was not so generous. "Lou's mother thought she was dumb," recalled a family friend. "I don't think she was dumb. Lou thought she was dumb for thinking that his father was so clever. I think it was just jealousy. I think it was the boy who wanted all of his mother's attention." According to another friend, not only was Sidney Reed a wit, but he maintained a great rapport with Toby, who loved him dearly—much to the chagrin of the possessive, selfish, and often jealous Lewis. "I remember his mother was always amused by his father. His mother admires his father and thinks it's too bad that Lou doesn't see his father the way he is."

One friend who accompanied Lou to school daily recalled that Toby

Reed smothered her son with attention and concern. "I think his mother was fairly overbearing. Just in the way he talked about her. She was like a protective Jewish mother. She wanted him to get better grades and be a doctor." Such attentions, of course, were fairly typical of full-time mothers in the family-oriented fifties. Allen Hyman never found her unusual. "I always thought Lewis's mother was a very nice person," he said. "She was very nice to me. I never viewed her as overbearing, but maybe he did. My experience of his parents was that they were very nice people. He might have perceived them as being different than they were. My mother and father knew his parents and my mother knew his mother. They were very involved parents. His mother was never anything but really nice. Whenever we went there, she was anxious to make sure we had food. His father was an accountant and seemed to be a particularly nice guy. But Lewis was always on the rebellious side, and I guess that the middle-class aspect of his life was something that he found disturbing. My experience of his relationship with his parents when we were growing up was that he was really close to them.

"His mother and father put up with a lot from him over the years, and they were always totally supportive. I got the impression that Mr. Reed was a shy man. He was certainly not Mr. Personality. When you went out with certain parents, it was fun and they were the life of the dinner and they bought you a nice meal, but when you went out with Sidney Reed, you paid. When you're a kid, that's unusual. The check would come and he'd say, 'Now your share is . . .' Which was weird. But that was his thing, he was an accountant."

Lou's father was very quiet; his mother had a lot more energy and a lot more personality. She was an attractive woman, always wore her hair short, had a lovely figure and dressed immaculately. "He'd always found the idea of copulation distasteful, especially when applied to his own origins," Lou wrote in the first sentence of the first short story he ever published. The untitled one-page piece, signed Luis Reed, was featured in a magazine, *Lonely Woman Quarterly,* that Lou edited at Syracuse University in 1962. It hit on all the dysfunctional-family themes that would run through his life and work.

His quixotic/demonic relationship to sex was clearly intense. Lou either sat at the feet of his lovers or devised ingenious ways to crush their souls. The psychology of gender was everything. No one understood Lou's ability to make those close to him feel terrible better than the special targets of his inner rage, his parents, Sidney and Toby. Lou dramatized what was in 1950s suburban America his father's benevolent dominance into Machiavellian tyranny, and viewed his mother as the victim when this was not the case at all. Friends and family were shocked by Lou's stories and songs about intra family violence and incest, claiming that nothing could have been further from the truth. In the story, Lou had his mother say, "Daddy hurt Mommy last night," and climaxed with a scene in which she seduced "Mommy's little man." Lou would later write in "How Do You Speak to an Angel" of the curse of a "harridan mother, a weak simpering father, filial love and incest." The fact is that Sidney and Toby Reed adored and enjoyed each other. After twenty years of marriage, they were still crazy about each other. As for violence, the only thing that could possibly have angered Sidney Reed was his son's meanness to his wife. However, these oedipal fantasies revealed a turbulent interior life and profound reaction to the love/hate workings of the family.

In his late thirties, Lou wrote a series of songs about his family. In one he said that he originally wanted to grow up like his "old man," but got sick of his bullying and claimed that when his father beat his mother, it made him so angry he almost choked. The song climaxed with a scene in which his father told him to act like a man. He did not, he concluded in another song, want to grow up like his "old man."

Reed's moodiness was but one indication that he was developing a vivid interior world. "By junior year in high school, he was always experimenting with his writing," Hyman reported. "He had notebooks filled with poems and short stories, and they were always on the dark side."

Reed and his friends were also drawn to athletics. Freeport High was a football school. Under the superlative coaching of Bill Ashley, the Freeport High Red Devils were the pride of the town. Lou would claim in *Coney Island Baby* that he wanted to play football for the coach, "the straightest dude I ever knew." But he had neither the size nor the athletic ability and never even tried out. Instead, during his junior year Lou joined the varsity track team. He was a good runner and was strong enough to become a pole-vaulter. (He would later comment on *Take No Prisoners* that he could only vault six feet eight inches—"a pathetic show.") Although he preferred individual events to team sports, he was known around Freeport as a very good basketball player. "Lou Reed was not only funny but he was a good athlete," recalled Hyman. "He was always kind of thin and lanky. There was a park right near our house and we used to go down and play basketball. He was very competitive and driven in most things he did. He would like to do something that didn't involve a team or require anybody else. And he was exceptionally moody all the time."

Allen's brother Andy recalled that it was typical of Lou to maintain a number of mutually exclusive friendships, which served different purposes. Allen was Lewis's conservative friend, while his friend and neighbor Eddie allowed him to exercise quite a different aspect of his personality. "Eddie was a real wacko," commented another high school friend, Carol Wood, "and he only lived about four houses away from Lou. He had all these weird ideas about outer-space Martians landing and this and that. During that time there was also a group in town that was robbing houses. They were called the Malefactors. It turned out that Eddie was one of them."

"Eddie was friendly with Lou and with me, but Eddie was a lunatic," agreed Allen Hyman. "He was the first certifiable person I have ever known. He was one of those kids who your mother would never want or allow you to hang out with because he was always getting into trouble. He had a BB gun and he would sit up in his attic and shoot people walking down the street. Lou loved him because he was as outrageous as he was, maybe more. He used to get arrested, he was insane."

"There was a desire on Lewis's part—of course I didn't know this at the time—to be accepted by the regular kinds of guys, and on the other hand he was very attracted to the degenerates," Andy recalled. "Eddie was kind of a crazy guy who was into petty theft, smoking dope at a very early age, and into all kinds of strange stuff with girls. And Lewis was into all that kind of stuff with Eddie while he was involved with my brother in another scene." Having managed to convince his parents to buy him a motorcycle, Lou would ride around the streets of Freeport in imitation of Marlon Brando.

According to his own testimony, what made Lewis different from the all-American boys in Freeport was the fact, discovered at the age of thirteen, that he was homosexual. As he explained in a 1979 interview, the recognition of his attraction to his own sex came early, as did attempts at subterfuge: "I resent it. It was a very big drag. From age thirteen on I could have been having a ball and not even thought about this shit. What a waste of time. If the forbidden thing is love, then you spend most of your time playing with hate. Who needs that? I feel I was gypped."

"There was no indication of homosexuality except in his writing," said Hyman. "Towards our senior year some of his stories and poems were starting to focus on the gay world. Sort of a fascination with the gay world, there was a lot of that imagery in his poems. And I just thought of it as his bizarre side. I would say to him, 'What is this about, why are you writing about this?' He would say, 'It's interesting. I find it interesting.' "

"I always thought that the one way kids had of getting back at their parents was to do this gender business," recalled Lou. "It was only kids trying to be outrageous. That's a lot of what rock and roll is about to some people: listening to something your parents don't like, dressing the way your parents won't like."

Throughout his adolescence, Lou was saved by his real passion, rock and roll. Lou had fallen for the new R&B sounds in 1954, when he was twelve. Almost instantly, he had started composing songs of his own. Like his fellow teenager Paul Simon, who grew up in nearby Queens, Lou formed a band and put out a single of his own composition at the age of fifteen, appropriately called "So Blue." To Lou's parents, these early signposts of a musical career were ominous. Their dreams of having their only son become a doctor or, like his father, an accountant were vanishing in the haze of pounding music and tempestuous moods. Since puberty Lou had honed a sharp edge, wounding his parents with both public and private insults. In his teens, Lou led Mr. and Mrs. Reed to believe he would become both a rock-and-roll musician *and* a homosexual—the stuff of nightmares for suburban parents of the 1950s. Actively dating girls at the time, and giving his friends every impression of being heterosexual, Lou enjoyed the shock and worry that gripped his parents at the thought of having a homosexual son. "His mother was very upset," recalled a friend. "She couldn't understand why he hated them so much, where that anger came from. At first, they had no malice, they tried to understand. But they got fed up with him."

Throughout his teens, Lou would try anything to break the tedium of life in Freeport, especially if it was considered outside conventional norms. Lou found other characters who were also desperate to elude boredom. One such moment came about indirectly through his interest in music. Every evening, the better part of the high school population of Freeport and its neighboring towns would tune into WGBB radio to hear the latest sounds, make requests, and dedicate songs. Often the volume of telephone calls to the station would be so great that the wires would get crossed, creating a teenage party-line over which friendships developed. On one occasion, Lou became friendly with a caller. "There was this girl who lived in Merrick," explained Allen Hyman. "She was fairly advanced for her time, and Lou ended up going out on a date with her. He came back from the date, and he called me up and he said, 'I've just had the most amazing experience. I took this girl to the Valley Stream drive-in and she took out a reefer.' And I said, 'Is she addicted to marijuana?' Because in those days we thought if you smoked marijuana, you were an addict. He said, 'No, it was cool. I smoked this reefer, it was really great.' "

The decades in which Lewis grew up, the fifties and early sixties, were characterized by middle-class unconsciousness and safety. Much like in the TV series *Happy Days*, most teenagers were more interested in having a good time than experiencing a wider worldview. "There was not a tremendous amount of consciousness about what was happening on the planet," commented Allen Hyman. "But Lou was always interested in questioning authority, being a little outrageous, and he was certainly a person who would be characterized as mildly eccentric."

Lou's eccentric rebellious side found a lot to gripe about within the conservative, white confines of his neighborhood. Hyman remembered that, though outwardly polite, Lou harbored a hatred of his environment that was manifested in an ill will for Allen's right-wing father. "The reason he disliked my father so much was because he always viewed him as the consummate Republican lawyer. He was very aware early on of political differences in people. We lived in an area that was Republican and conservative, and he always rebelled against that. I couldn't understand why that upset him so much. But he was always very respectful to my parents."

Mr. Reed, along with Mr. Hyman, discouraged musical careers for their sons. "He thought there were bad people involved, which there were," recalled Lou. However, as Richard Aquila wrote in *That Old Time Rock and Roll*, "adult fear of rock and roll probably says more about the paranoia and insecurity of American society in the 1950s and early 1960s than it does about rock and roll. The same adults who feared foreigners because of the expanding Cold War, and who saw the Rosenbergs and Alger Hiss as evidence of internal subversion, often viewed rock and roll as a foreign music with its own sinister potential for corrupting American society."

Lewis enjoyed the comforts of his middle-class upbringing, but acted as if he were estranged from the dominant values of suburban American life. Lou would rewrite his childhood repeatedly in an attempt to define himself. Some of his most famous songs, written in reaction to his parents' values, have a stark, despairing tone that spoke for millions of children who grew up in the stunned and silent fifties of America's postwar affluence. One friend put her finger on the pulse of the problem when she pointed out that Lou had an extreme case of *shpilkes*—a Yiddish term that perfectly sums up his contradictory nature: "A person with *shpilkes* has to scratch not only his own itch, he can't leave any situation alone or any scab unpicked. If the teenage Lewis had come into your home, you would have said, 'My God, he's got *shpilkes!* Because he's cute and he's warm and he's lovable, but get him out of here because he's knocking the shit out of everything and I don't dare turn my back on him. He's causing trouble, he's aggravating me, he's a pain in the ass!" According to Lou, he never felt good about his parents. "I went to great lengths to escape the whole thing," he said when he was forty years old. "I couldn't relate to it then and I can't now." As he saw himself in one of his favorite poems by Delmore Schwartz: ". . . he sat there / Upon the windowseat in his tenth year / Sad separate and desperate all afternoon, / Alone, with loaded eyes . . ."

Another charge Lou would lob at his unprotected parents was that they were filthy rich. This was, however, purely an invention Lou used to dramatize his situation. During Lou's childhood his father made a modest salary by American standards. The kitchen-table family possessed a single automobile and lived in a simply though tastefully furnished house with no vestiges of luxury or loosely spent funds. Indeed, by the end of the 1950s, what with the shock treatments, Lou's college tuition, and their daughter Elizabeth's coming into her teens, the Reeds were stretched about as far as they could reach.

*   *   *

THE YEAR OF HIS ELECTROSHOCK TREATMENTS, 1959, THROUGH THE SUM-mer of 1960 was a lost time for Lou. From then on, the central theme of his life became a struggle to express himself and get what he wanted. The first step was to remove himself from the control of his family, which he now saw as an agent of punishment and confinement. "I came from this small town out on Long Island," he stated. "Nowhere. I mean nowhere. The most boring place on earth. The only good thing about it was you knew you were going to get out of there." In August he registered and published a song called "You'll Never, Never Love Me." A gut resent-ment of his parents was blatantly expressed in another song, "Kill Your Sons." The music, he later said, gave him back his heartbeat so he could dream again. "The music is all," he wrote in a wonderful piece of prose called "From the Bandstand." "People should die for it. People are dying for everything else, so why not for the music. It saves more lives."

Chapter Two

PUSHING
THE EDGE

SYRACUSE UNIVERSITY: 1960—62

> *Lou liked to play with people, tease them and push them to*
> *an edge. But if you crossed a certain line with Lou, he'd*
> *cut you right out of his life.*
>
> —Allen Hyman

IN ORDER TO CONTINUE THEIR FRIENDSHIP, LOU AND ALLEN HYMAN HAD conspired to attend the same university. "In my senior year in high school Lou and I and his father drove up to Syracuse for an interview," recalled Allen. "We didn't speak to his father much, he was quiet. Quiet in the sense of being formal—Mr. Reed. We stayed at the Hotel Syracuse, which was then a real old hotel. There were also a bunch of other kids who were up for that with their parents. Would-be applicants to Syracuse. Lou's father took one room and Lou and I took another. We met a bunch of kids in the hall that were going to Syracuse and we had this all-night party with these girls we met. We thought this was going to be a gas, this is terrific. The following day we both knew people who were going to Syracuse at the time who were in fraternities, and the campus was so nice, I think it was the summer, it was warm at the time, it looked so nice."

The two boys made an agreement that if they were both accepted, they would matriculate at Syracuse. "We both got in," said Hyman. "And the minute I got my acceptance I let them know I was going to go and I called Lou very excited and said, 'I got my acceptance to Syracuse, did you?' And he said, 'Yes.' So I said, 'Are you going?' and he said, 'No.' And I said, 'What do you mean, no? I thought we were going, we had an agreement.' He said, 'I got accepted to NYU and that's where I'm going.'

I said, 'Why would you want to do that, we had such a good time up there, we liked the place, I told them I was going, I thought you were going.' He said, 'No, I got accepted at NYU uptown and I'm going.' "

In the fall of 1959, Lou headed off to college. Located in New York City, New York University seemed like a smart choice for a man who loved nothing more than listening to jazz at the Five Spot, the Vanguard, and other Greenwich Village clubs. But the Village was not the NYU campus Lou chose. Almost incomprehensibly, he signed up for the school's branch located way uptown in the Bronx. NYU uptown provided Reed with neither the opportunities nor the support that he needed. Instead, Lou was left floundering in a strange and hostile environment. One of his few pleasures came from visiting the mecca of modern jazz, the Five Spot, regularly, but he didn't always have the money to get in and often stood outside listening to Thelonious Monk, John Coltrane, and Ornette Coleman as the music drifted out to the street.

However, Lou's main concern was not college. The Bronx campus was convenient to the Payne Whitney psychiatric clinic on the Upper East Side of Manhattan, where he was undergoing an intensive course of postshock treatments. According to Hyman, who talked to him on the phone at least once a week through the semester, Lou was having a very, very bad time. "He was in therapy three or four times a week," Hyman recalled. "He hated NYU. He really hated it. He was going through a very difficult time and he was taking medication. He was having a lot of difficulty dealing with college and day-to-day business. He was a mess. He was going through a lot of very, very bad emotional stuff at the time and he probably had something very close to a minor breakdown."

After two semesters, in the spring of 1960, having completed the Payne Whitney sessions although still on tranquilizers, Lou couldn't take the NYU scene anymore.

One of the few people who encouraged Lou during his yearlong depression was his stalwart childhood friend, Allen Hyman, who now urged him to get away from his parents. Allen encouraged Lou to join him at Syracuse—a large, prestigious, private university, hundreds of miles from Freeport. In the fall of 1960, shaking off the shadows of Creedmore and the medication of Payne Whitney, Reed took Hyman's advice and enrolled at Syracuse.

*   *   *

THE COEDUCATIONAL UNIVERSITY, ATTENDED BY SOME NINETEEN THOU-
sand sciences and humanities students, had been established in 1870. It
was located on a 640-acre campus atop a hill, in the middle of the city.
Its $800 per term tuition was relatively high for a private university. Most
of the students lived in sororities and fraternities and were enjoying one
last four-year party before putting aside childish notions for the economic
responsibilities of adulthood. There was, among the student population,
a large and wealthy Jewish contingent, generally straight-arrow fraternity
men and sorority women bound for careers in medicine and law. There
was a small margin of artists, writers, and musicians with whom Lou
would throw in his lot, enjoying, for the first time in his life, a niche
in which he could find a degree of comfort. Among many other talented
and successful people, the artist Jim Dine, the fashion designer Betsey
Johnson, and the film producer Peter Guber all graduated in Reed's class
of 1964.

The Syracuse campus looked like the perfect set for a horror movie
about college life in the early 1960s. Its buildings resembled Gothic
mansions from a screenwriter's imagination. Indeed, the scriptwriter of
The Addams Family TV show of the 1960s, who attended the university at
the same time as Lou, used the classically Gothic Hall of Languages as the
basis for the *Addams Family* mansion. The surrounding four-block-square
area of wooden Victorian houses, Depression-era restaurants, stores, and
bars completed the college landscape. A pervasive ocher-gray paint lent
a somber air to the seedy wooden houses tucked away in side streets
covered, most of the time, with snow, wet leaves, or rain. The atmosphere was likely to elicit either poetic contemplation or depressive madness. It provided a perfect backdrop for the beatnik lifestyle.

The surrounding city of Syracuse presented no less smashed a landscape. The manufacturing town got dumped with snow seven months of
the year, and heavy bouts of rain the rest of the time. Only during the
summer, when most of the students had scattered to their homes on Long
Island or New Jersey, did the city receive warmth and sunshine. A thriving industrial metropolis popularly known as the Salt City, also special-
izing in metals and electrical machinery, it was two hundred miles
northwest of Freeport, forty miles south of Lake Ontario on the Canadian
border, and five miles southwest of Oneida Lake. Syracuse was aggres-
sively conservative and religious, but at the time of Reed's arrival it was
fast turning into the academic hub of the Empire State. The city proudly

supported its prestigious university, whose popular football team, the Orangemen, was undefeated during Lou's four years, and its residents turned out in great numbers for athletic events. Despite high academic standards, Syracuse was still primarily seen as a football school. "Where the vale of Onondaga / Meets the eastern sky / Proudly stands our Alma Mater / On her hilltop high" ran the opening verse of the school song, a ditty Lewis, as many of his friends called him, would not forget.

As a freshman, Lou was assigned to the far southwestern corner of the North Campus in Sadler Hall, a plain, boxlike dormitory resembling a prison. However, much of his time was spent in the splendid, gray-stone Hall of Languages, which overlooked University Avenue and University Place at the north end of campus and housed the English, history, and philosophy departments.

Syracuse University had excellent faculty and academic courses. Though Lou may have sleepwalked through much of the curriculum, he threw himself into the music, philosophy, and literature studies in which he excelled. In music appreciation, theory, and composition classes, Lou soaked up everything, even opera. First, Lou tried his hand at journalism, but he dropped that after a week when the teacher told him his opinions were irrelevant. However, Lou quickly immersed himself in philosophy. He devoured the existentialists, obsessed over the torturous dialectics of Hegel, and embraced the *Fear and Trembling* of Kierkegaard. "I was very into Hegel, Sartre, Kierkegaard," Reed recalled. "After you finish reading Kierkegaard, you feel like something horrible has happened to you—fear and nothing. That's where I was coming from." He also loved Krafft-Ebing and the writing of the beat generation, particularly Kerouac, Burroughs, and Ginsberg. To complete his freshman image, he took imagistic inspiration from the brash, tortured figures of James Dean, Marlon Brando, and, most of all, Lenny Bruce.

To his advantage, Reed already had the perfect agent to introduce him to the university, the smooth operator and prince of good times Allen Hyman, now entering his sophomore year. Another pampered suburban kid who drove both a Cadillac and Jaguar, Allen was generous, full of good humor, and sharp-witted. Furthermore, he genuinely appreciated Lou and was willing to put up with a lot of flak to remain his friend. Hyman was well connected with the straight fraternity set and eager to introduce Lewis to his world.

However, a highly uncomfortable introduction came about when Allen tried to get Lou to rush his fraternity, Sigma Alpha Mu (aka the Sammies). "Hazing was a really horrendous experience and most people were very intimidated by it," recalled Hyman. Inductees were forced to drink themselves into oblivion and were often humiliated physically, sexually, and mentally by the fraternity brothers. When Allen told Lou stories about what he went through to join a fraternity, Lou shot him a hard look, snapping, "What are you into—masochism?"

"He had said that he didn't want anything to do with it and that it was fascistic and disgusting," Hyman recalled, "and he couldn't believe anybody would be willing to go through hazing without killing the person who was hazing them." However, typically perversely, Reed agreed to attend a rush session.

From the outset it was clear that he intended to make a strong impression. Reed came to the socializer in a suit three sizes too small and covered in dirt. It was a radical departure from the blue blazer, smart tie, and neatly combed hair of the other rushees. Allen immediately realized how much Lou was getting off on being outrageous. When one of the brothers criticized Lou's appearance, Reed riposted, "Fuck you!" and his fraternity career came to an abrupt end. Hyman was asked to escort his friend out immediately. Walking Lou back to his dorm, a chagrined Allen hung his head regretfully, but Lou, far from being despondent, appeared exhilarated by the event. "I guess this isn't for you," Allen said.

"Yeah, that's right," Lou replied. "I told you I wouldn't get along with those assholes. How can you live there?"

Another freshman trial that Lou failed was with the Reserve Officers' Training Corps. As part of his freshman course requirements, he had to choose between physical education and ROTC. (In those days it was common to join ROTC in order to be able to go into the army as an officer and a gentleman.) Claiming that he would surely break his neck in phys ed or else kill somebody in ROTC, Lou attempted to evade either requirement, but in the end grudgingly signed up for the latter. ROTC consisted of two classes a week about how to be a soldier and possibly a leader. However, Lou's military experience was almost a short-lived as his fraternity stint. Just weeks into the semester, when he flatly refused a direct order from his officer, he was unceremoniously booted out.

But Reed managed to make an impact his freshmen year with his very own radio show. Employing a considerable boyish charm to overcome the severe doubts of program director Katharine Griffin, during his first semester Lou hustled his way onto the Syracuse University radio station, WAER FM, with a jazz program called *Excursions on a Wobbly Rail* (named for a wicked Cecil Taylor piece that was used as his introductory theme). The classical, conservative station, Radio House, was situated in a World War II Quonset hut tucked away behind Carnegie Library. Freezing his balls off through many icy Syracuse evenings, hunched over his ancient machinery like some WW II underground resistance fighter for two hours, three nights a week, Lou blasted a mélange of his favorite sounds by the avant-garde leaders of the Free Jazz movement Ornette Coleman and Don Cherry, the doo-wopping Dion, and the sexually charged Hank Ballard, James Brown and the Marvelettes. The mixture presented the essence of Lou Reed. "I was a very big fan of Ornette Coleman, Cecil Taylor, Archie Shepp," he recalled. "Then James Brown, the doo-wop groups, and rockabilly. Put it all together and you end up with me."

Unfortunately, the Reedian canon was not appreciated by the station's staff, and numerous faculty members, including the dean of men, lodged complaints about the—to them—hideous, unintelligible cacophony that was Reed's program. And the authorities' reaction was not Lou's only problem. Disguising his voice, Allen Hyman would often call Lou at the station and harass him with ridiculous requests. On one occasion, "I asked him to play something he hated and I knew he would never play," Allen recalled. "He said, 'No, I'm not going to play that, forget it.' So I said, 'Listen, if you don't play this, I'm gonna fucking have you killed. I'll wait for you myself and I'm gonna kill you!' And, thinking it was some lunatic, Lou got scared. Then I called him back and told him it was me and he screamed at me, saying that if I ever did that again he'd never speak to me."

As it turned out, Allen's pranks didn't last long enough to lose him Lou's friendship because before long Griffin, ever vigilant in her duties as WAER's program director, concluded that "*Excursions on a Wobbly Rail* was a really weird jazz show that sounded like some new kind of noise. It was just too weird and cutting edge." Before the end of the semester, she unceremoniously dumped it from the air, causing Lou considerable anguish.

In retrospect, Griffin and her contemporaries realized that Reed was simply ahead of his time. "Most of us who were in power on campus were children of the fifties," she explained. "Kids in those days wore chinos and madras shirts, a clean-cut Kingston Trio kind of thing. Lou looked more like what a rock person from later in the sixties would look like. Lou was presaging the sixties and seventies and we just weren't ready for it. He was right on the cusp of two generations. A little too far ahead to be admired in the fifties."

During his first year at Syracuse, the scholarly Griffin concluded, "It was just Lou versus everybody else."

Lou quickly defined himself as an oddball loner. Eschewing all organizations, he was creating an image that would in time become widely acknowledged as the essence of the hip New York underground man. Lou was a year older than most freshmen and fully grown. Measuring five feet eight inches (although he claimed to be five feet ten) he was a little chubby and some way yet from the Lou Reed of "Heroin." He wore loafers, jeans, and T-shirts, tending, if anything, to be a little sloppier than the majority of men at school, who wore the fraternity uniform of jacket and tie. His hair was a trifle longer than theirs. Otherwise, he would not have been noticed in a crowd. His looks tended toward the cute, boyish, curly haired, shy, gum-chewing. He had a small scar under his right eye. His most unusual feature was his fingers. Short and strong, they broadened into stubby, almost blocklike fingertips, making them perfect tools for the guitar.

Lou had already formed his ambition to be a rock-and-roller and a writer. The university's rich music scene consisted of an eclectic mix of talents like Garland Jeffreys, a future singer-songwriter and Reed acolyte two years younger than Lou; Nelson Slater, for whom Lou would later produce an album; Felix Cavaliere, the future leader of the Young Rascals; Mike Esposito, who would form the Blues Magoos and the Blues Project; and Peter Stampfel, an early member of the Holy Modal Rounders, who would become a pioneer of folk rock. While colleges in New York and Boston produced folksingers in the style of Bob Dylan, Syracuse created a bunch of proto-punk rockers.

Most importantly for Lou musically, it was at Syracuse he met fellow guitarist Sterling Morrison, a resident of Bayport, Long Island, who had a similar background. Just after Lou got kicked out of ROTC, Sterling, who was never actually enrolled at Syracuse but spent a lot of time there hanging out and sitting in on some classes, was visiting another student, Jim Tucker, who occupied the room below Lou's. Gazing out Tucker's window at the ROTC cadets marching up and down the quad one afternoon, Morrison suddenly heard "earsplitting bagpipe music" wail from someone's hi-fi. After that, the same person "cranked up his guitar and gave a few shrieking blasts on that." Excited, Morrison realized, "Oh, there's a guitar player upstairs," and prevailed on Tucker for an introduction.

When they met at 3 A.M. the following morning, Lou and Sterling discovered they shared a love for black music and rock and roll. They also loved Ike and Tina Turner. "Nobody even knew who they were then," Morrison recalled. "Syracuse was very, very straight. There was a one percent lunatic fringe."

Luckily, the drama, poetry, art, and literary scenes were just as alive as the music scene for that one percent fringe. Soon Lou was spending the majority of his time playing guitar, reading and writing, or engaging in long rap sessions with like-minded students. Many of Lou's conversations about philosophy and literature took place in the bars and coffee shops he and his friends began to call their own. Each restaurant had its social affiliations. Lou's crowd set up camp at the Savoy Coffee shop run by a lovable old character, Gus Joseph, who could have walked right out of a *Happy Days* TV episode. At night, they drank at the Orange Bar, frequented predominantly by intellectual students. According to Lou, he took two steps out of school and there was the bar. "It was the world of Kant and Kierkegaard and metaphysical polemics that lasted well into the night," he remembered. "I often went to drink alone to that week's lost everything." He had become accustomed to taking prescription drugs and smoking pot, but Lou was not yet a heavy user of illegal substances. At the most he might have a Scotch and a beer.

At Syracuse, Lou presented himself as a tortured, introspective, romantic poet. Following the dictate that the first step to becoming a poet is to look and act like one, Lou liked, for example, to give the impression that he was unwashed, but that wasn't true. According to one friend, "He wasn't about to go out unless he took a shower first." As far as his costume was concerned, he was still stuck somewhere between the suburban teenager in loafers and button-down shirts and the rumpled dungarees and work shirts of the Kerouac rebel. Observers remembered him as more chubby and cherubic than thin and ascetic. In fact, he didn't dress unusually at all. If anything, he dressed poorly, wearing the same pair of dirty jeans for months. As for his demeanor, Lou copped the uptight approach of the young Rimbuad. He was just beginning to swing with the legend of his electroshock treatments, turtleneck sweaters, and the whole James Dean inspired "I've suffered so much everything looks upside down" routine.

According to one student who occasionally jammed with him, "Part of his aura was that he was a psychologically troubled person who in his youth had had electroshock treatments which clearly had an effect on him. He used that as part of his persona. Where the reality and the fantasy of what he was crossed, who knew." For a sarcastic kid who had grown up with buck teeth, braces, and a nerd's wardrobe, Lou wasn't doing badly turning himself into the image of a totally perverse psycho. However, whatever he did with his wardrobe and his attitude to make himself hip, there was one nightmarish detail about his looks that seemed always to overwhelm him—his hair. His frizzy helmet had plagued him since he'd started looking into the mirror with intense interest in his twelfth year. What stared back at him throughout his adolescence was a Jewish version of Alfred E. Neumann.

Since America had been a largely anti-Semitic nation, the Jewish "Afro" was seen as geekishly ethnic. In the early sixties, Bob Dylan would single-handedly change the image of what a hip young boy could look like. Though the film industry and media characters like Allen Ginsberg had begun to turn the whole Jewish male persona into something ultrachic, nobody came close to having the pervasive influence of Bob Dylan. As Ginsberg explained to his biographer Barry Miles, when Dylan appeared, particularly in his 1965 *Bringing It All Back Home* incarnation, he made the hooked nose and frizzy hair the very emblem of the hip, intellectual avant-garde. By the time Lou got to college, however, and started to resculpt himself into the Lou Reed who would emerge in 1966 as the closest competition to Dylan for the hippest rock star in the world, he was ready to do something about his hair. At Syracuse he discovered a hairtreatment place in the black neighborhood and on several occasions had his hair straightened.

Just like his British counterparts Keith Richards of the Rolling Stones or John Lennon of the Beatles, Lou rejected the lifestyle that came before the bomb and was remaking himself out of a combination of his favorite stars. Such self-creation was not difficult for Lou, who often claimed he had as many as eight personalities. He now clothed these personalities in the costumes and attitudes of a cast of media characters who were as important to his image as the first creative friends he would hook up with at Syracuse.

First among them was Lenny Bruce. Though damned by his legal problems to a horrible fate, Bruce was at the apogee of his career. In the eyes of the public he was the hippest, fastest-talking American poet and philosopher around. Bruce spiked his act—a kind of Will Rogers on fast-forward—by injections of pure methamphetamine hydrochloride, which would in time become Lou's own drug of choice. Many of Reed's mannerisms, his hand gestures, the way he answered the phone as if he was asleep, the rhythm of his speech, came directly from Bruce.

As for the rest of Lou's media idols, you only have to look at a panel of head shots of the stars of the era to see what Lou would take in time from Frank Sinatra, Jerry Lewis in *The Bellboy*, Montgomery Clift, and William Burroughs, to name but a few of the more obvious ones. In fact, one of Lou's most attractive characteristics was the way he appreciated and celebrated his heroes. He was always trying to get Hyman, for example, a straight law student whose path would lead in a direction diametrically opposite to Lou's, to read Kerouac and then rap with him about it. Lou loved turning people on to the new sounds, the new scenes, and the new people.

A lot of the artistic kids who went to Syracuse look back upon it with disdain as a football school dominated by the "fucking" Orangemen. In fact, in that watershed period between the end of McCarthyism and the death of Kennedy, a new permissiveness swept through colleges across the country. Syracuse contained and nurtured a lot of different environments. Certainly the fraternity environment still dominated the American campus, and the majority of male and female students still aligned themselves with a fraternity or sorority in sheeplike fashion. There was, however, a vital cultural split between the Jewish and the non-Jewish fraternities. The Jewish fraternities were for the most part hipper, more receptive to the new culture and more open to alternative ways of living. Despite completely rejecting Sigma Alpha Mu and attaching himself primarily to the arty intellectual crowd, some of whom had apartments off campus,

Lou maintained a loyal friendship with Hyman and was, in fact, adopted as something of a mascot by the Sammies as their resident oddball. They weren't about to miss out completely on a character who had already, in the first half of his freshman year, carved out an image for himself as tempestuous and evil. In fact, Jewish fraternities in colleges across America would provide some of the most receptive of Lou Reed's audiences throughout his career.

The rules that governed a freshman's life at Syracuse were greatly to the advantage of the male students. Whereas the girls in the dorm atop Mount Olympus were locked in at 9 P.M., and any girl who dared break curfew was subject to expulsion, the boys, who had no curfew, were able to use the night to live a whole other life, exploring the town, drinking in the Orange or in frat houses and getting up to all sorts of mischief. Naturally Lou, who had developed the habit of staying up most of the night reading, writing, and playing music, lost no time exploring his new home. He quickly discovered the neighboring black ghetto where at least one club, the 800, presented funky jazz and R&B as well as a whole culture, centered around drugs, music, and danger, that appealed to the explorer of the dark side in Reed.

Lou's first college girlfriend was Judy Abdullah, and he called her The Arab. It may be that she was of more interest to him as an exotic object than as a person. Judy revealed an interesting quirk in Lou's sexuality. He was turned on by big women. Judy Abdullah was twice his size. She was a sensual woman and they apparently had a good time in bed, but at least one acquaintance added a shade to Reed's personality profile when she pointed out that his attraction to big women offered both a challenge and an escape route. Lou could take the attitude that he had no responsibility to be serious about her or even try to satisfy her.

The relationship petered out before the end of the year. Lou, who persisted in not wasting time with dates and always coming on obnoxiously, was mean to Judy, and when they broke up, she was pissed off at him for good reason. Still, they remained acquaintances and Lou saw her occasionally throughout his college years.

By the end of his first year at Syracuse, according to one of the Sammies, "Lou's uniqueness and stubbornness made him different from anyone I had ever known. He marched to his own drum. He was for doing things for people, but his way. He would never dress or act in a way so

that people would accept him. Lou had an unbelievably wry, caustic sense
of humor and loved funny things. He played off people. He would often
act in a confrontational manner. He wanted to be different. Lou was a
funny guy in an extremely dry, witty sense. Certainly not the type of
comedian that would make you laugh at him. He wasn't making fun of
things but seeing the humor in things—the banal and the normal. There
was an undercurrent of saneness in everything he did. He was screwed up,
but that was schizophrenia too."

WHAT LOU REED NEEDED MOST WAS TO FIND A COCONSPIRATOR, AN
equal off whom he could bounce his ideas and behavior and receive
inspiration in return. Almost miraculously, he found such a person in
what would become the second golden period of his life (the first being his
discovery of rock and roll). Lou's first great soul mate, mirror, and collaborator, whom he roomed with in his sophomore year, was the brilliant,
eccentric, talented, but tortured and doomed Lincoln Swados. Swados
came from an upwardly mobile, middle-class, and, by all accounts, outstandingly empathetic Jewish family from upstate New York. Like Reed,
he had a little sister called Elizabeth, upon whom he doted (and to some
extent, like Lou, identified with). The two students fell into each other's
arms like lost inmates of some Siberian prison of the soul who finally
discover after years of isolated exile a fellow voyager. To make matters
perfect from Lou's point of view, Lincoln was an aspiring writer (working
on an endless Dostoyevskian novel); his favorite singer was Frank Sinatra;
Lincoln's side of the room was covered in more crap than Lou's; and—this
was the clincher—Swados was agoraphobic. He spent most of his time
holed up in their basement room either hunkered over a battered desk or
playing Frank Sinatra records and rapping with Lou. Whenever Lou
needed a receiver for one of his new songs, poems, or stories, Lincoln was
always there. Their relationship was the first of many constructive collaborations in Lou's life.
    One of Lou's strongest personalities was the controlling figure who
always needed to be the center of attention and the most outstanding
person in the room. Here again Lincoln was his perfect match, for if Lou
ever worried that he might not yet possess the hippest look in the world,
Lincoln presented no threat. He was usually togged out in a pair of pants

that ended somewhere above his ankles and were belted in the middle of his chest. His customary short-sleeve shirt invariably clashed with the pants. A pair of bugged-out eyes that made Caryl Chessman in the electric chair look like a junkie on the nod stared out of a cadaverous face capped by a head of dirty, disheveled blondish hair. Lincoln's body was as much of a mess as was his mind. He rarely bathed or brushed his teeth and at times emanated an odor that obviated any close physical relationships. The whole ensemble was tied together by a disembodied smile that clearly indicated, at least to somebody of Lou's perceptiveness, just how far out in space Lincoln really was most of the time.

Their basement room was furnished like some barren writer's cell out of Franz Kafka's imagination. The two black iron bedsteads, identical desks, and battered chairs ensconced upon a green concrete floor and lit by a harsh bare lightbulb could not have better symbolized both the despair and ambition at the heart of their twin souls. They both despised the world of their parents from which they had at least temporarily escaped. Both were intent upon destroying it and all of its values with some of the most vitriolic, driven pages since Burroughs spat *Naked Lunch* out of his battered typewriter in Tangier. The room became their arsenal, their headquarters, their cave of knowledge and learning, and the engine of their voyage into the unknown. In time, Lou would rip off Lincoln's entire repertoire of attitudes, gestures, and habits. Lou later confessed, "I'm always studying people that I know, and then when I think I've got them worked, I go away and write a song about them. When I sing the song, I become them. It's for that reason that I'm kind of empty when I'm not doing anything. I don't have a personality of my own, I just pick up other people's."

Having met his male counterpart, Lou now needed, in order to pull out the male and female sides warring within him, a female companion. Within a week of settling in with Swados, Lou saw her riding down the university's main drag, Marshall Street, in the front seat of a car driven by a blond football player who belonged to the other Jewish fraternity on campus and recognized Reed as their local holy fool. Thinking to amuse his date, a scintillatingly beautiful freshman from the Midwest named Shelley Albin, he pulled over, laughing, and said, "Here's Lou! He's very shocking and evil!" making, as it turned out for him, the dreadful mistake of offering "the lunatic" a ride.

Although in no way as twisted and bent as Lincoln Swados, Shelley was as perfect a match for Lou as his roommate was. Born in Wisconsin, where she had lived the frustrated life of a beatnik tomboy, Shelley had elected Syracuse because it was the only university her parents would let her attend. In preparation for the big move away from home, Shelley, along with a childhood girlfriend, had come to Syracuse fully intending to mend her ways and acquiesce to the college and culture's coed requirements. Discarding the jeans and work shirts she wore at home, she donned instead the below-the-knee skirt, tasteful blouse, and string of pearls seen on girls in every yearbook photo of the period. When Lou hopped into the backseat eager to make her acquaintance, Shelley was squirming with the discomfort of the demure uniform as well as her dorky date's running commentary.

She vividly recalled Lou's skinny hips, baby face, give-away eyes, and knew "we were going to go out as soon as he got into the car." She also knew she was making a momentous decision and that Lou was going to be trouble, but that it certainly wasn't going to be boring. "It was such a relief to see Lou, who was to me a normal person. And I was intrigued by the evil shit."

The feeling was clearly mutual. As soon as the couple let Lou off in front of his dorm, Reed sprinted into their room and breathlessly told Swados about the most beautiful girl in the world he had just met, and his plans to call her immediately.

Lincoln had a strangely paternal side that would often appear at inappropriate moments. Seeing his role as steering Lou through his emotional mood swings, Swados immediately put the kibosh on Reed's notion of seducing Shelley by informing him that this would be out of the question since he, Lincoln, had already spotted the pretty coed and, despite not yet having met her, was claiming her as his own.

Lou, for his part, saw his role in the relationship as primarily to calm the highly strung, hyperactive Swados. Reasoning that the nerdy Lincoln, who had been unable to get a single date during the freshman year, would only be wounded by the rejection he was certain to get from Shelley, Lou wasted no time in cutting his friend off at the pass by calling Shelley at her dorm within the hour and arranging an immediate date. That way, Lou told himself, he would soon be able to give Swados the pleasure of her company.

Shelley Albin would not only become Lou Reed's girlfriend through his sophomore and junior years—"my mountaintop, my peak," as he would later describe her—but would remain for many years thereafter his muse. "Lou and I connected when we were too young to really put it into words," Shelley said. "There was some innate connection there that was very strong. I knew him before everything was covered up. My strongest image of Lou is always as a Byronesque character, a very sweet young man. He was interesting, he wasn't one of the bland, robotic people, he had a wonderful poetic nature. Basically, Lou was a puffball, he was a sweetie." For all of Lou's eccentricities, Shelley found him "very straight. He was very coordinated, a good dancer, and he could play a good game of tennis. His criteria for life were equally straight. He was a fifties guy, the husband of the house, the God. He wanted a woman who was the end-all Barbie and would make bacon when he wanted bacon. I was very submissive and naive and that's what appealed to him."

But Lou also had his "crazy" side, which he played to the hilt. Like many bright kids who have just discovered Kierkegaard and Camus, he was the classic, arty bad boy. Alternating between straight and scary, Lou reveled in both. "There was a part of Lou that was forever fifteen, and a part of him that was a hundred," Shelley fondly recalled. Fortunately for Lou, she embraced both parts equally. And going out with Lou gave Shelley the jolt she needed to throw off her skirt and pearls for jeans and let her perm return to her natural long, straight hair. Seeing her metamorphosis, the boy Shelley had left so brazenly for Lou was soon chiding her, "You went to the dogs and became a beatnik. Lou ruined you!" In fact, Shelley, an art student, had simply reverted to being herself. But she enjoyed the taunt, knowing how much Lou liked it when people accused him of corrupting her and enjoyed the notoriety it won him. Shelley was also astonishingly beautiful, and to this day, Lou's Syracuse teachers and friends remember above all else that Lou Reed had an "outrageously gorgeous girlfriend who was also very, very nice."

Shelley Albin had a unique face. Looked at straight on, what struck you first were her eyes. An inner light glimmered through them. Her nose was straight and perfect. Her jawline and chin were so finely sculpted they became the subject of many an art student at Syracuse. It was an open and closed face. Her mouth said yes. Yet her eyes had a Modigliani/Madonna quality that bayed, you keep your distance. Her light brown hair reflected in her pale cream skin gave it at times, a reddish tint. At five feet seven inches and weighing 115 pounds, she was close enough in size to Lou to wear his clothes.

"We were inseparable from the moment we met," Shelley recalled. "We were always literally wrapped up in each other like a pretzel." Soon Shelley and Lou could be seen at the Savoy, making out in public for hours at a time: "He was a great kisser and well coordinated. I always thought of him as a master of the slow dance. When we met, it was like long-lost friends." For both of them it was their first real love affair. They quickly discovered that they could relate across the boards. They had a great sexual relationship. They played basketball and tennis together. When Lou wrote a poem or a story, Shelley found herself doing a drawing or a painting that perfectly illustrated it. She had been sent to a psychiatrist in her teens for refusing to speak to her father for three years. Lou wrote "I'll Be Your Mirror" two years later about Shelley. And Shelley was Lou's mirror. Just as he had rushed a fraternity, she, much to his delight, rushed a sorority and then told them to go fuck themselves an hour after she got accepted.

"His appeal was as a very sexy, intricate and convoluted boy/man," Shelley said. "It was the combination of private gentle lover and romantic and strong, driven thug. He was, however, a little too strong, a dangerous little boy you can't trust who will turn on you and is much stronger than you think. He had the strength of a man. You really couldn't win. You had to catch him by surprise if you wanted to deck him.

"The electroshock treatments were very fresh in his mind when we met. He immediately established that he was erratic, undependable, and dangerous, and that he was going to control any situation by making everyone around him nervous. It was the ultimate game of chicken. But I could play Lou's game too, that's why we got along so well.

"What appealed to me about Lou was that he always pushed the edge. That's what really attracted me to him. I was submissive to Lou as part of my gift to him, but he wasn't controlling me. If you look back at who's got the power in the relationship, it will turn out that it wasn't him."

Whereas the entrance of a stunning female often offsets the male bonding between collaborators, in the tradition of the beats established by Kerouac and his friend Neal Cassady, Lou correctly presumed that Shelley would enhance, rather than break up, his collaboration with

Lincoln. In fact, it became such a close relationship that Lou would occasionally suggest, only half-jokingly, that Shelley should spend some time in bed with Lincoln. Their relationship mirrored that of the famous trio at the core of their generation's favorite film, *Rebel Without a Cause*, with Lou as James Dean, Shelley as Natalie Wood, and Lincoln as the doomed Sal Mineo.

Lou presented Lincoln to Shelley as an important but fragile figure who needed to be nurtured. Lincoln was homely, but Shelley's vision of him in motion was "like Fred Astaire, Lincoln was debonair and he would spin a wonderful tale and I think Lou could see this fascination. Lou felt very responsible and protective toward Lincoln because nobody would see Lincoln and we liked Lincoln." The first thing Lou said to Shelley was, "Lincoln wants you, and if I were a really good guy, I should give you to Lincoln because I can get anybody and Lincoln can't. Lincoln loves you, but I'm not going to give you to him because I want you." Shelley realized that many of Lou's ways of being charming and his gestures were taken straight from Lincoln. "A lot of what I really loved about Lou was Lincoln, who was in many ways like Jiminy Cricket standing on Lou's shoulder, whispering words into his ear. They were going to take care of me and straighten me out and educate me."

The most important thing about Lincoln and Shelley was their understanding and embracing of Lou's talent and personality. If Lincoln was a flat mirror for Lou, Shelley was multidimensional, reflecting Lou's many sides. Perceptive and intuitive, she understood that Lou appreciated events on many different levels and often saw things others didn't. For the first time in his life Lou found two people to whom he could actually open up without fear of being ridiculed or taken for a ride. For a person who depended so much on others to complete him, they were irreplaceable allies.

Initially, Lou's first love affair was idyllic. Lou rarely arose before noon, since he stayed up all night. He and Shelley would sometimes meet in the snow at 6 A.M. at the bottom of the steps leading to the women's dorm. Or else in the early afternoon she would take the twenty-minute hike from the women's dorm to Lou and Lincoln's quarters. Like all coeds on campus, she was forbidden to enter a men's dorm on threat of expulsion, so she would merely tap on their basement window and wait for Lou to appear. When he did, he would gaze up at one of his favorite views of his lover's face smiling down at him with her long hair and a scarf hanging down. "I liked looking in on their pit," she recalled. "It was truly a netherworld. I liked being outside. I liked my freedom. And Lou liked that I had to go back to the dorm every night." From there, the threesome would repair to a booth at the Savoy where they would be joined by art student Karl Stoecker—a close friend of Shelley's—and English major Peter Locke, a friend of Lou's to this day, along with Jim Tucker, Sterling Morrison, and a host of others, to commence an all-day session of writing, talking, making out, guitar playing, and drawing. Lou was concentrating on playing his acoustic guitar and writing folk songs. The rest of the time was spent napping, with an occasional sortie to a class. When the threesome got restless at the Savoy, they might repair to the quaint Corner Bookstore, just half a block away, or the Orange Bar. But they always came back to home base at the Savoy, and to the avuncular owner, Gus Joseph, who saw kids come and go for fifty years, but remembered Lou as being special.

LOU WAS SO ENAMORED OF SHELLEY THAT IN THE FALL OF 1961 HE DE-cided to bring her home to Freeport for the Christmas/Hanukkah holidays. Considering the extent to which Lou based his rebellious posture on the theme of his difficult childhood, Shelley was fully aware of how hard it would be for Lou to take her to his parents' home. She remembered him thinking that he would score points with his parents: "It was sort of subtle. He was going to show his father that he was okay. He knew that they would like me. And I suspect in some ways he still wanted to please his parents and he wanted to bring home somebody that he could bring home."

Much to her surprise, Lou's parents welcomed her to their Freeport home with open arms, making her feel comfortable and accepted. Lou had given her the definite impression that his mother did not love him, but to Shelley, Toby Reed was a warm and wonderful woman, anything but selfish. And Sidney Reed, described by Lou as a stern disciplinarian, seemed equally loving. They appeared to be the exact opposite of the way Lou had portrayed them. In her impression, Mr. Reed "would have walked over the coals for Lou."

At the same time Shelley realized that Lou was just like them. He not only looked like them, but possessed all their best qualities. However, when she made the mistake of communicating her positive reaction, commenting on the wonderful twinkle in Mr. Reed's eyes and noting how similar his dry sense of humor was to Lou's, her boyfriend snapped, "Don't you know they're killers!?"

Given their kind, gracious, outgoing manner, the Reeds were sitting ducks for Lou's brand of torture. He would usually begin by embracing the rogue cousin in the Reed family called Judy. As soon he got home, Lou would enthusiastically inquire after her activities and prattle on about how he wanted to emulate her more than anyone else in the family, often reducing his mother to tears. Next, Lou would make a bid to monopolize the attentions of thirteen-year-old Elizabeth. Confiding to her his innermost thoughts, he would make a big point of excluding his parents from the powwow. "She was cute," thought Shelley, "she looked just like Lou. So did his mother and father. They all looked exactly like him. It was hysterical. Lou was very protective of her. And she was so sweet. She didn't have that much of a personality, but she was not unanimated." Every action aimed to cut his parents out of his life, while keeping them prisoners in it. Meanwhile, like every college kid home on vacation, Lou managed to extract from them all the money he could, and the freedom to come and go as if the house were a hotel. As soon as everybody at 35 Oakfield Avenue was in position ready to do exactly as he wanted, Lou began to enjoy himself.

In fact, so extreme was the situation that, on this first visit, Toby Reed, looking upon her as the perfect daughter-in-law, took Shelley into her confidence. "They were very nervous about what was he bringing home," she remembered. "So they really took it as a sign that, 'Oh, God, maybe he was okay.' We recognized with each other, she and I, that we both really liked him and we both loved him." Mrs. Reed filled her in on Lou's troublesome side and tried to find out what Lou was saying about his parents. Shelley got the impression that the Reeds bore no malice toward Lou, but just wanted the best for him. Mrs. Reed seemed completely puzzled as to how Lou had gotten on the track of hating and blaming them. Pondering the strange state of affairs unfolding behind the facade of the Reed's attractive home, Shelley drew two conclusions. On the one hand, since his family seemed quite normal and had no apparent problems, Lou was moved to create psychodrama in order to fuel his writing.

On the other hand, Lou really did crave his parents' approval. He was immensely troubled by their refusal to recognize his talent and needed to break away from their restricted life. One point of Lou's frustration was the feeling that his father was a wimp who gave over control of his life to his wife. This both horrified and fascinated Lou, who was a dyed-in-the-wool male supremacist. Lou was secretly proud of his father and wanted more than anything else for the old man to stand up for himself. But Lou simply could not stand the thought of sharing the former beauty queen's attention with his father.

After spending a wonderful, if at times tense, week in the Reed household, Shelley put together the puzzle. In a war of wits that had been going on for years, Lou went on the offensive as soon as he stepped through the portals of his home. Attempting by any means necessary to horrify and paralyze his loving parents, Lou had learned to control them by threatening to explode at any moment with some vicious remark or irrational act that would shatter their carefully developed harmony. For example, one night Mr. Reed gave Lou the keys to the family car, a Ford Fairlane, and some money to take Shelley out to dinner in New York. However, such an exchange between father and son could not pass without conflict straight out of a cartoon. As Lou was heading for the door with Shelley, Sid had to observe that if he were going to the city, he might, under the circumstances, put on a clean shirt. Instantly spinning into a vortex of anger that made Sid feel like a cockroach, Lou threw an acerbic verbal dart at his mother before slamming out the door.

On the way into New York he almost killed himself and Shelley by driving carelessly and with little awareness of his surroundings. "I remember him taking this little flower from the Midwest to the big city," Shelley said. "Chinatown. We drove in a hair-raising ride I'll never forget in my whole life. Lou showed me how to hang out on the heating grate of the Village Gate so you could hear the music and stay warm."

His parents, she realized, "had no sense of what was really in his mind, and they were very upset and frightened by what awful things he was thinking. He must have been really miserable, how scary." As a result, in order to obviate any disturbance, Lou's tense and nervous family attended to his every need just as if he were the perennial prodigal son. The only person in the house who received any regular affection from Lou was his little sister, Elizabeth, who had always doted on Lou and thought he was the best.

However, at least for the time being, Lou's introduction of Shelley into their lives caused his parents unexpected joy. Ecstatic that his son had brought home a clean, white, beautiful Jewish girl, Mr. Reed increased Lou's allowance.

If he had had any idea of the life Lou and Shelley were leading at Syracuse, he would probably have acted in the reverse. As the year wore on, sex, drugs, rock and roll, and their influences began to play a bigger role in both their lives, although Shelley did not take drugs. Already a regular pot smoker, Lou dropped acid for the first time and started experimenting with peyote. Taking drugs was not the norm on college campuses in 1961. Though pot was showing up more regularly in fraternities, and a few adventurous students were taking LSD, most students were clean-cut products of the 1950s, preparing for jobs as accountant, lawyers, doctors, and teachers. To them, Lou's habits and demeanor were extreme. And now, not only was Lou taking drugs, he began selling them to the fraternity boys. Lou kept a stash of pot in a grocery bag in the dorm room of a female friend. Whenever he had a customer, he'd send Shelley to go get it.

Lou was by now on his way to becoming an omnivorous drug user and, apart from taking acid and peyote, would at times buy a codeine-laced cough syrup called turpenhydrate. Lou was stoned a lot of the time. "He liked me to be there when he was high," Shelley remembered. "He used to say, 'If I don't feel good, you'll take care of me.' Mostly he took drugs to numb himself or get relief, to take a break from his brain."

Meanwhile, having presented himself as a born-again heterosexual, Lou now wasted no time in making another shocking move by shoring up his homosexual credentials. In the second semester of his sophomore year, he had what he later described as his first, albeit unconsummated, gay love affair. "It was just the most amazing experience," Lou explained. "I felt very bad about it because I had a girlfriend and I was always going out on the side, and subterfuge is not my hard-on." He particularly remembered the pain of "trying to make yourself feel something towards women when you can't. I couldn't figure out what was wrong. I wanted to fix it up and make it okay. I figured if I sat around and thought about it, I could straighten it out."

Lou and Shelley's relationship rapidly escalated to a high level of game playing. Lou had more than one gay affair at Syracuse and would often try to shock her by casually mentioning that he was attracted to some guy. Shelley, however, could always turn the tables on him because she wasn't threatened by Lou's gay affairs and often turned them into competitions that she usually won for the subject's attentions. If Shelley was a match for Lou, Lou was always ready to up the stakes. They soon got out of their depth playing these and other equally dangerous mind games, which led them into more complexities than they could handle.

Friends had conflicting memories of Lou's gay life at Syracuse. Allen Hyman viewed him as being extraordinarily heterosexual right through college, whereas Sterling Morrison, who thought Lou was mostly a voyeur, commented, "He tried the gay scene at Syracuse, which was really repellent. He had a little fling with some really flabby, effete fairy. I said, 'Oh, man, Lou, if you want to do it, I hate to say it but let's find somebody attractive at least.' "

Homosexuality was generally presented as an unspeakable vice in the early 1960s. Nothing could have been considered more distasteful in 1962 America than the image of two men kissing. The average American would not allow a homosexual in his house for fear he might leave some kind of terrible disease on the toilet seat, or for that matter, the armchair. There were instances reported at universities in America during this time when healthy young men fainted, like Victorian ladies, at the physical approach of a homosexual. In fact, as Andy Warhol would soon prove, at the beginning of the 1960s the homosexual was considered the single most threatening, subversive character in the culture. According to Frank O'Hara's biographer, Brad Gooch, "A campaign to control gay bars in New York had already begun in January 1964 when the Fawn in Greenwich Village was closed by the police. Reacting to this closing by police department undercover agents, known as 'actors,' the New York Times ran a front-page story headlined, 'Growth of Overt Homosexuality in City Provokes Wide Concern.' " Besides the refuge large cities such as San Francisco and New York provided for homosexuals, many cultural institutions, especially the private universities, became home to a large segment of the homosexual community. Syracuse University, where there was a hotbed of homosexual activity, led by Lou's favorite drama teacher, was no exception.

"As an actor, I couldn't cut the mustard, as they say," Reed recalled. "But I was good as a director." For one project, Lou chose to direct The Car Cemetery (or the Automobile Graveyard) by Fernando Arrabal. Reed could scarcely have found a more appropriate form (the theater of the absurd) or subject (it was loosely based on the Christ mythology) as a reflection of his life. The story line followed an inspired musician to his ultimate betrayal to the secret police by his accompanist. Everything Lou wrote or did was about himself, and had the props been available, perhaps Reed would have considered a climactic electroshock torture scene. In giving the musician a messianic role against a backdrop of cruel sex and prostitution, the play appealed to the would-be writer-musician. "I'm sure Lou had a homosexual experience with his drama teacher," attested another friend. "This drama teacher used to have guys go up to his room and put on girls' underwear and take pictures of them and then he'd give you an A. One dean of men himself either committed suicide or left because he was associated with this group of faculty fags who were later indicted for doing all kinds of strange stuff with the students."

The "first" gay flirtation cannot simply be overlooked and put aside as Morrison and Albin would want it to be. First of all, it had happened before. Back in Freeport during Lou's childhood, he had indulged in circle jerks, and the gay experience left him with traits that he would develop to his advantage commercially in the near future. Foremost among them was an effeminate walk, with small, carefully taken steps that could identify him from a block away.

Despite an apparent desire originally to concentrate on a career as a writer, just as his guitar was never far from his hand, music was never far from Reed's thoughts. Lou's first band at Syracuse was a loosely formed folk group comprising Reed; John Gaines, a striking, tall black guy with a powerful baritone; Joe Annus, a remarkably handsome, big white guy with an equally good voice; and a great banjo player with a big Afro hairdo who looked like Art Garfunkel.

The group often played on a square of grass in the center of campus at the corner of Marshall Street and South Crouse. They also occasionally got jobs at a small bar called the Clam Shack. Lou didn't like to sing in public because he felt uncomfortable with his voice, but he would sing his own folk songs privately to Shelley. He also played some traditional Scottish ballads based on poems by Robert Burns or Sir Walter Scott. Shelley, who would inspire Lou to write a number of great songs, was deeply moved by the beauty of his music. For her, his chord progressions were just as hypnotic and seductive as his voice. She was often moved to tears by their sensitivity.

Though he was devoting himself to poetry and folk songs, Lou had not dropped his initial ambition to be a rock-and-roll star. In addition to how to direct a play, Lou also learned how to dramatize himself at every opportunity. The showmanship would come in handy when Lou hit the stage with his rock music. Reed's development of folk music was put in the shade in his sophomore year when he finally formed his first bona fide rock-and-roll band, LA and the Eldorados. LA stood for Lewis and Allen, since Reed and Hyman were the founding members. Lou played rhythm and took the vocals, Allen was on drums, another Sammie, Richard Mishkin, was on piano and bass, and Mishkin brought in Bobby Newman on saxophone. A friend of Lou's, Stephen Windheim, rounded out the band on lead guitar. They all got along well except for Newman, a loud, obnoxious character from the Bronx who, according to Mishkin, "didn't give a shit about anyone." Lou hated Bobby and was greatly relieved when he left school that semester and was replaced by another sax player, Bernie Kroll, whom Lou fondly referred to as "Kroll the troll."

There was money to be made in the burgeoning Syracuse music scene, and the Eldorados were soon being handled by two students, Donald Schupak, who managed them, and Joe Divoli, who got them local bookings. "I had met Lou when we were freshmen," Schupak explained. "Maybe because we were friends as freshmen, nothing developed into a problem because he could say, 'Hey, Schupak, that's a fucking stupid idea.' And I'd say, 'You're right.' " Soon, under Schupak's guidance and Reed's leadership, LA and the Eldorados were working most weekends, playing frat parties, dances, bars, and clubs, making $125 a night, two or three nights a week.

Lou was strongly drawn to the musician's lifestyle and haunts. Just off campus was the black section of Syracuse, the Fifteenth Ward. There he frequented a dive called the 800 Club, where black musicians and singers performed and jammed together. Lou and his band were accepted there and would occasionally work with some of the singers from a group called the Three Screaming Niggers. "The Three Screaming Niggers were a group of black guys that floated around the upstate campuses," said Mishkin. "And we would pretend we were them when we got these three black guys to sing. So we would go down there once in a while and play. The people down there always had the attitude, the white man can't play the blues, and we'd be down playing the blues. Then they'd be nice to us." The Eldorados also sometimes played with a number of black female backing vocalists.

However, at first what made LA and the Eldorados stick out more than anything else was their car. Mishkin had a 1959 Chrysler New Yorker with gigantic fins, red guitars with flames shooting out of them painted on the side of the car, and "LA and the Eldorados" on the trunk. Simultaneously they all bought vests with gold lamé piping, jeans, boots, and matching shirts. Togged out in lounge-lizard punk and with Mishkin's gilded chariot to transport them to their shows, the band was a sight when it hit the road. They had the kind of adventures that bond musicians.

Mishkin remembered, "One time we played Colgate and we were driving back in Allen's Cadillac in the middle of a snowstorm, which eventually stopped us dead. So we're sitting in the car smoking pot around one A.M., and we realized that we can't do that all night because we'd die. The snow was deep, so we got out of the car and schlepped to this tiny town maybe half a mile away. We needed a place to stay so we went to the local hotel, which was, of course, full. But they had a bar there. Schupak was in the bar telling these stories about how he was in the army in the war, and Lewis and I are hysterical, we are dying it was so funny. Then the bartender said, 'You can't stay here, I have to close the bar.' We ended up going to the courthouse and sleeping in jail."

The Eldorados further distinguished themselves by mixing some of Lou's original material into their set of standard Chuck Berry covers. One of Lou's songs they played a lot was a love song he wrote for Shelley, an early draft of "Coney Island Baby." "We did a thing called 'Fuck Around Blues,' " Mishkin recalled. "It was an insult song. It sometimes went over well and it sometimes got us thrown out of fraternity parties."

LA and the Eldorados played a big part in Lou's life, providing him with many basic rock experiences, but he kept the band separate from the rest of his life at Syracuse. At first Lou wanted to make a point of being a writer more than a rock-and-roller. In those days, before the Beatles arrived, the term *rock-and-roller* was something of a put-down associated more with Paul Anka and Pat Boone than the Rolling Stones. Lou preferred to be associated with writers like Jack Kerouac. This dichotomy was spelled out in his limited wardrobe. Like the classic beatnik, Lou usually wore black jeans and T-shirts or turtlenecks, but he also kept a tweed jacket with elbow patches in his closet in case he wanted to come on like

John Updike. However, in either role—as rocker or writer—Lou appeared somewhat uncomfortable. Therefore, in each role he used confrontation as a means both to achieve an effect and dramatize an inner turmoil that was quite real. For Hyman and others, this sometimes made working with Lou exceedingly difficult.

According to Allen, "One of the biggest problems we had was that if Lou woke up on the day of the job and he decided he didn't want to be there, he wouldn't come. We'd be all set up and looking for him. I remember one fraternity party, it was an afternoon job, we were all set up and ready to go and he just wasn't there. I ran down to his room and walked through about four hundred pounds of his favorite pistachio nuts, and then I found him in bed under about six hundred pounds of pistachio nuts—in the middle of the afternoon. I looked at him and said, 'What are you doing? We have a job!' And he said, 'Fuck you, get out of here. I don't want to work today.' I said, 'You can't do this, we're getting paid!' Mishkin and I physically dragged him up to the show. Ultimately he did play, but he was very pissed off."

Reed seemed to at once want the spotlight and to hate it.

"Lou's uniqueness and stubbornness made him really different than anyone I had ever known," added Mishkin. "He was a terrible guy to work with. He was impossible. He was always late, he would always find fault with everything that the people who had hired us expected of us. And we were always dragging him here and dragging him there. Sometimes we were called Pasha and the Prophets because Lou was such a son of a bitch at so many gigs he'd upset everyone so much we couldn't get a gig in those places again. He was as ornery as you can get. People wouldn't let us back because he was so absolutely rude to people and just so mean and unappreciative of the fact that these people were paying us to get up and play music for them. He couldn't have cared less. So we used the name Pasha and the Prophets in order to play there again. And then the people who hired us were so drunk they wouldn't remember. He would never dress or act in a way so that people would accept him. He would often act in a confrontational manner. He wanted to be different.

"But Lou was ambitious. He wanted to be—and said this to me in no uncertain terms—a rock-and-roll star and a writer."

·   ·   ·

IN MAY 1962, SICK OF THE STODGY UNIVERSITY LITERARY PUBLICATION and keen to make their mark, Lewis and Lincoln, along with Stoecker, Gaines. Tucker, et al., put out two issues of a literary magazine called the *Lonely Woman Quarterly*. The title was based on Lou's favorite Ornette Coleman composition, "Lonely Woman."

Originating out of the Savoy with the encouragement of Gus Joseph, the first issue contained an untitled story, mentioned in the previous chapter, signed Luis Reed. It described Sidney Reed as a wife-beater, and Toby as a child molester. Shelley, who was involved in the publication, was convinced that just as Lou's homosexual affair was mostly an attempt to associate with the offbeat gay world, the story was a conspicuous attempt to build his image as an evil, mysterious person. He was smart enough, she thought, to see that this was going to make readers uncomfortable. "And that's what Lou always wanted to do," she said, "make people uncomfortable."

The premier issue of *LWQ* brought "Luis" his first press mention. In reviewing the magazine, the university's newspaper, the *Daily Orange*, had interviewed Lincoln, who boasted that the magazine's one hundred copies had sold out in three days. Indeed, the first issue was well received, but when everyone else on its staff apparently got lazy, Lou put out issue number two, which featured his second explosive piece, printed on page one. Called "Profile: Michael Kogan—Syracuse's Miss Blanding," it was the most attention-grabbing project Lou ever pulled off at Syracuse: a deftly executed, harsh attack upon the student who was head of the Young Democrats Party at the University. Allen Hyman recalled, "It said something like he [Kogan] should parade around campus with an American flag up his ass, which at the time was a fairly outrageous statement." Unfortunately, Kogan's father turned out to be a powerful corporation lawyer. "He decided that the piece was libelous," remembered Sterling, "and he'd bust Lou's ass. So they hauled him before the dean. But . . . the dean started shifting to Lou's side. Afterwards, the dean told Lou to finish up his work and get his ass out of there, and nothing would happen to him." By May of 1962, Reed's literary career was off to a running start.

Despite this, Lou's relationship with Shelley—not his classes—had dominated his sophomore year. They had spent as many of their waking hours together as was possible, camping out over the weekends in friends' apartments, using fraternity rooms, cars, and sometimes even bushes to make love. Lou received a D in Introduction to Math and an F in English History. Then he got in trouble with the authorities again when a friend was busted for smoking pot and ratted on a number of people, including Lewis and Ritchie Mishkin.

"We smoked all the time," admitted Mishkin. "But we didn't smoke and work. We may have played and then smoked after and then jammed. Anyway, the dean of men called Lou, me, and some other people into his office and said, 'We know you were smoking pot, so give us the whole story.' We were terrified, at least I was. But nothing happened. Lou was angry. With the authorities and with the informer. But they were pretty soft on us. We were lucky, but then all they had to go on was the 'he said, she said' kind of evidence, so there was a limit to what they could do. But they had us in the office and they did the old, 'We know because so-and-so said . . .' "

As a result of these numerous transgressions, and with his apparent academic torpor at the end of his sophomore year, Reed was put on academic probation.

THE SUMMER OF 1962 WAS SOMEWHAT DIFFICULT FOR LOU. THIS WAS THE first time he had been separated from Shelley for more than a day, and he took it hard. First, in an attempt to exert his control over her across the thousand miles that separated them, he embarked on a zealous letter-writing campaign, sending her long, storylike letters every day. They would begin with an account of his daily routine—he would go to the local gay bar, the Hayloft, every night—and tweak Shelley with suggestive comments. Then, in the middle of a paragraph the epistle would abruptly shift from reality to fiction and Lou would take off on one of his short stories, usually mirroring his passion and longing for Shelley. An exemplary story sent across the country that summer was "The Gift," which appeared on the Velvet Underground's second album, *White Light/ White Heat*, and perfectly summed up Lou's image of himself as a lonely Long Island nerd pining for his promiscuous girlfriend. "The Gift" climaxed with the lovelorn author desperately mailing himself to his lover in a womblike cardboard box. The final image, in the classic style of Yiddish humor that informed so much of Reed's work, had the boyfriend being accidentally killed by his girlfriend as she opened the box with a large sheet-metal cutter.

Shelley, a classic passive-aggressive character, rarely responded in kind, but she did talk to Lou on the phone several times that summer, and he did not like what he heard at all. Lou had expected Shelley to remain locked in her room thinking of nothing but him. But Shelley wasn't that kind of girl. Despite having commenced the vacation with a visit to the hospital to have her tonsils out, by July she was platonically dating more than one guy and at least one was madly in love with her. Despite the fact that Shelley was really loyal to Lou, the emotions Lou addressed in "The Gift" were his. He paced up and down his room in frustration. He couldn't stand not having Shelley under this thumb. It was driving him insane.

Then he hit on a plan. Why not go out and visit her? After all, he was her boyfriend, he was writing to her every day or so and had called her several times. It sounded like the right thing to do. His parents, who had kept a wary eye on their wayward son that summer, still frowning on his naughty visits to the Hayloft and daily excursions on the guitar, were only too happy to support a venture that they felt was taking him in the right direction. At the beginning of August he flew out to Chicago.

Shelley had been adamantly against the planned visit, warning Lou on the phone that her parents wouldn't like him, that it was a big mistake and wouldn't work out at all. But Lou, who wanted, she recalled, "to be in front of my face," insisted.

By now Lou had developed a pattern of reaction to any new environment he entered. His plan was to split up any group, polarizing them around him. In a family situation, as soon as he walked into anybody's house, he took the position that the father was a tyrannical ogre whom the mother had to be saved from. On his first night in the Albins' home, he cleverly drew Mr. Albin into a political discussion and then, marking him for the bullheaded liberal Democrat that he was, expertly lanced him with a detailed defense of the notorious conservative columnist William Buckley. While Shelley sat back and watched, half-horrified, half-mesmerized, Mr. Albin became increasingly apoplectic. Lou was obviously not the right man for his daughter. In fact, he didn't even want him in the house.

The Albins had rented a room for Lou in nearby Evanston, at Northwestern University. Using every trick in his book, Lou pulled a double whammy on Mr. Albin, driving his car into a ditch later the same night when bringing Shelley back from the movies at 1 A.M., forcing her father to get up, get dressed, come out, and help haul out the mauled automobile.

Things went downhill from there. Lou made a valiant attempt to win over Mrs. Albin. Having dinner with her and Shelley one night when the man of the house was absent, Lou launched into his classic rap, saying, "Gee, you're clearly very nice. If it wasn't for the ogre living in the house . . ." But Mrs. Albin was having none of his boyish charm. She had surreptitiously read Lou's letters to Shelley that summer and formed a very definite opinion about Lou Reed: she hated him with a passion—and still does more than thirty years later. In her opinion, Lou was ruining her daughter's life.

As an upshot of Lou's visit, Shelley's parents informed her that if she continued to see Lou in any way at all, she would never be allowed to return to Syracuse. Naturally, swearing that she would never set eyes upon the rebel again, Shelley now embarked upon a secret relationship with Lou that trapped her exactly where Reed wanted. Since Shelley had no one outside of Lou's circle in whom she could confide about her relationship with him, she was essentially under his control. From here on Lou would always attempt to program his women. His first move would always be to amputate them from their former lives so that they accepted that the rules were Lou's.

Chapter Three

SHELLEY, IF YOU JUST COME BACK

SYRACUSE UNIVERSITY: 1962–64

The image of the artist who follows a brilliant leap to success with a fall into misery and squalor, is deeply credited, even cherished in our culture.

—Irving Howe, from his foreword to In Dreams Begin Responsibilities and Other Stories by Delmore Schwartz

WHEN LOU RETURNED TO SYRACUSE FOR HIS JUNIOR YEAR, HE RENTED A room in a large apartment inhabited by a number of like-minded musicians and English majors on Adams Street. The room was so small that it could barely contain the bed, but that was okay with Lou because he lived in the bed. He had his typewriter, his guitar, and Shelley, who was now living in one of the cottage-style dorms opposite Crouse College, which were far less supervised than the big women's dorm. She was consequently able to live with Lou pretty much full-time.

The semester began magically with Shelley's arrival. Lou whipped out his guitar and a new instrument he had mastered over the summer, a harmonica, which he wore in a rack around his neck, and launched into a series of songs he had written for Shelley over the vacation, including the beautiful "I Found a Reason." Shelley, who was completely seduced by Lou's music, was brought to tears by the beauty and sensitivity of his playing, the music and the lyrics. Lou played the harmonica with an intense, mournful air that perfectly complemented his songs, but was unfortunately so much like Bob Dylan's that, so as not to be seen as a Dylan clone, he had to retire the instrument. It was a pity because Lou was a great, expressive harmonica player. In his new pad, he played his music as loud as he wanted and took drugs with impunity. It also became another stage on which to develop "Lou Reed." He rehearsed with the band there, often played music all night, and maintained a creative working environment essential to his writing. He was really beginning to feel his power. His band was under his control. He had already written "The Gift," "Coney Island Baby," "Fuck Around Blues," and later classics like "I'll Be Your Mirror" were in the works.

By the mid-1960s, the American college campus was going through a remarkable transformation that would soon introduce it to the world as one of the brighter beacons of politics and art. One of the marks of a particularly hip school was its creative writing department. Few American writers were able to make a living out of writing books. Somewhere in the 1950s some nut put together the bogus notion that you could haul in some bigwig writer like Ernest Hemingway or Samuel Beckett and get him to teach a bunch of some ten to fifteen young people how to write. However, it had succeeded in dragging a series of glamorous superstars like T. S. Eliot (a rival with Einstein and Churchill as the top draw in the 1950s) to Harvard for six weeks to give a series of lectures about how he wrote, leading hundreds of students to write poor imitations of *The Waste Land*. The concept of the creative writing program looked good on paper, but it was, in reality, a giant shuck, and the (mostly) poets who were on the lucrative gravy train in the early sixties were, for the most part, a bunch of wasted men who had helped popularize the craft during its glorious moment 1920–50, when poets like W. H. Auden had the cachet rock stars would acquire in the second half of the century.

Delmore Schwartz was one of the most charismatic, stunning-looking poets on the circuit. He had been foisted on the Syracuse University creative writing program by two heavyweights in the field—the great poet Robert Lowell and the novelist Saul Bellow, who would go on to win the Nobel Prize—who had known him in his prime as America's answer to T. S. Eliot. Unfortunately for both him and his students, Schwartz had by then, like so many of his calling, expelled his muse with near-lethal daily doses of amphetamine pills washed down by copious amounts of hard alcohol. Despite having as recently as 1959 won the prestigious Bollingen Prize for his selected poems, *Summer Knowledge*, when he arrived on campus in September 1962, Schwartz was, in fact, suffering through the saddest and most painful period of his life.

Sporting on his forty-nine-year-old face a greenish yellow tinge, which gave the impression he was suffering from a permanent case of jaundice, and a pair of mad eyes that boiled out from under his big, bloated brow with unrestrained paranoia, on a good day this brilliant man could still hold a class spellbound with the intelligence, sensitivity, and conviction of his hypnotic voice once it had seized upon its religion—literature. Schwartz once received a ten-minute standing ovation at Syracuse after giving his class a moving reading of *The Waste Land.* Unfortunately, by 1962 his stock was so low that none of the performances he gave at Syracuse—in the street, in the classroom, in bars, in his apartment, at faculty meetings, anywhere his voice could find receivers—was recorded.

Until the arrival of Delmore Schwartz, Lou Reed had not been overly impressed by his instructors at Syracuse. However, Lou only had to encounter Delmore once to realize that he had finally found a man impressively more disturbed than himself, from whom he might be able to get some perspective on all the demons that were boiling in his brain.

If Lou had been looking for a father figure ever since rejecting his old man as a silent, suffering Milquetoast, he had now found a perfect one in Delmore Schwartz. In both Bellow's novel about Schwartz, *Humboldt's Gift,* and James Atlas's outstanding biography, *Delmore Schwartz: The Life of an American Poet,* many descriptions of Schwartz's salient characteristics could just as well apply to what Lou Reed was fast becoming.

As Lou already did, Delmore entangled his friends in relationships with unnatural ardor until he was finally unbearable to everyone. Like Lou, Delmore ultimately caused those around him more suffering than pleasure. Like Lou, Delmore possessed a stunning arrogance along with a nature that was as solicitous as it was dictatorial. Both possessed astonishing displays of self-hatred mixed with self-love and finally concluded in concurrence with many of their friends that they were evil beings. Both were wonderful, hectic, nonstop inspirational improvisators and monologuists as well as expert flatterers. Grand, erratic, handsome men, they both gained much of their insights during long nights of insomnia.

But there the comparison ended. For Delmore Schwartz was already singing himself in and out of madness, and when his heart danced, it never danced for joy, whereas Lou possessed a marvelous ability for unadulterated joy and a carefully locked hold on reality. He had no doubt that he was going to succeed, and most of his friends equally believed in his talent. Lou may have shared with Delmore moments of sublime inspiration alternated with moments of indescribable despair, but unlike Schwartz, Reed had not read himself out of American culture.

In his junior year, Reed took a number of courses with Schwartz apart from creative writing. They read Dostoyevsky, Shakespeare, and Joyce together, and when studying *Ulysses*, Lou saw himself as Dedalus to Schwartz's Bloom. They developed a friendship that would go on until Lou graduated.

At first Schwartz would attend classes in which it was his duty to entertain students. Soon, however, rather than attempting to teach them how to write, he would fall into wandering, often despondent rants about the great men he had known, the sex life of the queen of England, etc., conveying his information in tones so authoritative and confiding that he convinced his astonished audiences that he really knew what he was talking about. When he grew tired of these exercises of nostalgia for a lost life, he would often fill in the time reading aloud or, on bad days, mumbling incoherently. He also set up an office at the far back left-hand corner table of the Orange Bar, where, usually sitting directly opposite Lou, who was one of the few students able to respond to him, and surrounded by several rows of chairs, Schwartz would do what he had now become best at. Saul Bellow called him "the Mozart of conversation."

Shelley, who was always at the table with them, recalled that Lou and Delmore "adored each other. Delmore was always drinking, popping Valiums, and talking. He was kind of edgy, big, he would move but in a very contained manner. His hands would move, picking things up, putting them down; he was always lurking over and I always got the feeling he was slobbering because he was always eating and talking and spitting things out. He was very direct to me. He said, 'I love Lou. You have to take care of Lou because he has to be a writer. He is a writer. And it is your job to give up your life to make sure that Lou becomes a writer. Don't let him treat you like shit. But tolerate everything he does to stay with him because he needs you.' "

Later in his life, perhaps to some extent to disarm the notion that he was just a rock-and-roll guitar player, Lou liked nothing better than to reminisce about his relationship with Delmore. "Delmore was my teacher, my friend, and the man who changed my life. He was the smartest, funniest, saddest person I had ever met. I studied with him in the bar. Actually, it was him talking and me listening. People who knew me would say, 'I can't imagine that.' But that's what it was. I just thought Delmore was the greatest. We drank together starting at eight in the morning. He was an awesome person. He'd order five drinks at once. He was incredibly smart. He could recite the encyclopedia to you starting with the letter A. He was also one of the funniest people I ever met in my life. He was an amazingly articulate, funny raconteur of the ages. At this time Delmore would be reading *Finnegans Wake* out loud, which seemed like the only way I could get through it. Delmore thought you could do worse with your life than devote it to reading James Joyce. He was very intellectual but very funny. And he hated pop music. He would start screaming at people in the bar to turn the jukebox off.

"At the time, no matter how strange the stories or the requests or the plan, I was there. I was ready to go for him. He was incredible, even in his decline. I'd never met anybody like him. I wanted to write a novel; I took creative writing. At the same time, I was in rock-and-roll bands. It doesn't take a great leap to say, 'Gee, why don't I put the two together?' "

Schwartz's most famous story, "In Dreams Begin Responsibilities," was a real eye-opener for Lou. The story centers around a hallucination by a son who finds himself in a cinema watching a documentary about his parents and flips out, screaming a warning to them not to have a son. " 'In Dreams Begin Responsibilities' really was amazing to me," Lou recalled. "To think you could do that with the simplest words available in such a short span of pages and create something so incredibly powerful. You could write something like that and not have the greatest vocabulary in the world. I wanted to write that way, simple words to cause an emotion, and put them with my three chords."

Delmore, for his part, clearly believed in Lou as a writer. The climax of Lou's relationship with Delmore came when the older poet put his arm around Lou in the Orange Bar one might and told him, "I'm gonna be leaving for a world far better than this soon, but I want you to know that if you ever sell out and go work for Madison Avenue or write junk, I will haunt you."

"I hadn't thought about doing anything, let alone selling out," Reed recalled. "I took that seriously. He saw even then that I was capable of writing decently. Because I never showed him anything I wrote—I was really afraid. But he thought that much of me. That was a tremendous compliment to me, and I always retained that."

Close though they were, they had two serious differences of opinion. As a man of the forties, Delmore was an educated hater of homosexuals. The uncomprehending attitudes common among straight American males toward gays in the early sixties put homosexuals on the level of communists or drug addicts. Therefore, Lou was unable to show Delmore many of his best short stories, since they were based on gay themes.

Then there was rock and roll. Delmore despised it, and in particular the lyrics, which he saw as a cancer in the language. Delmore knew Lou was in a band but wrote it off as a childish activity he would outgrow as soon as he commenced his graduate studies in literature.

Delmore Schwartz was thus barred from two of the most powerful strands of Lou's work.

Lou's relationship with Shelley reached its apotheosis in his junior year when, she felt, he really gained in confidence and began to transform himself. Ensconced together in the Adams Street apartment debris of guitars and amps, books, clothing, and cigarettes, Lou now lived in a world of music accompanied by the spirit of Shelley. She knew every nook and cranny of him better than anybody, and before he put his armor on. She had become his best friend, the one who could look into his eyes, the one he wrote for and played to.

Lou needed to be grounded because although Lincoln could be cooler than whipped cream and smarter than amphetamine, he was a lunatic. Lou always needed a court jester nearby to keep him amused, but he also required the presence of a straight, 1950s woman who could cool him down when the visions got too heavy. Shelley Albin became everything to Lou Reed: she was mother, sister, muse, lover, fixer-upper, therapist, drug mule, mad girl. She did everything with Lou twenty-four hours a day.

Lou was drinking at the Orange as Delmore told stories of perverts and weirdos and fulminated over the real or imaginary plots that were afoot in Washington. Lou was flying on a magic carpet of drugs. Pages of manuscripts and other debris piled up in his room, which Shelley felt was a purposeful pigsty. Lou was having an intensely exciting relationship with

Lincoln, who was going bonkers, lost in a long, hysterical novel mostly dictated by a series of voices giving him conflicting orders in his head. Lou was also displaying that special nerve that is given to very few men, getting up in front of audiences three or four times a week, blowing off a pretty good set of rock and roll, playing some wild, inventive guitar, becoming a lyrical harmonica player, turning his voice into a human jukebox.

Everything was changing. Rock was "Telstar" by the Tornadoes, "Walk Like a Man" by the Four Seasons, "He's So Fine" by the Chiffons—all great records in Lou's mind—but what was really happening on campuses across the USA was folk music. Dylan was about to make his big entrance, beating Lou to the title of poet laureate of his generation.

At this point, Lou appeared to have several options. He could have gone to Harvard under the wing of Delmore Schwartz and perhaps been an important poet. He could have married Shelley and become a folksinger. He could have collaborated with any number of musicians at Syracuse to form a rock-and-roll band. Instead, he began to separate himself from each of his allies and collaborators one by one.

THE TROUBLE STARTED WITH LOU'S ACQUISITION OF A DOG, SEYMOUR, A female cross between a German shepherd and a beagle cum dachshund, three and a half feet long standing four inches off the ground. If you believe that dogs always mirror their owners, then Seymour was, in Shelley's words, "a Lou dog." Lou appeared to be able to open up more easily and communicate more sympathetically with Seymour than with anybody else in the vicinity. As far as Shelley could tell, the only times Lou seemed to feel really at peace with himself were when he was rolling on the floor with Seymour, or sitting with the mutt on the couch staring into space. Soon, however, Lou's love for the dog became obsessive, and he started remonstrating with Shelley about treating Seymour better and paying more attention to her.

Meanwhile, Lou's behavior increasingly hinted at the complex nature Shelley would have to deal with if she stayed with him. "I mean he got crazy about being nice to that dog," she commented later. "He was a total shit about it, so that was a clue." But then he couldn't be bothered to take the dog out for a walk in the freezing cold. It soon became evident that it fell to Shelley to feed and walk the dog. Even then the mercurial Lewis decided to dump the dog. Shelley had to persuade him not to. Then Lewis hit on another diabolical plan. He would take the dog home to Freeport and dump it on his family, without warning. And he knew exactly how to do it.

That Thanksgiving, Lou and Shelley returned to Freeport with the surprise gift. Displaying its Lou-like behavior, at La Guardia airport the dog rushed out of the cargo area where it had been forced to travel and immediately pissed all over the floor, leading Lou's mother to start screaming, "A dog! Oh my God, a dog in my house! We don't need a dog!" Riposting with the artful aplomb that would lead so many of Reed's later collaborators to despair, Lou presented an offer that could not be refused, announcing that the dog was, in fact, a gift for Bunny.

Dismayed at first by this invasion of their domain, the Reeds were, in time—much to Lou's chagrin—unexpectedly delighted by the new arrival. As it turned out, the dog possessed some of Lou's charm without any of his less attractive attributes. Soon Seymour was scurrying around the Reeds' living room or snuggling up to Toby as if she were her long-lost mother. In short, Seymour became the light of Toby's life in a way Lewis never could be.

"Can you imagine," Lou ad-libbed in a 1979 song, "Families," "when I first took her there nobody wanted her, but soon she became more important than me!"

Naturally, as soon as Lou saw how much his family liked the dog, he quickly reversed his decision to bestow her on Bunny and insisted on taking her back to Syracuse where she would live with him until he graduated, after which Seymour would live out the remainder of her life as the most popular member of the Reed household.

During their visit Lou took Shelley into Harlem to pick up drugs. "He said, 'Come on, we've got to pick something up,' " she recalled. "I remember going up to One Hundred and Twenty-fifth Street. Really vile, nasty hallways. It was a guy who was a musician, I remember him sitting at this grand piano in his apartment in Harlem. I think there was a connection between the guys in the bar in Syracuse and the guy there. I knew we were going to pick up drugs, my memory was that it was heroin, but I couldn't swear to it. I was more worried about his driving. And I knew I wasn't supposed to be in Harlem. I had a bad attitude. For white kids to do that at the time was stupid. It was dangerous. I could have gotten raped or killed. He loved that."

It was, however, neither the drugs nor the dog that finally caused his relationship with Shelley to break down. Although there was no doubt that Lou was in love with Shelley and their relationship was enlightening for both of them, Lou experimented sexually. According to Mishkin, for example, Lou had a thing for big girls, especially "one big fat ugly bitch who he also really loved to fuck on the side." He also occasionally had sex with one of the black female singers who accompanied the Eldorados. "I never observed him being particularly nice to Shelley," Hyman commented, "but then I never observed him being particularly nice to anyone."

When Lou wasn't nice to a woman, he could, it turned out, be particularly cruel, constantly pushing them to an edge, thereby testing the strength of their love. His idea, Shelley said, was, "I'm going to remake you and then I'm not going to like you, and I'm going to push you around and see when you're going to leave me. The worse I treat you the more it proves to me that you love me and you'll stay with me forever. He clearly got very obnoxious. He had to have somebody to kick around so he felt big, and at that point I was the kickee."

She was not the sort of girl to take this kind of treatment lying down, and she retaliated with several thrusts of her own. On one occasion the Eldorados were booked to play a fraternity at Cornell. Shelley had been dating one of the fraternity brothers sporadically on the side and decided to go along for the ride. When Lou walked in with the slightly effeminate walk he had mastered, the brothers were enraged to see Shelley on his arm. She had spent several weekends at the fraternity house and now this little Jewish fag . . . Shelley had not told Lou about the predicament, and even he was impressed by the hostility that greeted him. "Jesus, they're so nasty, they're a bunch of animals," he told Shelley. Somewhere during the evening she casually explained, "They're so hostile because I've been here on various weekends with this guy Peter. I'm his girlfriend." They barely got out of there alive.

Back at Syracuse the relationship between Lou and Shelley came to a climax one night at another fraternity job, when Lou came up to her between sets and said, "I'm going to go into the back room with that girl. Do you want to watch?" Seeing Ritchie Mishkin smirk at her, Shelley finally snapped, decided that she had taken enough abuse from Lou, and left the fraternity. It was February 1963 and bitterly cold. Lincoln accompanied her on the long walk back to her dorm telling her not to worry, that he was still there and that she was right to leave. That she shouldn't have let Lou treat her so badly for so long.

"Lou and I had such dire things going on between us for the previous few months," Shelley explained. "The groupie thing just finally put me over the edge. I never had any doubt that Lou was going to be a rock star and that if I was going to stay with Lou, I was going to be a rock star's wife. I made the decision to leave him and to stay away from him based on the next ten years of my life.

"The next day he said, 'I was so stoned I don't remember doing that. Why are you mad at me? Did I do that?' "

But Shelley had finally come to understand what made Lou tick, and she didn't like what she understood at all. The struggle to conquer and control was much more important to him than the possession, just as being a voyeur was becoming more important to him than natural sex. Basically, Lou was incapable of maintaining any kind of normal, nurturing relationship. Like a shark, he had an urge to poke at bodies until he found a live one, then devour it as ferociously and completely as he could, letting the blood run down his chin.

By the middle of his junior year, Lou had turned himself into a monster with eight different faces. It was in these various guises that he would slither through his life, building up great bands only to tear them down, devouring and destroying everybody he could seduce, because he resented the whole situation of life and didn't want anybody else to have any fun if he wasn't able to.

Ever since Lou had moved into his own apartment, the relationship with Lincoln Swados had been less close. As the junior year ground on, Lincoln showed alarming signs of having a real nervous breakdown. "I don't think either of us knew that Lincoln was truly schizophrenic," Shelley remembered. "Lou was so busy pulling so much of his drama from Lincoln that I don't know how much he realized Lincoln was truly ill, or whether he just thought Lincoln just had a better scam going. He was trying to pick up on Lincoln's traits and abilities. Much of Lou is Lincoln." Shelley claimed that for both men, the trajectory of a love relationship went something like this: "I'm going to stroke you and treat you

kindly and bless you with my knowledge and presence, and then kill you."
Allen Hyman agreed that Lou had picked up many of his twisted ideas
about life from Lincoln. "You couldn't get much weirder than Lincoln,"
he said, "without being Lou."

Shortly after Shelley left Lou, Lincoln was carted off to the bughouse
by his parents, who found him in a state of agitation far beyond their
wildest fears. According to Swados's sister, Elizabeth, he had got into "a
helplessly disoriented state. He was unable to go to classes, unable to
leave his room. The voices in his head were directing him to do too many
different things."

In short order, Lou had lost his best friends, his two mirrors. Delmore
was still there, but he was going in and out of hospital himself and was
hardly in a position to give Lou a shoulder to cry on—although he did
give him one piece of important advice. He told Lou that he should see
a psychiatrist and that it should be a woman, because he wouldn't listen
to a man.

However, despite her determination to avoid her former lover, the
break-up threw Shelley into a black depression, and she went out and did
the one thing that was bound to draw Lou's attention back to her—she
dyed her hair orange. "I remember Lou seeing it and saying, 'Wow! Now
you're appealing, now you really look like Miss Trash.' " Typically, Lou
had to race back to Freeport to show his parents what he had done to the
nice Jewish girl they had so doted on. "They saw this nice, wholesome girl
turned into trash and they said, 'Oh my God, Lou has done it again. He
has ruined somebody, he has won, he has turned her into trash,' " Shelley
recalled. "At that point, his mother even said to me, 'I hope he doesn't
treat you like he treats us.' We did horrify his mother. He loved it."

As soon as they got back to school, they broke up again. By then she
was determined not to go back to him. "He was such a shit."

NOVEMBER 1963 WAS A CATHARTIC MONTH FOR LOU. IT STARTED WITH A
Syracuse concert by Bob Dylan. "Lou idolized Dylan when Dylan first
came on the scene with his first album," explained Mishkin. "We knew
every inch of his music inside and out. All of a sudden there was this
music and poetry together, and it wasn't folk music. Lou was blown away
by it. It was an exciting thing. And Lewis immediately got a harmonica

and was playing that. And I remember sitting in the apartment with [Eldorado] Stevie Windheim and Lewis figuring out the chords to "Baby Let Me Follow You Down," and we got them and we were playing it and it wasn't the kind of thing we were going to do for a gig, but we had a good time with it."

The assassination of President Kennedy on November 22, 1963, was a major turning point for Lou. The event struck a blow to Delmore from which he would never recover. Lou watched helplessly as his mentor cum drinking buddy fell into a paranoid depression. He gave up any pretense of continuing to teach and retreated permanently to the Orange Bar. Soon Lou was looking after Delmore, walking him home at night after long sessions at the bar, making sure he had his key, his cigarettes, sometimes picking up groceries or other sundries for him. When Schwartz left the Orange, he was often so transported to other realms he might head off in any direction like some human dowsing wand in search of companionship or, as often as not, trouble. Lou always made sure Delmore got home, got himself to bed, and was not in too much danger of burning down the premises with a carelessly dropped cigarette. After a while, however, this kind of care takes on a spooky quality as the young man begins to recognize his own fate in that of the older man. Suddenly Lou, who had been benefiting from Delmore's enlightened encouragement, taking seriously his recommendation to go to Harvard, found himself taking care of a man who was increasingly incapable of getting from A to B without assistance. "Lou always felt that he had to stay around and watch Delmore and take care of him," said Shelley. "I think Lou began to find that a little tedious."

Meanwhile, Lou had initiated his own decline. Ever since he had been put on medication following the electroshock treatments of 1959, Lou had been an inveterate drug user. Or, to use his own description, a "smorgasbord schmuck." If he wasn't popping pills, he was inhaling pot, dropping acid, eating mushrooms, horning coke, or dropping Placidyls— not to mention bolting down enough booze to keep the Orange Bar in business around the clock. Now, for the first time, he added heroin to his drug menu, whereas previously he had only sold it.

Shelley marked Lou's downslide from the time he started to inject heroin. He had always been petrified by needles and said that he would never shoot any drugs into his veins. Once he began taking heroin, he insisted he could control it all the time and stop whenever he wanted to simply because he had elected to do so. Shelley recalled, "He was getting into heroin on and off. The experience was pretty horrifying to him and he was having some bad LSD trips too."

Shelley had no sympathy for Lou's cries for help. However, Lou had gone into a decline when he realized that Shelley was not only not coming back to him, but was in fact living with two other adult men just three doors down from his apartment. On another occasion when she was sitting in the Orange Bar with her new lover and his Korean vet friends, an acolyte of Lou's came racing in frantically telling her that Lou was having a really bad time. Although she fully expected that he might not make it through the night, Shelley sent back the reply, "If you send somebody over here to tell me that you're dying, die!"

Still, Shelley felt sorry for him. "Lou can't have a good time, it's not in his genes," she stated later. "He feels that he doesn't deserve it. The moment you say Lou's okay, he thinks there's something wrong with you. Because if you say he's okay, then you don't see how evil he is, you don't see all the bad things. He can't have a wonderful time any more than he can accept that people like him. That's what's so sad about Lou."

Swados, after Schwartz the most perceptive man Reed knew at university, was the first to note (in a conversation with a girlfriend a year later) that beneath Lou's often waiflike desperation, his need to be mothered, existed a much tougher, harder, more realistic man. He possessed an ambition and drive of which very few people who knew him at Syracuse had any idea. The fact alone, for example, that he would continue to experiment with drugs for the next fifteen years and survive suggests that he was at heart not only a survivor, but a student of narcotics who took care to know what it was he was ingesting.

THE MOST IMPORTANT DEVELOPMENT IN HIS SENIOR YEAR WAS LITERARY. Lou leapt across a great gap when he switched from making the short story his primary form to song lyrics, taking his knowledge of the short story structure with him. In many ways Bob Dylan was a major influence on Lou in this decision as well as in his subsequent decision not to apply to the graduate writing program at Harvard, but to pursue his love of rock and roll as a career. Dylan not only showed him a way to write lyrics, he legitimized being a singer/songwriter with intellectual credentials. That was the vital point. Lou needed to be recognized intellectually. He was concerned about Delmore's response to his decision; he didn't want Delmore to think that he didn't consider his words valuable. And yet, Delmore's collapse may have freed him to journey into that region he had always aspired to—the combination of writing and rock-and-roll lyrics.

"I thought, look, all these writers are writing about only a very small part of the human experience," Reed pointed out. "Whereas a record could be like a novel, you could write about this. It was so obvious, it's amazing everybody wasn't doing it. Let's take *Crime and Punishment* and turn it into a rock-and-roll song!

"But if you're going to talk about the greats, there is no one greater than Raymond Chandler. I mean, after reading Raymond Chandler and going on to someone else, it's like eating caviar and then turning to some real inferior dish. Take the sensibility of Raymond Chandler or Hubert Shelby or Delmore Schwartz or Poe and put it to rock music."

Like any foray into oneself, writing proved to be more than exhilarating. It was, for Lou, a long and painful process. "I love writing," Lou would tell an interviewer, "except that it's excruciating. It's a very strange process, I've never really understood it myself. But I'm available for, I'm there for, I try to make things as easy as possible for it. I just try and stay out of the way. So once I start typing, I never stop. I don't try and stop to fix anything because it will go away and then I'll never get it back ever again. Raymond Chandler: 'That blonde was as pleasant as a split lip.' Hard to beat that. He's talking about a guy's thumbnail, he thought his thumbnail looked like the edge of a ice cube. Boom, you can see it. And that's what I try to do. I try to give you a very visual image in very few words, so that you can picture it in your mind really quick. I spend most of my time taking things out. Taking tons of stuff out. Really chopping it down. That's the goal. Besides communicating emotion and having a beginning, middle, and an end, I'm really hammering at those words to be concise and get it across to you as quickly and visually as possible."

During this time, Lou continued to mine his everyday experiences for song material. He spent a lot of time going into New York, scoring drugs and checking out bands. He was fixated on Ornette Coleman and used to try to see him whenever he performed in New York City. In his last semester, his writing, taking drugs, loneliness, and fascination with un-

---

derground jazz set off a creative explosion. He wrote at least two songs, "Waiting for My Man" and "Heroin." The precision and scope of these songs heralded the Lou Reed who would become known as the Baudelaire of New York.

"At the time I wrote 'Heroin,' I felt like a very rather negative, strung-out, violent, aggressive person. I meant those songs to sort of exorcise the darkness, or the self-destructive element in me, and hoped that other people would take them the same way. 'Heroin' is very close to the feeling you get from smack. It starts on a certain level, it's deceptive. You think you're enjoying it. But by the time it hits you, it's too late. You don't have any choice. It comes at you harder and faster and keeps on coming. The song is everything that the real thing is doing to you." It would take Lou a year to work up "Heroin" from rough lyrics and bare-bone chords into one of the greatest rock-and-roll songs of all time. Mishkin helped Lou by hammering out its unforgettable bass line. Not until Lou met John Cale in the fall of 1964 did he develop the two Syracuse songs into the form in which they were recorded.

Reed's senior year was pitted with conflicts and frustrations that emerged in several dramatic incidents. In October the Eldorados had gone down to Sarah Lawrence to play a series of weekend dates. Now that Hyman had graduated and had been replaced by another drummer, Lou was ever more impatient with his plodding bandmates. One night when they got to the venue, Lou didn't want to play. "So he said, 'Fuck you, I'm not going to play for these assholes,' " remembered Mishkin. "And suddenly, right in front of everybody, he smashed his hand through a plate glass window [in emulation of Lincoln, who had done the same thing years earlier]. Of course he couldn't play. We took him to the hospital and there were lots of stitches."

Lou continued to flaunt his bad attitude. Rather than masking his increasing drug consumption, he became its walking advertisement. At 8 A.M., while other students trotted off to class, he would stand outside the Orange Bar to wait for Delmore, on the unmistakable heroin nod. "I was sitting in the Orange one early-spring day," remembered Sterling. "Lou and this guy were sitting in the guy's red convertible with the radio on full blast, the top down, and they were both nodding out in the front seat, so I went out and put the top up and turned the radio off. I remember another time sitting in the Orange and Lou came in and thought he was

leaning on his elbow, except his elbow was about a foot above the table."
The local campus police, who were determined to crack down on drugs,
took note of this behavior and put Reed under surveillance.

"I had recently been asked by the Tactical Police Force of the city
which housed my large eastern university to leave town well before graduation because of various clandestine operations I was alleged to be involved in," wrote Reed in one essay. "In those days few people had long
hair and those who did recognized each other as, at the very least, a good
guy and one who smoked marijuana. They couldn't catch me."

In fact, Lou suffered police surveillance more than he knew. In 1963,
as drugs spread rapidly through college campuses across the country, the
Syracuse Police Department had taken a small group of officers lead by
Sgt. Robert Longo from the vice squad and created a brand-new narcotics
squad. The heat was closing in, to employ the opening sentence of Lou's
favorite book, William Burroughs's recently published *Naked Lunch*. To
counterbalance the police pressure, Shelley and a friend of hers had
developed a friendship with two of the members of this new Syracuse
narcotics squad. "The police squad car would pull up outside my apartment and they'd supposedly be working, but they'd be having a beer and
hanging out," she recalled. "And getting a little bit of nooky without my
having to commit myself in any way. They came up and got a few hugs
and kisses and thought they were making real progress with the lewd, evil
girls of the campus. Lou met the cops and knew them through his senior
year. He used to see them in the Varsity a lot. Lou was harassed by the
same police. They just plain hated Lou."

Shelley was more aware of how much the cops really wanted to get Lou
("They thought he was a gay faggot evil shit," she said) and knew that if
they got their hands on him, they would beat him up badly. She repeatedly made it a condition of seeing the cop that he promise they would not
touch Lou. "Touch Lou," she told him, "and you don't touch me."

At first, the fact that the heavies from the narcotics squad were on
Lou's tail was more of an amusement than a hassle for him. He enjoyed
entertaining friends with stories about how, after being tipped off about
an impending bust, he had buried his stash at a nearby Boy Scout camp.
Lou felt confident that he could outsmart the police just as he had out-
witted authorities throughout his life.

There were also signs that a calmer, more confident Lou was emerging, a Lou who had passed through the very center of some internal tornado and survived stronger, surer, and more his own man. Larry Goldstein, a freshman whose band the Downbeats won the battle of the bands at Syracuse in 1963, and who had briefly joined LA and the Eldorados, got a chance to hang out with Lou one night.

"We started playing together, doing mostly college gigs," Goldstein recounted. "We played Cornell for one, and we used to play the FI—the Fayetteville Inn—which was about twenty miles from Syracuse. Lou was really nothing but very nice to us. We were just kids in comparison, but he wasn't a prima donna or a rock-star type, he was very supportive. There was a restaurant called Ben's in the Fifteenth Ward near Lou's apartment that served really greasy soul food, and Lou used to go there a lot. One night after we played a gig we were sitting around Lou's apartment and I remember him as being very gentle and very nice, like a kind of father figure. And he suggested that we go to Ben's to get something to eat. Lou seemed a lot older than us. And he was much more mature in many ways. He had an alternative type of personality that was unlike anyone else. I never remembered him being arrogant about it. He was just advanced."

In June 1964, Reed graduated with a bachelor of arts degree from the Syracuse College of Arts and Sciences. The richness of Lou's character, and yet at the same time its awful limitation, was revealed in Lou's last act of human kindness at Syracuse. According to Reed, "As soon as exams were over, at the graduation ceremony, I was told by the Tactical Police Squad that if I wasn't gone within an hour, they'd beat me up. They couldn't get me, but they'd break every bone, every movable part of my body. So I split, but I still graduated with honors."

However, according to Shelley, Lou in fact stayed after graduation strictly to take care of her through a particularly bad illness. The two of them had been living half a block apart. Shelley was installed on McDonald Street with her killer boyfriend; Lou was living alone on the corner of Adams. Near the end of the semester, Shelley's boyfriend had gone on a trip. Lou visited and found her unable to attend classes. He scooped her up and moved her into his apartment. Knowing she'd fail her course with Phillip Booth if he didn't do something drastic, Lou took her over to Booth's house. "I remember being bundled over there and being plunked down on the couch and being told, 'Just sit there and look hopeless,' " she recalled. "Which was no effort. My eyes must have been rolling in my head. He just told Booth, 'Pass this person,' and he did." As the other students left campus, Shelley was still too ill to travel, so Lou stayed with her and, she said, "really put me back together."

Shelley remembered thinking, "I really love him, he's really fantastic," but also being exhausted and foggy. "You know how it is when you get back together with someone. He was just terrific. We were really pigs in shit, like two kids let out of jail. He was adorable. It was a perfect time. We were really amazed at having such a good time."

She stayed with him for one to two weeks. Unfortunately, it was too long, and Shelley found herself being unpleasantly reminded of Lou's need to be in control and had an intuitive feeling that things would never work out between them. And so, when he put her onto the plane to Chicago, she waved good-bye to Lou without wondering when she would see him again.

Chapter Four

THE PICKWICK
PERIOD

WITH PICKWICK INTERNATIONAL:

1964—65

The Pickwick experience was the first plateau of Lou's maturation as a musician. It gave him a point of departure that I think was critical to his becoming what he became.

—Donald Schupak

INSTEAD OF GOING INTO NEW YORK LIKE THE MAJORITY OF THE OTHER bright English-literature graduates coming down from Syracuse University, Lou retreated to the comfort and safety of his parents' home. In the summer of 1964, he turned his full attention toward evading the draft. He knew he'd have to put on a good show at the draft hearing to convince the army officials he was sick, crazy, or both. He chose both.

Providentially, he was aided in his cause by a real illness that struck a few days after he got home to Freeport. Feeling feverish and exhausted, he was diagnosed as having a bad case of hepatitis, which he later claimed to have acquired in a shooting gallery by sharing a needle with a mashed-faced Negro named Jaw. Upon receiving this news, Lou immediately placed an expensive long-distance phone call to Shelley, warning her that she too might have acquired the disease during their recent rapprochement. Then he set about lining up medical evidence sufficient to stave off his recruitment into the army.

According to Lou, he managed to pull off his feat in a record ten minutes by walking into his local draft board chewing on his favorite downer, a 750-milligram Placidyl, a large green pill prescribed for its

hypnotic, calming effects and to induce sleep. The effects of the pill come
on within fifteen minutes to an hour and may be greatly enhanced when
combined with alcohol, barbiturates, and or other central nervous system
depressants. Although Placidyl was available over the counter through
the 1960s, due to its potential to cause severe, often suicidal depression,
as well as drug dependence, it is now available in America by prescription
only. "I said I wanted a gun and would shoot anyone or anything in front
of me," Reed recalled. If this smart-aleck claim didn't do the trick, the
yellow pall cast over his visage by the incipient hepatitis did. "I was
pronounced mentally unfit and given a classification that meant I'd only
be called up if we went to war with China. It was the one thing my shock
treatments were good for."

It was the summer of 1964. His father offered him a job in his tax
accountancy business, which he insisted Lou take over and inherit upon
his retirement. Lou did not fancy sitting behind a desk peering at a
calculator. He told Sidney that he should give his business to Elizabeth
(aged sixteen) because she had a better head for such things. Instead, Lou
put together a band and hacked his way through the summer playing local
shows, which included, as often as possible, gay bars. Resenting his family's earlier embrace of electroshock treatments and their current disapproval of his lifestyle, Lou set about stinging them with rejection. As he
would sing in one of his catalogs of contempt, "Families," that families
who dwell in the suburbs often reduce each other to tears.

However, the battle was not over. Summer fun was one thing allowed
the indolent rich graduates on the island, but come fall, every one of
them was expected to take up a calling. Hyman was already in law school.
Lou's parents presumed their son would also buckle down to some kind of
acceptable career.

How wrong they were! In a move calculated to upset both Delmore
Schwartz and his parents, Lou took a job writing made-to-order pop songs
for a cheap recording company called Pickwick International and, in their
eyes, threw away an expensive education.

The agent of this first step on Lou's path to becoming a songwriter was
none other than Lou's old friend from Syracuse, the manager of LA and
the Eldorados, Don Schupak. "I introduced Lou to a guy who I had
developed a partnership with back here in the city, Terry Phillips," Schupak recalled. Phillips, who had roomed with the record-producing genius

Phil Spector in the early 1960s, had convinced Pickwick to venture into the rock business. "They were taught the notion of rock and roll by Terry Phillips and me," Schupak continued. "They eventually became Music-land, and the people we had to convince to start this studio at the cost of eighty dollars have made tens if not hundreds of millions of dollars in the rock-and-roll business since then."

Reed was hired on Schupak's recommendation. "Pickwick started Lou's career," Donald recalled. "It taught him the discipline of showing up. It put him into the industry."

The grand, British-sounding Pickwick International consisted, in fact, of a squat cinder-block warehouse in Long Island City, across the river from Manhattan. The whole operation was run out of this warehouse full of cheap, slapdash records, with a small basement recording studio in a converted storeroom containing, as Schupak, who also worked there as a "record executive," recalled, "a shitty old spinet piano and a Roberts tape recorder." Lou, who received $25 a week for his endeavors—and no rights to any of his material—made the twenty-five-minute commute from Free-port to Long Island City every day. Once there, he would find himself locked into the tiny studio with three collaborators: the pasty-faced Phillips, whose pencil mustache, slicked-back hair, and polyester suits evinced his weird distance from life, and two other songwriters, Jerry Vance (alias Jerry Pellegrino) and Jimmie Sims (Jim Smith). While Schupak tried to figure out what he was supposed to be doing, Phillips took it upon himself to direct the fledgling rock arm of the Pickwick label.

Pickwick specialized in producing bargain-basement rip-off albums for a naive mass audience. For example, something like *Bobby Darin Sings the Blues* featured Darin crooning on exactly one song, squeezed in amidst ten other sung by Jack Borgheimer; the album of ten hot-rod songs by the Roughnecks sported a cover (minus Lou) of four gallivanting lads who looked, at a distance, suspiciously like the Beatles, but were in fact a bunch of pasty-faced session musicians wearing wigs. In other words, the album would say it featured four groups and it wouldn't really be four groups, it would just be various permutations of the writers, and they would sell them at supermarkets for ninety-nine cents or a dollar. In retrospect, observed Phil Milstein, one of Lou's most informed and appreciative critics and the founder in 1978 of the Velvet Underground Appreciation Society, "in many ways this is the craziest part of the entire crazy story. No work Lou has done is so trivial, so prefabricated, so tossed off, as what he did at Pickwick."

The Roughnecks' song "You're Driving Me Insane" opened with a tuneless buzz of guitars and then applied the unschooled, scratchy sound of the Kinks to some riffs refined from Chuck Berry. Over the dense, muddy instrumental came the lyrics—half-spoken, half-forced—droned-out words that were supported by the eerie abandon of a rabble of party-goers in the background: "The way you rattle your brain / You know you're driving me insane." Another contribution by another fake group, the Beachnuts' "Cycle Annie," with lyrics by Lou, mixed the surf sound with the first hints of the Velvet Underground. The song allowed Reed to assert himself lyrically with a tale of "a real tough chick" who "just didn't come any meaner." Filled with Reedian characters and his playful love of three-chord rock and roll, "Cycle Annie" would have fitted just as well on *Loaded.*

Lou and his fellow songwriters wrote as fast as they could. Although the setup lacked the glamour of the rock-and-roll lifestyle, it had redeeming educational value. "There were four of us literally locked in a room writing songs," Reed recounted. "We just churned out songs, that's all. They would say, 'Write ten California songs, ten Detroit songs,' then we'd go down into the studio for an hour or two and cut three or four albums really quickly, which came in handy later because I knew my way around a studio, not well enough but I could work really fast. While I was doing that, I was doing my own stuff and trying to get by, but the material I was doing, people wouldn't go near me with it at the time. I mean, we wrote 'Johnny Can't Surf No More' and 'Let the Wedding Bells Ring' and 'Hot Rod Song.' I didn't see it as schizophrenic at all. I just had a job as a songwriter. I mean, a real hack job. They'd come in and give me a subject, and we'd write.

"I really liked doing it, it was really fun, but I wasn't doing the stuff I wanted to do. I was just hoping I could somehow get an in, which, in fact, worked out. It's just worked out in an odd way. But, at least it was something to do with music."

Naturally, Lou told friends that he hated working at Pickwick and expressed endless bitterness over Phillips's failure to see any merit in Reed's own compositions. "I'd say, why don't we record these?" remembered Reed. "And they'd say, 'No, we can't record stuff like that.'" (One can only wonder how *Johnny Don't Shoot No More, Ten Drug Songs* would have gone over in that halcyon era.) But the truth is that the detached observer in Lou was making out like a bandit in this situation. In fact, he should have been paying them for the very useful education in how to use a recording studio and work with helpful collaborators for whom he would in time come to realize a strong need. Never was he more prolific than during his Pickwick days. Over the course of a few months Reed and his three collaborators published at least fifteen songs. The five months he spent at Pickwick from September 1964 to February 1965 provided the best on-the-job training he could possibly have had for a career in rock and roll.

Chapter Five

THE FORMATION OF THE VELVET UNDERGROUND

ON THE LOWER EAST SIDE: 1965

The best things come, as a general thing, from the talents that are members of a group; every man works better when he has companions working in the same line, and yielding to stimulus and suggestion, comparison, emulation.

—Henry James

IT WAS THROUGH PICKWICK THAT LOU MET THE MAN WHO WOULD BE THE single most important long-lasting collaborator in his life, John Cale. One day in January 1965, Lou, who had not let hepatitis slow him down, had ingested a copious quantity of drugs. As he felt the rush of creativity coming on, he leafed through Eugenia Sheperd's column in a local tabloid and came across an item about ostrich feathers being the latest fashion craze. Flinging down the paper and grabbing his guitar with the manic pent-up humor that fueled so much of his work, Lou spontaneously created a new would-be dance craze in a song called "The Ostrich." It joyously told the dancer to put his head on the floor and let his partner step on it. What better self-image could Lou have possibly come up with than this nutty notion, except that the dancers give each other electroshocks?

Although it appeared unlikely that even rock-crazed teenagers, currently dancing the twist and the frug, would go for this masochistic idea, Shupak's partner, Terry Phillips, desperate for a hit to exonerate his claim that the wave of the future was in rock, immediately snapped that this could be the hit single they had been looking for. With his spacey head full of images of millions of kids across America stomping on each other's head (he was ten years ahead of his time), the ersatz Andrew Oldham (the Rolling Stones' equally young and inexperienced producer) got the rock executives out in the warehouse to agree to his proposal that they release "The Ostrich" as a single by a make-believe band called the Primitives. When the record came out, they received a call from a TV dance show, much to their surprise, requesting a performance of "The Ostrich" by "the band." Eager to promote his project, Phillips persuaded the Pickwick people to let him put together a real band to fill the bill. He saw the pleasingly pubescent-looking Lewis as a natural for lead singer. But he was less than enthusiastic about the other musicians, who did not have the requisite look to con the teen market into spending their spare dollars on "The Ostrich." Frantic to get the show on the road, Phillips began to search for a backup band for Lou Reed.

From the Pickwick studio the story cuts to Terry Phillips at an Upper East Side Manhattan apartment jammed with a bunch of pasty-faced party people all yukking it up and trying to be cool despite having no idea at all about anything. Ensconced among them, highly amused and somewhat above it all, were the unlikely duo of a big-boned Welshman with a sonorous voice named John Cale and his partner and flatmate, the classic nervy-looking underground man, Tony Conrad. In their early twenties and sporting hair unfashionably long for those days, Cale was a classical-music scholar, Conrad an underground filmmaker, and they were both members of one of the midsixties most avant-garde music groups in the world, La Monte Young's Theatre of Eternal Music. On the trail of female companions and good times, they had been brought to the party by the brother of the playwright Jack Gelber, who had recently written a famous play about heroin called *The Connection.* Spotting these reasonably attractive and slightly eccentric-looking guys with long hair, Terry Phillips immediately asked them if they were musicians. Receiving an affirmative response, he took it for granted that they played guitars (in fact Cale played an electrically amplified viola as well as several Indian instruments) and snapped, "Where's the drummer?"

The two underground artists, who took their work highly seriously, went along with Phillips as a kind of joke, claiming they did have a drummer so as not to jeopardize the opportunity to make some pocket money. The next day, along with their good friend Walter De Maria, who would soon emerge as one of the leading avant-garde sculptors in the world and was doing a little drumming on the side, they showed up at Pickwick studios as instructed.

Cale, Conrad, and De Maria were highly amused by the bogus setup at Pickwick. To them, the Pickwick executives in polyester suits, who suspiciously pressed contracts into their hands, were hilarious caricatures of rock moguls. On close inspection, as Conrad recalled, the contracts stipulated that they would sign away the rights to everything they did for the rest of their lives in exchange for nothing. After brushing aside this attempt to extract an allegiance more closely resembling indentured servitude than business management, Conrad, Cale, and De Maria were introduced to Lou Reed. He assured them that it would take no time at all to learn their parts to "The Ostrich" since all the guitar strings were tuned to a single note. This information left John Cale and Tony Conrad openmouthed in astonishment since that was exactly what they had been doing at La Monte Young's rigorous eight-hours-a-day rehearsals. They realized Lou had some kind of innate musical genius that even the salesmen at the studio had picked up on. Tony got the impression that "Lou had a close relationship with these people at Pickwick because they recognized that he was a very gifted person. He impressed everybody as having some particularly assertive personal quality."

Cale, Conrad, and De Maria agreed to join "The Primitives" and play shows to promote the record on the East Coast. It was primarily a camp lark, but it would also give them a glimpse into the world of commercial rock and roll, in which they were not entirely uninterested.

And so it came about that in their first appearance together, Lou Reed and John Cale found themselves, without prior rehearsal, running onto the stage of some high school in Pennsylvania's Lehigh Valley following a bellowed introduction: "And here they are from New York—The Primitives!" Confronting a barrage of screaming kids, the band launched into "The Ostrich." At the end of the song the deejay screamed, rather portentously, "These guys have really got something. I hope it's not catching!"

Far from being catching, "The Ostrich" died a quick death. After racing around the countryside in a station wagon for several weekends getting a taste of the reality of the rock life without roadies, the band packed it in. Terry Phillips and the Pickwick executives ruefully left off their dream of seeing "The Ostrich" sail into the hemisphere of the charts and returned to the dependable work of Jack Borgheimer.

The attempted breakout had its repercussions though, primarily in introducing Lou to John, who held the keys to a whole other musical universe. The fact was that Lou, like many creative people, had a low threshold for boredom and realized that Terry Phillips's vision was too narrow to allow him to grow.

When Lou started to visit John Cale in his bohemian slum dwelling at 56 Ludlow Street in the deepest bowels of Manhattan's Lower East Side, Reed knew nothing of La Monte Young, or his Theatre of Eternal Music, and had little sense of the world he was entering. In keeping with the egocentric personalities he had been cultivating since his successes on the Syracuse University poetry, music, and bohemian scenes, Lou was out for his own ends and at first showed little interest in whatever it was that John was into. Instead, the rock-and-roller set about seducing the classicist.

Cale, for his part, was taken by Reed's rock-and-roll persona and what little he had witnessed of his spontaneous composition of lyrics, but took a somewhat snooty view of Reed's initial attempts to strike up a collaborative friendship. "He was trying to get a band together," Cale said. "I didn't want to hear his songs. They seemed sorry for themselves. He'd written 'Heroin' already, and 'I'm Waiting for My Man,' but they wouldn't let him record it, they didn't want to do anything with it. I wasn't really interested—most of the music being written then was folk, and he played his songs with an acoustic guitar—so I didn't really pay attention because I couldn't give a shit about folk music. I hated Joan Baez and Dylan. Every song was a fucking question!"

Despite having been a musical prodigy and, before the age of twenty-five, studied with some of the greatest avant-garde composers of the century, by 1965 Cale felt his career was going nowhere. "I was going off into never-never land with classical notions of music," he said, desperate for a new angle from which to approach music. The sentiment was shared by his family, putting additional pressure on him to get a job. Just like Lou's mother, Mrs. Cale, a schoolteacher in a small Welsh mining village

married to a miner, complained that John would never make a living as
a musician and should become a doctor or a lawyer.

Like a bullterrier nipping at pants legs, Lou kept after John, feeling
intuitively that the Welshman might provide a necessary catalyst for his
music. Eventually, Lou got his way and Cale began to take Lou's lyrics
seriously. "He kept pushing them on me," Cale recalled, "and finally I
saw they weren't the kind of words you'd get Joan Baez singing. They were
very different, he was writing about things other people weren't. These
lyrics were very literate, very well expressed, they were tough."

Once John grasped what Lou was doing—Method acting in song, as he
saw it—he glimpsed the possibility of collaborating to create something
vibrant and new. He figured that by combining Young's theories and
techniques with Lou's lyrical abilities, he could blow himself out of the
hole his rigid studies had dug him into. Lou also introduced John to a
hallmark of rock-and-roll music—fun—and his youthful enthusiasm was
infectious. "We got together and started playing my songs for fun," Reed
recalled. "It was like we were made for each other. He was from the other
world of music and he fitted me perfectly. He would fit things he played
right into my world, it was so natural."

"What I saw in Lou's musical concept was something akin to my own,"
agreed Cale. "There was something more than just a rock side to him too.
I recognized a tremendous literary quality about his songs which fascinated me—he had a very careful ear, he was very cautious with his words.
I had no real knowledge of rock music at that time, so I focused on the
literary aspect more." Cale was so turned on by the connection he started
weaning Reed away from Pickwick.

Cale immediately got to work with Reed on orchestrations for the
songs. The two men labored over the pieces, each feeding off the fresh
ideas of his counterpart. "Lou's an excellent guitar player," Cale said.
"He's nuts. It has more to do with the spirit of what he's doing than
playing. And he had this great facility with words, he could improvise
songs, which was great. Lyrics and melodies. Take a chord change and
just do it." Cale was an equally exciting player. Unaware of any rock-
and-roll models to emulate, he answered Reed's sonic attacks with illog-
ical, inverted bass lines or his searing electric viola, which sounded, he
said, "like a jet engine!"

Meanwhile, as he got to know Lou, and Reed began to unwrap the elements of his legend, John discovered that they had something else in common, "namely," Lou would deadpan, "dope." Reed joked dismissively about their heroin use, commenting that when he and Cale first met, they started playing together "because it was safer than dealing dope," which Reed was apparently still dabbling in. Whilst fully admitting his involvement with heroin, Lou always insisted, and friends tended to concur, that "I was never a heroin addict. I had a toe in that situation. Enough to see the tunnel, the vortex. That's how I handled my problems. That's how I grew up, how I did it, like a couple hundred thousand others. You had to be a gutter rat, seeking it out."

While rationalizing his drug use, Reed also made it clear that it provided him with a shield necessary for both his life and work: "I take drugs just because in the twentieth century in a technological age, living in the city, there are certain drugs you can take just to keep yourself normal like a caveman. Not just to bring yourself up and down, but to attain equilibrium you need to take certain drugs. They don't get you high, even, they just get you normal."

Despite the fact that drug taking was widely accepted, practiced, and even celebrated among the artistic residents of Cale's Lower East Side community, because it was addictive, dangerous, and could be extremely destructive, heroin had a stigma attached to it that led users to keep it private. Thus Cale and Reed found themselves bonded not only by a musical vision and youthful anarchy, but by the secret society heroin users tend to form. The cozy, intimate feelings the drug can bring on magnified their friendship.

Lou started spending a lot of his spare time at John's. Before long he was staying there for weeks at a time without bothering to return to his parents' house in Freeport. Lou had long since become fed up with his parents, avoiding them at all costs, and stopping by their house only when in need of money, food, clean laundry, or to check up on the well-being of his dog. Even his involvement with Pickwick was fading under the spell of the Lower East Side rock-and-roll lifestyle. "Lou was like a rock-and-roll animal and authentically turned everybody on," recalled Tony Conrad. "He really had a deep fixation on that, and his lifestyle was completely compatible and acclimatized to it."

Cale's was a match for Reed's mercurial personality. Moody and paranoid, he too was easily bored and looking for action. John responded to

Lou's driving energy with equal passion, not only sharing Reed's musical explosions but also providing a creative atmosphere and spiritual home for him. Conrad saw that Lou "was definitely a liberating force for John, but John was an incredible person too. He was very idealistic, putting himself behind what he was interested in and believed in in a tremendous way. John was moving at a very, very fast pace away from a classical training background through the avant-garde and into performance art then rock."

The relationship between John and Lou grew quickly, and it wasn't long before they started thinking about Lou's getting out of Freeport, where he was still living very uncomfortably under the disapproving gaze of his parents. Lou was eager to get something happening. "I took off, so there was more room in the pad, and John invited him to come over and stay where I had been staying," said Conrad. "Lou moved in, which was great because we got him out of his mother's place."

"We had little to say to each other," Lou said of the deteriorating relationship with his parents. "I had gone and done the most horrifying thing possible in those days—I joined a rock band. And of course I represented something very alien to them."

The hard edge of the Lower East Side kicked Lou into gear. The neighborhood was the loam, as Allen Ginsberg had said, out of which grew "the apocalyptic sensibility, the interest in mystic art, the marginal leavings, the garbage of society." As Lou discovered John's ascetic yet sprawling Lower East Side landscape with its population of what Jack Kerouac described as like-minded bodhisattvas, he found himself walking in the footsteps of Stephen Crane (who had come there straight from Syracuse University at the end of the previous century to write *Maggie: A Girl of the Streets* and wrote to a friend "the sense of a city is war"), John Dos Passos, e. e. cummings, and, most recently, the beats. Indeed, Reed could have walked straight out of the pages of Ginsberg's *Howl* for he too would, like one of the poem's heroes, "purgatory his torso night after night with dreams, with drugs, with waking nightmares, alcohol and cock and endless balls." Most importantly, the Ludlow Street inhabitants shared with Lou a communal feeling that society was a prison of the nervous system, and they preferred their individual experience. The gifted among them had enough respect for their personal explorations to put them in their art, just as John and Lou were doing, and make them new. Friends from college who visited him there couldn't believe Lou was living in these conditions, but among the drug addicts and apocalyptic artists of every kind, Lou found, for the first time in his life, a real mental home.

The funky Ludlow Street had for a long time been host to creative spirits like the underground filmmakers Jack Smith and Piero Heliczer. When Lou moved in, an erratic but inventive Scotsman named Angus MacLise, who often drummed in La Monte's group, lived in the apartment next door. Cale's L-shaped flat opened into a kitchen, which housed a rarely used bathtub. Beyond it was a small living room and two bedrooms. The whole place was sparsely furnished, with mattresses on the floor and orange crates that served as furniture and firewood. Bare lightbulbs lit the dark rooms, paint and plaster chipped from the woodwork and the walls. There was no heat or hot water, and the landlord collected the $30 rent with a gun. When it got cold during February to March of 1965, they ran out into the streets, grabbed some wooden crates, and threw them into the fireplace, or often sat hunched over their instruments with carpets wrapped around their shoulders. When the toilet stopped-up, they picked up the shit and threw it out the window. For sustenance they cooked big pots of porridge or made humongous vegetable pancakes, eating the same glop day in and day out as if it were fuel.

As he began to work with Cale to transform his stark lyrics into dynamic symphonies, he drew John into *his* world. John found Lou an intriguing, if at times dangerous, roommate. What they had in common was a fascination with the language of music and the permanent expression of risk. "In Lou, I found somebody who not only had artistic sense and could produce it at the drop of a hat, but also had a real street sense," John Cale recalled. "I was anxious to learn from him, I'd lived a sheltered life. So, from him, I got a short, sharp education. Lou was exorcising a lot of devils back then, and maybe I was using him to exorcise some of mine."

Lou maintained a correspondence with Delmore Schwartz that led his mentor to believe that he was still definitely on the path to distilling his essence in words. Lou wrote in one letter in early 1965, just after moving to New York City, "If you're weak NY has many outlets. I can't resist peering, probing, sometimes participating, other times going right to the edge before sidestepping. Finding viciousness in yourself and that fantastic killer urge and worse yet having the opportunity presented before you is certainly interesting."

With John in tow, Lou would befriend a drunk in a bar and then, after
drawing him out with friendly conversation, according to Cale, suddenly
pop the astonishing question, "Would you like to fuck your mother?"
John recalled this side of Lou during his early days at Ludlow Street,
commenting, "From the start I thought Lou was amazing, someone I
could learn a lot from. He had this astonishing talent as a writer. He was
someone who'd been around and was definitely bruised. He was also a lot
of fun then, though he had a dangerous streak. He enjoyed walking the
plank and he could take situations to extremes you couldn't even imagine
until you'd been there with him. I thought I was fairly reckless until I met
Lou. But I'd stop at goading a drunk into getting worse. And that's where
Lou would start." This kind of behavior got them into some hairy situations, abhorred by Cale—who was not as verbally adroit as Lou and was
at times agoraphobic and lived in fear of random violence. "I'm very
insecure," said Cale. "I use cracks on the sidewalk to walk down the
street. I'd always walk on the lines. I never take anything but a calculated
risk, and I do it because it gives me a sense of identity. Fear is a man's best
friend."

Money was a constant problem. Although Lou had use of his mother's
car and could return to Freeport whenever he desired, and kept working
at Pickwick until September, he had nothing beyond his $25.00 per
week. He picked up whatever money he could in doing gigs with John,
some of them impromptu. Once, they went up to Harlem to play an
audition at a blues club. When the odd-looking couple were turned down
by the club management, they went out to play on the sidewalk and raked
in a sizable amount of money. "We made more money on the sidewalks
than anywhere else," John recalled.

"We were living together in a thirty-dollar-a-month apartment and we
really didn't have any money," Lou testified. "We used to eat oatmeal all
day and all night and give blood among other things, or pose for these
nickel or fifteen-cent tabloids they have every week. And when I posed
for them my picture came out and it said I was a sex-maniac killer and
that I had killed fourteen children and had tape-recorded it and played it
in a barn in Kansas at midnight. And when John's picture came out in the
paper, it said he had killed his lover because his lover was going to marry
his sister, and he didn't want his sister to marry a fag."

Lou was creating the myth of his own Jewish psychodrama. It had become a custom of Lou's to sicken people with stories of his shock treatment, drug use, and problems with the law. This was the sort of image-building Reed would, in a search for a personality and voice to call his own, perfect in the coming years, culminating in a series of infamous personas in the 1970s. "At that time Lou was relating to me the horrors of electric-shock therapy, he was on medication," Cale recounted. "I was really horrified. All his best work came from living with his parents. He told me his mother was some sort of ex–beauty queen and his father was a wealthy accountant. They'd put him in a hospital where he'd received shock treatments as a kid. Apparently he was at Syracuse and was given this compulsory choice to do either gym or ROTC. He claimed he couldn't do gym because he'd break his neck, and when he did ROTC, he threatened to kill his instructor. Then he put his fist through a window or something, and so he was put in a mental hospital. I don't know the full story. Every time Lou told me about it he'd change it slightly."

Lou and John resolved to form a band, orchestrate their material into a performable and recordable body of work, and venture out into the world to unleash their music. "When we first started working together, it was on the basis that we were both interested in the same things," said Cale. "We both needed a vehicle; Lou needed one to carry out his lyrical ideas and I needed one to carry out my musical ideas. It seemed to be a good idea to put a band together and go up onstage and do it, because everybody else seemed to be playing the same thing over and over. Anybody who had a rock-and-roll band in those days would just do a fixed set. I figured that was one way of getting on everybody's nerves—to have improvisation going on for any length of time."

WHILE LOU WAS WRAPPING HIMSELF IN THE TROUBLED DREAMS AND screams of his music, elevating himself, as one friend saw it, to another level of anger and coolness, and becoming progressively weirder, he began to put some distance between himself and his past. True, he still borrowed his mother's car to go into dangerous parts of town to score drugs, and made the occasional trip or phone call home, but he began to amputate those friends with whom he had maintained contact post-Syracuse. The first to go was the stalwart Hyman. Living in Manhattan with his wife and going to law school, his former buddy had lost the ability to provide anything for Lou (save a free meal). Mishkin still fulfilled a function in that he had a big space in Brooklyn where Lou sometimes rehearsed, and a yacht called the *Black Angel* tethered at the Seventy-ninth Street Boat Basin where they sometimes socialized, but Mishkin was maintaining contact with Lou at a price. "At that point he was putting me down more than he would have at Syracuse," Ritchie recalled. "He was on the way to what he became."

Parting ways is common among former schoolmates who move on to new jobs and allegiances. The amputations that struck more deeply and perhaps more definitively were made by Lou of the people who had been most influential, the ones who knew too much about him.

After a period of psychiatric rehabilitation, Lincoln Swados had re-emerged on the New York scene, living in the East Village not far from Lou. For a short time he was making a reputation for himself as a comic-strip illustrator and stand-up comedian. But soon he beat Lou hands down in the lunatic sweepstakes by stepping in front of an oncoming subway train, saying, "I am a very bad person, I am a very bad person . . ." Moving aside at the last minute, he survived—minus an arm and a leg. Subsequently, he became something of a fixture on the Lower East Side as a crippled street performer. Lincoln's sister, Elizabeth, who had gone on to a distinguished career as a playwright, was apparently quite upset by the extent to which Lou, rather than opening up to Lincoln after this tragic episode, put even more distance between them. Lincoln, though, apparently had a perceptive understanding of his friend's motives. "Lou pretends to be like us," he told his ex-girlfriend, the journalist Gretchen Berg, "but he's really not, he's really someone else. He's really a businessman who has very definite goals and knows exactly what he wants."

Interestingly, Delmore Schwartz, who was now in the final year of his life, had drawn a similar conclusion. A Syracuse classmate of Lou's who ran into Schwartz in Manhattan one day was astonished to discover that "he looked really bad. He had on a black raincoat which looked like it was covered with toothpaste stains. He seemed to have been drinking, maybe he was drunk. And the only thing he was interested in discussing was his dislike for everyone at Syracuse; how Lou Reed and Peter Locke were spies paid by the Rockefellers." When Lou discovered that Schwartz was living in the dilapidated fleabag Dixie Hotel on West Forty-eighth Street, he went there to make contact, but Delmore let him have it with both barrels, screaming, "If you ever come here again, I'll kill you!" scaring off a shaken Reed, who recalled, "He thought I'd been sent by the CIA to spy on him, and I was scared because he was big and he really would have killed me."

The third mind in his life at Syracuse, Shelley Albin, reversed the amputation, cutting Lou out of her life when she married Ronald Corwin, who had been a big wheel on the Syracuse campus from 1963 to 1965 as the head of the local chapter of CORE, and whom Lou subsequently characterized as an "asshole airhead." The marriage was a blow to Lou in as much as he still considered Shelley to be "his" girlfriend, even though he had neither seen nor apparently made any attempt to contact her since the summer of 1964. Still, he had not carried on a romantic relationship with anyone else. Shelley would remain a thorn in his side at least throughout the end of the 1970s, inspiring some of his most poignant, if vicious, love songs.

The only people Lou seemed incapable of amputating were his parents, who were vividly remembered by friends as a pair of never seen but constantly present just off stage ogrelike specters threatening at any moment to have Lou committed (despite the fact that he was now twenty-three years old and legally beyond their reach).

A MONTH INTO HIS COLLABORATION WITH CALE, ONE OF THOSE CHANCE meetings that have often formed rock groups took place when Lou bumped into his friend from Syracuse Sterling Morrison, walking in the West Village. Lou invited Sterling to Ludlow Street to play some music. By then Angus MacLise was playing drums around Lou and John. The next time Tony Conrad dropped by, he discovered that the Reed-Cale relationship had blossomed with MacLise and Morrison into what they were beginning to call a group. They had even made a first stab at a name, trying on for several months the Warlocks (which, incidentally, was the name being used at the same time on the West Coast by the proto–Grateful Dead), and were taping rehearsals. The music, heavily influenced by La Monte Young via MacLise and Cale, but equally by the doo-wop and white rock favored by Reed and Morrison, was ethereal and passionate.

Lou and Angus collaborated on an essay called "Concerning the Rumor That Red China Has Cornered the Methedrine Market and Is Busy

Adding Paranoia Drops to Upset the Mental Balance of the United States," a nutty, stoned credo of the band's basic precepts. It read, in part, "Western music is based on death, violence and the pursuit of PROGRESS. . . . The root of universal music is sex. Western music is as violent as Western sex. . . . Our band is the Western equivalent to the cosmic dance of Shiva. Playing as Babylon goes up in flames."

Their original precepts were to dedicate themselves with an almost religious fervor to their collective calling, to sacrifice being immediately successful, to be different, to hold on to a personality of their own, never to try to please anyone but themselves, and never to play the same song the same way. The group discovered and exploited musical traditions lost to their contemporaries, rejecting outright the popular conventions of the day. "We actually had a rule in the band," Reed explained. "If anybody played a blues lick, they would be fined. Everyone was going crazy over old blues people, but they forgot about all those groups, like the Spaniels, people like that. Records like 'Smoke From Your Cigarette,' and 'I Need a Sunday Kind of Love,' the 'Wind' by the Chesters, 'Later for You, Baby' by the Solitaires. All those really ferocious records that no one seemed to listen to anymore were underneath everything we were playing. No one really knew that."

"Our music evolved collectively," Sterling reported. "Lou would walk in with some sort of scratchy verse and we would all develop the music. It almost always worked like that. We'd all thrash it out into something very strong. John was trying to be a serious young composer; he had no background in rock music, which was terrific, he knew no clichés. You listen to his bass lines, he didn't know any of the usual riffs, it was totally eccentric. 'Waiting for the Man' was very weird. John was always exciting to work with."

Their first complete success in terms of arrangements was "Venus in Furs." When Cale initially added viola, grinding it against Reed's "ostrich" guitar, illogically and without trepidation, a tingle of anticipation shot up his spine. They had, he knew, found their sound, and it was strong. Cale, who applied the mania to the sound, recalled, "It wasn't until then that I thought we had discovered a really original, nasty style." With the words of this song, wrote the British critic Richard Williams, "Lou Reed was to change the agenda of pop music once and for all. But it wasn't just the words either. 'Heroin' and 'Venus in Furs' were given music that fitted their themes, and that didn't sound like anything any-body had played before. Out went the blues tonality and the Afro-American rhythms, the basic components of all previous rock and roll. The prevailing sound was the grinding screech of Cale's electric viola and Reed's guitar feedback, while the tempo speeded up and slowed down according to the momentary requirements of the lyric."

The chemistry of their personalities was more fragile. On one occa-sion, Lou played a new song he had written and John immediately started adding an improvised viola part. Sterling muttered something about its being a good viola part. Lou looked up and snapped, "Yeah, I know. I wrote the song just for that viola part. Every single note of it I knew in advance." Although unable to outdo Lou verbally, John stuck to his guns through music. Several observers of the scene believed that John did more than that—he actually brought Lou Reed out of himself, completed him as it were. Some believe that without John Cale, the Lou Reed who became a legend would not have been born.

"It's a fascinating relationship," commented one friend. "That John worked with Cage and La Monte Young would be interesting enough if his career ended there, but that he met Lou and saw something in Lou despite the fact that Lou did not have the same kind of training that he had. I think he recognized that and must have done much in his way to nurture it and allowed it also to change the course of his life."

Sterling Morrison hid this nervousness under a cloud of silence when anything went wrong. His personality often made him a useful buffer between Reed and Cale, but it could also cause problems when, without informing anybody that he was upset, he would simply clam up. Insecure about his playing, and in need of constant encouragement, Sterling stood in the background and tentatively muttered the choruses he was supposed to sing. One friend recalled that "it was typical of Sterling to play a wonderful solo and pretend he didn't care, but then after an hour sidle up and ask, 'How was the solo?' "

The joker in the deck was Angus MacLise. Not only did the band get the majority of their electricity from his apartment, but Angus was, by all accounts, a lovely, whimsical, gnomelike man inspired, inspirational, and a serious methedrine addict. As a drummer, he was intuitive and complex, pounding out an amazing variety of textures and licks culled from cultures around the world. He was influenced a lot by his travels, by the dervishes of the Middle East and people he had met in India and Nepal. A visionary poet and mystic who also belonged to La Monte Young's coterie, MacLise believed in listening to the essence of sound and relating it to one's inner being. "Angus had dreamy notions of art—I mean real dreamy," commented Sterling. "So did we, otherwise we could have made a whole lot more money. We were never in it for the money, we felt very strongly about the material, and we wanted to be able to play it. We said screw the marketing."

Both Cale and MacLise continued to play with the Theatre of Eternal Music through 1965 in between rehearsing with the Warlocks, although this contravened Lou's need for total allegiance and commitment. This made La Monte Young almost a third mind in the construction of the band's basic precepts. It was characteristic of that period and place— specifically the East Village—that certain figures, such as La Monte Young, Andy Warhol, Robert Rauschenberg, Allen Ginsberg, were ensconced with an adoring, disciplelike entourage of followers and fellow workers. It is significant that despite his two bandmates' close connections with one of the most charismatic figures of the period, Lou Reed never met La Monte Young during his entire carer with the Velvet Underground. Reed understood that people who really wanted to make it on their own—to be stars—had to keep their distance from the vortex of such strong groups.

In fact, the central paradox of Lou's career—particularly in the 1960s— was that by entering the highly competitive, fast-paced world of rock and roll, he was by definition entering the one art form that relied completely and uniquely on intense, rapid, often nerve-racking collaboration—the thing he had the most trouble with. Soon his new bandmates would discover what the Eldorados had collided with at Syracuse—that Lou could be the sweetest, most charming companion socially, but he was virtually always a motherfucker to work with. His biggest problem, apart from demanding complete control and having a Himalayan ego, was the matter of credit. Just as the Rolling Stones had done when creating their music, the Velvet Underground worked up almost all of their songs collectively. Reed, who composed the simple, inspirational chord structures or sketchy lyrics, was under the impression, however, that he had single-handedly crafted masterpieces like "Heroin," "Venus in Furs," "Waiting for the My Man," "Black Angel's Death Song," etc. In truth, although

----

Reed undoubtedly supplied the brilliant lyrics and chord structures, the various and greater parts of the music—Cale's viola; Morrison's guitar; MacLise's drumming—were invented by each individually. In short, Reed should have shared the majority of his writing credits with other members of the band. At first, of course, before the question of signing any contract came up, everything was copacetic—since there was nothing to argue about. The group was also under the impression, due to the nature of the material, that no one would ever record or cover their music. In time, however, this vital subject of artistic collaboration, credit, and, most importantly, of publishing rights (which is where the most money is made in rock and roll in the long run) would become the deepest wound in the band's history of battles.

Still, in early 1965, Angus became a devoted, if crazy, friend to Lou, in the tradition of Lincoln Swados. Angus turned Lou on to the easily available pharmaceutical methamphetamine hydrochloride, which was the drug of choice of a particularly intense group of visionary seekers centered around Jack Smith, and later, Andy Warhol. Methamphetamine hydrochloride—speed—is a key to understanding what set Reed and Cale's sound aside from the mainstream of American pop in the second half of the 1960s, which was based more on soft and hallucinogenic drugs.

The tension between these four disparate personalities became the emotional engine of their music. Twenty years later, Reed would vigorously deny that the friction, particularly between him and Cale, was constructive. But this was simply one of his many attempts to write or control his own history. Morrison remembered, "I love Lou, but he has what must be a fragmented personality, so you're never too sure under any conditions what you're going to have to deal with. He'll be boyishly charming, naive—Lou is very charming when he wants to be. Or he will be vicious—and if he is, you have to figure out what's stoking the fire. What drug is he on, or what mad diet? He had all sorts of strange dietary theories. He'd eat nothing, live on wheat husks. He was always trying to move mentally and spiritually to some place where no one had ever gone before. He was often very antisocial and difficult to work with, but he was *interesting,* and people were *interested* in the conflict and some of the good things that came out of it."

Some of the good things that came out of it were the songs that began to soar out over the gritty, dangerous drug supermarkets next to Ludlow Street from Eldridge to the Bowery. Lou, Sterling, Angus, and John hammered away at songs day in and day out, honing down the ones that would appear on the first Velvet Underground album two years later. According to Cale, "We actually worked very hard on the arrangements for the first album. We used to meet once a week for about a year, just to work on arrangements. I felt when were were doing those first arrangements back in Ludlow Street, '65, that we had something that was going to last. What we did was unique, it was powerful. We spent our entire weekends going over and over and over the songs. We had no big problem with the work ethic; in fact, we were hanging on to the work ethic for dear life."

By the spring of 1965, the music began to soar. John Cale remembered these earliest days of playing as their best. Cale contributed his unique electric viola, Morrison his hauntingly beautiful electric guitar, MacLise his ethereal Far Eastern drumming, and Reed his raw lyrics and hard delivery of them. Often the band improvised a riff and Reed simply made up the lyrics as he went along. "He was amazing," Cale said. "One minute he'd be a southern preacher, then he'd change character completely and be someone totally different."

"In my head it would be great if I could sing like Al Green," Reed said. "But that's in my head. It wasn't true. I had to work out ways of dealing with my voice and its limitations. I wrote for a certain phrase and then bent the lyric to fit the melody. Figured out a way to make it fit." In 1965 he was remarkably creative, carving a dark, macabre, Poe-like beauty out of Cale's orchestration of the band's musical chaos. "We heard our screams turn into songs," Reed later wrote, "and back into screams again."

Meanwhile, Cale, traveling back and forth between London and New York on his classical-scholarship funds, was bringing back the latest singles of the most exciting new British groups—the Who, and the Kinks with whom they felt some affinity. It was an intensely creative, highly energized moment in rock history, and the band gorged themselves on everything they liked. In fact, Reed, who admired a wide range of musicians from Burt Bacharach to the Beach Boys, insisted that the best popular music should be as artistically recognized as poetry. "How can they give Robert Lowell a poetry prize?" he complained in another essay written the following year for *Aspen* magazine. "Richard Wilbur. It's a joke. What about the Excellents, Martha and the Vandellas (Holland, Dozier, Jeff Barry, Elle Greenwich, Bacharach and David, Carole King and Gerry Goffin, *the best songwriting teams in America*). Will none of the powers that be realize what Brian Wilson did with the CHORDS. Phil Spector being made out to be some kind of aberration when he put out the best record ever made, 'You've Lost That Loving Feeling.' "

Drugs were both a catalyst and inhibitor for the music. "There were no heavy addictions or anything, but enough to get in our way, hepatitis and so on," Sterling recalled. "I would take pills, amphetamines, not psychedelics, we were never into that. Drugs didn't inspire us for songs or anything like that. We took them for old-fashioned reasons—it made you feel good, braced you for criticism. It wasn't just drugs, there were vitamins, ginseng, experimental diets. Lou once went on a diet so radical there was no fat showing on his central-nerve chart . . . his spinal column was raw!

"We took a lot of downers—that's what I used to do. We did all sorts of junk. There was just so much going on, you had to keep up with it, that was all. I never got really A-headed out. But if you had two members of the band heavily sedated and the other on uppers, it is gonna affect your sensibilities. They wanted to do slow dirges and I wanted to do up-tempo songs!"

That summer two parallel events catapulted the Warlocks, who also occasionally used the in-your-face drug-innuendo name the Falling Spikes, out of the obscurity of Ludlow Street toward the limelight that would soon illuminate them.

First, through MacLise's connections in the Lower East Side underground-film scene, the most potent movement of the moment embracing arguably the largest, most intelligent, and creative audience in New York, they were invited to play their rehearsal tapes or sometimes perform live to accompany screenings of the mostly silent underground films by Jack Smith, Ron Rice, Andy Warhol, Stan Brakhage, and Barbara Rubin, which were making a big splash that season. Nineteen sixty-five was the climactic year of the Lower East Side art community and in particularly the underground-film scene. One of the scene's most outstanding, enigmatic figures, the poet and filmmaker Piero Heliczer, who often screened films at his enormous art factory loft on Grand Street, three blocks from 56 Ludlow Street, first offered the group a venue to play. Soon they were

playing regularly at Heliczer's and other artists' spaces, sitting behind the
film screens or off to the side. The most popular underground-film theater
space at the time was Jonas Mekas's Cinémathèque, which became the
band's most regular venue. "Center stage of the old Cinémathèque was a
movie screen, and between the screen and the audience a number of veils
were spread out in different places," recalled Sterling. "These were lit
variously by slide projections and lights, as Piero's films shone through
them onto the screen. Dancers and incense swirled around, poetry and
song rose up, while from behind the screen a strange music was generated
by Lou Reed, John Cale, Angus, and me, with Piero back there too
playing his sax." Occasionally they would play bare-chested with painted
torsos or try to look outrageous in some other way. They gained enthusiastic audiences, among whom Barbara Rubin would become their most
influential fan.

Their second breakthrough came in July when they recorded a demo
tape at 56 Ludlow Street that included early versions of "Heroin," "Venus
in Furs," "Black Angels Death Song," and "Wrap Your Troubles in
Dreams." " 'Wrap Your Troubles in Dreams,' that's relentless," said John
Cale. "Lou's often said, 'Hey, some of these songs are just *not worthy* of
human endeavor, these things are best left alone.' He may be right." The
tape also included a song that Morrison later recalled as "Never Get
Emotionally Involved With a Man, Woman, Beast or Child." Cale took
the tape over to London in the hope of securing a recording contract with
one of the most adventurous British companies (after all, the Who and
the Kinks used similar techniques), and there was considerable interest
from, among others, Miles Copeland, who would go on to manage the
Police.

By the fall, with their music mature and their audience growing, they
felt that something was happening. This seemed confirmed in November
when they stumbled upon the name they would keep, the Velvet Underground, "swiping it," as Lou put it, from the title of a cheap paperback
book about suburban sex Tony Conrad literally picked out of the gutter
and brought to Ludlow Street. The name *Velvet Underground* seemed to fit
perfectly their affiliations and intentions. That same month they got their
first media boost when filmed playing "Venus in Furs" for a CBS documentary on New York underground film, featuring Piero Heliczer and
narrated by Walter Cronkite. When the prestigious rock journalist Alfred
G. Aronowitz offered to manage them, they accepted.

Al Aronowitz, who had an influential pop column in the *New York Post* and had written extensively about the Beatles, Stones, and Dylan, was an important player on the New York rock scene. "Aronowitz was famous," wrote one onlooker. "Aronowitz was the man who'd introduced Allen Ginsberg to Bob Dylan and Bob Dylan to the Beatles. He'd known Billie Holiday and Jack Kerouac and Paul Newman and Frank Sinatra. He could get Ahmet Ertegun, George Plimpton, Clive Davis, or Willem de Kooning on the phone. He'd been Brian Jones's American connection and Leon Russell's New York guru and the one who introduced Pete Hamill to Norman Mailer. Only Aronowitz could write a rock column in a daily newspaper that'd make the whole country snap to attention." His interest in the Velvets was a sure sign of impending success.

Suddenly, however, their unorthodox background clashed with their progress. As soon as Aronowitz presented them with their first paying job, opening for another group he managed, the Myddle Class, Angus Mac-Lise, as Lou recalled, "asked a very intriguing question. He said, 'Do you mean we have to show up at a certain time—and start playing—and then end?' And we said, 'Yes.' And he said, 'Well, I can't handle that!' And that was it. I mean, we got our electricity out of Angus's apartment, but that was it. He was a great drummer."

Lou, who put his beloved group before anything and anyone, never forgave MacLise. But as it developed, Angus's withdrawal set in motion one last chance meeting that would perfectly complete the band. With the Aronowitz date booked for December 11, only days away, Lou and Sterling suddenly remembered that their Syracuse friend Jim Tucker had a sister who played drums and wondered if she might be able to fill in. Cale, horrified by the mere suggestion that a "chick" should play in their great group, had to be placated by the promise that it was strictly temporary. When he acquiesced, Lou shot out to the suburbs of Long Island to audition Moe Tucker. "My brother had been telling me about Lou for a while, because he had known him for a few years before that," Maureen recalled. "I was nineteen at the time, living at home and had a job, keying stuff into computers. Lou came out to my house to see if I could really play the drums. He said, 'Okay, that's good.'"

When she first went to John's apartment in New York to hear the band play their repertoire, Maureen, whose favorite drummer was Charlie Watts, was knocked out. She could see that Lou was a bona fide rock-and-roll freak, and the whole band was amazing. "When they played

---

'Heroin,' I was really impressed. You could just tell that this was different."

Maureen's drumming was a distillation of all the rock and roll that had gone before, and yet, influenced by African musicians, she played with mallets on two kettledrums while standing up. "I developed a really basic style," she said, "mainly because I didn't have any training—to this day I couldn't do a roll to save my life, or any of that other fancy stuff, nor have I any wish to. I always wanted to keep a simple but steady beat behind the band so no matter how wild John or Lou would get, there would still be this low drone holding it together." Methodical and steady as a person and a drummer, Maureen kept up the backbeat. But, young as she was in comparison to her older brother's friends, she held her own, rarely keeping her opinions to herself when they mattered. Though bowled over by the Velvets' music, she was not always impressed with the lifestyle that went along with it. She thought it was crazy for John and Lou to go out and look for firewood to heat their apartment. "It wasn't very romantic," she commented later about the flat. "It stank."

The Velvet Underground's first job took place at Summit High School in Summit, New Jersey, on December 11, 1965. They were squeezed in between a band called 40 Fingers and the Myddle Class. "Nothing could have prepared the kids and parents assembled in the auditorium for what they were about to experience that night," wrote Rob Norris, a Summit student. "Our only clue was the small crowd of strange-looking people hanging around in front of the stage."

What followed the gentle strains of 40 Fingers was a performance that would have shocked anyone outside of the most avant-garde audiences of the Lower East Side. The curtain rose on the Velvet Underground, revealing four long-haired figures dressed in black and poised behind a strange variety of instruments. Maureen's tiny hermaphroditic figure stood behind her kettledrums, making everyone immediately wonder uneasily whether she was a girl or a boy. Sterling's tall, angular frame shuffled nervously in the background. Lou and John, both in sunglasses, stared blankly at the astonished students, teachers, and parents, Cale wielding his odd-looking viola. As they charged into the opening chords of the cacophonous "Venus in Furs" louder than anyone in the room had ever heard music played, they rounded out an image aptly described as bizarre and terrifying. "Everyone was hit by the screeching urge of sound, with a pounding beat louder than anything we'd ever heard," Norris continued. "About a minute into the second song, which the singer had introduced as 'Heroin,' the music began to get even more intense. It swelled and accelerated like a giant tidal wave which was threatening to engulf us all. At this point most of the audience retreated in horror for the safety of their homes, thoroughly convinced of the dangers of rock and roll music." According to Sterling, "The murmur of surprise that greeted our appearance as the curtain went up increased to a roar of disbelief once we started to play 'Venus' and swelled to a mighty howl of outrage and bewilderment by the end of 'Heroin.' "

"Backstage after their set, the viola player was seen apologizing profusely to an outraged Myddle Class entourage for scaring away half the audience," Norris concluded. "Al Aronowitz was philosophical about it, though. He said, 'At least you've given them a night to remember,' and invited everyone to a party at his house after the show."

Observing that the group seemed to have an oddly stimulating and polarizing effect on audiences, Aronowitz advised them to get some experience playing in public by doing a residency at a small club. Four days later they started a two-week stand at the Cafe Bizarre on MacDougal Street in New York's Greenwich Village. "We played some covers, 'Little Queenie,' 'Bright Lights Big City,' the black R-and-B songs Lou and I liked—and as many of our own songs as we had," Sterling reported. "We needed a lot more of our own material, so we sat around and worked; that's when we wrote "Run Run Run," all those things. Lou usually would have some lyrics written, and something would grow out of that with us jamming. He was a terrific improvisational lyricist. I remember we had the Christmas tree up, but no decorations on it, we were sitting around busy writing songs, because we had to, we needed them that night!"

This fortuitous opportunity was pivotal for their career. First, since there was so little time between the two dates, they decided to keep Maureen, initially much to Cale's chagrin. Moe remembered standing in the street with John, who kept saying, "No chicks in the band. No chicks." Second, at the very time they were playing at the Cafe Bizarre to unreceptive tourists twice a night for $5 apiece per night, the pop artist and entrepreneur Andy Warhol was looking around for a group to manage for a nightclub he had been asked to host by the theatrical impresario Michael Myerberg (who had brought Beckett's *Waiting for Godot* to the

USA in 1956). Barbara Rubin, for whose film *Christmas on Earth* the band had played in their previous incarnation, was spending a good deal of time at the Warhol studio, the famous Silver Factory, and thought the Velvets would be the perfect band for Warhol's upcoming discotheque. She took two of Warhol's leading talent scouts, the film director Paul Morrissey and the underground film star Gerard Malanga, to see them. Malanga, who has just started in Warhol's version of *A Clockwork Orange, Vinyl,* was an outstandingly handsome young man with a potent sexual aura. Combining the looks of Elvis Presley and James Dean with the long hair of Mick Jagger, Malanga dressed head to foot in black leather and carried, purely for dramatic effect, a black leather bullwhip, which he wore wrapped around the shoulder of his jacket. During the Velvets' set, Gerard suddenly leapt up from his table onto the empty dance floor. All of the other customers were too terrified by the music to move. Making ample use of his whip, he undulated in a sinister, erotic dance that perfectly illustrated the visceral, throbbing music. The band was dumbfounded by Gerard's mind-blowing performance. In the intermission Lou and John went over to his table and told him to come back and dance anytime. Instantly spotting a starring role for himself in the scenario, Malanga thought the group would be perfect for Warhol.

The following night Malanga returned to the Cafe Bizarre with Rubin, Warhol's business manager Paul Morrissey, and Warhol himself, accompanied by an entourage including his reigning superstar Edie Sedgwick. They were thrilled by the weird and raucous performance of the Velvet Underground. Not only did the group do the same thing Warhol's films did—make people uncomfortable—but their name, and the fact that they sang about taboo subjects, perfectly fit Warhol's program. To top it off, Morrissey was intrigued by the band's androgynous drummer. After the set Barbara brought the Velvets over to Andy's table. The curly-haired Lou Reed with his shy smile, shared a temperament with Warhol. He sat next to the pop artist and the two of them immediately hit it off. "Lou looked good and pubescent then," Warhol recalled. "Paul thought the kids out on the Island would identify with that."

Morrissey, who was the most influential person in Warhol's world after Malanga, was fascinated: "John Cale had a wonderful appearance and he played the electric viola, which was a real novelty; but best of all was Maureen Tucker, the drummer. You couldn't take your eyes off her because you couldn't work out if she was a boy or a girl. Nobody had ever had a girl drummer before. She made no movement, she was so sedate. I proposed that we sign a contract with them, we'd managed them and give them a place to play."

"We looked at each other," Lou Reed remembered, "and said, 'This sounds like really great fun.' "

Chapter Six

FUN AT THE FACTORY

1966

Reality was the key.

—Lou Reed

WHEN ANDY MET THE VELVETS, THEY WERE UNGLAMOROUS AND UN-known. "Andy, the problem is these people have no singer," said Paul Morrissey. "There's a guy who sings, but he's got no personality and nobody pays the slightest attention to him." In the following days Warhol and Morrissey transformed them from a four-piece unit led by Lou to a band fronted by the stunningly beautiful singer-actress Nico, a statuesque German blonde who had walked into Warhol's studio a week earlier. Lou initially didn't want her to be their chanteuse, but the arrangement was worked out under the convincing influence of Warhol's business manager, Paul Morrissey, who "just didn't think Lou had the personality to stand in front of the group and sing. The group needed something beautiful to counteract the screeching ugliness they were trying to sell, and the com-bination of a beautiful girl standing in front of all this decadence was what was needed. Right away that sour little Lou Reed bristled. He was hostile to Nico from the start. I told them I thought that Nico could be part of the Velvet Underground and just fit in there under that name." Quick to grasp the essence of the problem, Lou replied, "Let's keep Nico separate in this. The Velvet Underground—and Nico."

"Andy was this catalyst, always putting jarring elements together," Lou noted. "Which was something I wasn't so happy about. He wanted us to use Nico. Andy said, 'Oh, you've gotta have a chanteuse.' I said, 'Oh, Andy, give us a break.' But we went along with it at the time. Andy wanted her so he got her." Unbeknownst to Lou, back in 1963 Andy had tried to put together his own rock-and-roll band with none other than La Monte Young and Walter De Maria. Now, in as much as Warhol saw himself in Nico, Andy could fantasize that he was fronting the band.

The most remarkable thing about Lou Reed's progress in 1966 was his uncharacteristic willingness to accept Warhol's control in order to achieve the extraordinary success it would bring him. But, in the process, Lou made something of a Faustian bargain with Andy. Warhol had miraculously pulled the group out of the toilet, elevating them to his level when he was at the height of his fame. In exchange, however, Andy demoted Lou from fronting the band to being, employing a phrase by Nico, its "janitor of lunacy." Imagine what would have happened if Andrew Loog Oldham had tried to pull the same moves on Mick Jagger, promoting, for example, Brian Jones over his head as the front man, or indeed if Brian Epstein had suggested to John Lennon that he take a backseat in the Beatles and let George Harrison come up and front them. It is very rare that rock groups in their first flush of success find lead singers and songwriters willing to bow into a background role at the very moment of their initial triumph. It revealed several sides of Lou. First, his ambivalence about being in the spotlight. Second, his unusual ability to accept what would be best for the band without thinking about his own fame. Third, his discipleship to Andy Warhol.

Andy choreographed his group within a context that had been predicted by one of Lou's favorite writers, Edgar Allan Poe, who wrote one hundred years earlier, "The next step may be the electrification of all mankind by the representation of a play that may be neither tragedy, comedy, farce, opera, pantomime, melodrama or spectacle, as we now comprehend these terms, but which may retain some portion of the idiosyncratic excellence of each, while it introduces a new class of excellence as yet unnamed because as yet undreamed of in the world." It was also based on—some people said ripped off from—the 1965 multimedia performances of La Monte Young and Piero Heliczer as well as the "happenings" that were rife in the art world of the early sixties. In the band's first performance, at a dinner for a psychiatrists' convention at the elegant Delmonico's Hotel on Fifth Avenue in New York on the night of January 13, 1966, the group turned the tables on their audience, putting on an act of resentment and rage that Lou characterized as "fun."

Originally, the psychiatrists had invited Warhol to give an after-dinner speech at their convention. When the artist had enraged the underground film community by screening epics like *Sleep* and *Blowjob* asked if he could show some films instead, they indulged him. Now, as one hundred of the leading psychiatrists in America settled behind coffee and snifters of brandy ready to analyze the contents of the blank screen at the far end of the dining area, their tranquillity was shattered by Barbara Rubin, who came screaming into the room brandishing a movie camera with a powerful sun-gun lamp atop it. The seemingly crazed woman rushed from table to table shoving the camera into their faces and barraging them with questions like, "Do you eat her out?" and "Is your penis big enough?" No sooner had they been blown out of their after-dinner stupor by this horrible spectacle than an unbelievably loud cacophony erupted at the far end of the room, and they swiveled in their seats to see a brand of mangy-looking young men in dirty denim jeans and jackets performing a howling song about heroin. In back of them was a starkly lit, high-contrast black-and-white film of a man tied to a chair being tortured, in front of which a real man was brandishing a whip. Embarrassed, insulted, and perplexed, the psychiatrists reacted by grabbing their partners and storming the exits, or sitting forward with benevolent smiles trying to "understand" the spectacle in front of them. As Warhol stood off to the side, staring impassively at the panicked throng with a trace of a smile, and Nico stared impassively from the stage, Lou reached the climax of his paean to nullification, intoning, "And I guess that I just don't know, and I guess that I just don't know." The event was reported in the *New York Times* the following day under the title "Shock Treatment for Psychiatrists."

The tension between the band and Nico was somewhat ameliorated in the following weeks when Lou fell madly in love with the tall European with long flaxen hair. According to Richard Mishkin, to whom Lou expressed his emotions about her, Lou loved the fact that Nico was big. According to Lou, "Nico's the kind of person that you meet and you're not quite the same afterwards. She has an amazing mind."

Lou, John, and Sterling had all moved to 450 Grand Street at the end of 1965. Now Lou would often stay at the apartment Nico was subletting on Jane Street, where he wrote three songs for her. "One night Nico came up to me and said, 'Oh, Lou, I'll be your mirror,' " he recalled. "A close friend of mine always said that I bring out the idiocy in people, but I can also bring out something in them which is the best they've ever done. It's like with Nico and John Cale. They were fantastic with the Velvet Underground. They helped produce a great sound then. When I gave Nico a song of mine to sing, I knew she would totally understand what was being said and perform it from that standpoint." Nico described Lou as "very soft and lovely. Not aggressive at all. You could just cuddle him like a sweet person when I first met him, and he always stayed that way. I used to make pancakes for him. Everybody loved him around the Factory; he was rather cute, you know, and he said funny things."

According to Cale, "We had no idea what Nico could bring to the band, it was just something Andy came up with and it was very difficult to accept. Lou kind of fell in love with the idea, but we didn't understand it." In fact, with Warhol's encouragement, Nico became something of an inspiration for Lou. "Andy said I should write a song about Edie Sedgwick. I said, 'Like what?' and he said, 'Oh, don't you think she's a femme fatale, Lou?' So I wrote 'Femme Fatale' and we gave it to Nico." But this also caused conflicts within the group. The tough-minded Moe felt Nico "was a schmuck, from the first. She was this beautiful person who had traveled through Europe being a semistar. Her ego had grown very large. The songs Lou wrote for her were great, and she did them very well. Her accent made them great, but there was a limit! I kept to myself until she wanted to sing 'Heroin.' But then I had to speak my piece." "There were problems from the very beginning," added Sterling, "because there were only so many songs that were appropriate for Nico, and she wanted to sing them all—'I'm Waiting for the Man,' 'Heroin,' all of them. We said, 'No, no!' She wasn't very egotistical, she was out of it. I always explained it by saying she's not very good at English."

"When I started with the Velvets, I wanted to sing Lou's song 'I'm Waiting for the Man,'" said Nico, "but he wouldn't let me. I guess he thought I didn't understand its meaning, and he was right. And we had the song 'Heroin,' which I thought was a provocation. But I have to say that Lou and John took heroin, and those songs were songs of realism."

Cale looked on at what transpired with Welsh amusement. "Lou and Nico had some kind of an affair, both consummated and constipated," he said. "At the time he wrote these psychological love songs for her like 'I'll Be Your Mirror' and 'Femme Fatale,' which gave the band a new dimension. It was a difficult situation, I must admit, and sometimes I don't know how we accepted it. Still, Andy brought her into the band, and we nearly always accepted Andy's decisions. He was so much on our side, so enthusiastic about everything we did, that we couldn't help it."

"My favorite Lou Reed song is . . . aah . . . 'All Tomorrow's Parties,' " Warhol told an interviewer many years later in a mild put-down. "By Nico. She wrote it, I think."

Lou himself recalled most vividly two memories of Nico and Andy that had an eerie similarity: "I sat in an ice cream shop late one night watching Andy take the hand of a less than ordinary person sitting opposite him and slap his [Andy's] own face with it. It somehow reminded me of Delmore raging in a bar, asking me to call the White House to tell them we were aware of the plot.

"I loved after-hours bars. It's where I first saw someone beaten to death. The woman I was with, Nico, threw a glass that shattered in a mob guy's face. He thought the man in back of me did it."

January to April 1966 was the golden period for the Velvet Underground and Andy Warhol. After the psychiatrist's convention, Warhol shot a scintillating film of the band rehearsing at the Factory, *Symphony of Sound,* which remains the single best visual record of the Velvet Underground. They also recorded sound tracks for two of Warhol's best movies shot at the beginning of the year, *Hedy* and *More Milk Yvette.*

In February 1966, Andy appeared on WNET TV in New York, coyly announcing in his usual deadpan voice, "I'm sponsoring a new band. It's called the Velvet Underground. Since I don't really believe in painting anymore, I thought it would be a nice way of combining music, art, and films all together. The whole thing's being auditioned tomorrow at nine o'clock. If it works out, it might be very glamorous." That week, with the help of Barbara Rubin, he launched the Velvets at the underground film center the Cinémathèque, as part of a multimedia show called *Andy Warhol Uptight,* a paean to conflict, which developed out of the psychiatrists' convention. Gerard Malanga came into his own as the whip dancer, improvising a series of story dances that illustrated Lou's songs. Behind the band was a backdrop of Warhol films, most of which starred Edie Sedgwick, like *Beauty #2.* Nico sang three songs and rattled a tambourine. "They also played the record of Bob Dylan's song 'I'll Keep It With Mine,' " she said, "because I didn't have enough to sing otherwise. I had to stand there and sing along with it. I had to do this every night for a week. It was the most stupid concert I have ever done."

According to one disappointed observer, these shows amounted to nothing more than "ritual dances devised by dope fiends with nothing better to do." But as the photographer Nat Finkelstein, who was working on a photo documentary of the Factory, remembered, "From the first time I saw them I said, 'Wow! Wow! Wow! They're going to kick these guys out on their ass for the next ten years!' Everybody hated them. The whole macho East Village group really hated the Velvets—just put-down after put-down—the hatred had nothing to do with their music; a lot of it had to do with the gay image. Also, Lou and John were really good musicians, whereas Ed Sanders and Tuli Kupferberg [of the Fugs] wouldn't have known music if it bit them on the ass."

The engagement was a hit on every level. Warhol successfully launched his multimedia show, and the group managed to make some money while sending shock waves through the city. "They made twelve thousand dollars, I think," recalled Morrison. "A lot of people would come to see any kind of Warhol endeavor. The first time we played 'Heroin,' two people fainted. I didn't know if they OD'd or fainted. So that was our real debut—playing in Manhattan." Reed characterized the band's performance at the Cinémathèque as "a dog whistle for all the freaks in the city."

Outside of a small coterie who recognized him, Lou was not seen as the leader of the group. Nico became the Mick Jagger of the Velvet Underground, while Lou took the more humble Keith Richards role. This initially caused some tension, but Lou may not have minded being left out of the spotlight since he often felt uncomfortable onstage. "At the age when identity is a problem some people join rock and roll bands and perform for other people who share the same difficulties," he later wrote in a revealing essay on the pitfalls of pop stardom. "The age difference between performer and beholder in rock is not large. But unfortunately, those in the fourth tier assume those on stage know something they don't. Which is true. It simply requires a very secure ego to allow yourself to be loved for what you do rather than for what you are, and an even larger one to realize you are what you do. The singer had a soul but he feels he isn't loved off-stage. Or, perhaps worse, feels he shines only on stage and off is wilted, a shell as common as the garden gardenia." Also, by this time Lou was so taken by Andy and his world that he would probably have done anything Andy suggested. The same month Andy signaled Lou's acceptance into his domain by making him the subject of one of his Screen Tests—three-minute films focusing on the frozen gaze of a Factory citizen.

Warhol's studio, a large, floor-through single room in a factory building on West Forty-seventh Street in Manhattan, was called the Factory. Here Warhol painted his pop pictures, made his movies, and held court as the hippest, hardest bellwether of his times. The famous room was painted and tinfoiled silver. The people who worked with him and hung around him were the most hard-core group in New York at the time. They all dressed in black jeans and black T-shirts. Their drug of choice was amphetamine. The majority of them were gay. They were exotic, talented people, young, full of energy and ideas, satellites.

When Lou Reed joined Andy Warhol, Warhol was thirty-six, wealthy, and the successful driving force behind a devout cult of artistic collaborators. Reed was twenty-three, strong as stainless steel, confident, and as ambitious as his new mentor. Lou Reed had been described by friends and enemies over the years as "a control freak," "a schizophrenic," "an asshole." Not one of those descriptions was "fun." Andy Warhol had been described as "a mad queen," "a Zen warrior," "a creep." None of them was "fun," either. And yet, essentially, over the next four months, from January to April 1966, *fun* was exactly what Lou and Andy had together. Their relationship was exemplified by a photograph at the Factory that year in which they stood eyeballing each other with face-splitting grins in front of a life-size, full-figure Warhol painting of Elvis Presley with a drawn six-gun. Andy, the Lionhearted Leo—his head, with its strong, high cheekbones and muscular jaw, cocked slightly to one side—revealed the Draculian character he possessed in the pencil-thin, sinewy body beneath his trademark black outfit. He looked, one observer later noted, like Sylvester staring at Tweety Pie. Lou, the uncharacteristically shark-hearted Pisces, stared in turn at Andy with all the gaminlike love he had been withholding from his father since he was twelve, with the adoration of a disciple who has just met the master who will open the gates of heaven and hell.

Andy seduced Lou by showering his prodigious ego with the highest compliments. "Andy told me that what we were doing with music was the same thing he was doing with movies and painting, i.e., not kidding around," Lou recalled. "To my mind, nobody in music was doing anything that even approximated the real thing, with the exception of us. The first thing I liked about Andy was that he was very real. His ideas would stun me. His way of looking at things would stop me dead in my tracks. Sometimes, I would go for days thinking about something he said."

Lou seduced Andy into spending the next five months trying to make Lou into a marketable persona that would make the most money in the shortest time—in short, a rock-and-roll star. "If Andy had been able to achieve the Walt Disney Hollywood status, Lou would have been able to change his persona to be like an Elvis," pointed out Factory manager Billy Name. "Andy would have put out Lou Reed movies: Lou in Hawaii, Lou in the army, Lou as a half-breed trying to decide whether he should like the Comanches and stay with the family that raised him."

Lou would make a career out of finding mentors. In Warhol, Reed found the all-permissive father-mother-protector-catalyst-collaborator he had always craved. In turn, Warhol saw his younger self in Reed and wanted to recapture that vitality. They were both isolated people who kept their innermost thoughts to themselves, and each could empathize with the other's masked vulnerability. Each had had nervous breakdowns. For Lou a whole new world of possibilities opened up.

He made himself completely available to Warhol—just as he had done with Delmore Schwartz at Syracuse—without selling him his soul. For a time he was able to drop his need to be the only genius in the room. Warhol taught Reed that an artist was a person who had to work hard and not waste time. Whenever Andy asked Lou how many songs he'd written that day, whatever the answer, he would urge, "You should do more." He taught Lou that work was everything, and that Lou came to believe that his music was so beautiful that people should be willing to die for it. It was the kind of effect Andy Warhol often had on his followers.

Lou's position at the Factory was significantly different from that of the other members of the band. "When the Velvets came over to the Factory, Lou was the only one I talked to," recalled Factory manager and photographer Billy Name. "Sterling rarely talked much. John would talk occasionally, and Moe was fun—she would talk—but Lou and I always had the bond thing." Of all the Velvets, Lou spent the most time at the Factory and was the closest thing to Warhol.

Warhol was not, however, an easy man to work with. Despite taking great joy in his success, he had, like Reed, a resentment of the conditions of his life that never stopped bugging him. "He was an artist who was neither understood nor accepted at the time but who, having been ridiculed and laughed at, had perseverance and ambition for success and 'la gloire,' as strong as that of any king in Shakespeare's history plays," wrote Gerard Malanga in an introduction to his *Secret Diaries*. "It was a desire that neither his coterie nor his celebrity could satisfy. Warhol was a man of parts, most of them contradictory, which accounts for his nickname, 'Drella,' composed equally of Dracula and Cinderella. He was a person of much generosity and kindness—yet he could slice a person at a glance. Warhol would try to organize other people's emotions in the same way he drew up shopping lists. He had the unique power of playing people off one another. He could be kind, cruel, friendly, catty, humane, overriding, passionately wild for 'la gloire.' And he was also all that was truly vulnerable. Warhol was painfully shy, which accounted for the group of young people he surrounded himself with. He was possessed by the people he had gathered around him, yet he was habitually exploiting, betraying, or otherwise mistreating those who were close, or seemed close to him."

In an essay, "From the Bandstand," he wrote about music that year, Lou drew attention to one of the key concepts they both emphasized in their work, repetition. "Every head in America must know the last three drum choruses of 'Dawn' by the Four Seasons. Paradiddles. Repetition. Repetition is so fantastic. . . . Andy Warhol's movies are so repetitious sometimes, so so beautiful. Probably the only interesting films made in the U.S. Rock and roll films. Over and over and over. Reducing things to their final joke. Which is pretty. 'Sally go 'round the roses / roses they won't hurt you.' "

"The real idea was to listen all the time," Reed said. "He had great ideas at the drop of a hat. But so did I. The thing was, he was there. There were a couple of people who were floating around who were there who always seemed to get in touch with one another one way or another. In other words, no other band could have been able to hold it up. It would have been overwhelmed by the lights or the movies. That's not, in fact, what happened. And that's because what we did was very strong."

"You scared yourself with music," Warhol told him. "I scared myself with paint."

"It was like heaven," said Reed of his early days at the Factory. "I watched Andy. I watched Andy watching everybody. I would hear people say the most astonishing things, the craziest things, the funniest things, the saddest things. I used to write it down."

All the Velvets seemed equally snowed by Andy. "It was like bang!" Warhol superstar Mary Woronov recalled. "They were with Andy and Andy was with them and they backed him absolutely. They would have walked to the end of the earth for him. And that happened in one day!"

Gretchen Berg, who often visited the Factory to interview Warhol, noticed that Reed maintained a strong position there. "Lou was very quiet. He almost never spoke to anyone, and when addressed, he would not answer," she recalled. "He would act as if you weren't there. I respected him. I saw that he was an artist of some kind and he had his group around him. They were always quite nice, but they always kept their distance. It was a bit snobbish. I also had the feeling that Mr. Warhol created the atmosphere of a family around him and there was a certain amount of competition. He had a lot of power with Andy on a one-on-one basis. You had the feeling that Lou was someone rather special. He was the brother who was away for many years and had to be caught when he came in. The father must now speak to Lewis, who's just come in, because Lewis will not speak to anyone else but father. It was exactly that feeling. No one else must speak to Lou. And then Lewis would speak to father and then leave. If you came up to him, it was not as if he was rude exactly, but he would just look at you and take a puff of his cigarette. Lou was very much in the background, but he kept himself in the background. There was always something that was being created in the background. While everyone else was going through their thing and living and having all this attention, this in the background was going on very quietly and very steadily. He was like Paul Morrissey in a way.

"There was tension between Paul and everyone. I think he felt that he must not say anything about Lou Reed because he had no power over Lou. Lou Reed came in when he liked, left when he liked."

In Warhol's Factory, Reed found a laboratory for his artistic and sexual explorations, a milieu full of psychodrama providing endless fodder for his songs, and a nurturing environment through which he could bring music to the world. "Everyone was very campy," Cale said. "There was a lot of game playing. Lou felt at home in that environment. I didn't really." Before the Factory, Reed had created scenarios for his songs; Warhol provided the cast and the telling details. More importantly, the Factory laid bare all the sexual fantasies and taboos that Reed had been struggling to conceal since his days on Long Island. In Warhol's light Lou metamorphosed from a rock musician with a negative attitude and a host of complexes into a glamorous member of the Warhol entourage. The fragile, gamin Reed was equally attractive to men and women, looking on the one hand like a pretty girl with his curly brown hair and tentative smile, and exhibiting on the other hand an insouciant attitude regarding sex that presented an ambivalent challenge. Reed soon abandoned the sweaters, casual jackets, and loafers he'd worn since leaving Syracuse and took on the Factory image—Warhol-inspired black leather jacket, boots, and shades. Like Warhol, Reed masked his vulnerable side within the armor of a tough, impenetrable image.

Warhol had often gone on the record saying that sex was too much trouble, but he was fascinated by the idea of sex, and many of his films were semipornographic in a distanced, ironic way. Reed also maintained a detached stance with regard to sex. As a friend recalled, "Lou was mostly a voyeur. In my experience he never had any sustained interest in either sex. Sex didn't offer Lou enough—he was just really bored by it." One budding transvestite, Jackie Curtis, tried to have sex with Lou. "He was very tall and heavily built, a big boy," recalled a mutual friend. "He was eighteen, but he looked about fourteen. And he would come right up to Lou and say, 'Hi, gee, how are you?' And Lou would not respond at all. And Jackie would say, 'Well, thank you very much.' And then he'd come back to me and say, 'God, what did I say?' He was very funny. Then he would go rushing up the next time and Lou would put his head back in an aloof manner."

Lou was not, however, always aloof. "Lou tried to put the make on me once," Malanga remembered. "It didn't go anywhere. He was the aggressor and I was gentle with him but . . . We came back from a gig real late—we were traveling somewhere and we came back to New York really late and he called up Barbara Hodes and Barbara put the two of us up that night. And I remember Lou making advances toward me under the sheet.

I think in the end we ended up just hugging each other. I kind of sent him the signal that I wasn't interested."

Reed was more interested in the sexual role-playing of transvestisms and S&M. Yet this didn't stop him from having a number of friendships with men and women. At the Factory he met Danny Fields, a young medical school dropout with whom he developed a connection that lasted over thirty years. "I first heard 'Heroin' and I thought it was beautiful music," Fields recalled. "But I was terrified of Lou. I was always trying to figure out things to say to him that would be sharp. Everybody was in love with him back then. Around 1966, he was the sexiest boy in town."

"Lou's relationship with Danny Field was collegial," explained Gerard Malanga. "They were in the same business and there was a lot of history between them. Lou and I may have crashed at Danny's one night. Danny's pad was basically a crash pad. Thank God for Danny. We would have been homeless. We always knew he could be relied on to put us up. He was living on West Twentieth Street between Fifth and Sixth Avenues above a coffee shop, which in those years was a very unfashionable place to live. So Danny was a pioneer. He had a floor-through loft in a two-story building. There were couches and pillows and mattresses on the floor with a few people staying there."

In the midst of all the ego collisions and role-playing, screaming guitars, and parties, Fields observed, "We all had this feeling about Lou—that he would bury us. He was much too smart to get sucked into the whirlpool. Others may have been too fragile, too beautiful to survive—but he knew what he was doing. I was ever so in love with Lou. Everyone was in love with him—me, Edie, Andy, everyone. I thought he was just the hottest-looking, sexiest person I ever had seen. He was a major sex object of everybody in New York in his years with the Velvet Underground. The Velvets were ahead of everybody. It was the only thing that ever, ever, ever swept me off my feet as music since early Mahler. They were a revolution.

"The anguish Lou was reflecting upon was not his own. He was personalizing what he'd seen. As an artist he kept his distance and refused to be destroyed by it. Oh, he'd had his ups and downs, but he's in no way a tragic figure. He simply had the brilliance to turn it all into art."

Another Factory denizen, Tally Brown, said, "Lou is one of the most interesting lyricists of urban life in the world. He also is one of the best theoreticians about rock and roll. I mean, he can write about it and talk about it. He's very verbal. Besides that, he's a fascinating, fucked-up guy."

After Warhol and Fields, Reed made strong, long-term connections with Billy Name, Ondine, and Gerard, the three strongest influences on Warhol. Each man had his separate function for Lou. Factory manager, photographer, and permanent resident Billy Name provided an outlet for Lou's mystical side. Lou and Billy spent hours hanging out and talking about their favorite subjects such as Eastern religion and matters of the occult. "When I first met Lou, we immediately bonded as if we were guys who grew up on the same block," Name recalled. "He's from Long Island, I'm from Poughkeepsie, with the same experience. We just got along so great we were like best buddies. We had a good love for each other and great respect. Lou was a great conversationalist, very congenial, very interested, never the type of person who would just say what he wanted to say—he explored what you were and heard what you said, always with camaraderie." Lou saw Billy as "a divinity in action on Earth. He did pictures that were unspeakably beautiful. Just pure space. For the people who have one foot on Earth and another foot on Venus, they would like that kind of picture because it was out-and-out space."

Gerard Malanga was a widely published and well-connected poet who was familiar with many of the poets Lou was interested in, including Delmore Schwartz. "I identified more with Lou on a poetry level than on a rock-and-roll level," said Malanga, "even when I was choreographing for the Velvets. I identified with Lou as a fellow poet as opposed to someone making music. Lou was a good guy to bring around. If you tapped him on the shoulder and said, 'Let's go here,' he would go. He wouldn't ask, 'Where are we going?' and 'What for?' and all that. He was good to have with you. He was good to hang out with. But he wasn't very humorous, and he didn't speak much. He wasn't an articulate person."

If Billy and Lou connected on a metaphysical level, and Gerard and Lou connected through poetry, then it was with Ondine that Lou shared his love of drugs. Like Lou and many denizens of the Factory, Ondine had chosen amphetamine as his drug of choice, and he became Lou's main supplier. "He was intelligent about his use of drugs," said Ondine. "He knew what he was doing, he studied it. I always thought that the whole heroin thing was an artistic expression. A lot of people experimented with heroin."

Lou's most famous song may be "Heroin," but the drug most associated with his image was undoubtedly amphetamine. It's easy to see why. According to the *Amphetamine Manifesto* by Harvey Cohen, "It is a drug for those who despair: shy, retarded, unhappy creatures who need love and had been rejected and had their natural instincts rejected and almost atrophied. Amphetamine is very much an overachiever's type of chemical. Methedrine rolls back the stone from the mouth of the cave. It is the most profound of all drugs, the most unexplored and the freakiest. It can be so many things; there's always a place to go behind methedrine that you've never been before. Amphetamine stimulates the central nervous system. It lessens the patient's inhibitions, relieving him of pent-up emotions often associated with some previously suppressed trauma. The ideal patient for this treatment has an obsessional, tense personality and has difficultly expressing his real feelings, particularly if they are aggressive. Patients with obsessional personalities become relaxed, but are awake and alert after injection."

Amphetamine had two vital functions for Lou creatively. By allowing him to stay up for three to five days at a time without sleep, it altered the synapses of his brain, cutting off a lot of static that had previously stymied the flow of words, and gave him—particularly in writing—the energy to pursue each vision to its conclusion. (One can see its effects in his essay "From the Bandstand," published in *Aspen Magazine*, December 1966, or in songs such as "White Light/White Heat"—pure amphetamine—or "Murder Mystery").

Methedrine is also, perhaps, the greatest male aphrodisiac, giving a man an erection that could break a plate, as well as Homeric duration in the act. On top of that, the methedrine available in 1966 was pharmaceutical and cheap. Being a favored customer, Lou could buy a film canister of the powder, which he cooked up and shot, for as little as $5.

The "amphetamine glories" who gathered around the central figure of Ondine at the Factory saw themselves as religious, heroic, and immortal. Of course they weren't, and many of them, like Ondine, died sad deaths. But when they lived, they lived beyond the barriers of society. As Lou wrote in one of his finest pieces of prose, the liner notes to *Metal Machine Music*, "For those for whom the needle is no more than a toothbrush.

Professional, no sniffers please, don't confuse superiority (no competition) with violence, power or other justifications. The tacit speed agreement with self. We did not start World War I, II, or III, or the Bay of Pigs for that matter. My week beats your year."

At first, the only dissenting opinion about Lou at the Factory came from Paul Morrissey, who felt that Nico was a far strong performer and presence onstage. "Lou was always ill at ease as a performer, and that's what his act still is—a remote, ill-at-ease person." The two of them shared a certain hardness, which led one observer to comment that Lou was "like Paul Morrissey with a guitar."

Nico was the first person at the Factory to taste the dregs of Lou's meanness just after her breakup with Lou following the show at the Cinémathèque. According to Cale, Lou was "absolutely torn up by it all. When it fell apart, we really learnt how Nico could be the mistress of the destructive one-liner." Cale recalled one morning rehearsal at the Factory shortly thereafter: "Nico came late, as usual. Lou said, 'Hello,' to her in a rather cold way, but just 'Hello,' or something. She simply stood there. You could see she was waiting to reply, in her own time. Ages later, out of the blue, came her first words: 'I cannot make love to Jews anymore.' "

"Lou was absolutely magnificent, but we quarreled a lot, he made me very sad then," she said later.

Lou may have lost his lover, but when it came to the Velvet Underground, he maintained control over Nico. "He wouldn't let me sing some of his songs because we'd split," she lamented. "Lou likes to manipulate women, you know, like program them. He wanted to do that with me. He told me so. Like, computerize me. Lou was the boss and he was very bossy."

"He was mean to Nico," said Malanga. "Lou could not stand to be around somebody who has a light equal to his or who shines more intensely."

According to Cale, he was intimidated by Reed. But despite Lou's immersion in the Warhol world, Cale was still the person who understood him best. "John idolized Lou," Paul Morrissey recalled. "He thought anything Lou said was wonderful." "John and Lou were very close," agreed a mutual friend. "They loved each other, but they also hated each other. It was competitive musically. John knew Lou got much more attention because he was the singer in the group, but then John cut a more flamboyant figure. Lou used to call him the 'Welsh Bob Dylan.' They were two guys fighting to be stars. They were the perfect match but they were the perfect mismatch in that their true deep-down directional head for music was very different."

"Andy and Nico liked each other's company," recalled John Cale. "There was something complicit in the way they both handled Lou Reed, for instance. Lou was straight-up Jewish New York, while Nico and Andy were kind of European. Lou was very full of himself and faggy in those days. We called him Lulu, I was Black Jack, Nico was Nico. He wanted to be queen bitch and spit out the sharpest rebukes of anyone around. Lou always ran with the pack, and the Factory was full of queens to run with. But Lou was dazzled by Andy and Nico. He was completely spooked by Andy, because he could not believe that someone could have such a goodwill and yet be mischievous in the same transvestite way that Lou was, all that bubbling gay humor. It was fun for the rest of us to watch all the shenanigans going on, with Rene Ricard and those spiteful games you just had to laugh at because they were so outrageous. But Lou tried to compete. Unfortunately for him, Nico could do it better.

"Nico and Andy had a slightly different approach, but they caught Lou out time and time again. Andy was never less than considerate to us. Lou couldn't fully understand this, he couldn't grasp this amity that Andy had. Even worse, Lou would say something bitchy, but Andy would say something even bitchier, and—nicer. This would irritate Lou. Nico had the same effect. She would say things so he couldn't answer back."

The month of March was spent on the road, doing shows at university art departments. The whole entourage was feeling cocky and took a defiant us-against-them attitude. "We all got along very well and had tremendous fun on the road," recalled Sterling, "Andy and the whole crowd. We used to rent those big recreational vehicles—and pack everyone in there and just roll. It was a self-contained world. We had a generator on the back so we could power all our stuff."

Warhol's death-squad entourage, all dressed in black, all on drugs, and all acting out ego traumas and fantasies, caused a sensation wherever they went. "We had a horrible reputation—they thought we were gay," said Sterling. "They figured we must be—running around with Warhol and all those whips and stuff. In order to eke out a career, you've got to start thinking about things like longevity, and markets and tastes. We were quite intelligent, I'm sure we were the most highly scholarshipped band in history. Which made it very difficult to manage us, because the usual bullshit shallow thinking wasn't going to work for an instant. You couldn't say, 'Do this.' Andy, oddly enough, probably could have, but he never operated that way."

During their trip to New Jersey's Rutgers University, a fight broke out in the cafeteria when the members of the group were not allowed to eat there, ensuring that the afternoon's performance would sell out. But it wasn't until they got to Ann Arbor, Michigan, that the whole thing finally came together and was a smash hit. "In March we left New York for Ann Arbor in a rented van to play at the University of Michigan," wrote Warhol. "Nico drove, and that was an experience. I still don't know if she had a license. She'd only been in this country a little while and she'd keep forgetting and drive on the British side of the road. A cop stopped us near a hamburger drive-in near Toledo when a waitress got upset and complained to him because we kept changing orders, and when he asked, 'Who's in charge here?' Lou shoved me forward and told him, 'Of all people—Drella!'

"Ann Arbor was crazy. At least the Velvets were a smash. I'd sit on the steps in the lobby during intermissions and people from the local papers would interview me, ask about my movies, what we were trying to do. 'If they can take it for ten minutes, then we play it for fifteen,' I'd explain. 'That's our policy. Always leave them wanting less.' "

BACK IN NEW YORK THAT APRIL, THE GROUP REACHED THE ZENITH OF their career when Warhol rented a Polish community hall, the Dom, on St. Marks Place in the East Village, and put on his climactic multimedia show, now called the *Exploding Plastic Inevitable*.

When the Velvet Underground performed for a month that April under Warhol's direction in the *Exploding Plastic Inevitable*, Nico undoubtedly became the star of the show. Onstage in her white pantsuit, she was the center of attention. She was an inch taller than Cale, and despite the fact that Reed sang most of the songs, everything was geared so that she just had to stand there to command attention. Every drug-induced movement she made became significant. It was a talent she had developed in her years as a model and with which Lou Reed could not compete. The musicians who stood out were the flamboyant and handsome Welshman John Cale, with his great hawk nose and mop of shiny black hair cut in the style of Prince Valiant, as he bowed his electric viola, and the androgynous little drummer, who stood up behind a bizarre-looking kit composed chiefly of kettledrums, banging away with the relentless ferocity of an insane fourteen-year-old. In fact, Warhol was the dominant influence because his films set the striking backdrop and his conduction of the light show played over the band and the films, creating a whole new way to look at rock-and-roll shows. And people came to see a Warhol show.

It was, for the mid-1960s, an incredible sight. Two of Warhol's films were projected side by side on a floor-to-ceiling white wall behind the band. The Velvets, all dressed in black, often turned their backs to the audience. Nico, all in white, sang under a single harsh spotlight. In front of them, two Warhol dancers in black leather, Malanga and Mary Woronov (a Warhol actress), one often brandishing a whip, acted out images from the songs. Over the stage Warhol hung a spinning mirrored ball. From a balcony at the other end of the hall, Warhol focused colored strobe lights on the stage. The colored lights played across the whole ensemble, and the spinning mirrored ball sent slivers of light splintering in a hundred different directions. This created a flickering effect, which, combined with the loudest rock music ever heard at the time, disoriented the audience, with mixed-up messages of love, peace, hate, and revenge. Nico sang trancelike, fixated, aloof, her beauty as removed from conventional concepts of warmth as Alaska; Warhol's show filled the space with images as disturbing and abrasive as Reed's songs.

Lou, who usually wore all black as well as sunglasses to avoid the punishing lights that occasionally flashed over his face, faded into the shadows and was primarily represented by his eerie, disembodied, monochromatic voice intoning the hymnlike lyrics to "Heroin" and "Venus in Furs." But since it issued from a mélange so new, so strange, so different, so revolutionary, the last thing an observer found himself wondering about was who's the singer?

The writer Stephen Koch, who was there, has given the most telling description of the performance's effects as it mirrored the essence of Reed and Warhol's artistic marriage. "The effort to create an exploding (more accurately, imploding) environment capable of shattering any conceivable focus on the senses was all too successful. It became virtually im-possible to dance, or for that matter do anything else but sit and be bombarded—'stoned' as it were. . . . Seeing it made me realize for the first time how deeply the then all-admired theories attacking 'ego' as the root of all evil and unhappiness had become for the avant-garde the grounds for a deeply engaged metaphor of sexual sadism, for 'blowing the mind,' assaulting the senses; it came home to me how the 'obliteration' of the ego was not the act of liberation it was advertised to be, but an act of complete revenge and resentment wholly entangled on the deepest levels with the knots of frustration. Liberation was turning out to be humilia-tion; peace was revealing itself as rage."

"I'd never seen a show like that," John Cale said. "You just ignored it and played. Lou and I had an almost religious fervor about what we were doing—like trying to figure ways to integrate some of La Monte Young's and Andy Warhol's conceptions into rock and roll. It was exciting be-cause what Lou did and what I did worked. What he put into words and what I put into music and what the band put together, the combination of everything and the mentality involved in it, was stunning."

DURING HIS FIRST WEEK AT THE DOM, ANDY OPENED A NEW SHOW AT LEO Castelli's, which had been conceived as his farewell to art. He wallpa-pered one room of the gallery with the repeated images of a cow's head, resembling the friendly Borden ice-cream trademark, Elsie. Another room was filled with free-floating helium-filled silver pillows. At the end of the show, Warhol opened a window and released a giant pillow which floated away as a symbolic end to his fine-art career.

The Dom was a financial success, earning $18,000 in its first week. "But our actual salary from Paul Morrissey, who handled the business side for Andy, was five dollars a day, for cheese or beer at the Blarney Stone," chuckled Sterling. "He had a ledger that listed everything, including drug purchases—'$5 for heroin.' When the accountant saw it, he said, 'What the hell is this?' "

The continuing tensions between Lou and Nico were evident during the shows. "Nico took an age in the dressing room, and then we had to wait while she'd light this candle," remembered Cale. "It was for her own good luck or something—and she held up the band, held up the gig. Lou had very little time for women and their accoutrements, and this ritual would really irritate him. The comic thing was, she'd do all this to help her performance, and then she'd start off singing on the wrong beat! Where she started in the song was a real focal point of the night! Lou would hiss across the stage, 'We know what we're doing, Nico.' There were always conflicts and presumably there always will be. Lou was the vocalist, front man, and songwriter for the band. I was just taking it easy and generally having fun. Now I look back on it all, I wasn't particularly enamored of the more garish aspects of, say, the *Exploding Plastic Inevitable* row, but then that's exactly what Lou was very into."

As much as Lou enjoyed playing at the Dom, not everything was always copacetic. One night on stage Sterling suddenly yelled at him, "Don't move!" "I take a look," Lou recalled, "and I'd just put on fresh strings, and one of the long ends had hit the microphone and just burned right up, and it was starting down the neck of the guitar! Well, I didn't move. They shut everything down, and I just stood there, and there was smoke and that terrible ozone odor in the air. I mean, people get knocked out, killed. It's incredible. I mean, that kind of jolt cannot be doing good things to your system. . . . I've always had a big fear of electric shocks."

As the show became successful, the band's unity broke under the pressure brought on by the unequal attention afforded certain members of the troupe—Malanga and Nico were more prominent than Cale and Reed for example. "John had the balance of the Velvet Underground charisma," pointed out a mutual friend. "Lou without John, it wouldn't have the edge. John gave it that romantic . . . I mean the sound of the Velvet Underground was John. The words and the music were Lou, but it was those weird nails-on-the-blackboard sounds and the holding of the notes and that La Monte Young/Terry Riley preface to the Velvet Underground—that cold, edgy Wales edge, and John just visually was the person I always looked at. I don't know if John knew that. . . . Lou knew it enough that he was jealous."

"They were outrageous times," Cale recalled. "Every day someone would do something outrageous to someone famous. It was characterized by this terribly camp, very flagrant behavior. I used to just stand there and watch and have a good laugh. And there was always Andy, who was a fantastic game player—so was Lou, but he had street sensibility. That was the big difference between them: Andy was a society person who didn't have a bad bone in his body, while Lou came with a streetwise outlook and was very close to having a bad bone in his body. It was a case of never the twain.

"I never felt marginalized. To me, it was just a marvelous collaboration, where everybody had an enormous amount of freedom. Lou felt marginalized, though. He has this thing in his persona about having to struggle alone, not as part of a group. At the time, he clearly felt that he was experiencing a lot of boundaries working with other people. It's something that was there for the duration of our time with Andy. He never really resolved in his mind the relationship between Andy and the band, and himself and the *EPI*.

"In some ways, if you're a protest writer like Lou is, then you need some spark of injustice to continue—and where one does not exist, then you find one. That makes one awfully close to being a malcontent, you know. I think that's always been Lou's problem, he's always tried to find something which he can work off."

At the time of the *EPI* performances at the Dom, Reed was struck by a small tragedy. "Lou had a Gretch, semihollow body, old, green," recalled Maureen. "He had taken the frets off of it. And it really had this odd sound. Fantastic sound. Of course you couldn't use it for many songs, but for what he wanted it was tremendous. And it got stolen while we were playing at the Dom. Along with his record collection. Lou must have been collecting singles since he was twelve. Songs, groups you'd never heard of, for the most part. I loved them, because we both liked the same music, and once in a while we would have sort of a party, and he would say, 'Listen to this!' He'd be half-drunk and I'd be half-drunk, and so would everybody, and he would put it on and I'd say, 'Yaaaaa, who is it?' and he'd say, 'The Goofballs,' or whoever. He must have had two or three hundred records, anyway.

"We called it the 'great sneaker robbery,' because there were actually sneaker prints on his bed. But they came and took his guitar and all of his records. Oh, it was heartbreaking. Some of those records, there isn't a copy left in the world."

The *Exploding Plastic Inevitable* became a sensation, attracting celebrities like Salvador Dalí and Jackie Kennedy to intellectuals, college kids, druggies, and members of the press. "We played music surrounded by people who were in every respect more glamorous than we were," commented Sterling. "Andy created multimedia in New York," said Reed. "Everything was affected by it. The whole complexion of the city changed, probably of the country. Nothing remained the same after that." The media pundit of the age, Marshall McLuhan, agreed and included a double-page-spread photograph of their performance in his classic book, *The Medium is the Massage,* with the statement, " 'Time' has ceased, 'space' has vanished. We now live in a global village . . . a simultaneous happening." Lou responded in a poem, "I'm an electric child / Of McLuhan. (Bullshit) / He's got no clue / To what's going on."

Some critics, jealous of Warhol's publicity and angered by his indulgence toward amphetamine and homosexuality, attacked the *EPI* as nothing more than an untalented evening of noise and insults. Warhol, they charged, was ripping people off at $6 a head just to make them feel uncomfortable. "People would tell us it was violent, it was grotesque, it was perverted," said Reed, laughing. "We said, 'What are you talking about? it's fun, look, all these people are having fun.' Right around the corner was Timothy Leary and some mixed-media event. He criticized us, saying, 'Those people are nothing but A-heads, speed freaks.' So the people talking for Andy Warhol said, 'Those people take acid. How can you listen to anything those people say?' It was that insane and ridiculous. We were always astonished in the first place that people were shocked by us. Andy and us were cut from somewhat the same cloth, and we wanted to shake people up a little bit. Just so much fun. When confronted with a—quote—really straight audience, that's what we went for. We were never playing to make enemies; we were playing to make music." On more than one occasion members of the group were attacked as they left the building by bottle-wielding malcontents.

For the most part, the mainstream press maintained a hostile stance when commenting on the show. The *New York Times* mentioned the event, but placed it on the Women's page. "The first story about the Velvet Underground was on the Women's page of the *Times* and it was all about Nico," recalled Paul Morrissey. "You can imagine how well that went down with Lou Reed." In fact, the *Times* review was one of the more kind reactions to the performance. "We were attacked constantly," said Reed. "No one ever wrote anything nice about us, or even looked at it very seriously, which was fine. You got tired of being called obscene. It just seemed to go on and on and on and on and on. Anyone who writes for a newspaper or something has to be sick. People who criticize other people. There must be a reason for it. They must have something else to do. Why don't they go and do something with themselves. They think it's so easy. Our favorite quote was, 'The flowers of evil are in bloom. Some-one has to stamp them out before they spread.' "

These were heady days for Lou. In four months he had gone from obscurity to being, as part of the Velvets, the center of a media blitz. They had every reason to believe that they were on their way to being as big as the Rolling Stones. The Lou Reed who created intelligent rock poetry of drugs, deviant sex, violence, and suicide now fully emerged. "That's when he was at his peak," remarked the writer Glenn O'Brien. "When Lou was the most good-looking, dressed in the best of taste, and did the most powerful work. He didn't show any signs of age or ravage, he was still undamaged and young."

As Reed's image grew, he developed a coterie of staunch supporters. For those who didn't know him, however, he presented an often contra-dictory and confusing image. "A bunch of us would leave the Dom really late and go to the after-hours clubs around the Village—Lou knew them all," recalled Warhol. "At the Tenth of Always [named after the Johnny Mathis song 'The Twelfth of Never'] there'd always been one same little blond boy every night who'd get drunk and turn to Lou and demand, 'Well, are you a homosexual or not? I am and I'm proud of it.' Then he'd smash his glass on the floor and get asked to leave."

Richard Mishkin, who had kept in touch with Lou and who had occasionally sat in on bass at the Dom, was under the impression that Lou was making progress in his drive to become a success. "Anybody who could tolerate what he was tolerating in terms of lifestyle would have to be driven," he said. "I remember playing at the Dom in front of strobe lights, and I had never been exposed to strobe lights, and thinking, this is really hard, this is not playing music. Lou was doing what he had to do. He knew that he wasn't Paul McCartney or Elvis Presley. He was Lou Reed, and if he was going to do what he wanted to do and become a rock-and-roll star, he had to do it the Lou Reed way. That's what he was doing, he was creating his place in history, so to speak, by being so different." (The irreverent teenager still lurked beneath the sleek surface, however. On one occasion when Lou and Ritchie were rehearsing at Lou's Grand Street loft, Mishkin's mother showed up in a fur coat and high heels to drag her recalcitrant son away from the den of iniquity, and Lou was so hysterical with laughter he almost fell on the floor.) Another man who sat in on several shows when Cale got sick, the avant-garde violinist Henry Flynt, recalled, "Reed taught me their whole repertoire in about five minutes, because basically he just wanted me to be in the right key. At one point I got in a fight with him onstage because I was playing a very hillbilly-influenced style on the violin and that upset him very much. He wanted a very sophisticated sound, he didn't want rural references in what was supposed to be this very decadent S-and-M image that they were projecting."

Reed had found a vitality in performing at the Dom. "Young people know where everything is at," he told a reporter backstage. "Let 'em sing about going steady on the radio. Let 'em run their hootenannies. But it's in holes like this that the real stuff is being born. The universities and the radio kill everything, but around here, it's alive. The kids know that."

AS SOON AS HE REALIZED THE GROUP WAS TAKING OFF, ANDY started producing *The Velvet Underground and Nico* album, which would become a rock classic. Warhol put up some of the revenue from the Dom engagement, and they found some other investors. "This shoe salesman, Norman Dolph, put up the money," recalled John Cale, "and he got a deal at Cameo-Parkway Studios, on Broadway. We went in there, and the floorboards were torn up, the walls were out, there were four mikes working. We set up the drums where there was enough floor, turned it all up, and went from there." The recording studio was rented for $2,500 for three nights, enough time to cut the whole album.

In order to claim royalties on a song, it first had to be published. A lead sheet of musical notation had to be written for each song, then the tax forms had to be registered. If this was not done, the writer could not earn any money from the song. One of Danny Field's closet friends, a musician by the name of Hope Ruff, who worked in this capacity for many songwriters including Bob Dylan and Sam the Sham, made it her responsibility to work up the lead sheets for Lou's songs "because nobody else was doing it," she said. "John was certainly capable of it, but I think he was really strung out a lot. I don't think Lou could do it. It's a real pain in the ass for most people. But it was nothing to me. I would write it as fast as they'd play it. I think Lou was concerned about it. He was not as crazy as he pretended to be. And I always said that. Danny would say, 'Oh, Lou, he did this, he did that,' and I always said to him, 'He is just a kid from Long Island.' He calls his mother up to make sure she fed the dog. And that's how I always thought of him. He'd say, 'I have to go make a phone call,' and I'd say, 'Who are you calling?' He'd say, 'I have to call my mother to find out how my dog is.' When you're really crazy, you don't worry about that kind of stuff. But everybody saw what they wanted to see. But he was not a nut case. I liked him. I thought he was a nice person. And Danny would look at me like . . . That was a big insult in the sixties. You don't say that about someone: 'He was a nice guy.' But he was. And I had great respect for him. He had a reputation for being mean to women, but he was always very nice to me. He was wild to Nico. He was never mean to me. I remember Lou talking to Nico like she was a pile of trash. I can't remember any specifics but I remember him yelling at her—she really couldn't sing and she couldn't play. At the Balloon Farm or in the back room at Max's—I'd always be there—and she'd say something stupid. He'd jump on her because he's very smart and he hated stupid. Put it this way, he was caustic with anybody who was weaker than he was. I don't think you just had to be a female. I mean, there were dumb guys around too—dumb rock stars. Lou had a sharp mouth as far as they were concerned because he wasn't mainstream famous and he was very talented and way smarter and that's the way it goes. So I think if he sensed that someone was weak, as a lot of us did in those days, he would sweep in for the kill because it was funny."

The Reed-Cale collaboration reached a peak during the recording. Because of his experience of making records since he was fifteen and his time in the studio at Pickwick, Lou seized the opportunity to act as engineer and producer. John Cale, who had a limited knowledge of the workings of a recording studio, also contributed significantly to the album's sound. His music training and love of experimentation perfectly complemented Reed's songs. "Basically, Lou would write these poppy little songs and my job was to slow them down, make them 'slow 'n' sexy,' " explained Cale. "Everything was deeper too. A song written in E would be played in D. Maureen used cymbals. I had a viola and Lou had his big drone guitar we called an 'ostrich' guitar. It made a horrendous noise, and that's the sound on 'All Tomorrow's Parties,' for instance. In addition, Lou and Nico both had deep voices. All of this made the record entirely unique."

The usual conflicts, however, quickly erupted. Lou didn't want Nico on the album, and she felt she didn't have enough material to sing. Then Nico kept insisting on singing "I'll Be Your Mirror" in what Sterling described as a "Götterdämmerung voice." There was near constant bickering between Lou and the Velvets and Nico and Warhol and Morrissey. "Everyone was nervous about it," Cale recalled. "Lou was paranoid and eventually he made everybody paranoid." "The whole time the album was being made," Warhol wrote, "nobody seemed happy with it."

Despite the fact that Reed and Cale were doing most of the work, Warhol played an important role. According to Lou, "Andy was like an umbrella. We would record something and Andy would say, 'What do you think?' We'd say, 'It's great!' and then he would say, 'Oh, it's great!' The record went out without anybody changing anything because Andy Warhol said it was okay. It's hilarious. He made it so we could do anything we wanted. But when we recorded the album, we had our sound. The first album, *The Velvet Underground and Nico,* was cut in three hours. We just wanted to make a record. We didn't know good equipment. It wasn't even a matter in those days whether it was good equipment, it was just, did it work? In those days, engineers would walk out on us anyway. 'I don't want to listen to this. I didn't become an engineer so I could listen to you guys jerk off. This is noise and garbage.' We ran into a lot of that."

Cale claimed Dolph ran the sessions, but "he didn't understand the first fucking thing about recording. He'd say, 'Hold it, I think we've got a hot one here!' He didn't know what the hell he had on his hands." According to Dolph—a former Columbia Records sales executive, not a shoe salesman—the sessions were held at the decrepit Scepter Records studio on Fifty-fourth street. He agreed that he may not have been the most together of producers, "but nobody knew what they were doing."

"We were really excited," said Cale. "We had this opportunity to do something revolutionary—to combine avant-garde and rock and roll, to do something symphonic. No matter how borderline destructive everything was, there was real excitement there for all of us. We just started playing and held it to the wall. I mean, we had a good time."

For Lou, the most important thing was "Andy made a point of trying to make sure that on our first album the language remained intact. He would say, 'Make sure you do the song with the dirty words, don't change the words just because it's a record.' I think Andy was interested in shocking, in giving people a jolt and not let them talk us into taking that stuff out in the interest of popularity or easy airplay. The best things never get on record. A couple of guys in the East Village made a tape of two girls screaming. That's all—just two girls screaming. Great. But when they took it to the record company, the man said, 'But it has no beginning and no end,' but that was the whole point. Andy said, 'Oh, you've got to make sure you leave the dirty words in.' He was adamant about that. He didn't want it to be cleaned up, and because he was there, it wasn't. And, as a consequence of that, we always knew what it was like to have your way as opposed to these other assholes trying to do exactly the opposite of what Andy wanted. By producing that LP, he gave us freedom and power. I was always interested in language, and I wanted to write more than 'I love you—you love me—tra la la.' He wasn't the record's producer in the conventional way, but when the record-company people would say, 'Are you sure that's the way it should sound?' he'd say, 'Sure, that sounds great.' That was an amazing freedom, a power, and once you've tasted that, you want it always."

Chapter Seven

EXIT WARHOL

1966—67

> *Andy Warhol's studio became the equivalent to Walt Disney studios. Lou was going to be Andy's Mickey Mouse, the idol-hero. But originally, in the first Tugboat Mickey cartoon, Mickey was a nasty guy. And so Lou in his Mickey Mouse period was never able to achieve the lovable one and had to live underground like Tugboat Mickey.*
>
> —Billy Name

WARHOL SPECIALIZED IN CAPTURING YOUNG, AS YET UNFORMED, ECCENtric, creative people on the edge of a nervous breakdown in a painting or on film. Now he had done the same thing in music, pulling out of Lou not only the three great songs that would balance out the content of the first album, but pushing him so that he played and sang like a man passing through the center of a storm of inner turmoil. However, there was one significant difference between Lou Reed and anyone else who worked and played with Warhol at the top of his game. And it was what would make Reed a star in time and give him the duration so rare in rock and roll. Whilst remaining open to all of Warhol's input, and taking all the death-defying trips he took during his season in "hell" (one of Reed's many descriptions of the Factory), Lou had, in fact, retained an inner control that nobody else had. Essentially this was because he was there primarily as a writer. "I watched Andy," he explained. "I watched Andy watching everybody. I would hear people say the most astonishing things, the craziest things, the funniest things, the saddest things. I used to write it down." The voyeuristic medium gave him the distance of an observer and allowed him to maintain control of his own craft. It would in time allow him to escape traps and hells far worse than anything he experienced at Andy Warhol's Factory.

Andy Warhol, Paul Morrissey, and even Lou Reed did not comprehend just how cutthroat and competitive the rock business was. They
reached the zenith of their collaboration in April with the dual triumph
of the Dom shows and the recording of the album, which would not be
released until the following year, only to have the rug pulled out from
underneath them by Charlie Rothchild—an associate of Dylan's manager, Albert Grossman—who promised to help them out by handling the
booking end of the business. He immediately got them a May-long job at
the Trip in Los Angeles. Despite the fact that the EPI was the hottest
thing happening in rock and roll in New York that spring, it made sense
to Reed and Warhol to go out to L.A. because major record companies
had their headquarters there.

On May 1, the entire EPI company packed their guitars and drums,
their whips and chains, and their thirteen selves onto a jet plane and
streaked across the continent. Brimming with enthusiasm, they were
confident that the rock gods were on their side and that in Lala Land they
would find an environment freaky enough to embrace their far-out sounds.
After all, what could be more plastic, more California, more Hollywood,
than Nico, Gerard Malanga, Andy Warhol, and songs about sex, drugs,
and paranoia?

They were wrong. From the moment they landed at L.A. International, signs that they had made a disastrous mistake erupted like cock
roaches out of the woodwork. Driving in from the airport, the first song
they heard on the radio was a soupy ballad called "Monday Monday" by
a leading West Coast group, the Mamas and the Papas. According to
Morrison, a chill ran through the group.

The truth was, everybody in the band despised the sixties West Coast
sound. Nobody hated it more than Lou Reed, who proved himself a
vituperative critic. "We had vast objections to the whole San Francisco
scene," he said. "It's just tedious, a lie and untalented. They can't play
and they certainly can't write. I keep telling everybody and nobody cares.
We used to be quiet, but I don't even care anymore about not wanting to
say negative things, 'cause somebody really should say something. Frank
Zappa is the most untalented bore who ever lived. You know, people like
Jefferson Airplane, Grateful Dead, all those people are just the most
untalented bores that ever came up. Just look at them physically. I mean,
can you take Grace Slick seriously? It's a joke." Asked what separated

----

them apart from distance, he snapped, "The West Coast bands were into soft drugs. We were into hard drugs."

Lou was not alone in despising the West Coast groups and the hippie styles they advertised. "Our attitude to the West Coast was one of hate and derision," said Cale. "We all hated hippies," affirmed Morrison. "We really despised all of the West Coast bands," concluded Tucker.

Despite this negativity, the *EPI*'s engagement at the Trip got off to a big start when showbiz celebrities (many of whom they hated—like John Phillips of the Mamas and Papas, Sonny and Cher) and movie stars like Ryan O'Neal showed up on opening night. Also in attendance were a host of unknowns, including a UCLA film student named Jim Morrison, who would shortly cop every inch of Malanga's act to turn himself into the Lizard King of rock and roll as the front man of the Doors. There was no question that Warhol's show had an enormous impact on the L.A. scene, but it was so intense it burned itself out in a record three days. Flouncing out of the club on the first night, a terrified Cher snapped that the music would replace nothing except, perhaps, suicide (a quote the Warhol people could not but relish). As soon as news spread that the Warhol gang was in town, every weirdo in L.A. gravitated toward them. Unfortunately, the local sheriff rapidly found reason to close the club. His action left the thirteen people who comprised the Warhol entourage stranded in their $500-a-week residence, the Castle. According to Musicians' Union rules, they had every right to collect their full fee as long as they remained in town for the duration of the booking.

Lou sat out the failed engagement at the Castle, listening to the Velvets' record over and over again, and socializing with Gerard Malanga. Reed and Malanga filled time in L.A. taking drugs and hanging out in the clubs. "Lou was the first person, and the last, to turn me on to Placydils," recalled Gerard. "He said, 'Gerard, I want to turn you on to something,' and then we went out on the town that night. It was a tranquilizer. It was legal and you could buy it over the counter. Now you've got to get it by prescription. My system just couldn't take experimenting with these drugs—and Placydils is a funny name for a drug because it comes from the word *placid* or *tranquil*—and it just put me in a state that made me feel clumsily numb. Not in control but in control. Lou obviously relished it."

One night, Gerard ran into two women he had met at the Trip and invited Lou to join in: "Lou and I were involved with these two babes, Linda [the mother of Brian Jones's child, and who would go on to marry Donovan] and Cathy. They had beautiful bodies and blond hair. Our initial situation took place in a motel room and then continued on at the Castle. And we had a wild sex scene in the motel room. The four of us were taking a shower in the motel and I peed down Lou's leg."

Relations between Reed and Warhol soured during this frozen time in the spooky environs of the Castle. Reed began to be persuaded by the sharks circling the wounded enterprise that Andy was not, perhaps, the most focused of rock managers. And it was true. The rock business was growing rapidly. Millions of dollars were at stake. Andy and Paul, for all their perspicacity, simply didn't seem to know how to get down in the dirt with the real rock-and-roll swine and root around to suck up the cash. Not only did Andy lack the temperament for this unpleasant job, he was overextended. He was the most famous pop artist and underground film-maker in the world, plus he had an enormous number of personal and financial problems to deal with on a daily basis.

Lou, on the other hand, was devoting all of his attention to the Velvet Underground. He was the only member of the group who saw what wasn't going on with the Velvets' album. "Lou had worked for his father's accounting firm, so he had a strong background in the business side of things and his feet never left the ground," noted Cale. "Mine definitely did."

At first, the band's immediate future did not look as disastrous as it would turn out to be. After having their album turned down by every rock mogul they could contact in New York, in L.A. they finally encountered the record producer Tom Wilson, who had created the folk-rock sounds of Bob Dylan and Simon & Garfunkel. Wilson heard the Velvet Underground music on a par with that of his other superstar clients. Explaining that he was about to move from Columbia to head a division of MGM, Verve Records, which was just attempting to enter the relatively new rock field, he guaranteed them a deal if they would be patient. Warhol, Morrissey, and the band were relieved to have encountered such a receptive and established producer.

Wilson suggested making the album more commercial by adding more songs by Nico and releasing one of them as the single. Lou complied, writing the relatively commercial "Sunday Morning." "Andy said, 'Why don't you just make it a song about paranoia?' " Lou explained. "I thought that was great so I came up with 'Watch out, the world's behind you, there's always someone watching you,' which I feel is the ultimate paranoid statement in that the world even cares enough to watch you."

" 'Surn-day Mourning' sounded all right for Nico because she brought something weird to everything," Morrissey recounted. "Tom said okay, and we went into a studio paid for by MGM-Verve. Somehow, at the last minute, Lou didn't let her sing it. I had a fight with him. I'd say, 'But Nico sings it onstage,' and he'd reply, 'Well, it's my song,' like it was his family. He was so petty. And then he sang it! The little creep. He said, 'I wanna sing it 'cause it's gonna be the single.' Tom Wilson couldn't deal with Lou, he just took what came."

Lou then proceeded to sing the song in a voice that was so full of womanly qualities that on first hearing it you paused, wondering just who the hell *was* singing.

The terms of the Velvet Underground's contract with Warhol specified that all moneys earned by them would be paid to Warvel (the corporation that Warhol and Morrissey had created specifically for that purpose). Warhol was to keep 25 percent and pass the rest on to the band. However, when it came time to sign the record contract, Lou refused to accept its terms unless it was revised to state that all moneys went first to the Velvets, who would then pass on 25 percent to Warhol and Morrissey. Reed was acting on his own in a show of remarkable determination and increasing leadership of the band, but he was also taking advice from several people who wanted to take over management of the VU.

Warhol grudgingly agreed to the demand over Morrissey's protestations. The contract was amended and the record deal signed. But Lou's victory over Warhol was shortsighted. The contract failed to stipulate the percentage of royalties the band would receive! As a result, it would be many years before anybody in the Velvet Underground would receive any royalties from their first album. Warhol never received a penny from sales of *The Velvet Underground and Nico,* which sold steadily around the world for the twenty years (1967–87) between the time of its release and his death.

Even though they all still believed that the record was going to be a big moneymaker, the hassle over the contract stripped the veneer off Warhol's artistic affair with Reed. "At a certain point Andy didn't take Lou as seriously as Lou wanted Andy to take him," claimed Malanga. "Because when you do something against Andy, Andy would cut you off. Andy distanced himself from Lou, he'd be gracious to Lou in his presence, but Andy never really involved Lou in anything after that. There were no portraits of Lou, there was no type of that stellar involvement that Andy had."

THE FINAL DEBACLE OF THE WEST COAST TRIP CAME IN SAN FRANCISCO. Begged by the rock impresario Bill Graham to play his Fillmore Ball Room, the *EPI* company, who had by then been stranded in L.A. for three weeks, were loath to further explore the West Coast. Then, when they finally agreed, arriving in San Francisco on May 26 for a two-night stand with the Mothers of Invention and the early Jefferson Airplane, they were met with a more vicious hostility than anything L.A. had thrown at them.

Before they even set foot onstage, the band provoked the considerable ire of Graham. Perturbed by Morrissey's sarcastic air and bold-faced recommendation that all rock musicians take heroin, he was incensed by the insular aura of the Warhol entourage, who traveled everywhere by limousine, rejecting what they saw as the phony hippie culture. Seconds before they went onstage, Graham screamed, "I hope you motherfuckers bomb!" Ralph Gleason wrote a particularly scathing review for the *San Francisco Chronicle,* saying the *EPI* was an East Coast poison intended to corrupt, defile, and destroy their pure innocence.

Gleason's review went on, "Warhol's *Exploding Plastic Inevitable* show was nothing more than a bad condensation of all the bum trips of the Trips Festival. Few people danced (the music was something of a dud, the Velvet Underground being a very dull group). It was all very campy and very Greenwich Village sick. If this is what America's waiting for, we are going to die of boredom because this is a celebration of the silliness of cafe society, way out in left field instead of far out, and joyless." On the second night, when the band leaned their instruments up against their amplifiers and left the stage to a barrage of sonic feedback, the great rock impresario Bill Graham finally pulled the plug.

To make matters worse, the San Francisco poet and playwright Michael McClure refused to sign a release allowing Warhol to show a film he had made of McClure's play *The Beard;* Gerard was arrested in a restaurant for carrying his whip, labeled an offensive weapon, and spent a nervous night in jail; and Lou shot up a drug that seized up all his joints. He was diagnosed (incorrectly) as having a terminal case of lupus.

A shattered *EPI* company, who had only four weeks earlier left New York in triumph, limped back across the continent separately, leaving behind one member, the lighting man Danny Williams, who would subsequently commit suicide. Back in New York, Lou checked into Beth Israel Hospital with a serious case of, as it turned out, hepatitis. Nico departed to Ibiza, her favorite island off the coast of Spain. The rest of the band rehearsed for an upcoming June booking in Chicago. Warhol, disappointed by the lack of money from his five-month investment in the group, returned to his first love, making films.

While Lou was laid up in the hospital undergoing a six-week course of treatment, he became increasingly paranoid about losing control of the group. Not only was he excluded from the one-week stint in Chicago, but the band adapted to cover his absence with relative ease. Angus MacLise was brought back in as drummer, while Maureen switched to bass. According to Sterling, Angus realized what a mistake he had made in quitting the group and hoped to be allowed back in. Lou, however, still angry about MacLise's defection, was adamant about punishing Angus and maintaining his loyalty to Moe.

When Warhol, Malanga, and MacLise stopped by Beth Israel Hospital to inform Reed of the alterations in the lineup, Gerard could see that he was disturbed by it. The reappearance of MacLise once again turned the power axis of the Velvet Underground against him. "Lou was sitting on the edge of his bed in a bathrobe," recalled Malanga. "Lou was yellow in the face, he had a yellow pall and looked sickly—he always looked sickly. Sitting at the end of the bed having this discussion about what was happening with the Chicago gig. And I remember distinctly Lou turning to Angus and saying, 'Just remember, this is only temporary.' Like, 'Don't think you're coming back into the group.' There was a real tug-of-war between Lou and John—not so much with John, but with Angus, which caused Angus to leave. Lou had a very specific agenda, and Angus was the antithesis of that agenda. Angus was too idealistic for Lou. Lou wanted the group to be rock and roll, and there was a real confrontation there."

The success of the band's Chicago dates at Poor Richard's provided a revealing glimpse into Reed's unusually well-hidden insecurity. Despite the absence of its stellar members—Nico, Warhol, and Reed—the band was so successful they were held over for an extra week. Back in the hospital, Lou's paranoia was fed with catty gossip. Andy called, saying, "Oh, they got great reviews. Gee, it seems okay without you. Everyone's happy." He was just trying to make him uptight. Lou worked himself into a rage.

In July 1966, Delmore Schwartz, to whom the Velvet Underground had dedicated "European Son," died of a heart attack in New York at fifty-three. Gerard called Lou in the hospital and suggested they make the wake. Lou, who had been told he couldn't leave the hospital for three weeks, donned a pair of black jeans, a black T-shirt, black jacket, and boots and cut out to the funeral. "I checked myself out of the hospital to go to Delmore's funeral and never went back."

"We were very informal," Gerard complained. "I think Lou relished the idea of bad taste. Lou was into anything that had a disguise to it. He just showed up like a slob. Lou didn't have much of a sense of sartorial splendor about him."

Malanga took Reed to the open-casket wake at Sigmund Schwartz Funeral Home, 152 Second Avenue. They arrived in the middle of a Dwight MacDonald eulogy. As they filed past the body afterward, the effects of alcohol and drug addiction were evident on Delmore Schwartz's ravaged, rutted, puffy face. Lou was silent, withdrawn, and didn't react. Outside afterward a former classmate of Lou's said, "Why don't you come to the burial?"

In one of his more telling descriptions of the emotional lives of his mentors as they mirrored his, Lou said, "Delmore Schwartz was the unhappiest man who I ever met in my life, and the smartest—till I met Andy Warhol. I'm just delighted I got to know him. It would have been tragic not to have met him. But things have occurred where Delmore's words float right across. Very few people do it to you. He was one. His mother wouldn't allow him to use curse words until he was thirty. His worst fear was realized when they put him in a plot next to her."

IN THE SUMMER OF 1966, LOU WAS SUPPOSED TO WRITE THE THEME song for Warhol's new film Chelsea Girls; Nico was to sing it. Strangely, despite the fact that he and John recorded part of its sound track, Lou failed to deliver. For a man who wrote songs as regularly as he ate breakfast (and preferred to write on assignment), it was a passive-aggressive signal of how he felt about any further collaboration with Warhol and Nico. If he could have sung it himself, it seems likely he would have written it.

Other factors helped create the split between Lou and Andy. Upon returning from California, the *EPI* company had discovered that Bob Dylan's manager had stolen their idea for a nightclub and taken over the Dom, renaming it the Balloon Farm. It was a terrible blow with severe, lasting consequences. Not only was potentially significant revenue lost, but it would be years before the Velvets would find as good a venue in the city. Out of sheer frustration and paranoia, the band would soon boycott New York shows altogether. Morrissey encouraged Warhol to support Nico's career. She was, he thought, a more marketable star than Lou.

When Morrissey arranged for Nico to sing solo in a small bar underneath the Dom called Stanley's and asked the band to provide a backup acoustic-guitar player, he slammed into Reed's wall of resentment. "Lou didn't want to do it," he recalled, "of course he didn't. And he didn't want Sterling to do it. And he knew that John was terrified of him, so that was difficult to negotiate. 'Oh, Lou, if you don't want me to . . .' It was so stupid. Lou said, 'It's not good for the group's image.' I replied, 'This is awful. She needs work, she has some songs. Couldn't one of you help her?' Then Lou said, 'We'll put it on tape.' "

Lou, John, Sterling, and Moe were working on their next album, *White Light/White Heat,* on which there were no songs for Nico. Hitting a creative roll, they made July and August highly productive months. Sterling, John, and Lou moved into a building on West Third Street, which they dubbed "Sister Ray house" after their favorite new song, to work on the album. Unlike rock stars who write on the road, Lou and John created their best songs when living either together or a few blocks from each other in New York. "Sister Ray" was worked up over the summer. They played music all day, going out at night to their favorite new haunt, the club on Park Avenue South and Seventeenth Street that had become Warhol's social headquarters, Max's Kansas City.

Run by Mickey Ruskin, a restaurateur and club owner who catered to the art world, Max's was divided into two sections. The first room was a standard bar-restaurant. The bar ran down the left-hand wall of the rectangular room, the rest of which was occupied by tables and chairs. The back room, which was guarded, usually by Ruskin himself, and into which only the hip elite were allowed, was smaller. Lit by a red Dan Flavin light sculpture in one corner and furnished by a series of booths along the left- and right-hand walls, its habitués included visiting Hollywood aristocracy like Roger Vadim and his wife, Jane Fonda, rock stars like the Rolling Stones, writers, plus top-of-the-line groupies, drug dealers, and drag queens. In 1966–68, the supercharged, Felliniesque atmosphere was dominated by the arrival, presence, and departure of Andy Warhol, who made it a habit of arriving between midnight and 2 A.M.

The artistic netherworld of Max's back room offered the perfect setting for Lou Reed's anthropological reports on the hell and heaven of the thriving sixties underground. Everybody was dressed to kill, and either blissfully content or raging with paranoia, lust, greed, hatred, and contempt. The room vibrated with all the elements of the sixties as they were in New York. Many an affair was started, carried out, and finished at Max's—often in the phone booths. Girls like the Warhol starlet Andrea Feldman would leap onto a table and entertain the crowd with a song and strip show, while Warhol superstar Eric Emerson would piss into a glass and bolt down his bodily fluid screaming that it tasted good! The half of the room held by the Warhol elite would be on speed, whilst the other half, representing an anti-Warhol faction, would be on acid or other hallucinogenics. The free-for-all atmosphere created eruptions that would in time sound the death knell of the sixties. It was here, for example, that one could encounter Warhol's hardcore lesbian would-be assassin, Valerie Solanas, slumped dejectedly at a corner table, or overhear beat poet Gregory Corso snarling at Warhol, "You and your faggots and rich women and Velvet Undergrounds, I don't understand!" only to be shushed into silence by the bardic presence of Allen Ginsberg. The background of Max's was an extension of the Factory. Here Lou was afforded the attention due a star of his caliber. Here he could be seen with his arm wrapped around a girl, a boy, or somebody of undetermined gender.

*   *   *

HOWEVER, IN THE FALL OF 1966, LOU SUFFERED A SERIES OF DISAP-pointments, the biggest being the nonappearance of *The Velvet Underground and Nico*. While Verve brought out the Mothers of Invention's first album, *Freak Out*, the Velvets' album was on hold. The band was alternately told that MGM/Verve was having difficulties in reproducing Warhol's cover portrait of a banana that actually peeled, and that the company had temporarily mislaid one of the master tapes. Meanwhile, the Velvets found their *EPI* performances transformed into a freak show that Warhol now rarely had time even to attend. "It wasn't very good when Andy started losing interest in the whole project," recalled Cale. "We were touring round the country and then he just wasn't interested anymore. For one thing, traveling with thirteen people and a light show is a kind of mania if you don't get enough money. And the only reason we got a lot of money, probably, while we toured was because Andy was with us. And there was a lot of backbiting going on in the band."

That summer Lou had had a brief affair with one of Gerard's girlfriends, creating more unspoken tension.

As they changed from an art rock band into a touring band, Lou grew weary of the mundane experiences that greet all such entertainers. In October and November the *EPI* did a short tour of the Midwest, playing in venues that sometimes paid less than $1,000 a night. A pall of bad humor hung over the whole event. Relations soured. Paul, acting as road manager, had to slog his way through an unglamorous Greyhound bus tour. Nico was now sleeping with Cale. That Nico had emerged as the new superstar of *Chelsea Girls* and become far more famous than both Reed and Cale also grated on Lou's nerves. He took to attacking her in public. According to one witness, Lou was at times wildly critical of Nico. During their unhappy tour he was relentlessly critical, yelling at her that she couldn't sing and she couldn't play. Meanwhile, the continued delay in the release of the album aggravated everyone.

It was a violent fall. Driving downtown in a cab with Malanga, Lou was in an accident that left him with cuts and bruises. Walking into Max's with Warhol in October, Lou was hit by a table aimed at Andy by some drunken freak screaming obscenities. In the fall of 1966, Warhol was pushing everybody to the edge, and violence had begun to erupt around him constantly.

As the watershed year 1966—the year of Dylan's *Blonde on Blonde*, of the Stones' *Aftermath,* and of the Beatles' *Revolver*—neared its end, it looked to Lou as if a great moment had been lost, perhaps forever. Then when Verve belatedly released two singles, "All Tomorrow's Parties"/"I'll Be Your Mirror" and "Sunday Morning"/"Femme Fatale," the company failed to give them the necessary promotion. "Sunday Morning" stalled at No. 103 on the *Cashbox* charts.

IN MARCH 1967, THE POORLY TIMED AND LITTLE PUBLICIZED RELEASE OF *The Velvet Underground and Nico* finally arrived. So little enthusiasm was left from the original Warhol collaboration, begun fifteen months earlier, that there were no celebrations. Instead, the event became fodder for more negativity. The famous Warhol cover—consisting of a white field graced by a life-size bright yellow banana, prominently signed with his trademark rubber-stamp signature in the bottom right-hand corner—did little to publicize the band. Warhol was also credited as producer on the spine of the gatefold sleeve. Consequently, those lucky enough to catch a glimpse in stores of the poorly distributed record were confused about its contents. Had Warhol embarked on a recording career?

"We were all having fun and didn't care about credits, and things like that," Reed later explained. " 'Produced by Andy Warhol.' It was like being a soup can." Unfortunately, the cover contributed to a popular misapprehension that the Velvet Underground was Warhol's put-on band. "And if you really got into the sticks," Lou would bitterly joke, "they thought Andy Warhol was the lead guitar player." To top it all off, the album's appearance sparked the kind of critical backlash Andy was used to, but was new to Lou. The songs about drug use and sadomasochism drew intense criticism. The print media refused to run ads for the record apart from Grove Press's *Evergreen Review.* The majority of radio stations refused to play it. One deejay who played a cut snapped, "That was the Velvet Underground, a very New York sound. Let's hope it stays there." Scattered reviews were dismissive, and MGM/Verve further cut their scant marketing budget.

Although, as a person who specialized in making people feel uncomfortable, Lou may have wanted the album to elicit hostility, he asserted otherwise: "The Velvet Underground very consciously set out to put themes common to movies, plays, and novels into pop-song format. I thought we were doing something ambitious and I was taken aback that people were offended by it and thought I was causing some kids to become drug addicts. I used to hear people saying we were doing porn rock. What happened to freedom of expression? I remember reading descriptions of us as the 'fetid underbelly of urban existence.' All I wanted to do was write songs that somebody like me could relate to. Why not have a little something on the side for the kids in the back row? At the worst, we were like the antedated realists. At best, we just hit a little more home than some things."

In May, Warhol tried to re-create the heady nights at the Dom by renting a new hall, the Gymnasium, on Manhattan's Upper East Side. But with attendance low, it became clear that the *EPI's* initial magic was gone. Furthermore, people started to focus on the music, criticizing the band's unorthodox playing. The deejay Terry Noel, who had a considerable influence on the club circuit, vividly described the Gymnasium shows: "We went because it was a big deal and people were talking about the Velvets. Because of Andy. Normally I never went to any Andy Warhol things, but I was interested in new things and this was a new thing going on and it was hot. We all went there, and, *oh my God!* None of them can play instruments. They're all off-key. It wasn't like today, today they're all off-key because they mean to be—it was so bad I couldn't believe it. Nobody could believe it."

Recognizing yet another failure on the growing list, the Velvets decided they had had enough of the *EPI.* "As soon as the Gymnasium shows were over," recalled Morrissey, "the Velvets didn't want to work anymore. I was a manager of the goddamn thing for almost a year or more and I remember, because they never released the album, but once the album came out, I think that's when they wanted to go off and be themselves and not have any revenues go back to Andy and me."

When the album started to make some headway on the charts—despite bad reviews—a maverick Warhol superstar, Eric Emerson, sued MGM for putting his picture on the back cover without getting a release. Rather than paying him off or getting Warhol to shut him up, the company withdrew the album from the stores for six weeks while they had Emerson's face airbrushed off the cover. Embittered by the lack of support from both MGM/Verve and Warhol, who, like the record company, hadn't lifted a finger to dissuade Emerson from his legal action, Lou flicked his switchblade tongue. "The New York radio scene is so awful," he snapped. "A record won't be played unless it's already number seven all over. All over has phenomenal records no one in NY gets to hear. There's great music in the hills." Lou decided that in response to his album's rejection in New York, the band should no longer play in the city. They did not play New York again publicly until 1970.

Thus, they were left with an audience of totally unappreciative teen-agers at, for example, La Cave on Euclid Avenue in Cleveland. The writer Glenn O'Brien, then a student in Ohio, recalled the first time he ever saw them just after the release of The Velvet Underground and Nico: "That spring the Velvet Underground were on tour and they were com-ing to this club, La Cave, which I went to all the time to see people like Caroline Hester or Ian and Sylvia. It was a Saturday night and the club was full. They came out one at a time. John came out first and he looked so fucking weird. He had this really long hair and this diamond rhinestone collar, which you'd never seen anything like. And then Moe came out and you couldn't tell what sex she was. The first song took about twenty minutes and Lou was the last one to come out. He just looked amazing. His neck looked so muscular and he had this weird kind of Roman haircut. It was hip to have long hair then, but he had pretty short hair and these amazing sunglasses and a hollow-bodied Gibson guitar. We were all sitting there thinking, 'These are really junkies!' "

In fact, by this time the Velvets, at a performing peak, were an as-tonishing act to see live. The audiences who managed to discover the band experienced something they had never before witnessed in another rock band. Togged out in mean-looking black outfits, the Velvets ground out a wailing symphony of invention and power whilst standing rigidly stock-still.

As they began to play clubs without the EPI, the Velvet Underground put some distance between themselves and Andy Warhol. However, they remained open to continuing the arrangement if Warhol would turn his attentions in their direction. However, the final nail in the coffin of Lou Reed's collaborative relationship with Andy Warhol came at the end of

May 1967, when Warhol took an entourage to the Cannes Film Festival in France to show *Chelsea Girls*—excluding the Velvets, who had since 1966 been invited to play at several European venues. Among other offers, the Italian director Antonioni had wanted to film the band for a nightclub sequence in his famous movie *Blowup,* and Barbara Rubin had offered to put them on in London at the prestigious Albert Hall. Now, when Warhol had the opportunity, not only did he choose to leave them home, but in a move typical of the perverse way in which he operated, he included among his entourage Eric Emerson, who had caused the Velvets so much trouble only a month earlier.

With Warhol away for a month, Lou had some room to start looking for a new manager. Clearly, the Velvet Underground needed professional business help. An increasing number of managers on the expanding rock scene had the resources to make things happen. A number of them had approached Reed soon after he and the Velvets achieved their initial success at the Dom, whispering in his ear that he could be making more money. One of these go-getters was a young Bostonian named Steve Sesnick, who had part ownership of a popular club in that city called the Boston Tea Party. Sesnick had been involved in earlier discussions about Warhol's multimedia performance ideas. He was friendly with the Beatles' manager Brian Epstein's New York lawyer Nat Weiss. Unlike Warhol, who was unresponsive to Reed's questions on business matters, Sesnick made himself available to explain the machinations of the music business. Now, he virtually promised to deliver the Velvets success on a silver platter.

When Warhol returned, Lou got a minor, but symbolic, opportunity for retaliation. The night he got back from Europe, Warhol took Nico to Boston so she could join the VU onstage during a concert at the Boston Tea Party. In typical Warhol fashion, the two arrived late. Surprising both Andy and Nico, Lou refused to let her onstage. Nico blamed Lou's enlarged ego for the incident. "Everybody wanted to be the star," she said. "Of course Lou always was. But the newspapers came to me all the time. That's how I got fired—he couldn't take that anymore. He fired me." Reed's refusal to let Nico come onstage could have been excused by the fact that the band had only two more songs to go and they weren't songs that she could sing. But Andy did not see it that way and took Lou's action very badly.

This incident prompted a meeting between Warhol and Reed to decide what kind of financial and time commitment Warhol wanted to make to the *EPI*. He had many film plans in the works. He had a number of art shows coming up. Andy told Lou, "Look, you have to make a decision: Do you want to continue presenting your music in art museums and at colleges? Those are the only venues we can present to you. Don't you think that you should be moving into the Fillmores and the rock theaters of America?"

As Lou recalled the incident, "I fired him."

Billy Name, who attended the meeting, explained, "Andy said to everybody who worked with him: 'You have to start developing your own career and not just be dependent on what's going on here.' He had no problem with it because Andy was an artist. Lou was trying to get into the straight music scene and not be the puppet of an artist. So in a sense it was good. He wanted to have a real manager in the music business. There were no problems about leaving Andy."

However, as Lou remembered it, Warhol "was furious. I'd never seen Andy angry, but I did that day. He was really mad. He turned bright red and called me a rat. That was the worst thing he could thing of. This was like leaving the nest. In a way it was terrible to be without him. He wasn't there to take the criticism. And it was always such fun to be with him, it was a nicer environment. I never felt dependent because at that time I didn't have anything anyway, so I didn't having anything to lose, and it didn't matter. Nothing over here, nothing over there—what difference does it make? We worked until the show couldn't exist anymore because it was just so expensive. No one knew the business. No one could handle the business. No one could talk to the businesspeople. Businesspeople have a place in this world, and especially now you're getting a lot of businesspeople who are, let's say, easier to talk to. But the point is, if you're going to get involved in business, then you should get a business manager."

Lou was shaken by Andy's uncharacteristic display of emotion. The extraordinary thing, and one of the examples of Andy's generosity, was that he let Lou out of the contract with no argument. Nonetheless, he still presumed that Lou would honor the arrangement that they had made in California, namely, that Andy would receive 25 percent of all earnings from the Velvet Underground's music created under his management. The record had been produced under his management, and Andy even

put up some of his own money to pay for its production and contributed
the artwork. He really wanted the Velvet Underground to be successful,
so he let them go. Asked to explain this uncharacteristic financial laxity
years later, Warhol replied, "I liked them so much it didn't matter . . .
they just decided to find some other manager."

Chapter Eight

EXIT CALE

1967—68

The relationship between John and Lou was symbiotic.
They loved each other, but they also hated each other.

—Lynne Tillman

IN THE SUMMER OF 1967, DESPITE ALL THE MANEUVERING FOR CONTROL, the band was charged with the enthusiasm of a fresh start. Instead of dwelling on the poor response to *The Velvet Underground and Nico,* and the possibly adverse effects of breaking with Warhol, everyone had great expectations for Steve Sesnick and the new material they were working up for a second album. In turn, Sesnick had his own terrifically high hopes for the group. Maureen thought, "He was honestly convinced that we could be the next Beatles. He always talked up—never down. Of course, even I realized he was in it to get rich. He had such high, high hopes."

The dissenting opinion about Sesnick came from Cale, who instinctively distrusted the fast-talking, cigar-smoking entrepreneur who managed to manipulate everybody in the group as well as their record company with a smoke screen of promises, laughter, and exaggeration. "Steven just drove a wedge right between Lou and me," said Cale. "His main concern was to say, 'Look, Lou's the star, you're just the sideman.' Wrong, Steve." John found himself constantly arguing with Lou about arrangements for the new songs. Lou was pushing the band to appeal to a wider audience. John was resisting with all his might. "There were pressures building up, and we were all getting very frustrated," Cale recalled. "After the first record we lost our patience and diligence. We couldn't even remember what our original precepts were."

The Warhol crowd also despised Sesnick. "It was as if your daughter married someone from the wrong family," sniffed the man who continued to be the band's strongest supporter and Lou's staunchest friend, Danny Fields.

"The person they picked," Warhol noted icily, "was terrible."

Although not yet officially their manager, Sesnick immediately got to work behind the scenes on a number of Velvets projects. He sent a copy of *The Velvet Underground and Nico* to the Beatles' manager, Brian Epstein, with an eye to making a publishing deal with Epstein's company, Nemperor. The deal, backed by an Epstein-produced European tour, might have elevated the band to international stardom.

One night that spring Danny Fields found himself at Max's with the British impresario looking for an opportunity to encourage the deal. "I wanted Brian to manage them or promote them or get them to Europe or something!" Danny recalled. Spotting Lou in the crowded back room, he hurried over and urged him, "Pretend you have to go uptown and I'll get you a ride with Brian Epstein!" Although in the midst of an intense conversation, Lou complied.

In the limousine, Brian, who had just returned from Acapulco, leaned over and, fondling Lou's arm, murmured, "My lover and I spent our whole vacation listening to your record."

"Oh?" Lewis replied.

"Well, I like it very much."

"Why, thank you."

Reed sniffed dismissively to a friend the following day, "Everybody thinks we homosexuals are wanton perverts, but as a matter of fact we're all quite straight and selective." Sesnick continued to pursue a deal with Epstein in the ensuing months, cashing in on his friendship with Epstein's lawyer Nat Weiss. Tragically, Epstein died of a drug overdose before the end of the year, without having done anything about the VU.

In July, John helped produce and arrange Nico's first solo album, *Chelsea Girl*. It was a magical record and collaboration, containing three songs by Lou (who seemed willing to collaborate with Nico from a distance), as well as tracks by Dylan, Cale, Morrison, and Jackson Browne.

Browne recalled meeting Lou during the sessions: "Lou, who always had this incredible menacing scowl on his face, wouldn't say more than one or two syllables because that was how Andy was. But he was a sweetheart underneath. Afterwards he took me for a big Chinese meal and then on to see the *Murray the K Show* at RKO. There was Wilson

Pickett, the Blues Project, the Who, Etta James. What a day." Impressed by Jackson, Lou took the seventeen-year-old singer/songwriter under his wing. At one point he told Jackson about the recent "be-in" hippie celebration in San Francisco and revealed that he'd been to the simultaneous event in New York: "The way he described it, you realized there was a place for all that inside of him. He loved seeing Central Park full of people all just high and loving each other."

Unfortunately, when Nico's *Chelsea Girl* was released in October, Lou, John, and Nico were all disappointed by its production. "If they'd just have allowed Cale to arrange it and let me do more stuff on it," exclaimed Reed. "I mean everything on that song "Chelsea Girls," those strings, that flute, should have defeated it, but the lyrics, Nico's voice, managed somehow to survive. We still got "It Was a Pleasure Then"; they couldn't stop us. We'd been doing a song like that in our beloved show, it didn't really have a title. Just all of us following the drone. And there it sits in the middle of that album." Lou became more determined to make the next Velvet album a success no matter what the cost.

The Velvet Underground recorded their second album, *White Light/White Heat,* in September. They had been working up the material since the previous summer and took three days to complete it in the studio. Reed was quite taken with astrology at the time and would enthusiastically explain how a lot of his songs embodied the Virgo-Pisces opposition. Lou and John were Pisces, and Maureen and Sterling were Virgos. (All the songs on the second album were published by their company, Three Prong Music, representing the trident of Neptune—the ruler of Pisces.) "White Light/White Heat" was an obvious drug song showing the Pisces: suffering, self-indulgent, and living on the "road of excess." Virgo, on the other hand was about enlightenment, expressions of Christian purity, self-control, living in the "palace of wisdom," as expressed in songs like "Here She Comes Now" and "I Heard Her Call My Name."

The short, intense sessions lent the music a feeling of spontaneity. Nowhere was this more evident than on "Sister Ray," which Reed had written on a train coming back to New York from Connecticut. The lyrics echoed scenes from *Last Exit to Brooklyn* by Hubert Selby, one of Lou's favorite writers. " 'Sister Ray' has eight characters in it and this guy gets killed and nobody does anything. The situation is a bunch of drag queens taking a bunch of sailors home with them, shooting up on smack and having this orgy when the police appear."

In terms of musical arrangement, "Sister Ray" was Cale's greatest masterpiece with the Velvet Underground. Though Reed and Sesnick were pushing Cale to tone it down, he stood his ground and eventually forced both of them to see things his way. "When we did 'Sister Ray,' we turned up to ten flat out, leakage all over the place," said Reed. "That's it. They asked us what we were going to do. We said, 'We're going to start.' They said, 'Who's playing the bass?' We said, 'There is no bass.' They asked us when it ends. We didn't know. When it ends, that's when it ends. It did a lot to the music of the seventies. We were doing the whole heavy-metal trip back then. I mean, if 'Sister Ray' is not an example of heavy metal, then nothing is." Later Lou commented on just how far ahead of their time they were: "No one has ever attempted what we did on the second album, where we used raw electronics."

The seventeen-and-a-half-minute song, unrecognized when it was released, has been compared to Dylan's "Sad Eyed Lady of the Lowlands" and Ornette Coleman's "Free Jazz" as well as such rock classics as "Wooly Bully" and "96 Tears."

White Light/White Heat was the most manic, abrasive, and powerful album of the Velvet Underground. It reflected the internal tensions of a band ascending into prominence and "at each other's throats," as Cale said. The intelligence in the band, however, could not offset the daily antagonism of differing musical ideas. Some observers insisted that Lou, at this point, realized he wanted to make it as a solo performer, regarding a band as a necessary but supportive evil.

"I Heard Her Call My Name," which opened side two of the record, played a decisive role in the intensifying Reed-Cale battle. Lou, in an extraordinary move, went into the studio without telling any of the others and remixed the track so that he would appear prominent on it. According to the normally restrained Moe Tucker, the song "was ruined by the mix—the energy. You can't hear anything but Lou. He was the mixer in there, so he, having a little ego trip at the time, turned himself so far up that there's no rhythm, there's no nothing."

IN THE FALL OF 1967 THE BAND SPLIT UP THEIR COMMUNAL LIVING. STERling moved in with Martha Dargan and her brother Tom on East Second Street. John moved into the Chelsea Hotel with his girlfriend, Betsey Johnson. Moe was living on Fifth Avenue and Ninth Street. Lou bounced

from place to place, staying mostly on Perry Street, and later in a loft on
Seventh Avenue and Thirty-first Street. Lou's loft was "just me, a bed, and
our stuff, five or six huge amplifiers and guitars." Despite this separation,
the band still spent most of their time hanging out together. "We'd come
flying in at five in the morning and play 'Sister Ray' through them," Lou
continued. "I was the only guy living in the building, except for this big
black guy upstairs who had a gun. When it got too loud, he'd start jumping
up and down on the floor; you knew when the ceiling started buckling that
things were getting serious. Then he'd come down and start pounding on
the door. That was it: rehearsal canceled due to gun."

The major shift in the group came, however, not from the recording of
White Light/White Heat or from the breakup of their living situation, but
rather from their having signed a managerial contract with Steve Sesnick.
Cale's predictions were beginning to play themselves out with cata-
strophic consequences. "Lou was starting to act funny," said John. "He
brought in Sesnick—who I thought was a real snake—to be our manager,
and all this intrigue started to take place. Lou was calling us 'his band'
while Sesnick was trying to get him to go solo. Maybe it was the drugs he
was doing at the time. They certainly didn't help. Basically, Sesnick just
became an apologist for Lou. He was just a yesman, and he came between
us. It was maddening, just maddening. Before, it had always been easy to
talk to Lou. Now you had to go through Sesnick, who seemed pretty
practiced in the art of miscommunication. We should have been able to
sort out our own problems. He should never have been brought in.
Things had been bad between us for a while, but when Sesnick arrived,
they got worse. There was a lot of intrigue, a lot of duplicity, and a lot of
talking behind people's backs, a lot of plotting."

Cale later claimed that it was at this point, after the recording of *White
Light/White Heat* in the fall of 1967, that he first thought of leaving the
band. He realized that they weren't going to progress any further on the
path that he and Lou had embarked on in early 1965. Lou was beginning
to introduce to the group a light, much more pop style of playing. The
songs he was writing that fall signaled a clear backing away from the
material typified by "Sister Ray," and an increasing emphasis on his lyrics.

Cale's original idea—to create an orchestral chaos in which Lou could
spontaneously create lyrics—was being lost, because Lou wasn't looking
for an orchestral chaos anymore. He was looking for a group that would

follow his directions to create pop songs. Sesnick was also playing a large role in this, because Sesnick was supporting Lou's approach toward what he imagined to be a more popular and commercial form.

Making matters worse for John was that Lou, who demanded 100 percent allegiance and attention from his collaborators, resented John's close relationship with Betsey Johnson. Betsey had a great belief in John and encouraged him to step out of Lou's shadow and make his own music, write his own songs, and sing them himself. A fashion designer of international fame who had recently been written up in *Time* magazine, Johnson had a shop called Paraphernalia, which was said to be the hippest clothes shop in America. John was very photogenic, and Betsey enhanced this greatly by designing clothes for him. She also designed clothes for the rest of the band, but John's tastes and style became increasingly flamboyant. In one instance, he wanted her to make special gloves for him so that his hands looked as if they were on fire when he was playing. Sometimes he wore dramatic masks onstage. Sterling recalled that after being dressed by Betsey Johnson, John became astonishing to look at and even more charismatic onstage next to the diminutive, uncomfortable Lou.

John's outshining Lou onstage was counterbalanced by the fortuitous appearance of *Andy Warhol's Index Book,* by Andy Warhol, published in December, which helped pave Lou's way as a solo star. Less a study than a celebration of the Factory, the book contained interviews with Andy and his clique and was packaged with a number of Warholesque objects and a flexidisc. The record was decorated with a photo of Lou Reed, clad in the Factory-standard impenetrable shades. The recording consisted of an interview with Nico, with the Velvets' music playing in the background. The book, which made an enormous media splash when it hit the stores, raised Lou's profile.

WITH THE ROCK FIELD EXPANDING RAPIDLY, THE STAGE WAS SET FOR A successful debut of *White Light/White Heat* on January 30, 1968. But, to everyone's dismay, it too was banned on the radio. Lou, however, was still confident that they would succeed and, if anything, took this rejection as a sign that he was right to move further into the mainstream.

White Light/White Heat turned out to be another severe commercial disappointment, receiving an even harsher response than the first album.

Because of the lyrics, there was almost a complete blackout on the radio. Moreover, the lack of association with Warhol limited their channels of publicity. With no Warhol or Nico publicity boosting it, the record had to rely on the standard conduits for rock music, where *White Light/White Heat* was largely ignored. Even *Rolling Stone* magazine refused to review the album. "Most of our singles were never distributed," noted Morrison. "However, where they appeared on jukeboxes, people have really liked them. 'White Light/White Heat' as a single is nice. That single was banned everyplace. When it was banned in San Francisco, we said, the hell with it. That's as far as it ever got." Aside from neglect, the album faced competition from an enormous pop market that was being flooded with all sorts of flash-in-the-pan products, soaking up the teen market's dollars. As the rock-and-roll industry came into its own, alternative groups like the Velvets found it increasingly difficult to break in. Making matters worse was the fact that the band was still being put down for being Warhol acolytes—drug-taking, homosexual, S&M devotees—without the advantage of Warhol's umbrella protection and buoyant encouragement.

The Velvet Underground, though, knew how good they were and maintained a positive outlook despite the reviews. Fortunately, by the end of January, their financial situation had improved significantly. When managed by Warhol, the Velvets had lived on paltry per diem handouts from the Factory. But after Sesnick became their manager, they began to make some money. Lou especially, as the songwriter and lead singer, got enough money to live a reasonable life.

Most of their money came from touring. In one bright moment of an otherwise terrible relationship with MGM/Verve, Sesnick persuaded the company to take the money that they would have used in publicity and devote it to the expenses of the Velvets' touring. As a result, they flew first-class, stayed in the best hotels, and ate in nice restaurants. Moreover, they were sure they would sell out and get a great response at several of their regular venues—La Cave in Cleveland, the Tea Party in Boston, the Second Fret in Philadelphia, and a number of other places on the West Coast and Texas.

"We never did tour Europe, but it vexed us beyond imagining that we never made inroads in the U.S.," said Sterling. "It was tilting at windmills. We were obsessed by the idea of somehow changing California. We were always sallying forth to the West Coast for months, living well and playing occasionally. The longest we were ever away was two months, and that was hell. If we went out to the Coast, we couldn't afford to fly back and forth so we'd stay out there and play for six weeks and play up and down the Coast a little bit. Being on the road is mostly real boring. The only real good thing is playing."

The band, who received no royalties from their albums, earned $600 one week, $2,500 the next on the road. It was the only way they could make money, and they liked to play, but the pressures of touring did little to assuage the developing tensions.

Like any rock group spending large amounts of time on the road, they had problems getting along with each other. Whenever they got to a hotel, for example, Sterling would virtually knock everyone over in his attempt to get the best room in the suite. He usually shared a room with John, while Maureen would team up with Lou. Cale and Reed fought about the musical direction. According to Morrison, "One time in Chicago the club had a circular stage. I was playing the solo on 'Pale Blue Eyes,' Cale was lurching around on bass and stepped on a distorter, which quadrupled my volume. It was an accident. Everybody staggered back. John shuts it off and kicks the box across the stage. I look over at Lou and Lou's eyes were saying, 'What an asshole.' But for Cale, offense is the best defense, so when confronted, he attacks. I said, 'John, I wish you wouldn't come lurching over, blah, blah, blah. Oh, forget it.' Cale was really getting into it. On one occasion he drank nineteen whiskey sours. They had a big argument in Chicago. They may have thrown a few punches at each other. The first time they did that in California, I was horrified. I wasn't alarmed by the fighting, I was enraged. Sesnick and I felt like throttling the both of them."

Indeed, Cale found himself fighting more than Reed and Sesnick about maintaining the band's radical sound. Facing the extreme counter-avant-garde while touring the Midwest, he found that an element of compromise crept into their original precepts. "To make audiences feel comfortable," John explained, "we ended up putting a backbeat on everything, as if to say, 'We may be crazy, but we're still rock and roll.' "

During the early months of 1968, with Steve Sesnick egging him on, Lou Reed chipped away at the Velvets' democratic foundations. Sesnick and Reed decided where the band should play, setting up a surfeit of gigs at the Boston Tea Party, broken by occasional visits to California, Cleveland, and Canada. They also masterminded a subtle shift in the band's musical axis, away from the explorations of sound toward an emphasis on lyrics. Lou stepped into the forefront with his poetic investigations of a human spirit burdened by obsession and guilt.

John recalled it as an unhappy time. "Lou and I couldn't see eye to eye anymore. We weren't rehearsing, we weren't working, we were flying all over the place, and we couldn't concentrate on anything long enough to work. It was a result of touring day in and day out—which can be a detrimental influence. In terms of emotional balance, there was no more room in the band for anyone else—Lou and I did enough fighting for all. We weren't very compatible writing together, but we did turn out a number of songs."

In 1968, in two recording sessions that served to harvest the seeds of their breakdown, they attempted to cut a single. During the first session they recorded "Ferryboat Bill" and "Temptation Inside Your Heart," poppy, crowd-pleasing rock-and-roll songs that indicated the direction Lou wanted to take. In the second session they produced "Mr. Rain," Cale's recording swansong with the Velvets, a return to the prominent drone and viola. None of the songs were particularly inspired. Whereas they had previously gone into a recording studio and recorded an album in a day or two, they were now hacking around for days getting nowhere just trying to record a single.

In defending his turf musically, John went to extremes that even Sterling found intolerable. He recalled how John drove them all crazy: "One thing that really rankled was John insisting on building this bass amp of his with band money. Something to do with acoustic suspension speakers producing this great wall of sound. Thousands were spent on these goddamn things—and then they didn't work. Meanwhile, we were on endorsement to Acoustic Amplifiers, who made this fabulous bass amp, the Acoustic 360. John refused even to accept a free one from the factory. Later on, John found out that if he'd only had a preamp, it would have worked. All this money for what I called the Tower of Babble. There was a general dissatisfaction with his free-spiriting—and free spending. It really did piss everybody off. What the hell was he up to? Ha ha ha! But it was an ugly business, stupid and counterproductive."

According to John, "Because there was less and less finesse of anything

----

we were doing onstage, we lost sight of the music. There were a lot of soft songs and I didn't want that many soft songs. I was into trying to develop these really grand orchestral bass parts. I was trying to get something big and grand and Lou was fighting against that, he wanted pretty songs. I said, 'Let's make them grand pretty songs then.' All of that was just irritating, it was a source of a lot of friction. It was unresolved, it was a constant fight of who was gonna play what. They were creative conflicts. I think egos were getting bruised."

Even for Moe, Lou could be hard to deal with, primarily because she could never tell whether he was going to be superfriendly or withdrawn. Just like Lou's childhood friend Allen Hyman, Moe felt that Lou was overly influenced by his surroundings, too sensitive to anything that happened to him. Whereas this left her simply feeling sorry for Lou, whom she characterized as "a kind of sad person" at this time, Sterling found Lou's mood swings harder to handle. If Lou was down, Sterling would go down too. This dynamic combined with the pitched battle between Reed and Cale for control of the music transformed the Velvet Underground from being a band that had had a lot of fun together to being a band that began suffering together.

In February, John and Betsey Johnson announced that they planned to be married. Lou, she realized, "was not happy that John was getting married. Period. To me. Period."

"When you're in a band," Cale explained, "you're married to the band."

In Betsey's words: "The Velvets were totally insecure all the time anyway. It was an on-the-edge kind of time every day. Now it was like the girl breaking up the group."

The wedding was postponed when Cale came down with hepatitis and spent several weeks in the hospital, but John and Betsy finally got married in April. Lou attended the ceremony, but the Reed-Cale relationship was clearly under siege. Watching from the sidelines, Betsey sensed "a real edge with Lou all the time. Ego jealousy. Lou was definitely the star. Any guy who is out there singing is the star. It was hard for John because he was backup star. He had so much charisma."

If the Velvet Underground was a family and Lou was the husband, it raises the question of whether Lou had a personal life beyond the band. Mary Woronov, who saw him occasionally through the speed circle that centered around Ondine, recalled that Lou did not date, and other friends had the impression that Lou was no longer interested in sex. However, the truth is that from 1966 on, when Shelley Albin moved to New York City with her husband, Ronald Corwin, Lou had a relationship with her.

At first Shelley hoped that she could maintain an open, honest friendship with Lou that would include her husband, but when Corwin rejected the notion of having anything to do with Reed because he was a bad influence, she found herself having to reject Lou's overtures since she could not imagine being dishonest. Consequently, through 1966 and 1967 they rarely met. However, by 1968 she crossed the border and entered into a secret affair with Lou. Despite its occasional moments of satisfaction and inspiration for a number of outstanding songs, the relationship tortured Lou, who felt that she possessed everything he wanted but could not keep. "Are you going to come and spend your life with me," Lou would ask, "or are you going to stay with that asshole?"

Shelley felt ambivalent. Part of her was so relieved to be with an intelligent and real person with whom she could have a conversation, but another overriding part was scared off by Lou's lifestyle and all it entailed. "You're more interested in security than love," Lou would often chide her, and Shelley had to admit he was right.

What kept the relationship alive for Lou as much as the magic effect her presence had on him was the challenge. "Leave Ron," Lou would urge her. "What are you doing with him? Why don't you just come out the door and stay out the door?" Shelley, who still knew him better than anybody else, was quite sure that if she had agreed to move in with him, Lou would have made her life a living hell as he had done at Syracuse and pushed her out again. That was the curse of being Lou. He was, she was convinced, miserable throughout the sixties and obsessive about his misery to boot, rooting around in it like a pig in shit.

One striking difference Shelley found in Lou was that wherever he was with her, walking down the street, sitting at a lunchroom counter, he appeared to be constantly composing music in his head. Suddenly out of the blue he'd bark out: "You beat on the Coke glass, boop boop de boop. You sing, doo wah doo." In other words, either help me write this song or shut up. Actually, Shelley reflected, nothing had really changed. The bottom line was, if you were with Lou, you had to resign yourself to being an instrument.

Months would pass in which they would not see each other. Then they would get together in the simplest way, meeting for a Coke or a walk in the Central Park Zoo. In order to protect herself from being seduced against her will, Shelley had stopped listening to the radio altogether for fear that Lou's music would have the effect upon her that the sirens had on anyone who heard their song.

That summer the band toured the West Coast. Lou had hardly recovered from John's wedding when one morning in Los Angeles, riding down to breakfast in the elevator with Sesnick at the exclusive Beverly Wilshire Hotel, he glanced at a stack of newspapers piled on the floor to see a glaring headline announcing that on the previous day, June 3, Andy Warhol had been shot at the Factory and had less than a fifty-fifty chance of surviving. Badly shaken, Lou found his jumbled emotions difficult to sort out. Part of him wanted to rush to the phone and call New York to find out what the prognosis was, while another part of him was frightened of being rejected by his former mentor.

Shortly after Warhol was shot, Lou, back in New York, met Shelley at Max's and told her he was hiding out because Warhol's would-be assassin, a radical-feminist writer named Valerie Solanas, who had penned the manifesto of the Society for Cutting Up Men (SCUM), was after him.

Before the end of the month, Lou mustered the courage to call Warhol in the hospital. "I was scared to call him," he remembered, "and in the end I did and he asked me, 'Lou, Lou, why didn't you come?' " Reed felt terrible, but after a few minutes Andy started to gossip, and Lou realized Andy would be all right. Already tinged with guilt, Reed's relationship with his former mentor grew even more complex after the attempted assassination. Father figures weren't meant to be mortal, so Reed distanced himself from the wounded Warhol by avoiding him. "I really love him," Lou confessed on many occasions, and the emotion was always reciprocated by Andy. But there was also an inhibition on both sides, an awareness that some boundary of behavior had been breached.

Reed was among the most outspoken of Warhol's disciples about the shooting. In his song about the assassination attempt on *Songs for Drella,* written twenty years later, he concluded that he wanted to execute Valerie Solanas. In an extensive interview with the British writer John Wilcock, who compiled a book of interviews with Warhol's friends in the wake of the tragedy, Lou spoke about his feelings for the man who was—

after Cale—perhaps the most important influence on his life. "Andy's gone through the most incredible suffering. They let her [Solanas] off with three years. You get more for stealing a car. It's just unbelievable. But the point is the hatred directed at him by society was really reflected." Lou also revealed his own fears about the relationship between success and persecution. "I had to learn certain things the hard way. But one of those things I learned was work is the whole story. Work is literally everything. Most very big people seem to have enemies, and seem to be getting shot, which is something a lot of people should keep in mind. There is a lot to be said for not being in the limelight."

AFTER THE WARHOL SHOOTING, LOU DECIDED TO TAKE EXTREME MEA-sures to get rid of Cale. The question of who was really in command of the Velvet Underground had to be definitely settled. John felt strongly that they'd worked constructively to capture something rare on the first two albums, but that the motivating spirit was gone. By the summer, Reed and Cale were blocking each other's progress. Cale felt the problem could be solved; the more aggressive, business-minded Reed did not.

Once again their conflict centered on Sesnick's role. Reed, of course, wanted Sesnick in, whereas Cale continued to find his presence unbear-able. "Whenever a new song came around, it was like picking at sores. It was very badly handled and exacerbated constantly by Steve Sesnick. Sesnick built up a barrier between Lou and the rest of the band. Lou and I were very close and running the band, and gradually Sesnick came along and said, 'Lou's the songwriter, he's the star.' " After a year with Sesnick at the helm, Cale admitted, "I felt like a sideman, more or less. It was a mishandling of the situation." However, although Cale felt demoralized, he did not think things were irreconcilable. He wanted to go on.

The Reed/Cale conflict was as common in the rock world as the clap. Most partners resolved it in some manner that allowed them to continue. Undoubtedly the VU's commercial failure exacerbated the tension. Whatever, in September, Lou called a meeting of the band at the Riviera Cafe on Sheridan Square in the middle of Greenwich Village. When Sterling arrived, he found Maureen and Lou waiting, but no John. "Lou announced that John was out of the band," Morrison recalled. "I said, 'You mean out for today, or for this week?' and Lou said, 'No, he's out.'

I said that we were a band and it was graven on the tablets. A long and agonizing argument ensued, with much banging on tables, and finally Lou said, 'You don't go for it? All right, the band is dissolved.' "

For a blind second Sterling and Maureen were shocked by the finality of Lou's decision. In retrospect they both admitted they saw the split coming and had been paralyzed to do anything about it. It was a black moment in the band's history; Morrison and Tucker yearned for the lost sound of Cale's viola and organ. Yet both admitted that their desire to keep the band going was more powerful than their loyalty to Cale.

What upset John most was the way Lou handled the situation. It fell to Sterling to deliver the news. "We were supposed to be going to Cleveland for a gig," Cale remembered. "Sterling showed up at my apartment and effectively told me that I was no longer in the band. Lou always got other people to do his dirty work for him. Lou never confronted me, saying, 'I don't want you around anymore.' It was all done by sleight of hand. As for resentment, I dunno. Things had been pushed pretty far between us and I can't say I was entirely blameless, but I felt that was treason."

Disgusted with Lou, and creatively frustrated, John stormed off, claiming, "I left because the music was getting redundant, we weren't really working on the music anymore—and I decided I was going to find another career."

"It was really John's music and then Lou's music," concluded Betsey Johnson. "It seemed like they went as far as they could go in a way being the Velvet Underground. There was no kind of growth for them. Now they're heroes for what they did, but then, to keep a group together for what—a record contract, social acknowledgment, acceptance? Not people like that."

In retrospect, Reed laid the blame for the split on management problems. At the time, however, he felt triumphant enough to say, "I only hope that one day John will be recognized as . . . the Beethoven of his day. He knows so much about music, he's such a great musician. He's completely mad—but that's because he's Welsh."

As a result of the brutal betrayal of the man who had offered him his home and introduced him into a world he had only benefited from, Lou gained complete control of the Velvet Underground, but at the same time was eternally alienated from Sterling Morrison, which would turn out to be perhaps the biggest mistake he made. When he would need Sterling's support in the years to come, Sterl would not be there.

John's reflections about the episode were dismissive and bitter. "It was just a flash in the pan," he reflected on his four-year investment in the Velvet Underground. "It came and it went, and all of it had gone on without anybody really noticing that it had been there."

Ironically, at the time Cale left the band, their influence was just beginning to get a foothold on the front ranks of rock. The Rolling Stones, who had lost themselves in psychedelic rock in 1967, made a superb return to form in 1968 with *Beggar's Banquet*. "Lou's basic influence on songwriting was his use of plagal cadence," asserted Robert Palmer. "Plagal cadence is a one-chord—four-chord. C to F to C to F. 'Heroin' is that. 'Waiting For the Man' is basically that. An awful lot of Velvet songs are basically that. Lou really taught everyone to use the plagal cadence with a drone. The other people who really mastered the plagal cadence were Keith and Mick. 'Street Fighting Man,' 'Sympathy for the Devil,' 'Jumpin' Jack Flash,' are all plagal-cadence songs."

However, Cale was convinced the experiment had been a failure. "We never really fulfilled our potential. With tracks like 'Heroin,' 'Venus in Furs,' 'All Tomorrow's Parties,' and 'Sister Ray,' we defined a completely new way of working. It was without precedent. Drugs, and the fact that no one gave a damn about us, meant we gave up on it too soon."

"I think he's right in a way," Lou would admit twenty years later.

Chapter Nine

THE DEFORMATION OF THE VELVET UNDERGROUND

1968–70

*It became less fun when we had a manager. I think he
destroyed the group. He took two or three years, but he
destroyed it and made it so it wasn't any fun.*

—Lou Reed

PLAYING ROCK AND ROLL AT THE LEVEL LOU WAS (IN TWENTY YEARS THE
Velvet Underground would be judged the second most influential rock
band of the 1960s after the Beatles) is dependent on the musician's
confidence. The more confident he is, the stronger his performance. By
firing Cale, Lou had, like a lion expelling a competitor from the pride,
revealed his most confident self, a self so confident that it labored under
the illusion that it could do without John Cale (which is like Mick Jagger
thinking in the mid-1980s that he could do without Keith Richards).

At this moment, Lou Reed was at the peak of his career. He had
collaborated with three people who brought out the best in him: Cale,
Nico, and Warhol; he had written and recorded two of the most influential albums in the history of rock and roll (the first has often been listed
in polls as the single greatest rock album of all time). On top of that he
had gained complete control of the band he had worked so hard on,
molding it into the crack unit it was, and he had in place, as far as he

knew, a manager who adored him, agreed with his plans, and was eager to fulfill his every whim. Steve Sesnick was still convinced that with Lou's prodigious songwriting talents and with the great playing of Maureen and Sterling, the band would become in time as big as the Beatles.

It is at this stage in the story that Lou betrays one of the weakest links in his character: he is both the best and worst collaborator. Throughout his career Lou has revealed over and over again fantastically good taste in people he needed to help him put himself together. From Shelley Albin to Delmore Schwartz, from John Cale to Andy Warhol, he had chosen terrific people to work with. However, just as much as Lou was screaming out to play with the best of them at the top of the game, he was always finally incapable of staying too long around anybody who was as good as, or heaven forbid, better than, him. Clearly Lou had dismissed John because even though Cale was intimidated by Lou, he still shone too brightly and contributed too much for Lou. Aged twenty-six, four years into his career, Lou, perhaps understandably, was under the impression that he possessed that indefinable "it" that is rock and roll, and that he could do anything he wanted with it. Like so many egocentric maniacs, or young people, he could not see what he was doing. His vision at the crucial turning point may have been further blurred by the dramatic resumption of his love affair with Shelley Albin, which led him to write what many consider his most beautiful, enduring love song, "Pale Blue Eyes."

In the fall of 1968, through Steve Sesnick, Lou brought Doug Yule, a young bass player brought up on Long Island but now living in Boston where he played in the Glass Menagerie, into the band. Naturally, Sterling and Moe were concerned that the introduction of a new member could upset the delicate balance of the band's musical and personal relationships. "I just found it totally acceptable if Lou was being crazy, or being a pain in the ass, to say, 'Oh, well,' and forget it, because Lou was special and different," said Maureen, "whereas Sterling couldn't do that." Doug was impressed by Lou: "The best and worst thing about Lou as a person to work with is he has a lot of creative will power and drive. He gets an idea and he does it. He could make you laugh or cry, depending on what he wanted."

"It was never the same for me after John left," Sterling Morrison complained. "He was not easy to replace. Dougie was a good bass player, and I liked him, but we moved more towards unanimity of opinion. I don't think that's a good thing. I always thought that what made us good were the tensions and oppositions. Bands that fight together make better music."

In fact, Doug was an interesting addition to the band because, being five years younger than Lou and snowed to be suddenly catapulted into such a (in his Boston music circle) prestigious band, he was such putty in Lou's hands that he would soon come to dress, look, and sound like Lou, although they had virtually nothing in common apart from coming from Long Island. Doug was a more than adequate musician and in fact played well and successfully with the band, going on tour with them in October only a week after joining, but his major role originally was to fulfill Lou's desire to have somebody onstage and in his studio who would do what he was told and not bother Lou in any way. Doug fit the bill so perfectly that Moe was convinced that outside of work Lou found Doug to be a bore.

The first fruit of Lou's new band was their third album, called *The Velvet Underground*, recorded at TT&G Studios in L.A. that November. The writing and recording of the album perfectly summed up both Lou's personal dilemma and the dilemma of the band. The songs themselves, commencing with "Candy Says," and ceasing with "Afterhours," focus on the subject that Lou Reed was most confused about: love.

The deepest roots of this problem obviously have to come at least in part from his relationship with his parents, the only people, according to his friends, whom Lou genuinely feared, but at the time Lou wrote the album, from the spring through the fall of 1968, his confusion was apparent in his active bisexuality. During and beyond this time Lou was having affairs with two of the most influential people in his life, whose characters pervade the album, Warhol Factory manager Billy Name and Lou's Syracuse girlfriend Shelley Albin. The basic theme of the album, according to Reed himself, is that all kinds of love are the same as long as they're love. The album catalogs all kinds of love from adultery to religious love. However, by "Beginning to See the Light," the album's protagonist (clearly Lou) claims that he doesn't know what it feels like to be loved and declines from there into isolation and loneliness, complaining that going through the motions with somebody (Shelley) for the second time is particularly sad. After pausing for a moment to claim that he is set free, and concluding with the words of Billy Name that there's no difference between wrong and right, he also characterizes "Afterhours" as a "terribly sad song."

The recording of the album was no less disturbing than its subject matter. First, according to Sterling Morrison, "Right before we went into the studio all of our electronic gear was stolen in their ammunition boxes at the airport. So we didn't have fuzzers and expressers and compressors. We were left with amps and guitars, so we made a straightforward record." To complicate matters, Lou's voice, never strong under any circumstances, was ragged from constant touring. Furthermore, Morrison got his back up when presented with the soulful "Pale Blue Eyes." "Cale's departure allowed Lou's sensitive, meaningful side out," Sterling sneered. "Why do you think that happened on the third album? 'Pale Blue Eyes' is about Lou's old girlfriend in Syracuse. I said, 'Lou, if I wrote a song like that, I wouldn't make you play it.' He was very vain about his gifts as a lyricist. He didn't want them swept by the wayside. I didn't argue hotly about this or that feature on the album. My contribution was as much as ever, probably even more, but I didn't try and get my own way all the time. Perhaps the Cale business left me all argued out, or perhaps I didn't feel that strongly about the material one way or the other. I tried to maintain some tension by instigating a tremendous paranoia because I was still hanging around with Cale. But my position on that album was one of acquiescence."

Despite these problems and tensions, the making of *The Velvet Underground* was clearly a seminal victory for Lou. He celebrated his dominance over the band by doing something that would plague the rest of his career. After the album had been recorded and mixed, Lou went back into the studio and remixed it to bring his guitar playing and voice into prominence, destroying all the hard work the others had put into bringing his compositions to fruition. Granted, the album contained two of Reed's classic VU songs, "Some Kinda Love," and "Pale Blue Eyes," but according to the other members of the band, the original mix was superior. Coming on the heels of his brutal betrayal of Cale, this arrogant overplaying of his confidence was to cost Reed dearly throughout the remainder of his career with the VU. In fact, it would not be going too far to say that rather than beginning to see the light, they had all caught a glimpse of the end.

Sterling Morrison rarely spoke to Lou for the remainder of their time together and psychically closed him out of his life. Maureen, who was by far Lou's best friend in the band, was stalwart, but if one hundred strands of friendship held them together, some strands were definitely broken when Lou remixed the record. Doug Yule was actually the major victor of the crisis for two reasons. First, since they had been playing nightly at the Whiskey in L.A. during the recording sessions, Lou's voice was ragged and Doug got to sing several of the key songs like "Candy Says," bringing him into prominence in the band and blowing a lot of hot air into his inflatable ego. Secondly, Sesnick, a shrewd manipulator who wanted above all success, power, and money, began to see in Doug a possible replacement for the tiresome Lou, whose arrogance was only offset by his permanent case of *shpilkes*.

The third album offered hints of the path Lou Reed would eventually follow to personal survival. "I've gotten to where I like 'pretty' stuff better than drive and distortion because you can be more subtle, really say something and sort of soothe, which is what a lot of people seem to need right now," he explained. "Like I think if you came in after a really hard day at work and played the third album, it might really do you good. A calmative, some people might even call it Muzak, but I think it can function on both that and the intellectual or artistic levels at the same time. Like when I wrote 'Jesus,' I said, 'My God, a hymn!' and 'Candy Says,' which is probably the best song I've written, which describes a sort of person who's special, except that I think that all of us have been through that in a way—young, confused, with the feeling that other people, or older people, know something you don't."

Nineteen sixty-nine looked as if it was going to be Lou's most successful year. *The Velvet Underground*, released in March, was of course a big surprise for their fans, being nothing at all like the previous two albums. In January, Nico had released her second solo album, *The Marble Index*, produced by John Cale, who recalled, "When we finished it, I grabbed Lou and said, 'Listen to this: this is what we could have done!' He was speechless."

At the same time the band was touring through a performing peak. That November, the guitarist Bob Quine, who would work with Lou in the 1980s, met him during the band's visit to San Francisco. "You could see the relationship during the rehearsals. Lou seemed to be closer with Doug Yule than with Sterling. Sterling seemed to be a little detached from things. When Lou was working on arrangements, he would direct more comments to Doug Yule. Doug Yule did a good job—he didn't get in the way of songs. Like 'Sister Ray,' and sometimes they would whip off a version of 'Black Angel's Death Song.' I don't think they were pleased to be in San Francisco, and they knew what awaited them," Quine recalled. "They were regarded as Andy Warhol's death-rock band. It was still the height of clichéd hippiedom—flowers and everything. I saw them at the Family Dog the first week and they were great. But it was fairly tragic. Hordes of hippies would just go there regardless of who was playing. They had their tambourines and harmonicas and they were all playing along with the band, who they didn't know of course. At one point Maureen was laughing. Lou said, 'She's laughing because the tambourine players can't keep time.' He was doing amazing choreography—stuff that would make Chuck Berry look like a cripple—way beyond the duck-walk types of things and amazing guitar solos.

"Then they did this long thing at the Matrix club. They were there two or three weeks and I saw them every night. The most inspiring thing for me was that Lou was writing a lot of songs like 'Sweet Jane,' 'Sweet Bonnie Brown,' and 'New Age,' some of which would show up on *Loaded*. And they would change from night to night. He would improvise lyrics on 'Sweet Jane' and they were very different each night. Sometimes they would be funny and sometimes very, very scary. One night they did a version of 'Waiting for the Man,' and instead of that up-tempo thing, it was very slow and bluesy. Instead of taking any guitar solos he'd whistle. He was making up whole new verses: 'Standing on the corner waiting for the sun to rise, Miss Gina and Miss Ann said that they had a surprise. It's no mystery, it's no mistake, I guess that I'll just have to wait. I'm waiting for my man.' He would go on and on and on. Two or three 'Sister Rays' where he would really cut loose on guitar."

If there was any key juncture at which they could have broken out into the mainstream, this was it. However, the music business was changing so fast it could make your head spin faster than Linda Blair's in *The Exorcist*. As it would turn out, the band was now nearing the end of its relationship with MGM/Verve. "They knew they were up against it," recalled Quine. "Mike Curb was at MGM. He was bubblegum mentality at best and they knew they had to get out. I had overheard a conversation in the spring of '69 where Lou was saying they were enthusiastic and were making a fourth album. Then I asked them about it in November, and he just canned it: no comment. Lou would occasionally give them little talks, like, 'If we just stick together, I know we'll make it.' It's hard for people to imagine how totally ignored they were. Then they had this image—despite songs on the third album that anybody should have been able to like, like 'Pale Blue Eyes,' 'Candy Says'—the image worked against them."

Consequently, they were getting little support from the company whose president, Curb, would win praise from then President Nixon later that year for his resolute stand against "drug music," and one of whose employees would describe Reed as "the most spaced-out person I have ever met in my life. I think he was on speed all the time they were here. And on top of that, he had the nerve to tell me what a fucked-up company MGM is, and how much he hates the way we're handling them." The bottom line was that the album lacked adequate distribution. The Velvets would pack a club in the Midwest or Texas, then on the following day discover that none of their albums were available anywhere in town. Some store owners even complained of not being able to get them when ordered.

It says a lot for Reed's self-confidence that, despite these disheartening developments, he soldiered on through the summer working hard and apparently enjoying his life. Billy Name recalled going out with Lou regularly to gay bars, often stopping by the Factory for quick, casual sex after a night spent enjoying the new freedoms engendered by the gay liberation movement, which had sprung to life that year along with its sister, the women's liberation movement. "We would go to a gay dance bar and gravitate towards getting our rocks off," recalled Name. "He would stay with somebody from the after-hours bars or we would walk down Eighth Street and I would say, 'Well, come over to the Factory.' The more intimate relationship happened only because of the after-hours bars. We wouldn't have had a relationship if we hadn't gone out to that type of place and got blasted and there was a place at the Factory for us to go back to. It was strictly a result of the cultural theme going on. We weren't lovers or anything. And we weren't necessarily intimate. We were making out and we were closely bonded.

"My favorite remembrance of Lou was at the second Factory. Lou came and everything and was getting ready to go and I said, 'Wait a minute, I didn't come.' So I made him sit on my face and he said grudgingly,

'Okay,' so I could get off. So it was a playful type of relationship. But he could turn it off. I would never turn it off. He had that little streak of his own mentality operating where he'll just say no where I would never say no. It really pissed me off one time. I said, 'Come over to the Factory,' he said, 'No.' He could do that after being very close and very friendly. He was a brat. Other than that, the relationship was purely bonding, real friends, love and respectful, really into art and esoteric literature and very young type things. I think that whole mean streak was in there though."

On the other hand, as Lou pointed out, "Billy also told me I was a lesbian, so you have to take these things with a grain of salt."

"Another important person to Lou was Mary Woronov," Billy recalled of one of the former *EPI* dancers. Billy, Mary, and Lou formed a vigorous threesome. "Lou used to like queers, and I used to hang out with queers, so we went to gay bars," Mary recounted. "He liked sleazy drag queens. We were crazy about drag queens like Jackie and Holly and Candy. We knew them as very funny people. Lou had a loyalty towards me not as a girlfriend or as a fuckable person, but in the same way as he had a loyalty to a person like Maureen. I was a girl he liked. In other words, he never made a pass at me. Once I brought him home to my parents' apartment in Brooklyn Heights. My parents were freaked out because he looked so strange. He looked horrible. He was kind of strong about his health. He could take major drug-abuse and not be bothered at all. But he looked skinny and he always slouched. And his hair was always that wiry conk stuff. He wasn't a good-looking guy. He never dated. No one would touch him with a ten-foot pole."

Lou's affair with Shelley reached something of a climax from the spring through the fall of 1969, as is reflected in a number of songs on the third and fourth VU albums, and albeit fleetingly they really did have some wonderful times together. Lou had a charming ability to reveal an encouraging interest in what she was doing. At the time Shelley was seriously into pottery, and although this seemed far removed from anything in Lou's world, he would apply his mind to it as if she were another Warhol, encouraging her to get an angle and go with it. He was, she recalled, heavily into his injections of methedrine from the Dr. Feelgood so many celebrities went to in the late sixties, subsisting otherwise on health foods—bee pollen, wheat husks, and other natural substances— way before it became fashionable.

His state of mind was reflected in the recording of another album that summer in New York. The record, subsequently referred to as the lost album since it was not released until 1985, was made primarily so that they could fulfill and thus get out of their MGM contract and find a new record company that could appreciate their special talents. Ironically, according to Maureen Tucker, it was the most pleasant recording session they ever did because they were given an unprecedented ten days in the studio and were for the first time aided by a sympathetic engineer, Gary Kellgren. MGM never released the album, buried in their vaults, because they no longer believed in the band's commercial potential.

The break with MGM and the tricky period in between leaving MGM and finding a new record company coincided with a parallel breakdown in the relationship between Lou and Steve Sesnick.

From the outset of their relationship Lou had formed that particular bond with Sesnick that would characterize all his relationships with managers. Essentially, Lou put himself in the position he had attained with Delmore Schwartz as the favored if often prodigal son. Sesnick in turn had always given Lou the extraspecial treatment that the Beatles' manager, Brian Epstein, had given John Lennon or the Stones' Andrew Oldham had given Mick Jagger. They had a special mental affiliation, further connected by a shared love of basketball.

However, just as Lou had turned upon the munificent Andy Warhol when the VU's first album had crash-landed, after the commercial failure of the Velvet Underground, with tentative negotiations being conducted by Sesnick with other record companies, Lou began, perhaps to some extent urged on by chemicals, to become paranoid about Sesnick. As his "love" for Steve turned into "hate," Sesnick, who turned out at the same time anyway to be something of a match for Lou, played his trump card.

As the Velvets had metamorphosed from the most advanced art rock band in the world to just another rock-and-roll band on the road, none other than Doug Yule had emerged as one of its most popular members. Bearing an appearance that put him in the category of your average perky rock star grade-B level, Doug had an innocent, friendly, unthreatening look that made him accessible to the increasingly pubescent and prepubescent rock audience to whom Lou looked and sounded too frighteningly like, as Glenn O'Brien had pointed out in 1967, "a real junkie." Snapping that in fact Doug could replace Lou in the band and then they would

really be successful, Sesnick went on a campaign to promote Doug, comparing his performance to Lou's favorably, etc.

In order to understand what happened you have to summon up four
factors. First, these people were all very young and impressionable. Second, being in a rock-and-roll band was absolutely the single hippest thing
you could possibly do in 1969. Third, they had been, or so Lou thought,
hovering on the edge of success, or total failure, for a nerve-grindingly
long time. Fourth, any drug, whether it be pot or speed, laid on this
particular group of people, was bound to vastly magnify the fear and
trembling that go hand in hand with the ecstatic exaltation of playing
rock and roll live.

Consequently, at first a confused Lou responded to Steve's gibes that
Doug was a better performer by trying to emulate Yule. Thus we stumble
upon the bizarre image of the control freak Lou Reed trying to copy his
clone Doug Yule and making himself, as it would turn out, sick in the
process. Sterling was amazed to see Lou, who had always stood pretty still
onstage to good dramatic effect, hauling out a repertoire of rock-performer
moves that dated back to Chuck Berry or were picked up from the Monkees. As the Sesnick/Yule/Reed drama pressed on, both Sterling and Moe
became increasingly irritated by how much Doug was turning into Lou,
becoming arrogant and dominant, and how much Lou appeared to be
regressing into an earlier version of Doug, becoming quiet, withdrawn,
just taking the blows without complaint. The confidence that had driven
Lou to attain his goals since he had become Lou Reed up at Syracuse was
clearly beginning to erode. As the end of the sixties loomed up, marked
forever by the shocking murder of Brian Jones that summer (the first
famous rock-star death of Lou's generation, and one that chilled him to
the bone lest he lose his own life in pursuit of such a high road), Lou Reed
looked into his future with sad, puzzled eyes.

Lou had moved into an expensive Upper East Side apartment. However, when Morrison visited him to check it out, he was stunned by the
glimpse of his colleague's private life. "He was paying an outrageous
amount of money for it," recalled Sterling, "so I thought I'd go over and
see what this place looked like. Well, you know how those high-rise
apartments are—they're real barren. And this was totally unfurnished,
nothing except some kind of pallet that he had pushed up against one
corner. And a tape recorder and some old tapes and I guess a notebook,

and an acoustic guitar. There was nothing in the fridge except a half-empty container of papaya juice. I mean nothing, not even vitamins. It was just the picture of isolation and despair. He is the despairing type. So maybe it helps him."

In fact, 1970 looked as if it really was going to be the year in which the Velvet Underground rose above ground, not in the the least because they signed a new recording deal with the great Ahmet Ertegun at Atlantic Records. Ertegun, perhaps the most cultured and intelligent man in the industry, had midwifed many of the greatest musical artists of the century through Atlantic. His enthusiastic endorsement of the VU was a potentially huge factor in the coming year's success. Furthermore, that summer they were scheduled to record their first studio album for Atlantic, *Loaded*, to be released in the fall, and to play a six-week engagement at Max's Kansas City, the first time they had played publicly in NYC since 1967. What better way could Lou Reed have begun the new decade?

Lou, however, was not one to seize upon the positives in a situation as much as the negatives. He soon turned what looked like it could have been a happy year into another sad one. Mind you, in this instance several outside factors contributed to his despair.

If Lou had begun the second half of the VU's career in the fall of 1968 as the dominant lion in the band, he approached the summer recording sessions in almost exactly the opposite state. Fragmented, weak, fragile, exhausted, levitating above his bed, stoned out of his mind, incapable of making it home alone night after night, are just a few of the words and phrases used to describe Lou's state by those who knew him best in 1970. And as one dolly's in on his position like a movie camera squaring off for the big final shot, one can easily see why. Whereas in 1968 he had strong support from Sesnick, Yule, and Tucker, and at least acquiescence from Morrison, as he approached the recording of *Loaded*, Reed and Sesnick were hardly speaking. Morrison had picked up his college studies where he had left off in 1965 and, apart from having little time and sympathy for Lou, was spending all of his time not playing or recording, reading Victorian novels. Yule, whose head was permanently wrapped in clouds of illusions partially created by Sesnick that he was now the star of the band, thought everything was fabulous. And Maureen Tucker got pregnant. She had to take a leave of absence and was replaced for the unbelievable fee of $6 per day by Doug Yule's brother, Billy. Suddenly the sensitive

Lou, to whom everything hurt, was, as he saw it, surrounded by a band of ravenous baboons who wanted nothing so much as to see him whither away. Steve Sesnick put it more directly. "I don't care if you live or die," he told Lou flatly one day. According to Sterling, Lou found this cold slap in the face hard to take. Reed was, as some witnesses at the Factory had once said, as tough as stainless steel, but he had been taking a pounding day in and day out for four years straight, and he was as near to the end of his tether as he could be and still write and perform such classics as the great autobiographical "Rock and Roll" and the triumphant "Sweet Jane," the two greatest songs on *Loaded.*

In a head as schizy and hyper as Lou Reed's, who can say what finally tipped the scales against him that summer. "Lou loves to dramatize," explained Ronnie Cutrone, one of Lou's Factory friends. "He loves to be the orphaned child, the orphaned genius." Certainly a lot of factors were piling up against him, although everybody who saw him play at Max's said he was great, but what brought him down may well have been the final curtain on his relationship with Shelley, which came down that spring when she too got pregnant, by her husband, in a definitive choice to stay with her family rather than move in with the hapless Lou. Lou finally had to accept that Shelley would no longer be available to him, that she had chosen her family over him. "He had too many places to go," she said. "He was very narcissistic, and I knew he could never pay attention to a child."

The rock world was in a state of flux. In July the Beatles' single "The Long and Winding Road" and the Bob Dylan album, *Self Portrait,* represented reflective views of those who had been undisputed leaders. It was obvious that something new was going to come along soon and surprise everyone, but in the summer of 1970 there was little indication of what it might be or where it would come from. Lou was working very much from out of his own complex, paranoid, and, some would say, drug-addled mind. He told Moe that he had been levitating several feet above his bed.

Reed's own memories of that summer are engraved in his harsh, bitter monologue: "There were a lot of things going on that summer. Internally, within the band, the situation, the milieu, and especially the management. Situations that could only be solved by as abrupt a departure as possible once I had made the decision. I just walked out because we didn't have any money, I didn't want to tour again—I can't get any writing done on tour, and the grind is terrible—and I'd wondered for a long time if we were ever going to be accepted on a large scale. Words can't do justice to the way I got worked over with the money. But I'm not a businessman. I always said, 'I don't care about it,' and generally I've gotten fucked as a result of that attitude.

"I hated playing at Max's. Because I couldn't do the songs I wanted to do and I was under a lot of pressure to do things I didn't want to and it finally reached a crescendo. I never in my life thought I would not do what I believed in and there I was, not doing what I believed in, that's all, and it made me sick. It dawned on me that I was doing what somebody else was telling me to do supposedly for my own good because they're supposed to be so smart. But only one person can write it and only that one person should know what it's about. I'm not a machine that gets up there and parrots off these songs. And I was giving out interviews at the time saying yes, I wanted the group to be a dance band, I wanted to do that, but there was a huge part of me that wanted to do something else. I was talking as if I was programmed. That part of me that wanted to do something else wasn't allowed to express itself, in fact was being cancelled out. And it turned out that that was the part that made up 90 percent of Lou.

"I plugged into objective reality, and I got very sick at what I saw, what I was doing to myself. I didn't belong there. I didn't want to be a mass pop national hit group with followers.

"It simply requires a very secure ego to allow yourself to be loved for what you do rather than for what you are, and an even larger one to realize you are what you do. The singer has a soul but he feels he isn't loved off-stage. Or, perhaps worse, feels he shines only on stage and off is wilted, a shell as common as the garden gardenia."

What Lou had lost in the confusion and transition of the previous year was his confidence and that elusive "it" of rock that he had gone hand in hand with throughout the 1960s. You can hear it on the unique *Live at Max's Kansas City*, which was recorded by remarkable coincidence on the last night Lou played there on a cheap cassette by Warhol superstar Brigid Polk, accompanied by Gerard Malanga. The record has been praised as a Warholianly accurate transcription of the night's performance, and that it is, but Lou sounds ineffably sad and, to paraphrase one of his greatest other songs, "Venus in Furs," as if he had not slept peacefully for a thousand years. Obviously to some extent the gloomhead personality that comes across on the album was caused by something that only he, and his parents, who were on their way in from Long Island to pick him up even as he played, knew, that this was it. This was the last night he would ever play with the VU.

After the show, during which he played an unusually large number of ballads, he announced to Steve Sesnick that he was leaving the band. Sesnick's immediate reaction is unrecorded, but it can be imagined to be one of relief. Now he, like Lou in 1968, was in control. As if by some seismic consciousness sent out by Lou's levitating body, not only had Brigid Polk recorded this last show, but Maureen Tucker had come in from Long island to see it. She was the first to get the news from Sesnick and hurried off to find Lou, whom she discovered sitting by himself, waiting for his parents, at the top of the stairs that lead to the restaurant's third-floor offices and dressing rooms. Putting her arm around him, she tried to persuade Lou to reconsider, but he remained firm, if extremely depressed by his decision. Meanwhile, Yule was in shock—he typically had no idea at all that anything was wrong—and Morrison, engrossed in Thackeray's *Vanity Fair* and a cheeseburger, remained in the dark until he suddenly saw Lou looming up saying, "Sterling, I'd like you to meet my parents," and introducing Toby and Sidney Reed. Sterling, catapulted out of the nineteenth century back into the twentieth, was instantly filled with intense paranoia, since Lou's parents had only ever entered his consciousness through Lou as horrifying specters there expressly for the purpose of carting him off to the loony bin. Mumbling a hasty hello, he watched in amazement as the trio walked away, pondering the strange introduction's meaning with the silent question, no doubt nicked from Thackeray, "What in the world can this portend?"

Chapter Ten

FALLEN KNIGHT

1970—71

*I'd harbored the hope that the intelligence that once inhab-
ited novels and films would ingest rock. I was, perhaps,
wrong.*

—Lou Reed

LOU HAD AS COMPLEX AND PROBLEMATIC A RELATIONSHIP TO HIS PAST AS
he had to his present. One of his music companies that held the copyright
to "Heroin," for example, was called Oakfield Music, after the street on
which his parents still lived in Freeport, and no less an authority on Lou
Reed than John Cale had pointed out that Lou's best music had always
been made in reaction to his parents. Thus, returning to his parents'
home at 35 Oakfield Avenue in August of 1970, after having so dramatically resigned from the VU, can be seen from several viewpoints. On the
one hand, Lou was returning to a sanctuary. His parents had always been
good to him. They would be good now. On the other hand, according to
long-term friends, Lou's parents were the only people he appeared to
really fear. And he was returning on their terms and at least to some
extent on his, a failure. The VU had not become commercially successful. He had no money.

There is no doubt that the fall of 1970 was a confusing and depressing
time for Lou. Having turned his back on the scene that had supported
him for the previous six years, unplugged himself from his music and his
drugs, and started seeing an analyst again, he was making himself frighteningly vulnerable to the demons of schizophrenia—the lures of heaven
and hell—that plague people who dedicate themselves to an artistic métier. And the fear came down on him like a black cloud making him, in
his own words, "sad, moody, amazed at my own dullness" while still
"spellbound by the possibilities."

In this fragile state Lou had little time, after spending his first forty-eight hours at home locked up in his room asleep or having nightmares, for respite since the world he had so arbitrarily left kept on turning, as he saw it, on him.

September was a terrible month. Jimi Hendrix, a guitar player Lou greatly admired, though claimed to be better than, died. *Loaded* came out and smashed him over the head with its back cover, showing a photograph of Doug Yule alone in the studio surrounded by instruments with the clear implication that he was the resident genius of the VU now, and giving credits for all the compositions exclusively written by Lou Reed to the band jointly—with Lou's name third, after Yule's and Morrison's. When he put it on the turntable, he was horrified to discover that Sesnick had remixed the album, butchering, in Reed's opinion, not only several of his compositions, but the whole concept of the record. "The end of 'Sweet Jane' was cut off, the end of 'New Age' was cut off, the guitar solo on 'Train Round the Bend' was fucked around with and inserted," he said. "How could anyone be that stupid? They took all the power out of those songs." Looking at the song listings, he realized that their sequence had been changed so that the thematic structure of the album, an element Lou considered vital to the presentation of material, was entirely missing. "Secondly, I wasn't there to put the songs in order," he complained later. "The songs are out of order. They don't form a cohesive unit, they just leap about. If I could have stood it, I would have stayed with them and showed them what to do." As if that were not bad enough, when Lou went back into New York in September to try to persuade Sterling, whom he had known since his halcyon days at Syracuse, to reform the band, Morrison was not even interested in discussing the subject with Reed.

It was a hasty, ill-timed move prompted, perhaps, more by emotions than foresight. "I had hardly talked to Lou for months, and I said, 'Man, I just don't want to talk,' " recalled Sterling. "He said that as long as I'd played with him, I'd never told him he'd played well. This was quite possibly true. I said, 'I didn't need to because other people told you.' And he said, 'Who do you think I wanted to tell me?' It pointed out to me a real failing in me—I didn't think he needed me to tell him. I was dumbfounded. But I was so mad at him I just didn't want to talk. I would never tell him why. Which is a strange way to behave. You know the 'Poison

Tree' by Blake? Like that. 'I was angry with my friend . . . I told it not . . .' I don't tell you and that's your punishment."

Sterling had been on a slow burn ever since 1968 when Lou had forced John out of the band. He had virtually refused to talk to Lou since. By pleading with Morrison from a weak position, Lou had begged to be rejected. And Sterling, who had an understandable if misplaced sense of revenge, snapped at the opportunity. "He was saying, 'Oh, it was this diet I was on. Wheat husks,' " Morrison continued. "He said, 'I take responsibility for all that. You and me, we'll put together some new band.' So I said, 'Lou, from what I see, it will take at least two years to get right back to where we are today.' I was right: it took him at least that long."

Lou set himself up for another horrible rejection when he called Shelley in November to congratulate her on the birth of her daughter, Sascha, and she hung up on him. "My mother was sitting next to me when he called," she explained. "I said, 'you have the wrong number.' He said, 'It's me.' And I said, 'I know.' He said, 'It's Lou!' He was absolutely devastated. I can still hear his voice today. He was crushed. It was such an awful thing to do, but I was just not duplicitous by nature, and it was not in my ability to carry on a conversation and not have her know that this was Lou. But he was really astounded and shocked and hurt. It was a terrible time in his life and I think the end came for Lou and me when I hung up on him. It was as if I was saying once again, 'I understand how rotten you feel, but I've done it, so go fuck yourself and die! And I'll watch quietly.' I completely lost my best friend when I did that, and I have just been sorry about it ever since."

Reed's identity crisis was exacerbated by the undaunted progress of the Velvet Underground. *Loaded* received positive reviews. The band continued touring. His absence went unnoticed and unmentioned. Doug could do a fairly good imitation of Lou. There also emerged a second factor that both depressed and motivated him. Throughout 1970 and 1971, as Lou sat on the sidelines of the music scene, Cale came out with his first solo album, *Vintage Violence*; Nico released her third, *Desertshore*; and Warhol produced *Trash*, a commercially successful (partially Lou Reed inspired) film about a heroin addict and a drag queen.

As Lou experienced the bends of acute withdrawal from drugs and the Velvet Underground, the rock world was going through its own difficult passage. Elvis embarked on his first tour since 1958, Elton John began his first U.S. tour in Los Angeles, and Jimi Hendrix played his last concert at the Isle of Wight Pop Festival. One reason Lou left the Velvet Underground was because he was afraid of dying. He had good reason to believe that he might. The years 1970 and 1971, the period of Lou's exile to Freeport, took an inordinate toll on the rock-and-roll industry. Following Hendrix, Janis Joplin, Jim Morrison, Gene Vincent, Slim Harpo, Duane Allman, Junior Parker, Alan Wilson, Tammi Terrell, Otis Spann, and King Curtis, who had played on Reed's first recorded single, "So Blue," met their deaths through disease, drug overdoses, or, as in the case of Curtis, violence.

In the month following Lou's resignation, the powers that be turned their attention to the very music he was most associated with. Vice President Spiro Agnew gave a series of speeches in the fall attacking liberal Democrats as "troglodyte leftists," charging them with "pusillanimous pussyfooting," with an emphasis on music and media as promoters of drugs. In November, President Nixon proposed that all pro-drug lyrics be banned. In response, the president of the Velvet's first label—MGM—canceled the recording contracts of eighteen artists accused of promoting drugs. A permissive era appeared to be coming to an end.

Meanwhile, fans, rock critics, and members of the Velvets were left trying to figure out just why Reed had deserted them. Strange rumors floated around the New York rock scene, such as: Lou really was dead and his manager had murdered him; he had cracked under pressure and split for parts unknown; he had finally succumbed to the lure of heroin. When the more mundane truth, that he had gone home to Long Island to live with his parents, emerged, one cynic quipped, "Oh, well, he writes all his best songs on Long Island," echoing Cale's sentiment that Lou wrote best in reaction to his parents. Meanwhile, according to his greatest champion, Lester Bangs, "Lou Reed, sitting at home in Long Island, probably watching *Hollywood Squares,* showed neither his face nor said a word."

The explanations Lou offered for his surprise departure were quite rational. He cited poor relations with the band, his manager, even the audience; a chronic lack of money; unendurable touring; and near categorical lack of acceptance. In truth, however, it was Reed's fragile emotional and physical state, exhausted and overburdened with these pressures, that was broken rather than aided by severe drug use. "I know a lot of people who experiment with a lot of these things as methods to solve problems or find outlets or whatever, but, when you find that they don't really work very well, you move on to something else," he told Lester. "Like I haven't got any answers but the same ones everyone else has: yoga, health foods, all of that."

Lou began to quietly reconnoiter New York. Meeting with old friends and checking on his connections, many of whom were shocked by Reed's confused state, Lou tentatively tried to reestablish himself. "I met Lou at the Factory," recalled the writer Glenn O'Brien, who was working for Andy Warhol's *Interview* magazine. "He was living with his parents. He came around the Factory and he was really pathetic. I don't know what he was on, but he was really out of it. He was my hero, but it was like his life was over. So I thought, 'He's a great poet and a great writer. I'll get him to write for *Interview*.' And he turned in this thing that was so embarrassing that I was really shocked. I had suspected that he had been on psychiatric drugs when I met him. It was like it was written by somebody on Thorazine. It just didn't make any sense at all. Then I had to call him up and say maybe you really didn't want to do this. He was kind of apologetic. 'Well, oh yeah, you know I knew it really wasn't good.' It was horrible."

Toward the end of 1970, Reed was asked to contribute an essay to a book called *No One Waved Goodbye*, about the deaths of Brian Epstein, Brian Jones, Jimi Hendrix, and Janis Joplin. Lou penned a sober reflection full of images of himself. It was a much more successful piece than he had done for *Interview*, and good therapy too. "One cannot get to the top and switch masks," it read in part. "Your lover demands consistency, and unless you've established variance as your norm a priori you will be called an adulterer."

Among many key points Lou made in this best written and most revealing of his prose pieces was that the rock audience was the most changeable of all audiences, and that anyone who dared face them should wear armor. "Or, as my analyst puts it, don't depend on anyone, not your lover, your friend, or your doctor."

"I must redefine myself," he added, "because the self I wanted to become is occupied by another body."

To state that a person as complex as Lou Reed had a nervous breakdown is tricky because one immediately wonders if all eight Lou's had the breakdown or was it just five, etc. However, in the opinion of a number of long-term friends who knew him before and after this period of exile in Freeport, Lou went through some kind of internal process that undermined the confidence he had had when he'd arrived as an authentic rock-and-roll animal on the Lower East Side back in 1965. Signs of his shaky self-image come from his own account of finally accepting his father's overtures to work for the family business, albeit as a typist at $40 a week, rather than the heir to the throne, and in an even more revealing incarnation as a trash collector on Jones Beach, although that assignment only lasted for one day.

REED'S STORY IS NOT POSSIBLE TO UNDERSTAND UNLESS ONE IS AWARE OF the extremely sensitive, easily hurt, vulnerable sides of his personality that were bound up in his deeply buried roots with his confused sense of himself as a homosexual who, because of the 1950s mentality he grew up in, desperately wanted to be heterosexual, and a little boy who felt that he had never gotten enough attention from his mother.

It should come then as no great surprise that Lou was blown away and to some extent woken up again musically in January of 1971 by the release of John Lennon's powerful solo single "Mother." With its opening bell and pitiful refrain, "Mother you had me but I never had you," it summed up much that Lou had been struggling to express ever since his first published piece of prose at Syracuse in which his mother seduced him. After a period spent largely in the company of his dog and his rolling inner thoughts, in 1971 Lou sprang into action.

Doug Yule once remarked that the best and worst things about Lou were his willpower and drive, that once he set his mind on a notion, he had an unusual ability to take it to its conclusion. Apparently this referred as much to the reshaping of his psyche as his career. The first firm step Lou made on the comeback trail was in finding a collaborator or mate who would accompany him on the hard task of returning to himself and New York to, as it were, face the music. This new companion, whom he met in a department store, was a young woman in her early twenties named Bettye Kronstadt. Bettye had grown up on Long Island in a mode similar to Lou, middle class, Jewish, suburban, and was at the time they met attending acting classes where she referred to herself as Krista. Ironically, this was Nico's real first name, which must have sent a flash through Lou's brain. However, the person Bettye most reminded him of, with her string of pearls and elegant clothes, was the young Shelley Albin. In other words here was a girl whom he could, he presumed, make over into whatever image best suited him. Skinny, flat chested, sexy, and most fittingly of all an actress, Bettye bore a look that was becoming popular at the beginning of the 1970s. She resembled a glamorous starlet in Andy Warhol's 1971 classic film, *L'Amour.*

No sooner had he found Bettye than Lou reacted as he always did when he found a new playmate: he totally overreacted, throwing himself into the affair with all the supportive charm and encouragement he could muster. Soon he had pitched Bettye onto an impossibly high pedestal from which she could only, in time, fall. From Lou's point of view, however, it was a totally positive development. It unleashed in him a whole new series of poems, which celebrated his relationship with Bettye.

"I think I am in love," Lou announced in a poem called "Bettye." "I seem to have the symptoms (ignore past failure in human relations / I think of Bettye all the time)." Another piece, "He Couldn't Find a Voice to Speak With," began, "I am sorry, princess, I am so slow in loving / Believe me, it is inexperience."

"Bettye," Lou announced in the trendy magazine *Fusion*, "is not hip at all, and I want to keep her that way. I believe in pretty princesses." He underscored the sentiment in a poem he published in the same magazine, but worried that he might sound like a "bisexual chauvinist pig."

Everyone who met Bettye remembered her as the kind of woman whom Reed's parents would have chosen for his wife. "I met Bettye once," recalled Gerard Malanga. "She was a very sexy-looking Jewish babe, but quiet. And Lou kept her in the background. She wasn't voluptuous, she was very thin and taller than Lou, at least five feet nine inches. She was a stylish babe, she knew how to dress." With her conservatively styled hair, string of pearls, and elegant clothes, Bettye lived in a different world from the violent landscape of Reed's writing. She reminded Lou's more skeptical friends of Betty in the Archie comic books. "Some part of Lou really does like stability and the old cozy kitchen and homey living rooms," concluded Sterling Morrison.

Meanwhile, several other developments in Lou's life helped further lift his spirits. He launched a successful lawsuit against Sesnick to win back songwriting credits and copyrights on *Loaded.* Reed eventually won the lengthy battle to gain sole copyrights to the songs on the two albums, *Velvet Underground* and *Loaded,* that listed the credits to the band collectively. "Lou really did want to have a whole lot of credit for the songs, so on nearly all of the albums we gave it to him," Sterling Morrison commented a decade later. "It kept him happy. He got the rights to all the songs on *Loaded,* so now he's credited for being the absolute and singular genius of the Underground, which is not true. There are a lot of songs I should have co-authorship on, and the same holds true for John Cale. The publishing company was called Three Prong because there were three of us involved. I'm the last person to deny Lou's immense contribution, and he's the best songwriter of the three of us. But he wanted all the credit, he wanted it more than we did, and he got it, to keep the peace." However, Lou found moral justification in the decision of the court and soon afterward was also able to free himself from his management contract with Sesnick, although in the process he lost the rights to the name Velvet Underground. "Every song on the album was written by me," said Lou. "And no ifs and buts, nothing about it. But I had to go to legal lengths to establish it."

The foundations were now laid for Reed's emergence into the world. "It was just obvious that whatever it was, *I had to have control,*" he concluded. Control became his mantra over the course of his entire solo career.

He received an offer to turn Nelson Algren's famous novel about heroin addicts and hookers, *Walk on the Wild Side,* into a Broadway show, which didn't pan out, but led to his writing "Walk on the Wild Side." And most importantly of all, as it would turn out, with Bettye by his side he started revisiting New York. Through the auspices of his old Factory friend Danny Fields, he met a couple named Lisa and Richard Robinson, who had set up a salon for rock writers centered around their apartment called Collective Conscience.

In the confusing transition between the 1960s and 1970s that would lead shortly to both glam and then punk rock, many of the rock writers associated with the Robinsons' group would have a vital impact on the rock world. Henry Edwards, for example, wrote for the *New York Times.* Richard Meltzer became, for a short time, almost as famous in rock circles as some of the stars he wrote about. Scribes like Patti Smith, Jim Carroll, and Richard Hell were beginning to move from writing into music. Lester Bangs and David Dalton were also having a vital impact.

The Robinsons and Fields, who were both trying to build a power base for themselves in the rock world, welcomed Lou into their fold with open arms, extending to him and Bettye the special attention normally reserved for Warhol superstars like Jackie Curtis or the up-and-coming Patti Smith.

Lou, who was still undecided about the exact path he intended to pursue now that he was getting back on his feet, naturally took to the Collective Conscience salon and basked in their recognition of him as a writer. This was pointedly underlined by his first public appearance in New York that March, when he gave a reading at St. Mark's Church Poetry Project. Standing behind a lectern in front of the church's nave, Lou commenced his reading before a top-of-the-line downtown crowd, consisting of poets like Allen Ginsberg, Warhol people, the Robinsons' coterie, and various fans of the VU, with his most famous lyrics. Then, egged on by his audience's enthusiasm, punching the air, he launched into a series of poems about Bettye and concluded the reading with a number of new poems with gay themes. At the end he grabbed the opportunity to announce that he never intended to sing again because now he accepted that he was a poet, adding that if he ever did anything as foolish as returning to rock and roll, the ghost of Delmore Schwartz would surely haunt him.

Meeting up with his old friend, Allen Hyman, Lou demonstrated just how far he had drifted from the sensibility of his parents and his Freeport self. "We hadn't seen each other in a couple of years and he called me up and said it was time we got together again," Allen recalled. "So he came out to the house with this girl, Bettye, and we were sitting in the living room and my brother Andy was there also, because Lou and Andy were very friendly. I was very fascinated because the Velvet Underground was one of my favorite rock-and-roll bands, and I wanted to know about 'Heroin,' and how he had come to write this music. He communicated to me how he had been addicted to heroin at the time, and I had no idea that he had been. We were talking about his obsession with drag queens. It was like he was more attracted to the lifestyle, rather than being involved. It sounded so outrageous.

"Lou and Andy were jamming and we were having a good time. Then suddenly his girlfriend said something to him and he started beating her up, slapping her around. And Suzanne, my wife, got so upset, she said, 'Stop this, what are you doing?' And it was clear that he wasn't kidding around. She'd interrupted a song or something like that, and he started smacking her around. My son, who was maybe four or five years old, was really upset by this whole thing going on, and Suzanne said to Lou, 'You're going to have to leave.' "

According to Lou's favorite writer on the downtown scene, Richard Meltzer, Lou used to needle Bettye constantly about his "gay past" and drive her crazy by telling her how much he missed sucking cock. Worse still, he started to lash out at her violently on the slightest provocation. Friends also recalled the bruises and black eyes Bettye hid behind dark glasses.

Lou was trying to reconcile his confused feelings about sex and love and his relationship with Bettye. In the process he worked out his own view of what being gay was all about: "Just because you're gay doesn't mean you have to camp around in makeup. That's just like platform shoes. You just can't fake being gay. If they claim they're gay, they're just going to have to make love in a gay style, and most of these people aren't capable of making that commitment. You can't fake being gay, because being gay means you're going to have to suck cock or get fucked. I think there's a very basic thing in a guy if he's straight where he's just going to say no. 'I'll act gay, I'll do this and I'll do that, but I can't do that.' Just like a gay person if they wanted to act straight and everything, but if you said, 'Okay, go ahead, go to bed with a girl,' they're going to have to get an erection first."

Meanwhile, Richard Robinson, who was a staff producer at RCA Records, imagined himself gaining considerable credence from producing successful Lou Reed solo albums. The emergence of David Bowie in the U.K., who had just been signed by an A&R man at RCA in the U.S. named Dennis Katz, opened the door a crack further.

Like many musicians who spend the majority of their time and energy inside their heads with their music, Lou was, as we have seen in his relationship with Steve Sesnick, more easily lead and manipulated than we might imagine given his fiery character and powerful will. No sooner had the poetry audience melted away and the Robinsons encouraged him to perform some of his "new" songs on acoustic guitar than Lou found himself playing what would ultimately end up on his first album (mostly outtakes from Loaded) to an appreciative audience at the Collective's salon.

With the support of the Robinsons and their coterie, Reed regained much of the confidence he had missed since his days with the Velvets. Before long he was holding court. Meltzer recalled one such evening when he made the mistake of insulting the new incarnation of Lou Reed: "He took hold of an acoustic guitar and played a good ten to fifteen new compositions—all of them really okay—he'd been fooling around with at home. He completely blew up every time I opened my mouth, couldn't fucking stand anything I had to say that didn't capture the essence of his oh-so-unique creative vision. Like I'd tell him, hey, it would be real good with just him and an acoustic playing the clubs, he'd claim I was calling him a goddamn folky—beneath his dignity. I'd tell him one particularly nifty song reminded me of the Monkees; he'd say the Monkees were just plastic shit—he being, on the other hand, a sensitive genius. I'd tell him he was handling a passage the way Ray Davies might; he'd insist he never plagiarized anyone—his every thought being original. Lots of fury in his reaction 'cause, besides, what right did I—a mere writer!—have to question the efforts of a musician?"

In retrospect, several observers of the Collective Conscience group believed that the Robinsons were too-cool-to-live snobs "who were using Lou for their own ends and thought that he was lucky to be around them." One friend remembered how they didn't want Lou, a phoneaholic, to have both their private phone numbers since he had started calling fifteen to twenty times a day. Nonetheless, the Robinsons provided a stage on which Lou could rehearse his comeback and an audience to applaud his sense of humor. Despite his essay on fallen rock stars, he took Jim Morrison's death that summer as a joke. "I didn't even feel sorry for Jim Morrison when he died. I remember there was a group of us sitting in this apartment in New York and the telephone rang and someone told us that Jim Morrison had just died in a bathtub in Paris. And the immediate reaction was, 'How fabulous, in a bathtub, in Paris, how *faaaantastic.*' That lack of compassion doesn't disturb me at all, he asked for it. I had no compassion at all for that silly Los Angeles person. How dumb, he was so dumb."

No sooner had the Robinsons decided that Lou's new songs were a top-notch batch of classic Reed material that simply needed the right production, than they invited Dennis Katz to meet Lou Reed. The major arm of Reed's talent throughout his career has been in seizing upon the right collaborator at the right time. From Cale through Warhol to, at least for a little while, Sesnick, he has, in his own words, brought out the best in people he worked with. Dennis Katz was to be Reed's most important single collaborator during the first half of the seventies. Katz had just become vice president of A&R at RCA. "I was musically oriented and had the ability to negotiate and structure deals that would give them an A and R head with both backgrounds," Katz explained. "An A and R head must be able to do more than evaluate acts and listen to tapes. He must have a feeling for an act's commercial potential, to know what they'll be worth." Everybody was in the right place at the right time. Having just signed the hottest new rock star in the U.K., David Bowie, Katz soon persuaded RCA executives that Lou Reed would be another perfect star for the new rock era. Katz was a bright light in an otherwise lackluster company. RCA had been living off Elvis Presley since the mid-1950s and had done little since then to consolidate their position. Other RCA artists during Lou's RCA years were John Denver, Harry Nilsson, Hall & Oates, and Alabama. Lou signed a two-album solo contract with the company and immediately set to work with his new mentor.

Dennis saw an outstanding potential in Lou Reed: "Up to that point he was basically a songwriter. I really liked the Velvet Underground, even if I became familiar with their work only after they disbanded. The original group with John Cale had a much wider effect on other artists, but the later band was much more commercial, in my opinion." He also found a personal connection to his new artist. "Dennis was straight," recalled one observer, "but he had a few kinky things about him." Both appreciated music, poetry, and maintained a strong work ethic. Katz and Reed formed the core of a team that would prepare the way for Reed's solo career.

It was taken for granted that Richard Robinson (an in-house producer at RCA), who had become obsessed with reviving Lou's career, would be Reed's producer. "To date," he said, "he has not been recorded in a way that enables him to communicate easily with those who want to listen. And he's written the best rock-and-roll songs I've ever heard."

Once Lou got back in touch with Danny Fields and found himself a star in the Robinsons' coterie, things moved forward rapidly and very positively. In September he met a man who was to play a vital supporting role in his career, David Bowie. Bowie was on the verge of taking off into superstardom. He was already making a big point of how much he thought of Lou. He came to New York with his wife, Angie, guitar player Mick Ronson, and manager Tony DeFries, to sign his RCA contract and meet Lou. Tony Zanetta, an American actor who had recently starred as Warhol in Warhol's play *Pork*, was the go-between. "To celebrate the signing, Dennis Katz arranged for this party at the Ginger Man," recalled Tony. "The big thing was the celebration of the signing and for Lou and David to meet. It was like going to a bar mitzvah. There were twelve to fifteen people, Richard and Lisa Robinson, Bob Ring who was A and R at RCA, Dennis, and other record-company people. Lou took Bettye and David had Angie with him. Rono, Tony, and David thought of me as his entrée to Lou and Andy. I didn't know Lou. I was very intimidated by Reed. That amphetamine cutting humor frightened me so I sat there quietly, smiling. David was also not used to the biting, caustic humor. David was flirtatious and coy. He was in his Lauren Bacall phase with his Veronica Lake hairdo and eye shadow. So he let Lou take the driver's seat conversationally. Plus Lou was one of David's idols from the Velvet Underground. David was very shy. Lou was very short haired. I remember him being in jeans and a denim jacket. No colored fingernails or any of that. He didn't even have long hair. And no one knew how to take Bettye. We all thought she was an airline stewardess. Very vapid. She didn't have much to say. She wasn't very hip looking. She was in pantsuits. Lisa Robinson was the social center of all this, she was pivotal in terms of conversation at the dinner. After the dinner, we went down to Max's so David could meet Iggy. It was in the back room seated at the big booth in the corner on the right when you went in. Danny Fields was officiating over the introductions."

As 1971 drew to a close, Reed looked around for a manager. The first person he approached was his beloved Danny Fields, who declined, explaining, "Lou was making me crazy. So at a party at the Robinsons' I went over and I told him, 'Lou, I love you but this won't work. I just want to be your friend.' This was best left to professionals who weren't so emotionally or aesthetically involved, who weren't so enraptured of him." Next, Lou turned to Fred Heller, who managed Blood, Sweat & Tears, whose guitarist was Dennis's brother. Dennis was clearly having a strong influence on Lou, who hired Fred on his advice. The perspicacity of this choice was intimidated by a buoyant, optimistic mood. Heller's inventive motto was: "Lewis is going to be big in the business."

The question underlying the venture, of course, was whether, when Lou emerged from his exile and hibernation, he still possessed, or indeed might have further harnessed, that elusive spirit, that "it" of rock and roll that he had possessed even through the final days of the VU. In short, did he have the confidence to get up onstage in front of an audience and make rock and roll not as a member of an—within their coterie—established and cherished group, but as a solo star in a new time when rock stars were beginning to look very different?

Chapter Eleven

THE TRANSFORMATION FROM FREEPORT LOU TO FRANKENSTEIN

1971—73

> My direction had always been rock and roll—I saw it as a life force. My goal is to play Vegas . . . be a lounge act . . . be like Eddie Fisher . . . get divorced . . . have a scandal . . . go bankrupt . . . end up in Moscow, marry Connie Stevens, and read about myself in the National Enquirer.
>
> —Lou Reed

CHUBBY, SHAGGY-HAIRED, THIRTY-SOMETHING LOU PRESENTED HIMSELF to British customs officers at Heathrow Airport as a musician on December 28, 1971. He did not look anything like a rock star, let alone the glitter rocker who would soon be the world-famous standard-bearer of a new movement. For a man whose image at the Factory had been pencil-thin behind sunglasses and black leather, being fat was the most blatant sign of an ambivalence to the task at hand.

Reed and his entourage checked into what was London's most popular hotel for top-of-the-line rock stars, the Inn on the Park. An ultramodern

American-style hotel, it was located on the same block as the London Hilton, overlooking Hyde Park. Throughout January, Lou and Bettye and Richard and Lisa lived in a world of their own focused on the making of the solo album and little else. Lou would walk around with Richard on one arm and Bettye on the other, introducing them to people as "my boyfriend and my girlfriend." The threesome might have made a brilliant collaboration, but as it turned out, Bettye did not have the mind or strength to be Lou's partner, and Richard was no John Cale.

Lou had often used the image of a chess game to describe his career. One of his daring moves on the board now was to record in London instead of New York. The decision made sense: In London he could avoid the prying eyes of RCA executives and get out from under the union pressure to use RCA's New York studios. Yet, for a man who was proud of being a control freak he was taking an enormous risk in choosing to work in a scenario he knew nothing about and therefore could not easily manipulate.

Reed's strategy of starting his campaign in London was smart in other ways as well. It would have been a mistake to launch his return in America, where his association with Warhol and the Velvet Underground was the kiss of death. He was also better known in Britain than in the United States. His work was highly appreciated in Britain, and the new generation of rock stars, spearheaded by Bowie, welcomed him like a hero. In London, where the atmosphere was tolerant, Lou was free to explore his sexual identity. England had a history of fondness for eccentrics and cross-dressers, who often played starring roles in music halls and pantomime. Lou would feel free to stretch the boundaries of convention in his music. Apart from refreshing himself by changing the backdrop, Lou chose to record in London because it was the most receptive city for rock experimentors. London studios were on the cutting edge and British producers and engineers appeared more willing to translate musicians' ideas in a collaborative way. Given the many factors pointing to success, Lou's arrival in London was as well placed, and played, as his entrance into the Factory six years earlier.

These factors did not, however, work in Lou's favor. Despite five years of experience and a fifteen-month furlough to get ready for this step, Lou was ill prepared for his first solo recording sessions. Instead of showing up with a powerful collection of new works with which to stake his claim on the 1970s, Lou brought in unreleased VU tracks and castoffs from other projects. Surrounded by yes-men, Lou got no word of protest. The people working with him were more like enablers than collaborators.

His musicians, for one, were a lackluster group chosen for him by RCA. When Lou arrived in the studio, unpacked his guitar, and turned toward the microphone, he was astonished to discover, peering at him from behind their instruments, a (by Velvet Underground standards) B-list band: Rick Wakeman and Tony Kaye, two keyboard players from the progressive band Yes; Caleb Quaye from Elton John's band; as well as Steve Howe and Paul Keough on guitars, Les Hurdle and Brian Odgers on bass, and Clem Cattini on drums. These men were orthodox professionals who knew how to play their instruments, but, as session musicians, they brought little spirit to the music. Lou found it difficult to work up a rapport with them. As a result, Reed, once described by John Cale as "a wild man on the guitar," did not play a single note on his first solo album. Throughout the Velvets' reign, his guitar had been an extension of himself. Now, that third arm was amputated.

Lou didn't seem to care. As long as he could bark orders to a quiescent band, he was satisfied: "Making a really good record is very, very difficult and it's a matter of control. If you don't have the right musicians and you don't have the right engineer, it's very hard. But you have to start someplace. The situation is not always one where you can call the shots or even half the shots. I didn't particularly know any musicians so it didn't matter who you got. If they played what I told them to play, then it might be okay, and if they didn't, then it wouldn't."

While Lou was sleepwalking through the recording sessions, Robinson was floundering at the control panel. Having scant experience as a producer, Robinson was confused by some of the more sophisticated British technology. Giving the impression that everything was under control, he assured Katz's assistant, Barbara Falk, in a letter that month, "We are into technical cutting stages. As far as I can tell it is the best album I've done to date. Lou is in ecstasy." Gerard Malanga, who visited Lou at his hotel near the end of the session, found him quiet and content in the encouraging presence of Lisa Robinson, who played the Warhol role in the collaboration, flattering Lou and assuring him that everything was "Great!" Lou, though, must have noticed that everything was not as cool as the Robinsons thought because he kept telling Richard, "This isn't the

way the record is supposed to sound, the album is not defined enough."
The truth, one observer noted, was that "he had not quite settled on a
voice."

"A lot of what I do is intuitive," Reed said about making the album.
"I just go where it takes me and I don't question it." This admission about
his lack of direction, combined with the weak, raw material of the album,
cried out for a strong collaborator. However, Lou avowed, "I'm not con-
sulting anybody this time, it's a solo effort with my producer, Richard
Robinson." He felt confident that "this was the closest realization to what
I heard in my head that I ever did. It was a real rock-and-roll album."

Just how ambivalent Reed felt about his solo career was emphasized
near the end of the month when John Cale came to London and invited
Lou to join him and Nico in Paris to perform at the Bataclan Club on
January 29. Lou, who hated rehearsing, not only agreed to play with
them, but spent two days going over the material with John in London.
Richard Robinson videotaped Lou and John rehearsing, making music
that ranked among their best collaborations. As one critic, James Walcott, described it: "Reed's monochromatic voice, and Cale's mournful
viola, mixed with the dirgeful lyrics and the colorless bleakness of the
video image turned a casual rehearsal into a drama of luminous melan-
cholia. What was blurry before became indelibly vivid, and the Reed/
Cale harlequinade melted away so that one could truly feel their power as
prodigies of transfiguration. Listening to the Velvets, you may have been
alone but you were never stranded."

Lou also rehearsed for a whole day with Nico in Paris. The nightclub
show, filmed for French television, was one of his happier experiences.
Performing in a small, smoke-filled venue with his former soul mates, Lou
took off on a few solo flights in the tradition of the nightclub greats. He
noted later, "I always wanted to do a song like on the album *Berlin* that's
like a Barbra Streisand kind of thing. A real nightclub torch thing. Like,
if you were Frank Sinatra [whom Lou greatly admires], you'd loosen your
tie and light a cigarette. And when I was in Paris, that's how I performed
it. I didn't play at all. I had John play the piano and I sat on a stool with
my legs crossed. And during the instrumental break I lit a cigarette and
I puffed it and said, 'It was paradise. It was heaven. It was really bliss.' I
was just doing that Billie Holiday trip. Her phrasing, I mean that's singing. I think [he said in one of the more perceptive comments of his career]
I'm acting."

Lou was so moved by the experience with Cale and Nico that he suggested the three of them get back together, but they turned him down. At the time, Nico had already released two solo albums with great critical success, and Cale had made real headway as a producer and solo artist. At the time, they both appeared to be in a stronger position than Lewis.

During January 1972, Reed had lived inside a bubble—waited on hand and foot in a luxurious hotel at the center of a circle whose sole reason to be there was he—doing what he liked best: writing, singing, and recording. As soon as he returned to New York on January 30, however, the bubble burst.

Dennis Katz was appalled by how bad the album was. "The production did not come out the way I'd anticipated it," Katz explained. "It was much too sparse." Everybody in Reed's New York management organization agreed with Katz. "What are we doing wasting our time!" the salespeople at RCA screamed at Katz. "They made it clear that they were disappointed in Lou," he recalled. "They rejected the direction—and specifically the production—of the first album."

Listening to the album now, one can understand their concern. Whereas the record, titled simply *Lou Reed*, contained a number of fine songs such as "Lisa Says" and "Ocean," the performance and the production paled considerably in relation to anything Lou had previously released. Part of the problem was purely technical. Years later, when Reed remastered several tracks from *Lou Reed* for the 1992 boxed set *Between Thought and Expression*, he discovered the album had not been recorded in Dolby, but Dolby decoded, which robbed it of its high frequencies.

Technological mistakes aside, the album's artistic weakness arose from the fact that most of the songs were outtakes from VU albums that had sounded a lot better when Lou played them with the VU. The outstanding example is an outtake from *Loaded*, "Ocean," on which John Cale had played backup in 1970 at Steve Sesnick's invitation. The *Loaded* version, with Cale on organ and Lou in full command of an eerie and vibrant voice, was magisterial. The version on *Lou Reed* was dead by comparison. It was like comparing Janis Joplin singing "Bobby McGee" to Kris Kristofferson. Lou was very influenced by whomever he played with, and his inability to collaborate with people who were as good as or better than he had produced painfully obvious results on the album. In essence, the taut sound of Lou's songs on *Loaded* was obscured by the wrong musicians and poor production on *Lou Reed*.

Lou Reed almost destroyed Lou Reed's solo career before he got off the ground. The rock world was changing rapidly, and a lot of money was at stake for record companies, who were forced to make fast and merciless judgments. RCA's executives were so dismayed by the poor quality of *Lou Reed* they considered canceling his second album. Matters were made even worse by the fact that, for the cover, Lou insisted they use an illustration of a bird next to a jeweled egg by the artist who did the covers of Raymond Chandler books.

Back in New York, Lou found himself in a confusing place with nobody he could really talk to. Money was tight. Lou and Bettye squeezed into a cubiclelike studio apartment on Manhattan's Upper East Side on Seventy-eighth Street, popularly known as the airline-stewardess ghetto. Lou was trying on different disguises. "His life with Bettye and his apartment seemed to provide a kind of domestic security that Lou needed to sustain him in his transition from cult-group figure to solo artist," reported his friend Ed McCormack, who edited *Fusion*, a magazine that had recently published a number of Reed's poems. Ed remembered Lou, accompanied by a nervous, battered-looking Bettye, sitting in his apartment at midnight wearing a pair of sunglasses, keeping his fears at bay by bolting down copious quantities of booze.

"He had the most horrible apartment," recalled Glenn O'Brien, another writer Lou socialized with. "With shag carpeting going up the walls and really bad furniture. And Lou was boozing really heavy. He was a little bit more together, he didn't seem so pathetic, but he must have been doing a lot of booze and pills. He was the first person I ever saw who was really shaky like that, having double Bloody Marys at noon. The first time I met Bettye she had a black eye. She was cute, but I remember her always having a black eye."

The album was to be released in May, by which time it was Lou's job to put together a band and tour the U.S. Lou faced the near impossible question, What musicians do you hire to play with when you've played in one of the greatest rock-and-roll bands of all time? Lou's answer was to choose an unknown and unacclaimed band whose name, the Tots, said everything you needed to know about them. Not only were they pedestrian musicians, they were ugly and asexual. But the Tots provided Lou with exactly what he wanted—an unshared spotlight. No member of the band would question orders or arrangements, Lou would have total control. He also figured that teaching them his repertoire would be simple since the majority of his songs were repetitions and variations and stemmed off three, basic chords. Lou introduced the Tots as a great young and unknown band.

The ensemble made a nervous debut at the Millard Fillmore Room of the University of Buffalo. Lou's performance was uptight, rigid, and tentative, according to Billy Altman, the student who arranged the show. Togged out in black leather trousers and jacket, Lou's halo of ringlets hovered around a face covered by a layer of clown-white Pan-Cake makeup, lipstick and eye shadow. Having abandoned his guitar, Lou found himself thrust into the spotlight without the stage moves that are a crucial part of the lead singer's repertoire. Lou seemed trapped between personalities. At one moment he seemed to be copying Mick Jagger, then suddenly he looked like Jerry Lewis. When Altman, who had published a glowing review of the concert in the local paper, visited him the following day, Lou was curt, the five minutes they spent together excruciating. Despite proclaiming that he would never commit suicide because he was "in control," Lou was impressed by the suicide that month of the British actor George Saunders, who left a note explaining, "I'm so bored."

In May, when the album *Lou Reed* and two singles, "Goin' Down"/"I Can't Stand It" and "Walk and Talk It"/"Wild Child," were released, Dennis Katz's worst fears were realized. Initially *Lou Reed* sold around seven thousand copies, an embarrassing result in an industry where fifty thousand to one hundred thousand was considered reasonable.

It was a telling moment for the Robinsons and their collective. Lou was the mascot of the New York underground, whose inhabitants would have benefited from his success. Loyal critics like Donald Lyons gushed in *Interview* magazine that Lou was "a classic romantic—the smell of his work is the smell of Baudelaire's Paris—grappling, tempted, and sometimes happy, always human. It's a wonderful album." Robert Christgau gave it a B+ in the *Village Voice*, but added that it was "hard to know what to make of this. Certainly it's less committed—less rhythmically monolithic and staunchly weird—than the Velvets. Not that Reed is shying away from rock and roll or the demimonde. But when I'm feeling contrary he sounds, not just 'decadent,' but jaded, fagged out." "Edith Piaf he ain't," admitted the disappointed Lester Bangs.

Most reviewers lambasted the work. "The comeback album—the resurrection of [record company's label] 'The Phantom Rock' itself—was one of the more disappointing releases of 1972," wrote the leading British rock critic, Nick Kent, in the *New Musical Express*. "Reed's songwriting style has deteriorated—his dalliance with whimsical little love ballads are at best mildly amusing, at worst quite embarrassing, and always out of context."

Lou expressed a desire to kill Kent, but his defense of the album was lukewarm. "There's just too many things wrong with it," he lamented. "I was in dandy form and so was everybody else. I'm just aware of all the things that are missing and all the things that shouldn't have been there."

Nobody was willing to die for it and nobody claimed to be more upset than Sterling Morrison. "I really felt sad," he recalled. "I thought, 'Oh, man, you have blown it!' He used to be one of the great rock vocalists, but either his voice had seriously deteriorated or he can't or won't sing anymore." John Cale explained that the lyric about hiring a vet Lou sang at the end of "Berlin" was deadly serious. He noted that Lou would often get passionate about something everybody else found funny, then be highly offended by their laughter. But, particularly in light of the bad production of Velvets leftovers, he found the album lame.

To make matters worse, no sooner had Lou come rushing out of the gate with his first individual effort than he was unhorsed by the same hurdle the Beatles had come up against when they went solo—the specter of previous work. In Reed's case the invidious comparison between his earlier and current work was made painfully obvious when his last night with the Velvet Underground at Max's was released the same month. *Live at Max's Kansas City* enjoyed better reviews and sales than *Lou Reed.*

AT THIS AWFUL JUNCTURE, LOU PUT INTO PLAY ONE OF THE ELEMENTS that would always set him apart from the pack. When in trouble, he had an ability to charm and attract powerful people who believed in and were willing to go to bat for him. Dennis Katz, Lou's lawyer during the first half of 1972, was now leaving RCA and began to make overtures to become

Lou's manager. Katz's offer coincided with increasingly tumultuous relations between Reed and Fred Heller, with whom Reed had an explosive personality conflict. Bettye also complained about Fred pushing her around at Lou's shows. When Lou told Fred he was going to be replaced by Dennis, a lawsuit ensued, from which Lou extricated himself at considerable financial cost.

Lou now seized upon Dennis as a father figure, even though the two were roughly the same age. Poised, literate, happily married, and devoted to his career, Dennis represented a guiding strength. Lou would often visit him at his home in Chappaqua. Everyone around the two recalled with awe a friendship in which Lou initially never contradicted or challenged Dennis.

"I think Dennis liked the fact that Lou needed him and depended on him," said Katz's assistant Barbara Falk. "He really thought that Lou was fantastic. David [Bowie] was just starting to take off at RCA right after Dennis left. Now Dennis swung totally to Lou. I remember Dennis's wife saying that Lou was so much better than David Bowie, he wasn't all the frills and glitter and he was stark and black, he was the street poet. Being of the literary bent, one of the things that attracted Dennis to rock artists were their lyrics.

"Dennis started getting more interested in Lou, and when David Bowie expressed an interest in producing Lou, Dennis got even more involved. Dennis got more protective and there was more contact and a relationship developed. Lou's father came up to the office and wanted an accounting or reporting—because Lou had had problems with the guy who came before. He was a quiet, nondescript, businesslike fellow. He came on his own and he and Dennis went to lunch across the street. Mr. Reed was concerned and Dennis was trying to assure him that Lou was finally in good hands.

Considering that Dennis was so different from Lou, the strength of their bond was surprising. Falk described Katz as a bookish homebody: "He was very home-oriented and private, he didn't like to go out at night, he wasn't your typical rock-and-roller. He collected autographs and first editions. And he was very, very literary in his interests. That part of Lou interested Dennis, the fact that he had been published in the *Paris Review,* and the fact that they both read, which very few people in the rock world did. So they developed this strange relationship where they were both fascinated by each other's lifestyle and they kidded each other about them and joked and put each other down."

Lou loved the fact that Dennis was eccentric. He found that it was cool. He said, 'He's not like all the other guys, he's got something in here.' And there was this strange symbiosis between them. They got along really well, but then I could never picture Lou staying overnight in Chappaqua—with his hours. . . . But he used to stay over in this really nice house. And Dennis got up at seven, he fell asleep at eleven o'clock. I can also remember going out with the two of them to some gay bar and Dennis refused to go to the men's room. He was fastidious. When they got along, they were a funny pair. And Dennis was always a placater and a builder-upper. He was articulate and he could speak to Lou. He would get frustrated with Lou, but, let's face it, everybody would get frustrated with Lou. But Dennis always tried to make sure that Lou was aware of everything going on financially."

During the time that Lou was befriending Katz, Andy Warhol also approached him with a job offer. Thriving in a dramatic period of his comeback from the 1968 attempted assassination, the artist asked Reed to write some songs for a Broadway musical to be produced by Warhol and Yves Saint Laurent. Lou recalled, "Andy said, 'Why don't you write a song called "Vicious"?' I said, 'Well, Andy, what kind of vicious?' 'Oh, you know, like I hit you with a flower.' And I wrote it down, literally. Because I kept a notebook in those days. I used it for poetry and things people said." Lou also wrote two other songs that along with "Vicious" would appear on his second solo album, *Transformer;* "New York Telephone Conversation" and "Make Up."

Despite the support of these two men, Lou might have limped along indefinitely had it not been for the emergence of a new rock movement that swept him up in its vitality and high drama. 1972 had marked the entrance of glitter rock, which released sexual forces as potent as those let loose by the British pop explosion of 1964. In glam or glitter rock, male stars smashed open gender barriers by copying costumes and styles of camp 1930s film and stage icons. The results strained Lupe Velez and Mae West through a pastiche of drag queens and characters from the Warhol films *Flesh, Trash,* and *Heat.* Riding high on a creative wave brought on by the new gay liberation movement, glitter rockers—whether straight or gay— wore jewelry, makeup, high-heeled platform shoes, and sequined outfits.

Yet, despite the feminine trappings, these rockers acted just as macho and adolescent as performers like the Rolling Stones, strutting and preening like little red roosters. Exemplified in England by David Bowie with his 1971 album *Hunky Dory* and hit single "Changes," and in the U.S. by Alice Cooper, who had just released his album *Killer*, glitter rock changed rock's look and sound, blowing open the doors for a number of new groups and movements.

Reed would have been hard-pressed to compete had he too not donned an attention-getting image. But he didn't want to lose his hard edge or stoop to offering crass entertainment in the style of Alice Cooper. Lou hated Cooper's glitzy outfits and goofy stage histrionics, which included wrapping a snake around his neck and spattering himself with blood. David Bowie's smarter cooler demeanor appealed more to Lou. With his paler-than-pale skin, sensitive eyes, and floppy hair, Bowie looked appropriately androgynous. In Bowie, Reed would find a collaborator as important as Warhol—only much more commercial. And though at times losing sight of the thin line separating person from persona, Reed, like Bowie, would become a master of the seventies pageant.

In the summer of 1972, when Bowie returned to London from his triumphant American tour, bathed in the success of *The Rise and Fall of Ziggy Stardust* (which had come out in June), he proposed to RCA that he produce Reed's second album.

"David was very smart," noted his wife, Angie. "He'd been evaluating the market for his work, calculating his moves, and monitoring his competition. And the only really serious competition in his market niche, he'd concluded, consisted of Lou Reed and—maybe—Iggy Pop. So what did David do? He co-opted them. He brought them into his circle. He talked them up in interviews, spreading their legend in Britain." David (who had included a musical tribute to the Velvets on *Hunky Dory*) saw Lou as "the most important writer in rock and roll in the world."

According to Dennis Katz, RCA was receptive. "They had a lot of faith in Bowie because he produced both *Hunky Dory* and *Ziggy Stardust*. So they were then willing to take another shot at a Reed album—assuming David was working with Lou."

Tony Zanetta attended "another bar-mitzvah dinner" for David Bowie and Lou in New York at which they started talking about doing *Transformer*. Plans were made fast. David was still touring and planning on coming back to New York in September. They decided to record in July and August. "They wanted to work with Lou because they didn't like the first album and didn't think that it was what he should be doing," said Tony Zanetta. "But it was a sensitive issue because of Richard Robinson."

Lou's decision to have Bowie produce his next album was a shock to Robinson, who had been the only member of Lou's entourage to question Bowie's motives in January. Richard had taken it for granted that he would be producing Lou's second album, especially since Lou had told one interviewer, "Richard had the same goals I had. We knew we wanted the album to come out this way. We had it all plotted out before we even went to London." But once Lou became aware that Richard's involvement threatened to doom him to oblivion, he agreed to cut him from the team. "The Robinsons were rather possessive of Lou," Glenn O'Brien recalled. "They had a big problem because they thought he should have been eternally grateful to Richard for giving him his big break."

The Robinsons felt that they had brought Lou out of retirement and saw the move as the ultimate betrayal. When Richard was informed over the phone from Katz's office that his services would no longer be required, he screamed that Lou was an "aging queen."

"I can understand it," said Barbara Falk. "Richard thought, 'I brought him in, and it was my thing, and nobody wanted him, and part of my deal was that I would continue on. . . .' He thought he had an understanding. Lisa actually didn't speak to the Bowies for some time because of that—it was a big rift. Lou looked on her as the high priestess of the current rock scene. After the breach when they weren't speaking, he'd say, 'They're little pop people,' but he probably still read her religiously."

Lou suddenly found himself closed out of Lisa's collective. "I still love Richard," Lou groaned to Ed McCormack, "but I'm not so sure he loves me anymore. But then, I wouldn't really know what people think of me. I hardly see anyone anymore. There are dear friends who I no longer see, not because I don't love them, but because I can no longer be a part of that whole hip scene. These nights I hardly go out at all, except down to the liquor store to buy another fifth.

"Sometimes I have this horrible nightmare that I'm not really what I

----

think I am. . . . That I'm just a completely decadent egoist. . . . Do you have any idea what it's like to be in my shoes?"

WHEN LOU HAD LEFT THE VU, HE HAD REALIZED HE DID NOT WANT TO BE the kind of rock star Sesnick saw him as—a Beatle or a Monkee. David had shown him a way to be a star and carry his bisexuality as a weapon rather than a burden. When Lou flew to London in July for the August recording sessions, he immersed himself in the role with the glee he had felt as a newcomer at the Factory.

"Writing songs is like making a play and you give yourself the lead part," Reed said in an interview about working with Bowie. "And you write yourself the best lines that you could. And you're your own director. And they're short plays. And you get to play all kinds of different characters. It's fun. I write through the eyes of somebody else. I'm always checking out people I know I'm going to write songs about. Then I become them. That's why when I'm not doing that, I'm kind of empty. I don't have a personality of my own. I just pick up other people's personalities. I mean seriously, if I'm around someone who has a gesture that's typical of them, if I'm around them for more than an hour, I'll start doing it. And if I really like it, I'll keep it until I meet someone else who has something else. But I don't have anything myself."

Lou was dazzled by David, one of his brightest disciples. Lou was also mesmerized by David's management machine and deft manipulation of his press and fans. For a few weeks, Reed soaked up elements of the character and influence of his charismatic friend, adding them to his own, evolving day to day. "I had a lot of fun," Reed recalled, "and I think David did. He seemed quick and facile. I was isolated. Why were people talking about him so much? What did he do that I could learn? A lot of it reminded me of when I was with Warhol."

The two of them cruised London's seamy side. "Lou loved Soho, especially at night," Bowie said. "He thought it was quaint compared to New York. He liked it because he could have a good time and still be safe. It was all drunks and tramps and whores and strip clubs and after-hours bars, but no one was going to mug you or beat you up. It was very twilight."

By the time Lou and David got to hang out with each other that summer, Bowie had been praising Lou Reed to the sky for years. Now it was Lou's turn to be bowled over by David and his Warhol-like world in the high-powered, fast-moving London rock scene.

"David is a seductive person and that is his MO," explained Tony Zanetta. "And he used that with Lou because he wanted something from Lou. He looks you right in the eye and no one exists but you. But that's only for a few minutes. We all went for it and I'm sure Lou did. And I'm sure Lou was ignored—not out of lack of interest, but because David was so busy. David was interested in Lou, but he wanted everybody. That's what Ziggy was."

Very few artists are capable of the generosity David Bowie extended to Lou Reed in the summer of 1972. As proof of his devotion, Bowie invited Reed to guest-star at his headlining show at the Royal Festival Hall on July 8, a benefit for Friends of the Earth. At the end of the set David brought Lou Reed, dressed in black, onstage to perform "White Light/White Heat," "I'm waiting for the Man," and "Sweet Jane."

After Bowie introduced Lou to British audiences, he held a day of press interviews at the top-of-the-line Dorchester Hotel, to publicize their music and images. It was at this moment that Lou Reed minced officially into glitter rock, entering in his Bowie-influenced Phantom of Rock persona, made-up and sparkling in Bowie's designer's jumpsuit, six-inch platforms, and black nail polish. With studied deliberation, the Phantom deposited his two cents into the gay-liberation kitty by tottering across La Bowie's suite and firmly planting a kiss on David's mouth. Then, announcing that Bowie, "a genius," would be producing his next album, Lou withdrew.

"People like Lou and I are probably predicting the end of an era, and I mean that catastrophically," Bowie pontificated. "Any society that allows people like Lou and me to become rampant is pretty well lost. We're both very mixed-up, paranoid people—absolute walking messes. I don't really know what we're doing. If we're the spearhead of anything, we're not necessarily the spearhead of anything good."

Bowie then put himself at Reed's disposal, offering to help in any way he could, instructing his wife, for example, to find Lou and Bettye a flat. David's entourage was centered around his wife, Angie, and his guitar player, Mick Ronson. This triumvirate did everything they could to make Lou and Bettye comfortable in London. However, according to Zanetta, "Lou was pawned off on Angie; she was the human contact who would take care of things David didn't want to deal with. And Lou was one of those things. I don't know how involved David was with the record—I think it was mostly Ronson. He had a lot of things going on, gigs, touring, shows coming up, and recording. And the Mott the Hoople thing."

Angela Bowie, who vividly remembered, "We felt *extra*special, *intensely* alive, *incredibly* alert," was amused by Lou. "David introduced us and we shook hands, kind of. . . . Lou's greeting was a rather odd cross between a dead trout and a paranoid butterfly. My first clear impression of him was of a man honor bound to act as fey and inhuman as he could. He was wearing heavy mascara and jet-black lipstick with matching nail polish, plus a tight little Errol-Flynn-as-Robin-Hood body shirt that must have lit up every queen for acres around him."

Though they had very little money, Lou and Bettye moved into a furnished duplex in the tony London suburb of Wimbledon. Bowie was rehearsing for an upcoming tour, recording a new album of his own, and constantly working for greater international success, but took time to introduce Lou to people who would be useful to him. One contact, the writer and photographer Mick Rock, became Lou's long-term friend. Everyone in Bowie's set thought that Mick was brilliant and loved his work. "Mick," one commented, "was a lot of fun because he was in the ozone." In fact, Mick Rock was the perfect receiver for Lou Reed. Full of the good humor of the working-class Englishman straight out of a Charles Dickens novel, Rock possessed a mind that worked as fast as a camera, a charm that made people around him feel alive and at ease, and a detailed knowledge of Lou's work. He became Reed's primary social connection in London during the first half of the 1970s.

"Reed was staying in Wimbledon, a smart suburb of London favored by businessmen, film stars, and respectable hoodlums, and hating it there," Mick revealed of his first visit to Reed. "A prowler, he needed the rootless, strung-out city for stimulation. Echoes of Baudelaire. A poet of pavement and splintered nerves. His psyche was fragile, withdrawn and nurtured on gin and mascara."

Though he may have been uncomfortable in Wimbledon, Lou's entrée into London's rock world gave him a revitalized belief in himself. "People always come to me," he told Mick Rock. "They have to because I have the power on them. I mean, they can't stand me sitting here for too long doing nothing. Or they can't take what I have to say. I like to make believe I'm a gun. I calculate. I look for a spot where I can really do it. Then they suddenly know I'm really a person."

Not that he always had such a high opinion of himself. Later he would tell Mick, "I'm so dull really. That's why I don't write about myself. That's why I need other people. I need New York City to feed off. The actual state of things."

"Of the world?" Mick asked.

"No, just me. Fuck the world. I'm not interested in my problems or attitudes, 'cause other people's are so much funnier."

A week after the Dorchester press conference, Lou and the Tots set out on their first British tour with a show at the Kings Cross Sound in London. "When I saw Reed perform in London in the summer of 1972, the influence of Bowie's theatrical, sexually ambiguous aesthetic was apparent; Lou wore black eye makeup, black lipstick, and a black velvet suit with rhinestone trimmings," wrote one of Lou's most intelligent chroniclers, Ellen Willis. "The album *Transformer* referred directly and explicitly to gay life and transvestism. The subject matter was not new, but Reed's attitude toward it was—he was now openly identifying with a subculture he had always viewed obliquely, from a protective, ironic distance."

Lou was criticized for copying Bowie. "I did three or four shows like that, and then it was back to leather," he commented after the tour. "We were just kidding around—I'm not into makeup." These tentative forays into the glam scene were merely the beginning, however. The new, rude Lou Reed relished being grabbed onstage by both girls *and boys.*

Though audiences in Britain soaked up Lou's act, it was clear that he would have to work up some new songs to match it. The press was often critical of his material. "I'd rearranged my old songs just like Dylan and slowed some of them down, and the press branded the new versions as travesties of the originals," Lou protested. "They're *my* songs; surely I can do what I like with them. And I like them slower now."

Although he was accused of aping David Bowie in his appearance and stage act, Lou continued putting the finishing touches on the Phantom of Rock. "I'm not going in the same direction as David," Lou insisted. "He's into the mime thing and that's not me at all. I know I have a good hard-rock act, I just wanted to try doing something more—to push it right over the edge. I wanted to try that heavy eye makeup and dance about a bit. And how could anyone say I was letting my guitarist upstage me? He was doing it on my instructions. I told him to get up and wiggle his ass about and he did. Anyway, I've done it all now and stopped it. We all stand still and I don't wear makeup anymore." As an afterthought he added lugubriously, "They don't want me to have any fun."

Rock-and-roll records are born out of tension. By the time Bowie and Ronson took Reed into Trident Studios in August to record *Transformer*, which would turn Lou from an underground cult figure into a rock star, the collaboration was pitched on the edge it needed. On the one side was the authentic rock-and-roll animal Lou Reed. Fast, nervous, New York uptight, Lenny Bruce–like, sarcastic, hard, aggressive. On the other was the sensitive, high-strung Bowie, articulate, exotic, and strong, but not as sharp or hard as Lou. He was more of a dreamer. Between them stood the sturdy Mick Ronson—Ronno to his friends—from the shipbuilding town of Hull. Ronson could neither understand a word Lou said nor make his own densely crafted argot communicable to the wired little weasel. Lou seemed at times to be cracking up over convoluted private jokes told in another language altogether. Yet Ronno was the glue that cemented the three disparate figures to each other. "Ronson's nasally electric guitar, which he played through a half-closed wa-wa pedal, provided *Transformer*, with its instantly identifiable matrix," wrote Jon Levin. "The underrated Ronson provided the string and brass arrangements, as well as the all-important piano parts, from the languid arpeggios of 'Perfect Day' and 'Satellite of Love' to the comedic 'New York Telephone Conversation.' Lyrics aside, the music is almost perfect: Herbie Flowers's acoustic bass, acoustic guitars, a muffled electric, and jazzy brushes on the drums, all supported by Ronson's subtle, chillingly simple violin arrangements. Reed has credited coproducer Ronson with making the greatest contribution to the completion of *Transformer.*"

The impact of *Transformer*'s sexual content has been forgotten. It is hard to conjure up the shock resulting from David Bowie's confession of bisexuality in the *Melody Maker* interview of January 1972. The news catapulted Bowie into the front ranks of sexual role model for a generation or two. In *Ziggy Stardust*, with whom Bowie introduced an androgynous character (inspired by Warhol's cast of the play *Pork*). He became an icon anyone could lust for. When David took his Ziggy Stardust act into the Rainbow, a huge former cinema in London, on August 19, Lou described the show as "the greatest thing I've ever seen."

Bowie made bisexuality extremely hip, and Reed—who had sung lyrics such as "sucking on my ding-dong" as early as 1966—felt comfortable with the glam scene. In 1972, the lines "We're coming out. Out of our closets, out on the street" (from "Make Up") weren't simply a camp gesture, but were associated with the Gay Liberation Front's campaigning slogan—a rare political statement from the normally apolitical Reed.

The album had its rough edges and raw patches in the making. All three men were under a lot of pressure when they laid down its tracks. Bowie and Ronson, who were also recording with Mott the Hoople, were due to play concerts that month in London and New York. Their time was split between rehearsing and recording. For Reed, whose career depended on the outcome, every moment in the studio was vital. The fast, furious, drug-induced pace of their collaboration would have a lot to do with the album's ultimate success.

David was characteristically modest about his intentions: "All that I can do is make a few definitions on some of the concepts of some of the songs and help arrange things the way Lou wants them. I'm just trying to do exactly as Lou wants." Bowie was at the core of the production; it was his encouragement, like Warhol's, that brought Reed to the fore as a solo artist.

Bowie, who was more fascinated by Warhol than Reed, pulled out of Lou's nervous head a series of vignettes about the artist's life that were worthy of Reed's greatest role models—Raymond Chandler, Nelson Algren, and Jean Genet. Bowie got him to sing them at the top of his form. Enjoying himself, Reed was able to invent different attitudes and personalities for the album that found their way into the songs "Vicious" and "Walk on the Wild Side." "I always thought it would be kinda fun to introduce people to characters they maybe hadn't met before, or hadn't wanted to meet, y'know," Lou joked. "The kind of people you sometimes see at parties but don't dare approach. That's one of the motivations for me writing all those songs in the first place."

"Last time they were all love songs," he snapped, "this time they're all hate songs." Reed would play Bowie and Ronson the bare bones of the song, and together they would craft its eventual setting. Bowie and Ronson were attuned to what Lou's songs needed, and their arrangements reinforced his material.

Whereas Cale had drawn together the lyrics of "Heroin" and all the great songs on the first album, that task now fell to Ronson. Ronson wrapped the lyrics in confident, sparring music that leaped out of the speakers and grabbed you around the throat, just as the Velvets' music had. "Mick Ronson was really instrumental in doing the album," one observer confided.

Ronson described their approach: "We are concentrating on the feeling rather than the technical side of the music. He's an interesting person, but I never know what he's thinking. However, as long as we can reach him musically, it's all right." Reed's reaction to the collaboration with Bowie and Ronson was ecstatic. *"Transformer* is easily my best-produced album," he exclaimed. "Together as a team they're terrific." *"Transformer* was a very beautiful album that David did out of love for Lou," concluded Bowie's friend Cherry Vanilla. "What you have to worry about is insanity," Lou mused to friends later. "All the people I've known who were fabulous have either died or flipped or gone to India, Nepal, and studied and gave it all up, y'know, the whole trip. Either that, or else they concentrated it on one focal point, which is what I'm doing, which is what I think David is doing."

Though Lou and David managed to create a brilliant mix, they attempted to outdo each other in performing the roles of "tortured, creative artists." Angie Bowie, who frequently visited the studio, was often confronted with the sight of David curled into a fetal ball beneath the toilet bowl in deep depression, or Reedian tantrums so violent that she fled the studio before their velocity blew her out of the room. These throwbacks to childhood did not, however, faze the musical partners. Whenever David retreated to the john, Lou claimed he knew exactly how David felt and insisted that nobody disturb him. David in turn often talked Lou out of deep depressions. "David Bowie's very clever. We found we had a lot of things in common. He learned how to be hip. Associating with me brought his name out to a lot more people. He's very good in the studio. In a manner of speaking he produced an album for me."

When Lou entered David's world, the British charts had been dominated by Marc Bolan's T-Rex, Gary Glitter, Slade, Alice Cooper, The

Sweet, and Elton John. When *Transformer* was recorded and mixed, the single biggest star in the U.K. was David Bowie.

Whereas Reed's first solo album was a jumble of material the Velvets never recorded and patchy love songs, *Transformer* was much more of a unified whole. Its subject, introduced by the album's hit single, "Walk on the Wild Side," was the world of Andy Warhol after the 1968 attempt on his life as detailed in "Andy's Chest," and in particular the polymorphous sexuality of the early seventies in Warhol's films *Trash* and *Heat*.

Despite brief euphoric moments Lou had experienced during the making of *Transformer*, the album's release marked the end of the Bowie-Reed collaboration. "Once that album was done, I don't remember David ever mentioning Lou," said Zanetta. "Or wanting to go see Lou or wanting Lou to come see this. David was always hot and cold with people. I think he was always intimidated by Lou. Because Lou was sharp and David wasn't. David never pursued Lou the way he pursued Iggy. He would come and go with Lou."

In October, Lou and the Tots toured Britain. Lou's Bowie-influenced stage act, combined with his new material, propelled him into the pop limelight. Dressed, as one observer put it, "in leather and charisma," he delivered a series of devastating performances to rapt audiences. "I'm the biggest joker in the business," he said. "But there's something behind every joke."

After the tour, and before Lou left London, Mick Rock did a photo session with him that would supply Lou with his first successful solo publicity image. Lou had always had an image problem. The VU had a glowering, grungy glamour that had not meshed that well with mass rock audiences. Lou and Mick came up with a brilliant solution. Combining his love for science fiction and horror and mixing it with his electroshock experiences, in Mick Rock's cover photo for *Transformer*, Reed turned himself into a rock-and-roll Frankenstein.

In the photograph, the Lou Reed who had previously worn the black jeans, T-shirt, and rumpled corduroy jacket of a man uninterested in frills and stripped for heavy action, now appeared in the guise of a bisexual glitter rocker. Lou's face was painted with a mask of deathly white Pan-Cake, and he stared past the camera with haunted eyes underlined by black kohl. Black lipstick delineated his new Cupid's-bow mouth. His dyed jet-black hair was shaped in a stylish semi-Afro similar to Marc

Bolan's. Dressed from head to foot in a black jumpsuit, he also sported black nail polish. This powerful image so matched the era it was hijacked by Tim Curry, who put it to use in his starring role in the 1975 cult musical and film *The Rocky Horror Picture Show*. It would shortly lead Reed to the peak of his commercial career.

WHEN DENNIS KATZ AND THE PEOPLE AT RCA HEARD TRANSFORMER, THEY celebrated their decision to entrust Reed's future to David Bowie. Convinced it would be a success and even yield a hit single, they prepared the way for its release and a subsequent tour by the artist. The album, with the seminal cover photo by Mick Rock, came out in November 1972.

Transformer was an enormous success and opened up a new world for Lou Reed. "Both lyrically and musically, *Transformer* was less intellectual and more pop than Reed's work with the Velvet Underground," wrote Ellen Willis, who originally gave the album a poor review. "At first I thought it was disappointingly conventional, lacking in the Velvets' subtlety. That judgment turned out to be a joke on me; *Transformer* is easy to take as medicine that tastes like honey and kicks you in the throat. Take a song like 'Perfect Day,' a lovely, soft ode to an idyll in the park . . . or is it? But the album's deceptively ordinary surface had commercial appeal, which was no doubt part of the point."

To promote their hot new star, RCA came up with a clever label. They dubbed Lou Reed the Phantom of Rock. Ironically, this epithet underlined Lou's greatest weakness: He had fashioned himself in the image of what his English fans imagined he was—a sexy wolverine, homosexual junkie hustler, and advocate of S&M. However, Andy Warhol, a man with a telling eye for these things, pointed out, "When John Cale and Lou were in the Velvets, they really had style. But when Lou went solo, he got bad and was copying people." The figure he presented to the public didn't really exist.

Bowie had insisted that RCA release "Walk on the Wild Side" as a single—against Lou's wishes. Reed was sure it would be banned on the radio and didn't want to repeat the pattern of media neglect he had experienced with the great Velvets albums that were never heard on the radio. Fortunately, Lou relented, and as the record company predicted, the single began to climb the charts, peaking at no. 16 on the U.S. charts in late winter of 1973.

However, somewhat to Reed's chagrin, both in the U.K. and the U.S. the Bowie-Ronson influence was given more credit than Lou for the success of the work. "Thanks to their intelligence and taste," Tim Jurgens wrote in *Fusion,* "Lou Reed has found the perfect accompaniment to such flights of fancy that he's been lacking since John Cale went his own way." And the *Village Voice* noted that "you can cut the atmosphere surrounding each song with a knife . . . and the clue to this album's appeal lies in . . . a mix that has a chance of startling the listener and touching our common humanity."

The album rode the wave of gay liberation and the sexual awakening of the early seventies, so Lou became a mascot of the burgeoning gay community. "What I've always thought is that I'm doing rock and roll in drag," he stated. "If you just listen to the songs cursorily, they come off like rock and roll, but if you really pay attention, then they are in a way the quintessence of the rock-and-roll song, except they're not rock and roll."

Referring to another song, "Make Up," he commented, "The gay life at the moment is not that great. I wanted to write a song which made it terrific, something that you'd enjoy. But I know if I do that, I'll be accused of being a fag; but that's all right, it doesn't matter. I like those people, and I don't like what's going down, and I wanted to make it happy."

Not everyone bought this new act quite so unquestioningly. When *Transformer* was released in the U.S., Lisa Robinson got everybody in her writers' collective to give it a negative review. "As long as he played ball with Lisa and Richard, everybody supported him," recalled Henry Edwards. "But if you pull the reviews of *Transformer,* you have a little story, because she single-handedly turned the press against him. And she got everyone to pan his album, including me. And that's a good story, I think. No one thought at that moment he had a future. Everyone thought that he was a pop artifact to be manipulated—he was almost a golden oldie in a very short period of time. And he was desperate. . . . I do feel guilty about writing a bad review of his album for the *Times.* I did what everybody else did—we fucked the album."

"What's the matter with Lou Reed? *Transformer* is terrible—lame,

---

pseudodecadent lyrics, lame, pseudo-something-or-other-singing, and a just plain lame band," wrote Ellen Willis in *The New Yorker*. "Part of Reed's problem is that he needs a band he can interact with, a band that will give him some direction, as the Velvets did, instead of simply backing him up—in other words, not just a band but a group."

Andy Warhol was quick to realize that "Walk on the Wild Side" was the single strongest piece of publicity he could use for his trilogy of films starring various drag queens and Joe Dallesandro—*Flesh, Heat,* and *Trash.* "Walk on the Wild Side," would become the no. 1 jukebox hit in America in 1973, and every time it played in a restaurant or bar or came wafting out of an apartment or car, it reminded everybody that Warhol's movies were playing nearby. Warhol was happy about that, but it reminded him that Lou had now twice tapped into the Factory for material—where was the money Lou owed him from the first album? Thus, while embracing Lou publicly in his democracy of success, Andy harbored a hard-boiled resentment.

LOU WAS TRAVELING TOO FAST TO NOTICE. THE YEAR 1973 PROVED A momentous one in Reed's professional and personal life. As *Transformer* sales mounted—it would take six months to peak—Dennis Katz and the RCA machine swung into action, sending Lou out on a seemingly endless tour that winter. In January, at his first New York solo show at Alice Tully Hall, wearing black leather jeans and jacket, he was, by all accounts, electrifying.

In February, to everyone's surprise, the sexually ambiguous Reed, who thought of himself as a knight, who believed in pretty princesses and sparrows, married the woman another part of him looked upon as a Stepford wife. It was, he would later say, a pessimistic act. David Bowie was married, Mick Jagger was married. Maybe, Lou figured, it was the hip thing to do. "Yes, he's got the princess; she's Jewish, she likes making homey things," noted one skeptical friend. "He needed a companion tucked away to be there when he needed them, but Bettye really didn't understand him *at all.* He needed a person he could joust with, and ultimately Bettye really couldn't play the game. She'd be very boring. That's why he always ended up hitting her. He would never hit anybody who would smack him back."

Katz soon added to Reed's team his assistant Barbara Falk, who would be Lou's road manager through the midseventies and the indispensable member of his support team. In those days it was unusual for a woman to have such a powerful role, and Barbara suffered from both the macho businessmen who ran the rock-concert scene and Lou's wife, who was understandably jealous of another woman usurping her role as Lou's baby-sitter. However, Barbara Falk, who possessed seemingly unlimited energy and a tough sense of humor, found herself enjoying the wild ride that was Lou's life in those intense, successful years.

In 1973, Lou and his band played three to five concerts a week, for fees ranging from $6,000 to $7,000. Dennis Katz took 20 percent off the top. William Morris took 10 percent off the top. Barbara Falk, who collected and distributed the money, recalled that she was paying twelve people per diems of $100 per week: "There must have been money owed—rehearsal money to be paid. Guitars. It never seemed to me that there was enough. I used to do these budgets. There were as many expenses as there were receipts, and then some. Rent-a-cars or limos, hotels. In Europe and Asia, sometimes the promoter would pay hotels and cars; in Australia, we would get maybe $5,000 a gig. They paid flights. I never got paid all my salary. Then there was the accountant and the IRS. The accountant dealt with them; we never put money aside for them. And Lou could spend a lot on the road. I was doling it out, very petty cash. He'd come up to me with his hand full of receipts. I used to have Lou sign things like, 'Before money is paid to Lou, such and such amounts must be paid to Trans-former, Inc.' He read what was written and he could usually quote it back to me. I remember thinking of Lou that it was so sad that here was this guy with records and fans and all this, and he was living in this little sublet of a place with rented furniture. . . . And coffee ice cream."

To begin with, she genuinely adored Lou, who had a great sense of humor. He joked a lot. With a gift for mimicry, he would make fun of politicians, audiences, promoters, record-company people, and deejays. All were targets. She also quickly learned to get along with and respect Bettye, who was so obviously devoted to Lou. *Transformer* kept them pinned to the road for the next four months. By March 1973, Lou had reached a peak of success with his barnstorming tours turning into chaotic rock events. Although he had never possessed the charisma of Bowie or Jagger, Reed played a great rock-and-roll show. Above all, despite the chaos, the pressures, and the tight budgets, they all managed for the most part to have fun.

During one performance at Buffalo on March 24, Reed was bitten on the bum by a fan screaming, "Leather!" "America seems to breed real animals," Lou said afterward, laughing.

"The glitter people know where I'm at, the gay people know where I'm at," he explained. "I make songs up for them; I was doing things like that in '66 except people were a lot more uptight then." Barbara's favorite memory of the *Transformer* tour was Lou's being arrested onstage in Miami for singing "sucking on my ding-dong" while tapping the helmets of the policemen guarding the front of the stage with his microphone. As Lou was led away by a big cop with a serious expression intoning, "This man is going to jail," Lou could barely control his hysterical laughter.

The zenith of Lou's commercial success came between April and June of 1973 when *Transformer* and its single "Walk on the Wild Side" peaked, first in the U.S., then on the U.K. charts. Lou Reed was finally a pop star, but as the initial excitement of success waned, Reed considered the cost of stardom. Ever since *Transformer*, Lou's audiences had come to expect the "Son of Andy Warhol," a manufactured cartoon character Reed had never been comfortable with, but had nonetheless used to resurrect his flagging career. He was trapped in the Bowie-inspired Phantom persona, and much of his celebrity was tempered by comparisons between the two.

"It did what it was supposed to," stated the Phantom of Rock. "Like I say, I wanted to get popular so I could be the biggest schlock around, and I turned out really big schlock, because my shit's better than other people's diamonds. But it's really boring being the best show in town. I took it as far as I could possibly go and then o-u-t."

Chapter Twelve

NO SURFACE,
NO DEPTH

FROM BERLIN TO ROCK 'N' ROLL

ANIMAL: 1973–74

> *God isn't a Christian or a Muslim. He's the victim of cult*
> *followings. He's a bit like Lou Reed.*
>
> —Karl Wallinger, World Party

BY THE SPRING OF '73, REED KNEW THE GLITTER-ROCK SCENE WAS FADING.
And by now, his marriage to Bettye was collapsing.

The pressure of pioneering rock madness plunged Lou's marriage to the
abyss. By Reed's impossibly high standards, his wife had failed him mis-
erably. She did not understand him and she could not keep up with him.
She simply was not of his caliber, and he grew bored with her. "For a
while," one friend thought, "the nuptial plan had seemed like self-
preservation, but Lou had come to see it as a dreadful trap. The girl was
trying to housebreak him!" Cornered in a relationship he wanted to
slough off, Lou took to slapping her around in a fifties style. Lou's surly,
uncomfortable, distinctly uptight manner was a creation of the times—
the changing American male—that he shared, for example, with Sam
Shepard and Bob Dylan. He even flaunted his misogyny, despite the fact
that hitting women was not endorsed by Andy Warhol. "My old lady was
a real asshole," he rasped to one astonished interviewer. "But I needed a
female asshole around to bolster me up; I needed a sycophant who I could
bounce around, and she fitted the bill. . . . But she called it 'love,' ha!"

Years later, when Bettye was contentedly married with children, she
confessed that she could not understand how she got so deeply involved
with someone like Lou. But at the time, she was too young to have a

secure sense of herself in relation to her increasingly wild husband. She grew confused and despondent. Lou, who wore her tortured life like a badge of courage, bragged, "She tried to commit suicide in a bathtub in the hotel. It was someone standing there holding a razor blade. She looks like she might kill you, but instead she starts cutting away at her wrists and there's blood everywhere. . . .

"She lived," he complained, "but we had to have a roadie there with her from then on."

Lou responded to the disintegration and chaos with great material. In 1973, "Walk on the Wild Side" placed Reed among the top-selling artists on the lucrative rock-music scene, competing with "Frankestein" (the Edgar Winter Group), "Midnight Train to Georgia" (Gladys Knight), "Angie" (the Rolling Stones), and "Love Train" (the O'Jays) as the most popular single of the year. Lou knew that after a hit single his best move would have been to, as he put it, hand them down a boogie album. Common business sense would have told Lou to solidify his foothold in the rock field by making another record that sounded like *Transformer* and continuing to tour. Lou, however, chose to duck back inside the studio and record a depressing album about Bettye that would destroy his commercial credibility.

In ten songs, *Berlin* dramatized the breakdown of his marriage with Bettye by telling the story of two American drug addicts living in Berlin. Each song tore away another bandage from the mummy of Lou Reed. He challenged his audience to wonder how it felt to stay awake for five days on speed and booze, lonely, cold, miserable, but terrified of going to sleep because you could not stand to encounter yourself in the world of your dreams. The song sequence that eventually became *Berlin* revealed a darker, more introspective side of Lou than had his first two solo albums. "It was an adult album meant for adults—by adults for adults," Reed explained later. "I had to do *Berlin*," he insisted. "If I hadn't done it, I'd have gone crazy." Lou's management team and friends were against taking this direction. Lou's writing had never been better. He was taking, Lou explained, "the approach you would use in poetry. Instead of making a division between pop songs and a real story or a real poem, merging them so the separation didn't exist anymore. The fun I had in trying to write a really good short story or poem wasn't separate from writing a song. I put the two together and then I had the whole thing going on at once."

Much to the consternation of the RCA executives Reed also cut David

Bowie, along with his glitter-rock overtones, out of the equation. Reed and Bowie had put much distance between each other by the fall of 1972. As the media continued to compare them even after Lou's North American tour, Reed started to criticize and even insult Bowie by way of escaping the stigma of dependency. Each star hinted in the press that the other was exploiting the relationship. Bowie, for example, insinuated that Lou was borrowing too much of his identity: "I'm a ball of confusion, mentally, physically. Everything about me is confused, and Lou is very much the same way." Lou retaliated, calling David in *Circus* magazine "a very nasty person, actually."

To gain artistic control of the project, once again Reed entered into a Faustian agreement with RCA that would undermine the first half of the seventies for him. "Convincing the record company to finance the project was not easy," Reed recalled. "There was this big fight with RCA. I talked them into the veracity of the whole thing, of how astute it would be to follow up 'Walk on the Wild Side' with not just another hit single, but with a magnificent whatever. So I shoved it through." In exchange for being allowed to make this tortured and poetic album exactly as he wanted it, Reed promised to deliver two commercial products to RCA— one live and one studio album in the style of *Transformer*.

Fortunately, since Lou was at his commercial peak, all the doors in the rock world were open to him, particularly those of the new generation. After Bowie, Reed, and Iggy Pop, the most striking player on the scene was Alice Cooper. His comic-book translations of Reed's themes, combined with inventive management, had turned him into the biggest-selling rock star of the early seventies. Lou hated Alice and attacked him with the same vituperative humor he had directed at Zappa. This did not, however, stop him from hiring Alice's whiz kid twenty-four-year-old producer, Bob Ezrin, responsible for Cooper's classic hit albums *Love It to Death, Killer, School's Out,* and *Billion Dollar Babies*.

In April, Reed and Ezrin flew to London. The city was crackling with rock energy, and Lou, who had received more votes than Mick Jagger in a recent British music fans' popularity poll, had the rock world at his feet. But, rather than continuing with Phantom of Rock posturing and ego trips, Reed committed himself solely to getting his artistic self-portrait down on vinyl. According to Reed, Ezrin suggested Lou weave the songs into "a film for the ear" (as the album was eventually marketed), building them around movie images. Having their pick of musicians, Reed and Ezrin put together Lou's best recording band since the early Velvets. On bass, Jack Bruce; on keyboards, Steve Winwood; on guitars, two top-flight Detroit players who had worked with Ezrin on Cooper's records, Steve Hunter and Dick Wagner; B. J. Wilson, of the psychedelic band Procol Harum, played drums on two tracks before being replaced by the blues-based Aynsley Dunbar.

As he started burrowing into the dark tunnel of some of his greatest compositions, the harder, colder Reed emerged. What made Lou's work stand out was that despite portraying himself as a basket case, he was also portraying himself as a pioneer of pain, who was willing to take risks in order to bring back the pictures of his life. Like Warhol, he showed an extreme fascination with suicide; yet he claimed that he would never consider it: "It's so easy a way—the actual process. I mean, I've seen so many people like that. You either do it or you don't. And I know where I want to go. I'm in control. I know that there's this level and then there's this level. And I've seen over that level and I'm not even going to go near it. Ever. I'm in control, that's for sure."

Finding Lou's enthusiasm infectious, the studio musicians took the recording as seriously as Reed did. Jack Bruce read the song lyrics (many musicians do not bother to do this), and constructed an empathetic musical part. "Jack Bruce," Lou recalled, "wasn't supposed to be on the whole thing, but he went through the whole trip because he liked it a lot."

According to at least one musician, though, Lou was far from being in control at the *Berlin* recording sessions. Blue Weaver recounted how Lou was brought into the studio to record the vocal track over the instruments. "He couldn't do it straight, he had to go down to the bar and then have a snort of this or that, and then they'd prop him up in a chair and let him start singing. It was supposed to be great, but something went wrong somewhere."

"Blue Weaver is an asshole," Lou riposted. "He's a schmuck, a fucking ass. Blue Weaver ought to keep his fucking mouth shut, because he can't fucking play." But in fact Lou had such difficulty laying down the vocal tracks that he finally had to overdub them later in New York. "We killed ourselves psychologically on that album," he admitted. "We went so far into it that it was kinda hard to get out. It was a very painful album to make. And only me and Bobby really knew what we had there, what it did to us." What it did to Reed and Ezrin was leave them strung out and exhausted. Ezrin relied on heroin, which was cheap, strong, and easily available in London, to get him through. "I didn't know what heroin was until I went to England on this gig," he explained later. "We were all seriously ill. I would rather have had a nervous breakdown."

After the recording sessions, Dennis Katz spirited Lou off to Portugal for a much needed respite. They were joined by two friends from Amsterdam, with whom, according to friends, Lou had a tryst. In a postcard to Barbara Falk in New York, Lou wrote that both he and Portugal were divine, signing off, "Ha! Ha!"

Reed and Ezrin had planned *Berlin* as a double album with a gatefold sleeve and a booklet inside consisting of "film stills" of the story and lyrics. One week before Ezrin was due to deliver the final mix to RCA, he was informed that the RCA executives would not accept a double album because they didn't think the product merited that kind of outlay. RCA's turnaround left Bob Ezrin with the excruciating job of snipping fourteen minutes off the opus. He couldn't help but feel that the beautifully constructed work had been butchered. Lou recalled that "when Bobby Ezrin gave me the master, he said, 'Don't even listen to it, just put it in a drawer.' He went back to Canada and flipped out."

With his last words, "Awright, wrap up this turkey before I puke," Ezrin checked into a hospital suffering withdrawal from both the intensity of the project and heroin. However, according to a close friend, Bob's collapse had as much to do with rebounding from the intense involvement with Lou as it did with heroin: "Bob played the wrong game with Lou—he tried to be brilliant, to be his match. The only way to survive is to be the best you can and care for him deeply and hope that nothing goes horribly wrong. Nobody could ever be as brilliant as Lou."

Whatever the emotional cost, Lou had recorded the most moving, beautiful music of his career. It treated love, loss, betrayal, bitterness, and redemption in a more sophisticated manner than any other rock music. With *Berlin*, Lou expanded the borders of his métier, making something that would best be described as Lou Reed music.

RCA released *Berlin* that July in the U.K., Reed's strongest market, and he flew to London for the release. While there, he attended David Bowie's retirement party at the Cafe Royale. According to Tony Zanetta, "Lou and David were ships in the night. David's attention span is short.

And it was an intense period in his career. The party was part of the promotion. We flew Don Pennebaker over to film at the Hammersmith Odeon. And we planned this party at the Cafe Royale and invited every celebrity we could think of—and a lot of them came. The famous result was Mick Rock's picture of Lou, Mick Jagger, and David. But David didn't have a social scene. Maybe they had a chummy reunion that night, but that was the extent of it."

Berlin was released in the U.S. in September. Though the album was Reed's first solo masterpiece, at the time *Berlin* drew predominantly negative reviews, of which "the worst album by a major artist in 1973" was one of the more restrained. *Rolling Stone* pronounced it "a disaster." Another critic lamented, "I have difficulty caring about Reed's maladjustment," while Bruce Malamut considered it "the most naked exorcism of manic depression ever to be committed to vinyl." David Downing wrote in *Future Rock* that it contained "no hope. . . . [The protagonists] stare straight into each other's eyes and find only emptiness." And Roger Klorese regretted the range of Lou's vocals, "which sound, typically, like the heat-howl of the dying otter."

However, some more introspective writers recognized the spirit of Lou's genius. "Like most of the current crop of singer-writer-players, Reed suffers from the handicaps of having a poor voice, little singing ability, and even less instrumental technique," wrote the leading rock critic in the States, Albert Goldman. "His compositions are monotonously monochromatic, being, like most songs of the new rock theater, mere background music. But he does have the knack of twisting into sharp focus the imaginative substance of the current mania, which increasingly resembles the Berlin cabaret scene of the twenties."

"*Berlin* was full of insights you'd just as soon not have into the painful nuances of the war between the sexes," added Ellen Willis. "It was not on any level easy to take, and it was not popular. The metaphor of the divided city (which would be picked up by seventies rock-and-rollers from David Bowie to Johnny Rotten), and a loose narrative line, provided the framework for a stark record of emotional destruction closer in tone and spirit to the Velvets' first album than anything Reed had done since."

While being a token outlaw in the media, Lou could also be easily hurt. *Berlin*'s critical rejection twisted him into knots of Warholian resentment. During this period Lou maintained a fixed, sinister glare in public and rarely smiled. In interviews he developed his hard-line stance with rock journalists. His speech was abrupt, evasive. "Who cares about critics?" he snapped at one reporter. Another writer observed, "When he talks, he's polite but distant, never allowing those with him the privilege of feeling quite comfortable in his presence. He also enjoyed drinking particularly fearsome alcoholic concoctions and forcing writers to partake with him." To friends, however, Lou cried out, "Can you think of another rock star who inspires such hatred?" Some thought *Berlin* marked the major turning point in his solo career.

In his defense, Reed claimed, "Before *Berlin* came out, *Rolling Stone* said it was going to be the *Sgt. Pepper* of the seventies, and afterward they wrote a pan and then they had a huge article criticizing the pan. It won all kinds of awards . . . it won the Thomas Edison award in Holland, and the best album of the year in *Stereo* and *Hi-Fi*. So critically it did not get panned, not in my book. Not unless you look at some jerk-off magazine, a tit-and-ass magazine disguised as some junior hippie kind of thing. But outside of those morons—who are illiterate little savages anyway—it did really well.

"If the people don't like *Berlin,* it's because it's too real!" Reed continued. "It's not like a TV program where all the bad things that happen to people are tolerable. Life isn't like that. And neither is the album."

In an eloquent defense of the record in *Rolling Stone,* Timothy Ferris shot back at Reed's critics, noting, "Stephen Davis, writing in this magazine, characterized the record as 'a distorted and degenerate demimonde of paranoia, schizophrenia, degradation, pill-induced violence, and suicide.' Which it is. But I fail to see how that makes a bad record. *Berlin* is bitter, uncompromising, and one of the most fully realized concept albums. Prettiness has nothing to do with art, nor does good taste, good manners, or good morals. Reed is one of the handful of serious artists working in popular music today, and you'd think by now people would stop preaching at him."

In one of the few but important perceptive reviews, John Rockwell in the *New York Times* pinned both the dramatic, filmlike quality of the piece and its complex sexual overtones as impressive departures:

"The backings are clothed in rock dress, but the form is more operatic and cinematic than strictly musical in the traditional pop sense, and the sentiments are entirely personal. While others prance and play at provoking an aura of sexual aberrance, Reed is coldly real. *Berlin* is a typically dreamlike saga of a sadomasochistic love affair in contemporary Berlin. But the contemporary is enriched by a subtle acknowledgement of Brecht and Weill, and the potential sensationalism of the subject is calmly defused by a sort of hopeless matter-of-factness. It is strikingly and unexpectedly one of the strongest, most original rock records in years."

Berlin stalled at no. 98 on the U.S. charts. "The record sales, compared to *Transformer,* were a disaster for a normal person, but for me it was a total disaster," Reed explained. "The record company did a quick scurry round like little bunnies, but I went somnambulant. It wasn't brain rot like some people think. I just kinda did no more."

Lou's response to the criticism was so intense that it affected every major event in his career from 1973 to 1975. Realizing this in a moment of lucidity and honesty while performing in front of a packed audience, Lou announced, "*Berlin* was a big flop, and it made me very sad. The way that album was overlooked was probably the biggest disappointment I ever faced. I pulled the blinds shut at that point. And they've remained closed."

"I think Lou's power probably ended after *Berlin,*" opined one friend during the second half of 1973. "He had poetry and he had something to say and he said it and then he was finished saying it. It was an extraordinary moment, but he never went beyond it."

Despite negative reviews of *Berlin* in the U.S., Lou was still riding high on the wave of publicity surrounding that album and *Transformer,* and he was thrilled to scale his ambitious heights further when he came up with the ideal name for his midseventies persona—the Rock-'n'-Roll Animal. It fit him like a skin.

In August 1973, Lou and a new band moved up to Stockbridge, Massachusetts, and set about to rehearse for a tour in support of *Berlin.* "They rented a set of rooms at the Music Inn," Jim Jacobs, who would design and run the stage throughout the epic tour, remembered fondly. "He was drug-induced all the time. He hated rehearsing. He resented everyone and everything. He's not a nice guy and he can't help himself."

During the rehearsals Reed drunkenly stumbled around the stage, smashing microphones and barking at the road crew. Acting as if he didn't give a shit about the endeavor, he fomented strife among his musicians, staff, management, and friends at every opportunity. "Lou's very good theatrically," recalled one observer. "He's very good at staging. He was always a great director. I noticed on several occasions he would be in the middle of a situation, and without saying anything, or really doing anything, he had everyone around him fighting. He started some big chaos or commotion. And unless you were watching very, very carefully or from a distance, you would never have known that he was responsible for it."

The European tour had twelve scheduled dates in Paris, Copenhagen, Amsterdam, Brussels, and a handful of cities in the U.K. Despite receiving a plethora of bland or puzzled reviews and going down in rock history as a commercial disaster, Berlin did well in Britain, rising to no. 7 on the album charts by November and winning Lou a silver record. This rating was particularly good, considering that Transformer was still on the charts. Reed thought of Berlin as his version of Hamlet and dubbed himself "the Hamlet of Electricity." The comparison applied to the European dates on the 1973 Berlin tour, which Lou and his team called the Rock-'n'-Roll Animal tour.

Reed and his entourage flew into Europe and then drove from country to country. On the tour, the ecstatic but exhausted Lou, skirting drug and alcohol madness after touring continually for over a year and a half, played Hamlet to his royal-size entourage of twenty-three. Bettye, who was still holding on by her fingernails, was cast in the dual role of Ophelia and Gertrude. Dennis, who was beginning to look and sound to Lou like his parents, played Claudius; and the two young men who were hired to simultaneously run the lights and act as his bodyguards, Jim Jacobs and his partner, Bernie Gelb, became Lou's Rosencrantz and Guildenstern.

They played a different city every night, often driving on to the next venue after a show. Before going on tour, Lou had gone to see Andy Warhol at the Factory to ask advice on how to do the lights for the shows with a limited budget. Warhol advised Lou to use the stark, raw lighting Albert Speer designed for Adolf Hitler's speeches: intense white spotlights against a black background, setting the whole spectacle in high contrast. "I've seen Lou perform over the years, and that was close to the top of his performance peak, his stage personality," Gelb summed up. "He had it all together. Europe was just incredible. The whole tour was sold-out. On the European tour the lighting design involved a black stage and, for the most part, straight white spots right in Lou's face. He was the center of the

Lewis Reed, seventeen, 1959. "I don't have a personality."

Creedmore State Mental hospital. (*Victor Bockris*)

The house in Brooklyn where Lou was born. (*Victor Bockris*)

Reed playing in one of his high school bands, the C.H.D., or backward, Dry Hump Club.

Reed playing in his Syracuse college band, L.A. and the Eldorados, with Richard Mishkin (left). *(Archives Malanga)*

Where Lou spent his troubled teen years in Freeport. *(Victor Bockris)*

Film frame enlargement
from *Screen Tests* by Gerard
Malanga and Andy Warhol.
(Archives Malanga)

Lou Reed
performing in
the Parapher-
nalia footage
of Gerard
Malanga's
*Film Note-
books*, 1966.
*(Archives
Malanga)*

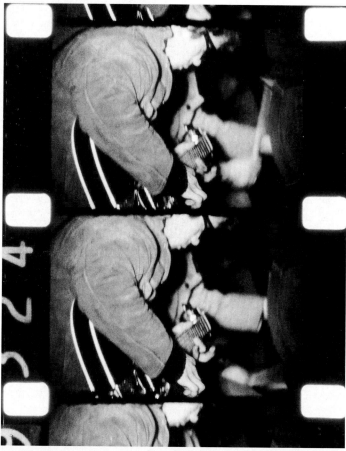

The E.P.I. core group in 1966 at the Castle, Los Angeles. From left to right: Andy Warhol, Nico, Danny Williams, Sterling Morrison, Mary Woronov, Paul Morrissey, Lou Reed, John Cale. In front: Maureen "Moe" Tucker. Kneeling: Gerard Malanga. *(Archives Malanga)*

Lou at *Loaded* sessions, 1970. *(Jim Cummins/Star File)*

Mickey Ruskin visiting Lou Reed and Barbara Falk prior to Lou's concert at the Music Inn, Lennox, in the Massachusetts Berkshires where Mickey maintained a country home. Summer, 1973. *(Gerard Malanga)*

Bettye and Lou in Florida, 1973. *(Barbara Wilkinson)*

Lou performing in New York, December, 1973. *(Chuck Pulin)*

Lou with Barbara Hodes
in New York, 1974.
(*Bob Gruen*)

Danny Fields with Rachel and Lou
in New York, 1976. (*Bob Gruen*)

Richard Robinson and Lisa
Robinson with Lou Reed in
New York, 1976. *(Bob Gruen)*

John Cale, Lou Reed, Patti
Smith, and David Byrne on
stage at the Ocean Club, 1976.
(Bob Gruen)

Lou Reed with Diana Ross and
Clive Davis, 1976. *(Bob Gruen)*

Andy Warhol holding a Lou Reed cornflakes box by Bobby Grossman. *(Bobby Grossman)*

William Burroughs and Lou Reed at Burroughs Bunker in New York, 1979. *(Victor Bockris)*

Left to right: Toby and Sidney Reed, Sylvia Morales, Mr. and Mrs. Morales, and Lou gesturing to and looking directly at his father during his wedding, to which Andy Warhol was not invited. New York, 1980. (*Roberta Bayley*)

Bob Quine, the guitar player who would pick Lou up, dust him off, and start him all over again in the early 1980s, particularly on *The Blue Mask*. (*Marcia Resnick*)

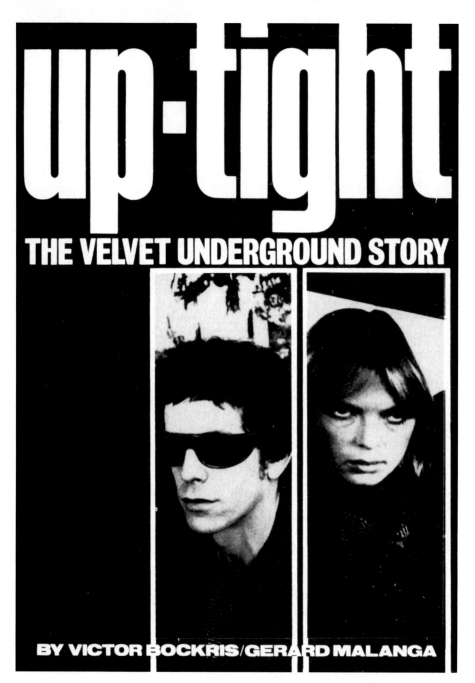

up-tight
THE VELVET UNDERGROUND STORY

BY VICTOR BOCKRIS/GERARD MALANGA

The cover of *Up-tight,* the book about the Velvet Underground that played a role in bringing them back into prominence again, published in England in 1983.

Sylvia Reed and Lou
Reed outside the church
after Andy Warhol's
memorial service,
1987. (*Bob Gruen*)

Lou Reed at the
time of the release
of *New York*, 1989.
(*Bob Gruen*)

Lou Reed at the photo session for *Between Thought and Expression*, 1991. *(Keith Miller)*

Lou playing at the opening of the Robert Mapplethorpe Room at the Guggenheim Museum in New York, 1993. *(Bob Gruen)*

Lou on the *Magic and Loss* tour in Holland, 1992. *(Marijn Van Rij)*

STING, STIPE & *MARR*??
Well, what *is* the ultimate Dream Team?

'So happy to be back'

THE VELVET UNDERGROUND
The VOX Interview & rare pictures

Shock
result of our
CD prices
survey • p7

eenage Fanclub • Dina Carroll • David Crosby
d Fripp • OMD • FILM INTERVIEW Michael Douglas

Cover of *Vox* magazine, 1993.

illumination on the stage, and anything else you saw was reflected light. There were some other small colored effects, but basically the band on that tour wore all black and stood at the back of the stage and Lou was front and center with the lights shining on him."

Lou spent most of his time with Jim Jacobs and Bernie Gelb, who took possessive care of him. Jim immediately connected with Lou, finding him wonderful to be with, bright and witty. "I thought that he was a first-rate intellect and a qualified and very fine American poet," Jacobs recalled. "I enjoyed listening to his music every night, because he was so crazy and so out of tune all the time. Lou really preceded punk rock by ten years. He was also very ambitious. And I cared about him." Gelb had similarly strong feelings for his charge: "I carried Lou offstage, I walked him to his dressing room and got him to the shows and I drove his car. Lou and Jim and I traveled separately from the band. And thus there was some jealousy from the other members of the entourage. But we were having a good time."

Uncharacteristically, Lou paid little attention to what was going on around him. Spending his time sleeping in the car, he allowed everything to be done for him. "He had no control and he didn't want it," said Gelb. "He was totally uninterested. He just wanted to show up, he wasn't interested in the opening act, didn't want to sit around too long before or after the gig. I think by the time we got to Europe we didn't even use him for sound checks. Lou would just show up, walk on, do the set, and split. Then he'd chill out and get in the car and go back to the hotel. He never asked a question or got involved with anything and was very cooperative. He did whatever we asked him."

Reed painted his face a stark white, blackened his lips, eyes, and hair, donned a black-on-black costume, and employed a number of props such as sunglasses and a leather jacket. His jerky, stumbling movements were combined with a catalog of rock clichés borrowed from classic performers like Jagger, Bowie, and Iggy Pop.

The three-week European tour met with universal success thanks, to a degree, to the supercharged band, led by the guitarists Steve Hunter and Dick Wagner. Their twin guitar riffs gave Lou's music a heavy-metal sound it had not had before and perfectly encased the Rock-'n'-Roll Animal onstage. Many Reed classics, such as "Sweet Jane," "Rock & Roll," "Waiting for the Man," and "Heroin," became current again.

"The band cooked," Gelb agreed. "They were fabulous. When I say Lou wasn't in control and he didn't pay attention to the details, that was true for everything except for onstage." Every show was sold-out, and the crush of fans caused riots.

The consensus was that Lou's shows were either brilliant or terrible, depending on how stoned he was. When he was on, he moved effortlessly from song to song like a spellbinding spinner of tales performing in sha-manistic ritual. When he was off, he had no rhythm, no flow. One moment he would be standing stock-still at the microphone, and the next he'd careen across the stage on a collision course with the amplifiers. Often he stuttered and stopped. The more outrageous Reed became on-stage, the more the audience applauded him. One Dutch journalist who interviewed Lou a number of times in the 1970s, Bert van der Kamp, commented, "There were people in awe of him, and he would act the part. He could hardly stand on his feet and they had to push him out onstage. People were very fascinated by this over here."

When the tour reached Paris, Bettye emerged briefly from the back-ground to play out her final tragic scene. During the first part of the European tour her presence was subdued, she still made a desperate over-ture to Lou; which roused him to a final act of cutting her off. Gelb, with Jacobs, steadfastly ignored Bettye, giving total allegiance to Lou. But even Gelb was surprised how quickly and irrevocably Lou turned on her: "Bettye made it a third of the way through, but then I saw the day he turned on her. It was in Paris. Nico came to visit. He turned on Bettye and the next day she was a nobody, a stranger to him. He had the ability to turn on you so completely and quickly as if he was turning it on and off. It was amazing. I have never seen anyone else cut someone out of their life so efficiently."

"I think the sexual thing was not important to Lou," Jacobs com-mented. "It wasn't the real issue. He didn't want anyone else to be getting sex, but it was more like not getting his fair share. I don't think he really cared."

In Paris they played the Odeon. "By then Lou could barely show up to the concert," Jacobs reported. "You just never knew if he was going to trip on the stage. He's not athletic, he's uncomfortable."

Gelb maintained a good record of keeping the fans away from Reed, who hated to be touched by them. "Only one fan was able to get to him on the whole tour," Gelb recalled proudly. "That was in Paris. One crazy young girl who jumped onstage and wrapped her arms around Lou. I got to her three seconds after she got to Lou. I grabbed her, pulled her offstage, ripped her shirt off in the process, and threw her out in the back alley topless and slammed the door."

In Amsterdam, Lou renewed his relationship with a man with whom he shared a number of interests. "One night in Amsterdam was the only night on the tour that he managed to get away from us," said Gelb. "He went out with this guy who was a speed freak."

"He would do any drug that was available," said Jacobs. "Coke, speed, pot, quaaludes, and a lot of booze. Speed and booze were his favorite drugs. He shot a lot of speed." The aftermath of this particularly wild night, however, threatened the next tour date in Brussels. Although Gelb and Jacobs managed to locate and transport Reed to the theater, his physical health and state of mind were significantly compromised. Jacobs recalled, "They stayed up all night doing really awful speed. The next day Lou was in the worst mood I had ever seen him in my life, and that's truly an awful thing to say. I had to dress him. I finally got all of his clothes on. We played some games together and I finally got him into a better mood. His time came and I literally shoved him onstage. He could barely walk, he stumbled around and sang, and this audience just loved him."

Unfortunately, drugs were just part of the problem during the stop in Brussels. "At one point he did some very odd maneuver and his leather pants ripped up the center," Jacobs recalled. "He wasn't wearing any underwear and he was standing onstage with his balls hanging out. Bernie ran out onto the stage with some silver gaffer tape and taped him right around the crotch. Lou was so pissed because this tape was around his balls. He sang one more song and he left."

"We didn't know, but just before he went onstage one night in Brussels, he did a massive dose of meth," Gelb added. "About a half hour into the show he started going into spasms, tachycardia, and he came over to the side of the stage and he said, 'Get me off the stage.' So I told everyone to shut it down. Then I picked him up over my shoulder and carried him up to the dressing room and locked the door. I laid him down and managed to bring him down to a state where I wasn't afraid he was going to die. And he was really fucked up. It was one of those things where he was saying, 'Don't let anyone see me, I can't talk to anyone. Don't let anyone in the room.' When I felt comfortable enough that he wasn't going to die, I stood outside the door for the next hour telling Dennis Katz, 'Yes, I understand you are his manager, but he doesn't want to see you now.' "

"And he would not do an encore," said Jacobs. "They destroyed the theater. They ripped the seats up and they threw everything at the stage and they even loved that! Because he was being such a bad boy."

Realizing that Lou was seriously endangering his health and thereby compromising the tour, and that he was losing touch with his meal ticket, Dennis Katz, who seldom joined the touring, once more assigned his most trusted assistant, Barbara Falk, to the task of tour manager and Lou baby-sitter. This relationship would last through the most hard-core mid-seventies touring and would become one of the most significant of Reed's professional life. "Lou was getting more and more difficult to handle," recalled Barbara Falk, who had known and worked with Lou for some time. "You could never get enough for Lou. And Dennis wasn't perfect either. He didn't do what Lou thought he should do. Lou resented the fact that Dennis didn't show up. Every once in a while Dennis would have to come to a gig somewhere, but he wasn't there hovering, saying, 'What can I do, what can I do?' Actually, Lou didn't like it when he came to gigs. Because we had a routine, and I had to pamper him. The rider said, 'Johnnie Walker Black. Don't give to Lou Reed, give to Barbara Falk'— and I would dole out one drink before he went on. I had to practically carry him onto the stage. But when Dennis would come, he would be jolly hockey sticks and all of this stuff. And it grated—it didn't help. Lou thought they were on totally different wavelengths altogether.

"Lou was feeling more and more alienated—as if Dennis didn't care enough about him. Dennis was getting paid and we weren't. He had a Bentley and a this and that. And we owed everybody. Band members were always knocking at my door because they had family at home and they weren't getting paid. It was always borrow from Peter to pay Paul, and who can I put off the longest. But Dennis always got paid. And I think Lou started to resent that."

Actually, Dennis Katz was the least of Lou's worries. To maintain the ferocious pace of touring, he had resorted to a wide variety of pharmaceuticals. "He was like Lenny Bruce," recalled Falk, who was astounded by the extent of Lou's involvement with drugs. "He used to carry around all these medical books about speed. And go into libraries. And in Europe where you could get works in drugstores. He was carrying all this around. He also had an enormous sense of fun and wit and chumminess. But he was usually coming up, down, or sideways. We had this mother-son thing, but it was also like a twisted marriage. He thought it was cool to have a girl—they didn't have girls on the road back then. I used to have to carry him around. He was very light. I would drag him, behind the shades, through immigration; I could have sworn he was asleep a couple of times."

The combined efforts of Gelb, Jacobs, and Falk aided greatly in the struggle to keep Reed sober. The trio's greatest success, in fact, lay in convincing him to swear off booze for the bulk of the European tour. "At the beginning of the tour in the States he was drinking really heavily," Gelb remembered. "At shows, at rehearsals—always bottles of Scotch or bourbon hidden in the amps and the PA. And one day we put our foot down—he was smashing equipment, breaking things, being a jerk: the alcohol did terrible things to Lou—and somehow we convinced him. It seems incredible that he would agree to stop drinking, but it was necessary. We were ready to drop him. He's a real survivor. He had good sense. He partied, met friends, got high. But he didn't get drunk for the rest of the tour."

By the time the show found its way to Britain toward the end of the tour, Lou was relatively clean and the show had honed itself into an incredible performance. After the Brussels show he had learned his lesson, and the English tour, where they were doing a city a night, demanded everyone's undivided attention. "He drove the fans nuts," Bernie Gelb said. "The Liverpool show—Jesus, that was the hardest show I ever had to get out of. The fans surrounded the hall, and they were tough there: every time we tried to leave, they would throw rocks at us. We were pinned in the back alley, there was an IRA bomb threat. There were twenty steps up to the front of the building, and I ended up driving the car up the steps, slipping out the front, and driving back down the steps. It was like a movie, like driving on the stairs in Rome or something. It was really insane."

Audiences across the country reacted in much the same way, making it abundantly clear that Lou Reed had become a major solo rock-and-roll star. "Lou was the mascot of people who liked to get down and dirty," Jacobs noted. "It was very difficult with Lou. He was on speed at the time

and his sexual ambiguity was always difficult. You didn't know whether he
would get drunk and be with a man one night or get drunk and be with
. . . But it was always very exciting to be involved on that total level."

"Lou is brilliant," concluded Bernie Gelb. "He's as highly intelligent
as any musician I have ever met. He can talk about any subject you want
to talk about. But like all great stars, Lou had a great ego. At the end of
the day, for all the good times spent watching him operate, Lou just isn't
the nicest guy to ever walk the face of the earth. But he lived a very
dramatic lifestyle."

Reed's success in Europe, especially the U.K., where *Berlin* lingered in
the charts' Top Ten and *Transformer* remained a steady seller, may have
been obvious to the fans, but to many journalists and celebrities, including the icons of mainstream rock, the Rock-'n'-Roll Animal persona
relegated Lou to second-class status. Feeling that he had done his time in
the trenches and had been an extraordinary influence on younger bands,
Reed resented being eclipsed by rock stars of the stature of Bowie and
Jagger. "He never got over the idea that he wasn't Mick Jagger or he
wasn't David Bowie," said Jacobs. "He was always overshadowed because
they were better performers. Lou was not a good performer. He doesn't
have a good voice. What Lou has is a devoted following of people who
appreciate and love his work. When we got back to America, he was
really fighting with Dennis. We were pretty tight, we lived together
basically for that whole six-to-eight-week period, but then there was
nothing left for us. There wasn't anything to do, and I was saying good-
bye to Lou and he was saying good-bye to me. We just got tired of each
other. I got tired of taking his shit."

The Rock-'n'-Roll Animal tour continued playing across the U.S.
through the summer. As Lou's popularity soared, however, the aggression
of his audiences followed. The primarily male audience erupted at each
concert in chants of obscenities and endorsements ranging from "Lou
Reed motherfucker!" to "It's your life, cocksucker!"

Reed began to act out in an increasingly crazed manner. "He was
drinking so heavily again, he would go piss in the corner of the room and
just drive you crazy," recounted Barbara Falk. "He did it up against the
wall in some place in Canada. I think he pissed under the table one time
on drummer Prakash John's foot. And Prakash was fastidious."

"I know why you're all here," he yelled at a bunch of friends, fans, entourage members, fellow musicians, and journalists in a hotel bar late one night. "You just want to get the headline story 'Lou Reed OD's in Holiday Inn,' don't you?"

IN THE AUTUMN OF 1973, LOU FINALLY WORKED OUT A DIVORCE AGREE-ment with Bettye, with the help of Dennis Katz. "When they split up," recalled Barbara, "she talked to Dennis a lot. And Lou's assistant Ernie and I had to up and try to pack stuff up in the apartment. I don't remember if he had started doing speed then."

Everyone who had ever spent any time with Bettye knew of her sweetness and emotional generosity. But Lou, who had moved into a whole new realm of existence, had come to resent her. The marriage, he said, had "kept me off the streets. And that's when I really started gaining weight. Then one day it dawned on me that it was all like a movie, and the thing about movies is that if you don't like 'em, you can always walk out. And as soon as that became clear, it was all very simple. Now I don't get headaches anymore and I'm poorer."

Lou later complained to friends that no sooner had he started earning money than he started losing it. "Sometimes you're better off without anything," he said. "Make a fresh start." Looking for someone to blame for his financial problems, he found Bettye as the obvious target. "Everyone should have a divorce once, I can recommend it," he snapped sarcastically. The alimony payments forced him to leave his Upper East Side apartment and live temporarily in hotels.

As soon as Lou shed the skin of Bettye, he went into self-destructive overdrive. His first thought was to go back on speed again so he could lose some weight and wail once more. For a while he had the drug sent to him from Amsterdam. When he resumed his steady use of methamphetamine, his physical and mental breakdown accelerated. His speed habits got a boost after a chance meeting between Lou and his old Syracuse friend and Eldorado bandmate Richard Mishkin. Mishkin introduced him into a speed circle that centered on a man who would become a major influence on Lou in the 1970s, Ed Lister. "I remember when I introduced them, it was a Sunday morning and I drove him down to Ed's house," Mishkin recalled. "Lister was one weird motherfucker. He was the largest user of speed that I had ever encountered. He would use needles meant for horses, deep-vein stuff so that he could get more in and just would use so much it was unbelievable."

Ed Lister came from an upper-middle-class family in upstate New York. He lived in and owned a brownstone that doubled as a shooting gallery. An accomplished thief, Lister also used the house to store and fence stolen merchandise in order to fund his lifestyle. "He would go steal cars and drive through the suburbs," Mishkin recalled, "and he'd have a long pole with a grasper on it which he'd use to open people's mailboxes and steal credit cards. Then he would dress up in a priest's outfit—Lister was a master of disguises—and go round to the department stores and buy everything. So he was a fence. If you wanted something, you could buy it from him."

Ed Lister was the leading member of a large New York speed scene made up of a bizarre cast of characters with whom Lou fit right in. One of its prominent members was the Turtle, who went to Columbia University. The Allen Ginsberg figure of the group, he was loving, gentle, and maternal. Turtle's apartment was a popular spot for the others to go sit in and talk for six to eight hours on amphetamines. He had a lot of records and books, and he always seemed interested in other people. Turtle distinguished himself by spending more time in jail than anyone else. Bob Jones, who was also on the speed scene, and unlike most of the others had an appreciation of Lou's music, described the relationship between Turtle and Lou:

"I don't think he liked Lou very much, although Lou sort of liked him. He was too gentle for Lou. He didn't have any of these macho pretenses, but he would shake his head in great sadness and say, 'Mike was shot the other day at Eddie's apartment.' He had a way of saying it that was very gentle. I think Lou wrote a song or two about Turtle. Another thing that was interesting was Turtle was gay and everyone around him was gay."

Reed and Lister immediately hit it off, primarily because Lou was fascinated by Ed. "It's not hard to believe they became friends, because Ed was a doll—a very charming guy," explained Andy Hyman, who had also been introduced to Lister by Mishkin. "And an extremely good-looking guy. A little like a young Michael Caine—big and powerfully built. Lou had a very romantic view of Lister. Lister came from a very rich family. Lister was a very educated man. Lister was godlike.

"There was a doctor who was the original Dr. Feelgood. He's dead now, or else he's in his late eighties. He was very old then. He was the guy who provided the amphetamine for the cast of *Hair*. On several occasions I saw Lewis at his office. The few times we actually sat down and had some conversation was in the waiting room. He was friendly then."

Lister, for his part, treated Lou abysmally, noted Jones: "He said that Lou couldn't sing, that nobody liked his music, and that he could understand why. He said, 'The guy's tone-deaf' and 'Who would listen to that shit? No wonder his records never sell.' He liked people like John Denver.

"Everyone just thought Lou was a bad singer and a pain in the neck. He was only a big shot to me, and I think he liked to have me around because he recognized that kind of adulation. I was the only person who would both bring him drugs, shoot up with him, and let him talk about rock-and-roll without sort of walking out of the room.

"Lou spent quite a lot of time proselytizing shooting up. He said, 'You're not really taking speed unless you're shooting up. You think you're taking speed, but you're not taking speed.' Somehow, though, Reed managed to retain a semblance of control."

"Lou, for the most part, used drugs very wisely," commented another friend. "The man really knew his own capacity. He would take pure methamphetamine hydrochloride and grind it down and include the whole experience in his music. Then after a month or two he'd decide to clean out his system. He'd stop entirely and move on to health foods and lifting weights. He knew exactly how to gauge the limits of his tolerance."

The popular sentiment in many amphetamine circles at the time was that speed was good, that it didn't harm one's health, and that the euphoric effects were perfectly natural. The only drawbacks, they argued, came through vitamin deficiency. As a result, Reed and the rest of the group would regularly ingest fistfuls of vitamins while shooting up—without, however, bothering to eat. The effects of chronic speed use and poor diet had particularly strong consequences for Lou, whose hands would become so dry that his fingers and fingernails cracked and bled. This made playing the guitar a near impossibility. He also experienced what the speed group called "a wandering jaw," where his mouth would unconsciously open and his jaw would hang loosely against his neck.

Although he managed to cope with speed's physical assault, Reed succumbed to the radical personality changes it induced. He would go from being a nice boy from Long Island to a paranoid maniac, hallucinating about Machiavellian plots. Real and imagined slights elicited violent reactions. Taking his reviews seriously, he wanted to kill the writers, no matter how much they adored him. His free-floating hostility reduced most communication to the basics, even to the point of threatening old and dear friendships. According to Mishkin, ever since they had left Syracuse, "Lou was never nice to me, and now he was more extreme. It was a straight line of development. But that was the speed, it made everyone awful. Your life loses meaning outside of the drug. Everything has to do with getting high and then getting more of it and then getting down without going crazy and then getting high again."

Through the end of 1973, in between speed binges and his divorce, Lou Reed and the Rock-'n'-Roll Animal tour continued their assault on cities across America. By this point Lou had stopped playing guitar at all onstage as well as in the studio. Instead, he had become a spindly-thin stand-up lead singer, whose eyes bulged out of his near-shaven bullet head as if they were plugged into an electric socket. His body was a shivering sack of anemic skin and bones clothed in a black T-shirt and jeans.

According to Lester Bangs, "He'd poke his arm so full of invigorating vitamins that he lost all the fat overnight, then cartwheeled onstage in spastic epic[ene]-choleric fits looking like some bizarre crossbreed of Jerry Lewis of idiot-movie fame and a monkey on cantharides. He moved in the short, clipped, violent motions of a speed freak." According to Cale, "Steady doses of amphetamine changed the muscle structure of Lou's face so he can't smile anymore. When he smiles, his face gets limp and sags. It looks like a weird Frankenstein grimace."

Reed continued to function as an artist, whether he was master of his senses or not. In fact, he used the long hours and increased concentration afforded him by amphetamine use to compose a number of new songs. Working in an idiom where success was measured by commercial acceptance, however, he soon found himself marginalized. His devoted (if maniacal) public wanted, not a hardworking artist, but a freak show. One reviewer described a show in Boston where Lou "clumsily lurch[ed] about the Orpheum stage, violently yanking his frame downward at exactly the wrong times, rhythmically speaking, and crouched froglike to serenade the front row as his band droned on." It was an uncomfortable spectacle, and one that, for all its appeal to the audience, brought Lou dangerously close to the edge. "They wanted to see me die," Reed repeated. "I like to think of us as Clearasil on the face of the nation. Jim Morrison would have said that if he was smart, but he's dead."

AROUND THE END OF HIS TOUR AND THE BEGINNING OF HIS SPEED RUN, Lou had become acquainted with Dennis Katz's brother Steve Katz, a star guitarist with Blood, Sweat & Tears. Lou and Steve talked and played guitar together. "Working with him," recalled Steve, "eased me out of the unhappiness with my own band. When he asked me to produce his next album, I went for it." Steve appreciated Lou and found it sad that *Berlin* was "a beautifully crafted album that was bombing. . . . I think it sold maybe twenty thousand copies. I told Lou we'd have to get rid of this old mystique and put out his songs to new people. He had a great band now and he could become a star with a hot live album." Lou accepted the strategy.

At the end of the U.S. leg of the Rock-'n'-Roll Animal tour, Reed's faith in *Berlin* combined with the burning drive that had produced two of his greatest solo works in a single year paid off on December 21 when he recorded a concert in New York at Howard Stein's Academy of Music on Fourteenth Street. Wrote John Rockwell in the *New York Times:* "With *Berlin,* Reed has proven conclusively that he must be counted as one of the most important figures in contemporary rock. His concert December 21 at the Academy of Music should be an event."

Guiding a Record Plant mobile unit, Steve Katz watched a capacity crowd explode into frenzy. A lot of fans still think it was one of the most spectacular concerts of their lifetime. Lou later characterized the performance as "manic." Lou and the Katz brothers realized that the Academy concerts would make the great live albums they had been searching for and set about mixing the tracks to get the record out as quickly as possible—to capture the moment.

According to Reed, who insisted on maintaining the recording principles first used in *The Velvet Underground and Nico,* "It was a perfect sound. Because I mixed it. The engineer just left. He didn't know how to record it. I couldn't stand what they were doing. Cleaning it up! And I went, 'Oh, no!' and there was another big fight."

On Christmas Eve, 1973, Lou was arrested in Riverhead, Long Island, for attempting to obtain drugs from a pharmacy with a forged prescription. Lou believed he had been sold out by another member of the speed scene. "The game never ended," said Barbara Falk. "I had to scrape up five hundred dollars of my own money to get him out of jail. He was pissed off, but in a humorous kind of way. Almost as if it was part of his image and act. Famous people get busted—that sort of thing. He wasn't scared or miffed about it, except that he was inconvenienced. He started kvetching a little bit. He was miffed that Dennis didn't come. He said, 'You come through for me, he never comes through . . . blah blah blah.' "

Lou got through the minor scrape with the law, but his drug habits were getting the better of him.

IN EARLY 1974, LOU MOVED IN WITH A NEW GIRLFRIEND NAMED BARBARA Hodes, at 45 Fifth Avenue, and immersed himself in the New York scene. He prided himself on knowing more hot-dog places than anyone else: "In New York I can pick up a phone and have anything I want delivered to the door. I can step a foot outside the door and get into a fight immediately. All the energy, people going crazy, guys with no legs on roller skates. It's very intense, the energy level is incredible. It's nice at five in the morning to be stoned on THC and go down to Hong Fows, have some watercress soup, then you take a taxi uptown with some maniac and say, 'Go ahead, drive fast, wise guy,' and you just zip around. When you go up to Park Avenue, there's a very funny turn and it's always fun to wonder if they'll make it."

In the wake of the Rock-'n'-Roll Animal tour publicity, Warhol seemed to take a renewed interest in Reed. Warhol was doing a series of videotape interviews for a projected TV show in which he'd usually sit silently staring into space or hiding behind a newspaper while the hapless interview victim was subjected to a series of banal questions by one of Warhol's minions. Reed had agreed to be videotaped on the stipulation that the interview be conducted solely by Warhol. Andy sat with his overcoat on, making it obvious that he couldn't think of anything to ask, while Lou, heavily made-up and looking as sick as one could without being locked up, made phone calls trying to find drugs in between trying to get a rise out of Andy. The artist merely responded with an occasional mirthless laugh that meant he was bored and thought you were corny.

The experience was excruciatingly uncomfortable. "It was very sad," Lou recalled, "because he said while we were doing it, 'You know, it can never happen again.' And he was right."

In January 1974, Reed and Andy Warhol discussed the possibility of making *Berlin* into a Broadway musical. Reed, Warhol, and Bob Colacello went to dinner at Reno Sweeney's, a cabaret-style restaurant in Greenwich Village that had just opened. Reed was characteristically obnoxious and paranoid. "Lou's opener was, 'I want you, Andy, your ideas—not Paul or Brigid's,' " Colacello recalled. "It was a very difficult dinner, with Lou hesitant to tell too much about his ideas, afraid Andy would steal them. He did explain the psychology of the lead character a bit: he only shows emotion when he's out of speed, Lou said, and when his drug dealer makes it with his girlfriend but not him. When his girlfriend commits suicide, he can only describe and feels nothing."

When the new live album, *Rock 'n' Roll Animal*, was released just five months after *Berlin* in the U.S. at the end of February, it won universal acclaim. The young Chrissie Hynde reviewing the album in the *New Musical Express* wrote, "He looks like a monkey on a chain, court geek—listen to him scramble to a corner, damaged and grotesque, huddled in rodent terror. Animal Lou. Lashing out in a way that could easily make the current S&M trend freeze in its shallow tracks. And the audience cheers after each song, we're with you, yeah, we always loved all those songs, ha-ha-ha. Well, he hates you." But, according to Timothy Ferris in *Rolling Stone* that March, he had finally become "a rocker and not a chanteuse." Ferris noted:

"*Rock 'n' Roll Animal*, an album of Reed's standards, opens with 'Sweet Jane' and a jam by the band before Reed takes the stage, which establishes that, unlike some of his past backup groups, this one is first-rate. The rest of the side is devoted to a towering, unsettling version of 'Heroin.' It is sinister and stunning, rooted in a treacherous organ and strung tautly on a set of vaulting guitar riffs. The piece has the atmosphere of a cathedral at Black Mass, where heroin is God. *Rock 'n' Roll Animal* is much less claustrophobic and oppressive than *Berlin*, but many people will probably loathe it anyway. Faggots, junkies, and sadists are not very pleasant, but theirs are the sensibilities Reed draws upon. His songs offer little hope. Nothing changes, nothing gets better."

The reviews of *Rock 'n' Roll Animal* were, however, among the best ever. For the first time in his solo career Reed was being praised for his Velvet Underground as well as his independent material. "At its best, Reed's live album brought the Velvets into the arena in a clean redefinition of heavy metal, thrilling without threatening to stupefy," wrote Robert Christgau. " 'Lady Day,' the slow one here, would pass for uptempo at many concerts, the made-in-Detroit guitars of Steve Hunter and Dick Wagner mesh naturally with the unnatural rhythms, and Reed shouts with no sacrifice of wit. This is a live album with a reason for living."

John Cale was still not impressed: "I'm amazed at just how different Lou and I were in our ideas now that I've heard everything he's done since that time. It all sounds just like weak representations of tunes and nothing more. I mean, some of his songs in the Velvets really made a point. Now he just appears to be going round in circles, singing about transvestites and the like. The only thing I've heard him do since where he put up a good performance was on 'Sweet Jane.' "

From February to March 1974, Lou hit the publicity trail doing interviews and photo sessions. He even made a TV ad for the new album in which, emulating a Warhol screen test, he stared blankly at the camera for fifteen seconds before blinking and making the startled viewers realize they were not looking at a photograph. Ironically, for a man who was famous for wanting to kill his critics, Lou befriended a number of rock writers, including Nick Kent, with whom he had a love-hate relationship. One day he would call him the Judy Garland of rock writers, the next he'd threatened to kill him.

Even when Lou was his most charming, he could not help but exude an eerie Poe-like quality. One scribe, who wishes to remain anonymous, recalled that talking with Reed was the weirdest interviewing experience he ever had:

> Lou resembled the young Frank Sinatra slightly. When I pointed this out to him, he seemed surprisingly pleased, joking, "Don't say that to Frank."
>
> Q: Are you interested in Frank Sinatra, Lou?
>
> R: Sinatra's fantastic. If somebody really gave him a really good song, with real lyrics, coming from him, and at this point he certainly could do it, you know, I mean, what the hell, come on, Frank.

Q: *Would you like to work with him?*

R: *I'd like to write for him. I would love to get to know him,*
then put lyrics in his mouth, then all he'd have to do would be sing
them, wouldn't matter if he understood them. Can you imagine if
Sinatra laid down "Heroin" in Vegas at the Sands with Nelson
Riddle conducting?

As he spoke, the mask of the young Sinatra superimposed itself
on his face like a ghost image, and for a split second Lou looked
exactly like Frank! The transformation was so abrupt it made me
nauseous. I ran up to the bathroom to be sick. I recovered enough
to conclude the interview. Before leaving, Lou invited me over to his
apartment the following day so he could teach me what I evidently
didn't know about rock and roll.

Barbara Hode's apartment, where he was staying, was an elegant one-bedroom, tastefully furnished in fashion-designer chic.
Lou seemed comfortable there, joking with the Jamaican maid, who
was dusting the European issues of Vogue. When she left, Lou
proceeded to take me through the history of rock, playing singles,
explaining their significance, meanwhile exulting in the music,
punching the air with a clenched fist, grinning from ear to ear at
certain notes. He was an intensely alive person who certainly knew
what he was talking about. He delivered the whole lecture with a
great deal of passion. However, I thought even then when Lou was
at his most serious, he could not help but stir up humor in his
interlocutors to such an extent that it was hard to get people to take
him seriously. In many ways, at least on the surface, Lou was an
extremely funny man. Like his mentor Andy Warhol, he was
constantly laughing and exulting in life.

As I got to know him, he turned at times into a fascinating bunch
of guys. Once I was talking to him backstage at the Bottom Line
when, in much the same fashion he had turned into Frank Sinatra,
he suddenly metamorphosed into Jerry Lewis. However, on this
occasion he was not so pleased when I commented on the resemblance. "Enough with the cheap shots!" he snapped, turning
abruptly back into Lou Reed. As we headed out the door, he
launched into a story about fucking a groupie who kept asking him,
"How come when you're inside me I can really feel it, but when-

ever Mick Jagger's inside me, I can't feel anything?" To which a
bug-eyed Lou said he complained, "Why are you telling me this?"

The overall question that cast a pall over Lou's progress through the
1970s was whether he had lost it after 1970. "Everything has been a
question of lack of confidence," confided an observer. "Lou thinks that
whatever 'it' is, he lost it."

To the press, Lou spouted the kind of contradictory reactions to
the live album that were his trademark, telling one journalist, "It was
like a walking time warp to me . . . but I had to get popular." The live
album, according to Reed, was payback for the deal he had made with
RCA in order to get *Berlin* released. Now, he said, he was paying his
dues.

By the end of March 1974, *Rock 'n' Roll Animal* had reached no. 45 in
the U.S. remaining in the Hot 100 for twenty-seven weeks. Steve Katz
was ecstatic with the success of his first production efforts.

The success of *Rock 'n' Roll Animal* redeemed Lou and gave him added
confidence enough to joust once again with his rival Bowie. One night in
February while Bowie was in town for his *Diamond Dogs* tour, the two got
together. Lou was wired, they were both very stoned, and the competition between them soon reached a fever pitch. Lou threw a drink on a
table and there was a big fight between them. According to Barbara Falk,
Reed was jealous of Bowie's success. "He was jealous," she recalled, "but
he also said he was the cool, underground, credible one. David stomped
out screaming."

To a friend Lou confided that he was having a good time by taking the
road of least resistance and going with things that annoyed him rather
than fighting them: "*Berlin* being a failure and *Rock 'n' Roll Animal* being
a smash hit had been hard to take. What he really liked was *Berlin. Rock
'n' Roll Animal,* what a degrading thing that was."

On March 2, 1974, the writer Jeff Goldberg presented a birthday cake
for Mr. Reed's thirty-second birthday. He recalled that Reed raised his
knife high and slammed it into the cake in mock-Peckinpah style. But,
careful about his diet, he didn't eat a piece. "He is very thin now, and he
pops his knuckles a lot and rubs his fingers nervously," Goldberg wrote.
"Maybe he is always itching to play the guitar. He sometimes seems
distracted, as if listening to music, and often breaks out with a dum-di-

dum movement, as if playing the drums in midair. Why are people so afraid of him?"

"He has no respect really for anyone, which is interesting," said Glenn O'Brien. "He's like Stalin in that he loves the people, he's filled with generosity for the human race, but not for any one person in particular. That's what he's all about to me. He loves being kind, but he hates your fucking guts."

Chapter Thirteen

THE NERVOUS YEARS

ELECTRICITY AND THE CELL

STRUCTURE: 1974—76

Life, as I had come to know it, had made me nervous.

—Lou Reed

LOU WAS TERRIFIC AT PUTTING TOGETHER A COLLABORATIVE RELATION-ship, but as soon as it succeeded, he had to subvert it. This need to demolish collaboration, his Achilles' heel, would soon find its way into his relationships with Steve and Dennis Katz. The Katz brothers had been responsible for maneuvering him onto the international rock charts. Now Lou would pay them back.

As a Jewish man of the fifties, Lou knew that the best way to upset Dennis Katz would be to taunt him for his interest in Nazi memorabilia, and that the best way to taunt him was to flaunt Nazi paraphernalia himself. To accomplish this new affront, Lou had his hairdresser shave off his locks and on the left and right sides of his skull chisel, into his new military crew cut, Iron Crosses that bore an unmistakable likeness to Nazi swastikas.

"Dennis and Lou did have a fall-out when Lewis appeared with those Nazi crosses in his hair," recalled Barbara Falk, who made Lou wear a hat whenever they went out. "We were worried when we first saw him like that, but what can you do? Lewis is such an extremist." At times, Lou's bizarre behavior and street-creep image broadened to such infantile and comic-strip proportions that people laughed at him, whether he wanted them to or not.

Lester Bangs had a friend working as a busboy at Max's Kansas City: "The guy called me up one day. 'Your boy was in again last night. . . . Jesus, he looks like an insect . . . or like something that belongs in an intensive-care ward . . . almost no flesh on the bones, all the flesh that's there's sort of dead and sallow and hanging, his eyes are always darting all over the place, his skull is shaved and you can see the pallor under the bristles, it looks like he's got iron plates implanted in his head.' "

One reason for Lou's extreme acting out was his frustration about having to fulfill his promise to RCA to deliver the two promised commercial albums—*Sally Can't Dance* and *Rock 'n' Roll Animal*. With Steve Katz once again to produce, RCA was sure they'd have a winning product. Yet in their plans and profit-loss calculations, they failed to factor in Lou's seething ire. In spring 1974, as soon as Lou started work on *Sally Can't Dance*, his resentment spilled out.

"I slept through *Sally Can't Dance*," Reed boasted. "I did the vocals in one take, in twenty minutes, and then it was good-bye. They'd make a suggestion and I'd say, 'Oh, all right.' I just can't write songs you can dance to. I sound terrible, but I was singing about the worst shit in the world."

Lou felt *Sally Can't Dance* was a mistake and that RCA had him up against a wall. As he saw it, the company heads were in cahoots with the Katz brothers to milk him for what he was still good for. Worse, they were trying to make him sound like Elton John! While halfheartedly fulfilling their expectations, Lou desperately held on to his identity. "*Sally Can't Dance* . . . with all the junk in there, it's still Lou Reed."

According to Steve Katz, Lou spent the majority of his studio time in the bathroom. Katz was becoming increasingly impatient. One weekend when Lou was staying at Katz's house in Westchester, Steve "accidently" walked into the bathroom and caught Lou injecting methedrine. Like his brother Dennis, Steve genuinely liked and respected Lou, but began to see that drugs were taking a toll on him. Even though Lou would regularly stop taking speed to clean out his system and follow a rigorous course of diet and exercise, his personality and work were being negatively affected. "We all loved him and understood him and tried to help him. But he simply refused to be there. The drugs were becoming just too much for me to deal with."

To make matters worse Lou was so desperate for money he constantly hit up friends for cab fares and restaurant bills. His behavior was surprising for a man who had two international albums and a single on the charts. The truth was that Lou's separation from Heller, divorce from Bettye, drug bills, and profligate spending habits had wiped him out. Never one to tackle financial matters like an accountant, Lou blamed the man who was handling his money, Dennis Katz. As Barbara Falk saw it: "Lou would say, 'Dennis doesn't get it and he's got to have all the money.' And then he became even more paranoid, there was a conspiracy to manipulate him and his money—full-blown!

"By then Dennis saw the handwriting on the wall, because that last year [1974–75] he was very particular about everything. And I remember when Dennis negotiated the publishing agreement with RCA where it was a lot of money, and they got twenty percent, then there were taxes, and there was very little left for Lou. The man had no real assets."

Steve Katz had always taken a supportive attitude toward Lou, but he could not supply him with the creative foil that Cale, Warhol, Bowie, and Ezrin had. Steve echoed Blue Weaver: "As an artist, Lou was not totally there. He had to be propped up like a baby with things done for him and around him."

Nobody could escape Lou's wrath. Not content with savaging his manager, his producer, and his musicians, Lou dragged Nico into his circle of torment. Back in 1973, Lou had told Nico that *Berlin* was about her. She responded so favorably that she reignited Lou's passion. When he showed friends an affectionate five-page scrawled letter from the Parisian foghorn, Lou's face split into a shit-eating grin as he raved that Nico's albums *Desertshore* and *The Marble Index* and her live version of "The End" were "incredible." Nico was not only a real star but a whole galaxy unto herself.

Now, a year later, Lou announced that he would produce an album of his songs by Nico. No sooner had this obsessive notion taken root than Lou threw the whole operation into high gear and dispatched a ticket to the poor, spooked-out Nico. Since last seeing Lou, the former beauty had become a penniless junkie who clung to remnants of the 1960s philosophy. In March 1974, inflamed once again by the notion that the Prince of Stories would rescue her from oblivion, Nico found herself strapped into a jumbo jet high over the Atlantic clutching her harmonium, her candles, and her drugs.

In an uncharacteristic move, the moody Lou invited the hapless chanteuse to stay with him in his pied-à-terre on East Fifty-second Street. She set her few belongings among his two electric clocks, each of which told a different wrong time, his stacks of electronic equipment (Lou was an early and avid fan of video games), his signed Delmore Schwartz volumes, his first editions of Raymond Chandler, from which he constantly quoted and appropriated words, his pints of coffee ice cream and cartons of Marlboros, and, of course, his supply of liquid amphetamine.

No sooner had Lou gotten Nico established in his spot than he embarked upon the task of dismantling her personality. His first act of cruelty was to deny her access to his amphetamine while letting her know how well supplied he was. She was tortured by a blissed-out Lou from whom she received a kind of contact withdrawal. When he had the wan diva just where he wanted her, trembling and in tears, he allowed her to have a tiny taste of his medication while he sat back and watched her dissolve.

To add to his amusement, Lou made a point of filling his apartment with a motley assortment of people: inarticulate and exhausted engineers lay sprawled across the furniture in various states of ugly-snoring sleep; eager young journalists astonished to be in the company of two living legends. According to Nico's blurred account of the three days she spent holed up with Lou, her final exit was precipitated by Lou's torturing her one too many times. Having been raped as a child amid the ruins of Berlin by a sergeant in the U.S. army, she lived in fear of male violence. She fled the chic doorman building, Lou's meanness, and any chance of being with Lou again. In her three-day stopover, Lou had succeeded in bringing her to her once proud knees and, having done so, evidenced a total lack of interest in her for the rest of her short life. He not only avoided producing a single track by her, but he refused to write or give her any more songs. The Lou Reed–Nico debacle marked a decisive turning point in her career, which plunged downward from its already low point.

Lou's harsh treatment of Nico occasioned at least one furious phone call from Cale, who harbored the Nico episode as a bone of contention between them throughout the decade. "Right through the seventies I hoped Lou would write her another song like 'All Tomorrow's Parties,' 'Femme Fatale,' or 'I'll Be Your Mirror,' but he never did," Cale said. "I'd tell him I was working with Nico on her new LP, whichever it was, and he'd just say, 'Really?'—nothing more, not a flicker of interest. He could have written wonderful songs for her. It's a shame and I regret it very much."

In April, seeking friendship elsewhere, Lou took a trip to Amsterdam to visit the brother and sister he had befriended the previous year and collect an Edison award for *Berlin*. However, he returned in three days, his anger and frustration flashing on dangerous levels. He had, he told one friend bitterly, made another mistake.

With Nico gone, Lou turned his attention to Barbara Hodes. Barbara had lived with him intermittently since early 1974, but she had known him since 1966. A sexy, intelligent woman in the fashion business, she offered him loyalty and support and was much closer to his level mentally than Bettye had been. He never forgot how she had sought him out during his 1971 exile and encouraged him to make a comeback.

Lou brought the full force of his personality to the rock-and-roll stage that year, the only place he could really unleash himself. In May and June, accompanied by an entourage of twenty-four people, including Hodes, Reed embarked on a tour of Europe that took him through Sweden, Denmark, the Netherlands, Britain, Belgium, France, and back to Britain. The climax of each show was Lou's rendition of "Heroin," to which he now added a theatrical twist. Extracting a syringe from his pants pocket and lashing the microphone chord around his skinny arm, he mimed the ritual of injecting the deadly poison. Although this was an act, Reed made it so convincing that some press people vomited. Others feared for his life. The image of a skeletal, peroxide-blond Lou Reed shooting up onstage became one of the emblematic images of rock and roll in the early 1970s.

"Lou Reed is the guy that gave dignity and poetry and rock and roll to smack, speed, homosexuality, sadomasochism, murder, misogyny, stumblebum passivity, and suicide, and then proceeded to belie all his achievements and return to the mire by turning the whole thing into a bad joke," wrote Lester Bangs in his most famous definition of his hero and bête noire. "Lou Reed is bound to be the best rock-and-roll star in America for the next five years, at least," wrote one addled, if accurate, devotee in Philadelphia's underground weekly, *The Disturbed Drummer*.

Having alienated Nico and Barbara, Lou desperately needed a companion who could keep pace with him as the pace quickened. Like his mentor Lenny Bruce, Lou had a little-boy side to his character who was frightened of being left alone lest he inadvertently do himself, or the building, harm. In fact, throughout the most dangerous years of his life, Lou would be alone only when he prowled the streets at dawn looking for an angry fix.

That autumn, back in New York, Lou met a tall, exotic drag-queen hairdresser from Philadelphia named Rachel (née Tommy). Rachel, a stunning half–Mexican Indian raised in reformatories, prisons, and on the streets, would become his nursemaid and muse through the midseventies.

"It was in a late-night club in Greenwich Village," Reed later rhapsodized to Mick Rock. "I'd been up for days as usual, and everything was at the superreal, glowing stage. I walked in and there was this amazing person, this incredible head kind of vibrating out of it all. Rachel was wearing this amazing makeup and dress and was absolutely in a different world to anyone in the place. Eventually I spoke and she came home with me. I rapped for hours and hours, while Rachel just sat there looking at me, saying nothing. At the time I was living with a lady and I kind of wanted us all three to live together, but somehow it was too heavy for her. Rachel just stayed on and the girl moved out. Rachel was completely disinterested in who I was and what I did. Nothing could impress her. He'd hardly heard my music and didn't like it all that much when he did."

"I thought Rachel was a mermaid," Lou wrote in a poem. "The Chemical Man." "Fins on Second Avenue. Will these pills bring relief. I am the chemical man." "Imagine," urged Steve Katz, "a woman in a man's body, getting by as a juvenile delinquent. Understanding Rachel was a question of understanding a person's orientation. I found her wonderful, and very quiet. That whole thing about, was Lou a homosexual, was he straight? . . . Rachel was physically gorgeous for any sex. Straight men were coming on to her all the time."

From Shelley Albin through Nico, Bettye, and Barbara Hodes, Lou maintained a pattern of dating blondhaired women with theatrical personalities. Rachel introduced an abrupt change. Not only was this a guy—very evidently a guy when he would stay up for a couple of days, forget to shave, and be drinking—but Rachel's coloring was dark and brooding. What Rachel had in common with her predecessors was a complete acceptance of Lou Reed across the board, an adoration of the little boy in him, and, most important of all, stamina. "I enjoy being around Rachel, that's all there is to it," Lou explained. "Whatever it is I need, Rachel seems to supply it, at the least we're equal."

According to Bob Jones, "Lou was having a sexual relationship with

Rachel. Rachel would come out of the bedroom with just a wrap around her and Lou would have just come out. They slept in the same bed, Rachel slept naked in the bed. Speed is the biggest aphrodisiac. Also, you can go for hours. It is very tactile and very erotic. You make out for two hours without coming, and you want to fuck daily. So I think Lou was having sex. There was never any talk about having sex, but it would be inconceivable that he would go three weeks without sex. In fact, it would be inconceivable to go a week without sex. Inconceivable."

With Rachel around, Lou never had to be alone. She did not speak much, but when she did, she put it across. Lou knew how to use her and benefited enormously from the relationship. "I think Andy's fascination with drag queens was behind Lou's interest in Rachel," said one close friend. "The thing that Lou comically got wrong was that Rachel wasn't a Warhol drag-queen type. The Warhol drag queens had a feminine side, or a drag-queen side. Rachel was sort of Native American, there was a very stone-faced-Indian aspect to Rachel. Rachel didn't really have a woman's attitude."

Mick Rock took a photograph that captured their relationship: clad in matching black leather, tottering on pencil-thin legs, the couple embrace. Lou in front faces the camera with a stoned smile on his face, Rachel, with a black hank of hair to her shoulder blades, supports him with a look of serene passion, her hands cupped possessively over his cock and balls.

Those who met Rachel found a tall, sweet person with a stoic nature. "In my experience of Lou," longtime friend Dave Hickey wrote, "all these supposed digressions from the 'norm' were just bullshit. Anyway, if you took that much speed for that many years, you don't know what the hell you are. Physically, you cannot get an erection. Whenever he'd start talking about his prowess, I'd know for sure he wasn't getting it up, and therefore going to extremes. Psychologically I don't think he's oriented one way or the other. But he had the brilliance to dip in and out of deviance and play with it, make an illusion of it."

However, Lou's sexual preferences had become important to his fans. Reed's roadies were constantly asked if their leader was bi. "Bi? The fucker's quad!" one joked in a bon mot that bounced around the rock world.

One observer believed some of his more outrageous behavior was a

----

deliberate ploy to boost his hard-edge image. Commented Hickey, "He was careful to observe all the feedback the 'Lou Reed persona' got in the press. He read an enormous amount of magazines. He knew he was carrying the weight of his image of the Velvet Underground; he knew Lou Reed had to be Lou Reed. If Lou Reed is supposed to take drugs and have a weird sex life—well, then, it has to be."

When *Sally Can't Dance* was released in August 1974, it got a lot of press. "Lou is adept at figuring out new ways to shit on people," wrote Robert Christgau in the *Voice*. "I mean, what else are we to make of this grotesque hodgepodge of soul horns, flash guitar, deadpan song-speech, and indifferent rhymes? I don't know, and Lou probably doesn't either— even as he shits on us, he can't staunch his own cleverness. So the hodgepodge produces juxtapositions that are funny and interesting, the title tune is as deadly accurate as it is simply mean-spirited, and 'Billy' is simply moving, indifferent rhymes and all. B+."

" 'Billy' is unusual even for unusual Lou," wrote Paul Williams in the *SoHo Weekly News*. "It's a ballad about an old school friend and what became of him—and, by extension, about what became of Lou as well. It works. This album, with 'Kill Your Sons' and 'Billy,' is among other things an acknowledgement of Lou's middle-class Long Island roots."

In an open letter in *Hit Parader*, Richard Robinson revealed an unlooked-for empathy, calling Katz's production "admirable" and telling Lou that it was "the closest thing you've been to being heard in some time." But Robinson regretted *Sally*'s lack of depth, energy, and rock-and-roll craziness, which had him virtually unable to distinguish one track from another.

As if to mock everything Lou stood for, *Sally Can't Dance* became Reed's biggest-selling album internationally and stayed on the charts for fourteen weeks, becoming the only American Top Ten LP of his career.

With *Sally*'s success, Lou became even more disillusioned with the charade his career had become, exhibiting a new level of raw self-loathing. During interviews at the time, Reed either went into Warholian catatonia or degenerated into verbal war. Lou's cynicism reached its zenith when he said to Danny Fields in *Gig* magazine, "This is fantastic— the worse I am, the more it sells. If I wasn't on the record at all next time around, it would probably go to number one."

After the album came out, Lou denigrated it, the musicians, and the producer. However, as Katz pointed out, Lou would work with some of them for years. According to Lou, "*Sally Can't Dance* wasn't a parody, that was what was happening. It was produced in the slimiest way possible. I like leakage. I wish all the Dolbys were just ripped out of the studio. I've spent more time getting rid of all that fucking shit. I hate that album. *Sally Can't Dance* is tedious. Could you imagine putting out *Sally Can't Dance* with your name on it? Dyeing my hair and all that shit? That's what they wanted, that's what they got. *Sally Can't Dance* went into the Top Ten without a single, and I said, 'Ah, what a piece of shit.' . . . I like the old Velvets records. I don't like Lou Reed records."

Reed attempted to justify the animosity he generated with a Warholian protestation of innocence. "I'm passive and people just don't understand that. They talk and I just sit and I don't react and that makes them *uncomfortable*. I just empty myself out so what people see is a projection of their own needs."

Lou retreated into his private world, finding refuge and solace in his relationship with Rachel and the group of addicts who centered around Ed Lister. Bob Jones, his only fan in the group, spent a lot of time with Lou in 1975, becoming Lou's on-again, off-again drug supplier as well as playmate throughout the long, hard summer: "One of my biggest clients right away was Lou. I would get prescriptions from Lister, from Turtle, from Rita, from Marty, and I had a network of pharmacies I would go to. And another thing that was always difficult was getting syringes, I used to be the big syringe man. You had to go to the Upper West Side for syringes. You'd go to a drugstore and buy them by the box."

Standard practice for the group was to shoot up first thing in the morning and then at some other point late in the day. The shots were so strong as to be considered lethal by conventional medical standards. A forged prescription of Desoxyn, for example, would consist of a bottle of one hundred yellow pills, of the highest (15-mg) potency. The ordinary recommended dosage, adjusted of course to meet the needs of the individual, was fifteen to twenty-five milligrams orally per day. The Lister amphetamine circle, on the other hand, would habitually use ten to twenty 15-mg pills at once and inject them directly into the bloodstream. These men were not messing about.

In order to inject the prescription pills, the amphetamine group prepared an intravenous solution. Essentially they put the pills in a pan on the stove and boiled them. The water would rapidly turn yellow from the drug released from the tablets, as much as three hundred milligrams of methamphetamine hydrochloride. The water could then be drawn into a syringe for injection into a vein.

The effects of such intense speed consumption were severe. "It was enough to take the top of your head off," remarked Bob Jones. The shots explained Reed's often temperamental states of being. "We never ate," stated Bob Jones. "We were very, very wired. Everyone's weight went right down. Lou weighed nothing. I lost forty pounds. And we never slept. The effect of having no REM, rapid eye movement sleep, was that we were deprived of dreams. So we would literally go for months without dreaming. The effect of this is that we would begin to have dreams in our waking state, which accounts for the paranoia and the delusionary style of the amphetamine addict."

The first soaking of the pills produced a dark yellow in the water, representing a strong dose. When for one reason or another, the Lister group became low on pills—which happened a few times in the two years Reed was involved—they would pour more water on the used pills, in what they called a second soak. The result would be a faint yellowing of the water. Shooting this diluted mixture produced a weaker effect and a limited amphetamine high. It was enough, however, to hold them for a few hours while they went looking for more pills.

When amphetamine could not be found, members of the Lister group would convince themselves that putting sixty twice-used pills in a tube and boiling them up would result in some small amount of speed. However, the third soaking of pills failed to yellow the water. Deceiving themselves into believing that there was some speed in there, they would end up shooting water into their veins. Of course, impurities would go into their veins along with the water, which wasn't such a good idea.

"What would happen," Jones explained, "was that your temperature would go through the roof almost immediately, within five minutes; you would feel a strange aching in your body and the next thing you'd know is your temperature would be about one hundred and three. You'd be drenched in sweat and in terrible, terrible pain in all of your joints. Appalling pain. And you would take your clothes off because it was too painful to keep them on and lie down on the bed racked with shivers and diarrhea and agony, drenched in sweat. That was called a bone crusher.

You would lie there with your knees drawn up to your chest and retch and cry out in pain. And this would go on for five or six hours. At the end of Lou's involvement with the amphetamine scene, this happened three or four times in a studio. He'd get a bone crusher and couldn't record. It was hopeless."

Jones believed that the drug created the fodder for Lou's songs, and the drug lifestyle was the ideal atmosphere for Lou's work. After taking their shots, Reed and Jones would often sit around the former's apartment. "There was nothing but drugs at Lou's place," Jones recalled. "There was never any eating. I guess in the course of time I gravitated towards Lou because I was interested in the way he spent his time in between shooting up, which was more interesting than what the rest of the group was doing. He was an international star at the time, it must have been hard to maintain his humility. Especially if you're whacked out on drugs all the time. There would be acts of friendship, but Lou was very selfish. Lou probably had a few real relationships which would fulfill some kind of purpose. And I think in a funny sort of way the relationship he had with Rachel was a symbolic relationship. The relationship I had with him didn't really exist except in the supplying him with drugs and with a pair of ears to listen to his speed rap about music and the drug world and crime. And someone who shared his interest in Warhol and was literate. There was a lot of strung-out, camp talk."

The two devoted a lot of time to listening to music and discussing their ideas of what was interesting about a particular piece. Lou showed Jones, who was an intelligent sounding board, the new, speed-induced lyrics he was working on, and he would also play the songs in draft. Lou was constantly playing, trying out songs, playing little riffs, and working the words into the music. He was extremely prolific and experimented with all sorts of different styles. On one occasion he recorded a whole cassette tape of Bob Dylan parodies. Lou also incorporated many of his experiences on the speed scene into songs of his "criminal" period. "If you analyze them, all of those songs on *Coney Island Baby* and *Rock and Roll Heart* are about this little crowd and its comings and goings," reported Jones. "Having an attitude was a big thing for Lou. Attitude was the sort of drug equivalent of what is called in the black world 'signifying.' Talking from the sides of your mouth."

According to Jones, Lou's social life outside this speed scene was limited. Although he was seeing some people in the music business, such as the singer Robert Palmer, his peculiar habits and long, erratic hours made it difficult for many friends to relate. He'd see guitarists, who'd come around and be moronic. He was very interested. They'd talk about music. He'd get interviewed and go into diatribes about lawyers. Outside of that, he'd see Rotten Rita, a real character from Warhol's novel *A,* an account of twenty-four hours at the Factory with Lou talking about desoxyn. "Rita was about six foot two, a hundred and ninety pounds," recalled Jones. "He lived under the elevated subway tracks in Queens in an absolutely terrible apartment. He had recently gotten out of jail in Bermuda, which he loved, and he had tapes of himself singing opera there. He was very wild, campy, and lonely. A very funny, potentially quite dangerous character, but at the same time quite sweet. You felt that he could tip a little bit and be capable of murder. And it was that side of him that was appealing to Lou. He was very much an outré camp figure who loved Callas; there was a lot of talk of Callas, there was a lot of playing of Callas albums, always opera, opera. He also became one of the main dealers."

For Lou, one of the appealing aspects of such large doses of amphetamine was the effect it had on making the most horrible, chilling experiences, as well as horrible, chilling people, interesting. This accounted for his attraction, for example, to Lister and some of the other characters on the scene, like Rotten. For a writer and rock star, faced with a constant assault of painful experiences such as the chaos of touring, as well as the ever-present need for new material, the drug was an effective tool. According to Bob Jones, "There seems to be some kind of deprivation of the normal blocks against certain kinds of interest in the macabre. I became fascinated with the police, for example; it was a fascination Lou and I shared. There was a big police book that I bought at Barnes and Noble about gunshot wounds. And it showed in color people who had put shotguns in their mouths and pulled the trigger. It showed people cut up, shot, all kinds of wounds. You'd see their brains spilling out all over the place. And it was very much that attitude that Lou was involved in at the time and that I became involved in, and I think understood as he did. It was that kind of erotic fascination with death."

Despite the drug's seeming ability to open new vistas of creativity, in reality it was wearing him out. As his health deteriorated, his mental state and professional responsibilities suffered. Lester Bangs noted that "Lou's

sallow skin was almost as whitish yellow as his hair, his whole face and
frame so transcendentally emaciated—he had indeed become a specter.
His eyes were rusty, like two copper coins."

A salesman in a record store in Cambridge, Massachusetts, described
the people who were buying Lou Reed records: "You get like these twenty-
eight-year-old straight divorcée types, asking for *Transformer* and *The
Velvet Underground,* but the amazing thing is that suddenly there's all
these fourteen-year-olds, coming in all wide-eyed: 'Hey, uh, do you have
any Lou Reed records?' "

In retrospect, while rejecting his two most commercial RCA albums,
Lou insisted that he made them in order to get the Velvet Underground
albums back into print, claiming, "I kept going with *Rock 'n' Roll Animal*
because it did what it was supposed to do. It got MGM to repackage all
those Velvet things, and it got the *1969 Live* album out."

That September, the double Velvet Underground album *1969 Live* was
released in the U.S. at the same time as several other Velvet Underground compilations were released in Europe. Patti Smith, on the verge
of her entrance into the rock world as the high priestess of punk, but then
still just a dog of a rock writer, reviewed the album in *Creem,* finding it
oppressive and likable.

By releasing his commercial solo albums, Lou was able to service the
audience who had come with him out of the sixties as well as the crazed
and dazed younger fans who were now attending his concerts like hyenas
in droves.

In retrospect, Lou was responsible for keeping the VU music alive by
recording his albums and by pressing his former bandmates to release the
music. His strategy was successful. Sterling Morrison, who had cut himself off from the music world, recalled with some annoyance that in early
1974 he began getting calls from Steve Sesnick: "And I thought, 'What
is this bullshit?' Then Lou even called. Apparently his lawyer had told
him to turn on the charm. They wanted me to sign the release for the
1969 Velvet Underground Live album. I did not want it released. There is
a certain clean feeling that comes from not dealing with the people you'd
have to, to collect royalties on anything like that. And I'd listened to the
tapes and I thought, 'Oh, man! I can't see this selling ten copies!' Musically I much preferred *Live at Max's Kansas City*—it has much more
energy. I said I was not going along with it. Then Steve Sesnick finally

convinced me. I signed the release for a pittance because he told me he needed the money. I'm sure he was in cahoots with Lou in some strange way."

Maureen Tucker got a phone call at work explaining that Lou wanted to put this album out, but that they all had to sign, giving their consent: "And we had to sign for like, two hundred dollars, or something. I said, 'No, no, I won't sign for two hundred dollars, what do you mean, two hundred dollars?' Then some agent type was calling me at work like mad: 'Well, how about three?' So I said, 'What, are you crazy? I broke my ass for seven years for three hundred dollars? Go to hell.' Sterling and I held out for more. We said we're not signing for anything less than fifteen hundred, which even then was stupid—fifteen hundred dollars, which we foolishly signed for."

IF LOU'S LONDON PERIOD CLIMAXED WITH RECORDING *BERLIN*, LOU'S *ROCK 'n' Roll Animal* period climaxed in his autumn-winter 1974 tour of the U.S. "He was very big in New York, New Jersey, Los Angeles, and part of the Midwest," recalled the ever-faithful Barbara Falk. Rachel, listed as his "baby-sitter," accompanied Lou on the tour. To dramatize his self-destructive motif, Lou kept "Heroin" in the tour repertoire, playing it for all it was worth. In a San Francisco column in *Melody Maker* of December 7, 1974, Todd Tolces described a "gory Guignol" before five thousand raving fans. Lou "pulled a hypodermic needle out of his boot . . . as the crowd erupted into cheers and calls for, 'Kill, kill!' he tied off with the microphone cord, bringing up his vein. As the writer ran for the gentlemen's toilet, Lou handed the syringe to a howling fan."

No one could be certain what had really happened, but the image lingered on and added fuel to the talk that these were Reed's final shows, that he would be unlikely to live beyond Christmas. For even if he wasn't actually shooting onstage, he was shooting up somewhere, and the drugs and lifestyle were killing him.

In the midseventies, Lou was hitting the zeitgeist smack on the nose day after day. Although at home Lou was still the sentimental little boy who liked nothing more than to play with his dog, onstage he appeared as ugly, violent, vicious, and stupid as the confused times seemed to call for. "The Stanley Theater was the perfect setting for rock's king of decadence—Lou Reed—and he knocked them dead last night," wrote Peter Bishop in Andy Warhol's hometown, Pittsburgh. "Once he got onstage, the crowd already standing on the seats applauding, he proved himself a star, embellishing the glitter-language lyrics with a choreographic blend of go-go, jitterbug, free-form, and street-fighting moves that threatened to shake the painted-on jeans from his scrawny hips. And how the audience loved it when he made the raunchy lyrics of 'Walk on the Wild Side' even raunchier. This song and Reed himself are definite vestiges of the decadent movement of the late 1800s, and how Oscar Wilde and Aubrey Beardsley would have loved to hear and illustrate that song. He gives you more than your money's worth of music and show; he's what rock and roll is all about."

In Cleveland, RCA got September 13 proclaimed Lou Reed Day. A couple of weeks later RCA proclaimed Lou Reed Impact Day in New York, where Lou played shows at the Felt Forum.

Lou was not often able to receive backstage guests after his shows because he was more often than not so profoundly moved by the emotional impact of the music and audience that Barbara would find him alone in his dressing room, unable to face anyone but her, sobbing uncontrollably. As Barbara described it:

"He'd be wrung out, drenched, shaking, and sometimes crying from sheer release of all this pent-up emotion. Especially if it was a good audience. Or if there was a really bad audience and he'd be upset that there wasn't anybody there. It was a physical and emotional release. After a while I would leave him alone to help pack up, and then he wouldn't want to leave. And he'd talk about it—he'd say, 'Did you see these moves or that step?' I think he fancied himself a good dancer, but he was terrible. He was best with just the cigarette.

"Other stars admired him greatly. He never came out and said it, but I think he was touched when they found him pretty nifty. I'll never forget Mick Jagger crouching down behind the amps at the Felt Forum so he didn't detract from Lou's performance. I would bring him little glasses of champagne. Mick wanted to come right back into the dressing room and tell him how fabulous he was.

"At the end of the year, he was more erratic. Dennis suggested that he go to his own doctor. Lou looked up to him so much that he trotted off. I can't imagine his doing this for anyone else. The doctor reported that

Lou had . . . slightly elevated cholesterol. Ha! Lou never let Dennis forget this. His idea of a real doctor, of course, was the notorious Dr. Feelgood. Sometimes he'd be waiting on that doctor's step at six A.M."

By the end of 1974, many sixties rock icons had moved into the mainstream. On December 13, for instance, former Beatle George Harrison had lunch with President Ford in the White House. Lou determined to defuse any attempt on the part of the record company or the critics to classify Lou Reed in the middle of the road.

IN JANUARY 1975, HE WENT INTO A NEW YORK STUDIO WITH A STRIPPED-down band and recorded the seeds of the raunchy *Coney Island Baby*— "Kicks," "Coney Island Baby," "She's My Best Friend," and "Downtown Dirt"—in four days. Dennis Katz told Lou flatly there was no way this music could be released. The songs were too raw, too negative. "Dirt," for one was an obvious and brutal put-down of Katz. As a result, *Coney Island Baby* was temporarily shelved and Katz sent Lou back on the road, telling him he was broke. It looked like an insensitive move. Sending the unstable, overloaded Reed on an international tour was likely to push him over an edge he had been teetering on all year. Behind him lay a crumbling relationship with Dennis Katz, and the slithering Rock-'n'-Roll Animal himself, whose skin he was painfully shedding. Reed was desperate to find a new image that would free him from the prison of glam rock. But, for the time being, the only reality that Lou could hold on to apart from his music was Rachel.

Accompanied by Rachel, the loyal Falk, and a surprise addition to the band, Doug Yule, Reed launched this tour in Italy. The country, unbeknown to Lou, was in political turmoil. On February 13, a Dada-influenced gang called Masters of Creative Situations disrupted his first concert in Milan. As Falk explained, "These riots had nothing to do with Lou; they just chose our arena as their battle site, because there were so many people there. The fascists and the communists were trying to influence the elections, so they threw tear gas at the stage. The riot police were all over the place with big shields." Throwing bolts and screwdrivers at the band, the rioters leaped onstage and denounced Reed as a "decadent dirty Jew." Lou left the stage in tears. He refused to proceed.

Barbara canceled the next show in Bologna and took him to Switzerland. Once he was in a neutral country, Lou demanded that somebody from the Katz team fly over to consult with him. Both Katz brothers declined the invitation. However, the bushy-eyed manager of David Bowie, Tony DeFries, who had been trying to manage Lou since 1972, jumped on a plane and went in their stead. "We were holed up in this very modern hotel in Switzerland," Falk recalled, "and Lou called De-Fries. Lou said Dennis should have been there, Daddy should have held my hand. Dennis was furious when DeFries came to Switzerland, that Lou would even consider talking to DeFries."

However, when DeFries arrived in Switzerland, Lou holed up in his Zurich-cocoon hotel suite and refused even to have a cup of coffee with Tony in the lobby. The unfazed DeFries flew back to New York without so much as clapping eyes on Reed. He'd made his point, and both Reed and Katz knew that he was serious.

From then on, the tour grew rapidly worse. The next concert was also aborted, the promoter claiming Reed had a nervous breakdown. Another riot ensued. In France, a fan jumped onstage and pulled a knife. In England, a fan bit him on the bum. But the final straw was when Dennis suddenly yanked Barbara Falk off the tour, replacing her with an antique-car mechanic named Alec. Lou went ballistic. First, he smashed up Coca-Cola bottles and stuffed the shards of glass in the hapless road manager's pockets, and Alec cut his hand. Then, taking a page from Elvis Presley's tour guide, Lou smashed up an RCA car that did not meet his requirements. Barbara Falk returned:

"Things were starting to go sour. Lou was having convulsions from the speed. Speed is insidious, and the personality changes are radical. Lou would go from being a nice Jewish boy from Long Island to a paranoid maniac. He would have hallucinations about intricate Machiavellian plots working against him. That's why he was always suing—when in doubt, litigate. Other occasions merited more violence. He took his reviews very seriously and sometimes wanted to kill the writers, no matter how much they adored him. Fortunately a member of his family was around to help me." His favorite cousin, Judy, who was traveling in Europe, joined him for a few shows, helping Lou through the ritual of preparing for his nightly performance. "He listened to her because he was going through a difficult time," said Barbara. "She said he'd listen to a strong woman. I remember shoving Valiums down him. Like all drug freaks, he felt he had complete control over the drug. In my experience, no matter how intelligent or visionary a person might be in other parts of his life, no matter how intimate his knowledge of the drug's effects, he still thinks he's stronger. And Lou had a much larger ego than your average speed freak."

Barbara had put the fear of God into the band about carrying drugs since they were bound to be strip-searched as they crossed borders daily. But "Europe, of course, is famous for easy prescriptions, so Lou would go to a different speed doctor in every country," she recalled. "He truly believed in it! He was forever proselytizing, trying to get me to take some. On tour he'd actually go to medical bookstores, he'd literally carry around written justification for amphetamine. Not only that, but he knew how to pronounce it correctly, in every language."

Despite his protestations, it was not a healthy life. He often stayed up for days at a time. In Europe that winter, as a result of clinical fatigue, he collapsed in convulsions on several occasions.

AT THE BEGINNING OF MARCH 1975, LOU RETURNED TO THE U.S. IN TIME for the release of *Lou Reed Live*, a second album culled from the December 1973 shows that produced *Rock 'n' Roll Animal*. *Lou Reed Live* was yet another commercial success, reaching no. 62 on the LP charts, where it hovered for several months. "Satellite of Love," "Sad Song," and "Vicious" placed him in the mainstream of rock between Elton John and the Rolling Stones. On the live album, Lou insisted that the producers keep the clear hollow ring of a youth's voice screaming out from the bleachers, "Lou Reed sucks!" at the very end of the second side.

The trilogy of *Rock 'n' Roll Animal*, *Sally Can't Dance*, and *Lou Reed Live* vaulted Lou from the hesitant commercial start of the early seventies to the rock mountaintop. His distinct following of the most mentally disturbed people in each country gave him a higher profile than he might otherwise have had. Lou Reed fans were loud, nasty, and exhibitionistic. "During the U.S. tour, mutual hostility rose in waves during some shows. The standard audience expression," according to Janet Macoska in the *Cleveland Commuter*, "was one of stunned boredom, hands barely holding up nodding heads. . . . And Lou, half the time, had no idea what he was supposed to be singing." But by the time he reached Detroit, then home turf of Lester Bangs, he had once again managed to focus his rage; Lester thought the show was superb.

At this midway point in the decade, Lou's famed interview slugfest with the writer Lester Bangs in *Creem* magazine reached its climax. "I always thought when Lou was being interviewed by Lester Bangs was the peak of his career," said the cartoonist John Holmstrom. "Lou hated Lester. They really hated each other. Lester had a love-hate thing. Lou just had the hate." "Bangs attempted to place rock within a cultural framework, pointing out its similarities to everything from Dada to Jack Kerouac," wrote critic Kyle Tucker. "For a critic like Bangs, Andy Warhol was as much of an aesthetic signpost as the Beatles; an understanding of Lou Reed, the Velvet Underground founder, was impossible without discussing Brecht's alienation effect."

Ever since the Velvet Underground played San Diego in 1968, Bangs had set himself up as the conscience of Lou Reed and the Velvet Underground. After celebrating the Velvets during their last two years, he had remained true to them through the first half of the seventies, writing obsessively about their influence and keeping tabs on the activities of Cale, Nico, and Reed. But when he met Reed during the U.S. tour, Bangs wrote, "Lou Reed is a completely depraved pervert and pathetic death dwarf and everything else you want to think he is."

"See, this to me is what rock journalists do, they rip off, make fun of musicians . . . y'know, and sell to morons," responded Reed in an interview. "Written by morons for morons. . . . The best way to get anything publicized is to tell Lester, 'Please don't print that.' And he'll print it. The very best way is to let him overhear something accidently on purpose." Asked, "Did you read the story Lester Bangs did on you?" Lou replied, "Oh, yeah. We both worked on it very hard. He thinks he won the last time, but that was only because I let him think that. He's the best PR agent I have. The worse things he writes about me, the better it is. If he ever started writing good things about me . . . it would be like the kiss of death. I mean, everyone has turned the old Velvet thing into much more than it ever was."

From then on, Reed's American concerts received critical raves. "Both Mr. Reed's concerts and his records have been up-and-down affairs over the last couple of years, and in that context Saturday night at the Felt Forum must be counted as a success," wrote John Rockwell in the *New*

York Times on April 28. "His singing was as tuneless as ever, but the phrasing remains gripping, and his backing quartet strikes a nice balance between professionalism and the out-of-tune raunch of his Warhol days. But in a large measure the risk has gone. Mr. Reed has made himself into a rock star—a strange, weird rock star, to be sure, but a rock star nonetheless. Still, in the old days he gave promise of something more daring, if more lonely."

As the graph of his record sales rose, however, Lou's emotional state plummeted. The break with Bettye, the rejection of *Berlin*, the struggle with the Katz brothers, the riot-torn tour, and the success of *Lou Reed Live*, another album he professed to loathe, reduced him to a fried geek. Meanwhile, the more he stumbled, the less capable he became of performing, the more audiences goaded him to fall. Pinned by the spotlight to the stage, he began to portray himself as rock's next sacrificial victim. He claimed that Bowie had told him "that 'Rock 'n' Roll Suicide' (on *Ziggy Stardust*) was written for me." Asked how it felt to be voted second only to Keith Richard in a Who Will be the Next Rock 'n' Roll Casualty in a recent magazine poll, Lou exclaimed, "Oh really, that's fabulous. It's a real honor to be voted after Keith. He's a real rock 'n' roll star."

Great rock stars often have the ability to respond to the very worst situation by performing at the top of their game. Lou was one such animal. With everything against him by the time he returned to New York, Reed was delivering a gripping set. "He was such a romantic figure at that point," said Bob Jones. "He was as good as you could be. He was very much a Rimbaud figure."

"By far his greatest work was composed when he was on drugs," pointed out Glenn O'Brien. "But who is successful using amphetamine over a long period of time?"

In the spring of 1975, after three years of relentless, amphetamine-fueled touring behind his most commercially successful albums, Reed faced a new contractual demand from his product- and profit-hungry record company, RCA: he had to deliver a new studio album. The "product" Lou came up with this time was way beyond anything any of his fans could have contemplated in their wildest expectations. A screeching cacophony of feedback and electronic noise that lasted for sixty-four minutes, it was called *Metal Machine Music*.

"As soon as he came walking into my office, I could see this guy was not too well connected with reality," recalled an RCA representative to whom the lot fell to steer Reed through this production. "If he was a person walking in off the street with this shit, I woulda threw him out. But I hadda handle him with kid gloves, because he was an artist in whom the company had a long-term commitment. He's not my artist, I couldn't get his hackles up, I couldn't tell him it was just a buncha shit."

The only thing the RCA executives knew about Lou was that Lou's last three albums—*Sally Can't Dance, Rock 'n' Roll Animal,* and *Lou Reed Live*—had been moneymakers. The company had high hopes that he would deliver another. Consequently, in a series of meetings about *Metal Machine Music,* they let Lou walk all over them. After talking the RCA people into presenting this highly unusual product, Lou told friends he had had to run to the men's room to explode with adolescent laughter.

"I told him it was a 'violent assault on the senses,' " continued the RCA executive. "Jesus Christ, it was fuckin' torture music! There was a few interesting cadences, but he was ready to read anything into anything I said. I led him to believe it was not too bad a work, because I couldn't commit myself. I said, 'I'm gonna put it out on the Red Seal label,' and then I gave him a lot of classical records in the hope that he'd write better stuff next time."

Everybody at the company was horrified by Lou's new weirdness. One marketing executive, Frank O'Donnell, recalled, "About twenty of us were seated around a vast mahogany conference table for a monthly new-release album meeting. The A-and-R representative at the meeting put on the tape and the room was filled with this bizarre noise. Everyone was looking at everyone else; people were saying, 'What the hell is that?' Somebody voiced that question and the answer came back, 'That's Lou Reed's new album, *Metal Machine Music.* His contract says we've got to put it out.'

"One day a middle-aged, very conservatively dressed and coiffed executive secretary asked me what I knew about 'this recording artist Lou Reed.' I told her, 'Well, I know he was involved with Andy Warhol and the Velvet Underground. One of his songs is called "Heroin," so I believe he has a pretty big following in the drug culture. He's kind of in the David Bowie groove—you know, eye makeup and lipstick and all that, so the homosexuals like him. His brand of rock and roll is pretty wild . . . why do you ask?' The lady looked side to side, warily. Then, sotto voce, she said, 'He's my nephew. But if you don't tell, I won't tell.' "

The company had wanted to issue *Metal Machine Music* on the Red Seal classical label, but Lou demurred, arguing that the venue was pretentious. Instead, they disguised the platter within a record sleeve showing Lou looking extracool onstage, clearly suggesting that this was his *Blonde on Blonde.* Included on the jacket was a list of the equipment putatively utilized in the recording, along with a bunch of supposed scientific symbols that Lou had copied out of a stereo magazine. "I made up the equipment on the back of the album," he later said, laughing hysterically. "It's all bullshit." After much gnashing of teeth and pulling of hair on the part of RCA's top brass, the album was released in July 1975. Those not prepared for what lurked beneath the cover of *Metal Machine Music* were in for a *big surprise.* According to Lou, "They were supposed to put out a disclaimer—'Warning: no vocals. Best cut: none. Sounds like: static on a car radio' "—but did not. The double album, subtitled "An Electronic Instrumental Composition," was mixed so that each side was exactly 16:01 in length—except that side four was pressed so the final groove would stick, repeating grating static screeches over and over until the needle was rapidly removed from the record by the hapless client.

Reed presented the album as a grand artistic statement, claiming that he had spent six years composing it, weaving classical and poetic themes into the noise. If one listened attentively, he promised, one could hear a number of classical themes making their way in and out of the feedback fury. "That record was the closest I've ever come to perfection," he stated. "It's the only record I know that attacks the listener. Even when it gets to the end of the last side, it still won't stop. You have to get up and remove it yourself. It's impossible to even think when the thing is on. It destroys you. You can't complete a thought. You can't even comprehend what it's doing to you. You're literally driven to take the miserable thing off. You can't control that record."

"I could take Hendrix," he told Lester Bangs. "Hendrix was one of the greatest guitar players, but I was better. If people don't realize how much fun it is listening to *Metal Machine Music,* let 'em go smoke their fucking marijuana, which is just bad acid anyway, and we've already been through that and forgotten it. I don't make records for fucking flower children."

Asked Lester, "Speaking of fucking, Lou—do you ever fuck to *Metal Machine Music?*" "I never fuck," Lou shot back. "I haven't had it up in so long I can't remember when the last time was." On another occasion when a fellow musician offered Lou access to his girlfriend, Reed claimed, "I'm a musician, man. I haven't gotten it up in seventeen years."

For the most part, the press's and the public's reaction to *Metal Machine Music* was a combination of outrage and contempt. *Rolling Stone* voted it the worst album of the year. Even John Rockwell, who had been a champion of Reed's since *Berlin*, delicately questioned its release. "One would like to see rock stars take the risk to stretch their art in ways that might jeopardize the affection of their fans," he wrote. "But one can't help fearing that in this instance, Mr. Reed may have gone farther than his audience will willingly follow." Lou, for his part, was of the opinion that *Metal Machine Music* would be the perfect sound track for the cult horror flick *The Texas Chainsaw Massacre*. And he may well have been right.

(NB: As an aficionado of movies, Lou listed as one of his favorite films of all time *The Ruling Class*, starring Peter O'Toole as a man who thinks he is Jesus Christ. Any serious fan of Reed's should make a point of seeing this film as an excellent example of Reed's self-image.)

Lou anticipated a strong reaction from his fans. He insisted, "I put out *Metal Machine Music* precisely to put a stop to all of it. It was a giant fuck-you. I wanted to clear the air and get rid of all those fucking assholes who show up at the show and yell 'Vicious' and 'Walk on the Wild Side.' It wasn't ill-advised at all. It did what it was supposed to do. I really believed in it also. That could be ill-advised, I suppose, but I just think it's one of the most remarkable pieces of music ever done by anybody, anywhere. In time, it will prove itself."

To anyone who would listen he said, "*Metal Machine Music* is probably one of the best things I ever did, and I've been thinking about doing it ever since I've been listening to La Monte Young" (whose name Lou misspelled on the back of the album). "That album should have sold for $79.99," he snapped to another astonished scribe. "If they think it's a rip-off, yeah, and I'll rip them off some more. I'm not gonna apologize to anybody! They should be grateful I put that fucking thing out, and if they don't like it, they can go eat rat shit. I make records for me."

The record, which would soon come to be seen as the ultimate conceptual punk album and the progenitor of New York punk rock, harkened back to the work of La Monte Young and the Velvet Underground's experimental track "Loop" (1966). "The key word was 'control,' " Lou concluded in *Metal Machine Music*'s liner notes.

In a conscious effort to present *Metal Machine Music* as a composition, Reed not only left the individual sides untitled, but offered a parody of classical liner notes. His first piece of published prose since his essay "No One Waved Goodbye," the *Metal Machine Music* "Notation" was a combination of arrogance, bluster, and inadvertent confessional. The writing was punk. Its subject shifted from Reed's complaints about the tedium of most heavy metal, through the symmetrical genius of his creation, to puns on his album titles, to insights about the gap between drug "professionals" and "those for whom the needle is no more than a tooth brush." It noted, "No one I know has listened to it all the way through including myself. . . . I love and adore it. I'm sorry, but not especially, if it turns you off. . . . Most of you won't like this, and I don't blame you at all. It's not meant for you."

In the end, almost one hundred thousand copies sold. "The classical reviews were fabulous," Lou reported.

In August, leaving his critics and fans with an unpleasant ringing in their ears, Reed went on another grueling tour of Japan and Australia. Every tour has a theme. This one was called the Get Down with Your Bad Self Tour. "In Japan, they greeted me by blaring the fucking thing [*Metal Machine Music*] at top volume in the airport," he claimed or hallucinated. Nobody in his entourage had any memory of this incident.

What they do remember is a press conference at the airport immediately following the grueling thirty hour flight from New York to Sydney at which Lou rivaled the midsixties Dylan in repartee:

> PRESS: It says in this press release that you lie to the press. Is that true?
>
> LOU: No.
>
> PRESS: Would you describe yourself as a decadent person?
>
> LOU: No.
>
> PRESS: Well then, what?
>
> LOU: Average.
>
> PRESS: Is your antisocial posture part of your show-business attitude?
>
> LOU: Antisocial?

PRESS: Well, you seem very withdrawn. Do you like meeting
    people?
LOU: Some.
PRESS: Do you like talking to us?
LOU: I don't know you.
PRESS: Would it be correct to call your music gutter rock?
LOU: Oh, yeah.

Joining the tour on bass was Doug Yule, back with Lou since the *Sally
Can't Dance* sessions. "When we traveled as the VU, we traveled as a
group," Doug recalled. "But here he and Rachel traveled together—they
were like the VIPs—and everybody else traveled behind. It was nice, it
was fun. He was a little more mercurial."

In fact, much distance had come between Reed and the rest of his
entourage, including the ever-present Barbara Falk. Unfortunately, this
was not an altogether healthy change, resulting in one of the few times
Lou was incapable of overcoming his drug-induced exhaustion to make it
to a show. "I once saw him consume fifteen straight tequilas—dou-
bles!—in a drinking contest with a drummer in New Zealand," recalled
Barbara. "And then he *walked* away."

"In New Zealand he couldn't perform," said Doug Yule. "So there was
an announcement that Lou wasn't going to play but the band was going
to play. Anyone who wanted their money back could have their money
back. We went out and played and I sang. The audience liked it a lot. But
it was not an attempt [as had been reported] to present it as if I were Lou,
nor were the people told I was Lou."

Meanwhile, in a series of frantic phone calls between New Zealand and
New York, Reed was given the impression that Katz was rapidly moving
to take control of his finances and tie up his recordings. The first casualty
of this escalating battle was Barbara Falk. Exhausted after three years of
baby-sitting Lou on twenty-four-hours-a-day call, she left the tour after
Lou accused her one too many times of being in cahoots with Katz to
cheat him. "Our last tour of Australia is what did it," stated Barbara Falk.
"I was exhausted—this was mid-'75, and we'd been pushing very hard, all
over the U.S. and Europe, behind *Sally Can't Dance*. My routine of being
the bookkeeper, the bouncer, and big mama wasn't covering the gaps. It
all really started with *Metal Machine Music*, an album I didn't particularly

like. I didn't tell him this, but I didn't praise it to the skies, either. Before this I was his biggest fan and strongest support, always convincing him that he was the cult musical figure of the century to be cherished and protected. But as I said, the instant the stroking stopped—and he noticed instantly that I wasn't carrying around the reviews of the album and passing them out to strangers on the street—he got progressively more nasty. It was awful at the end, and I had to abstain and just leave. I got on a plane and got out of Australia."

Extremely agitated by thoughts of betrayal, Lou was unable to go on with the tour. Returning to New York, he found himself, as it were, back at square one. While he had been touring, Dennis Katz had marshaled his chess pieces and presented Reed with what amounted to a checkmate. According to Reed, Dennis Katz's office had cut off his support payments. He discovered that he no longer had an apartment or money in the bank, then was informed that he was $600,000 in debt to his record company. Furthermore, RCA did not intend to proceed with his next album as planned.

Lou believed that the only way to face a storm was to drive right through its center at breakneck speed. Approaching RCA president Ken Glancy, Lou talked him into supporting him long enough to come up with a commercial album. Glancy, who knew Reed personally and believed in him in the same way that Katz once had, agreed to put him up in a suite at the Gramercy Park Hotel, an establishment that had seen better days but now exuded a louche charm as home for traveling rock bands and European tourists.

Lou was comfortable there. RCA picked up his room and restaurant bills and gave him $15 per day in cash. The hotel's restaurant had the air of a department store and served bland food, but the bar pulsed with cute groupies waiting for the appearance of any rock star. While Lou was there, Dylan's entourage was using it as a base for their Rolling Thunder tour and invited Lou to join them. He had to decline the offer.

The pecuniary difficulties strengthened the bond between Lou and Rachel. According to Lou, Rachel weathered hard times because she was "a street kid and very tough underneath it all." They also had a lot of fun together. Lou never tired of shocking people. One day a maid came into their suite unaware that they, Mr. and Mrs. Reed, were in bed. When she saw "Mrs. Reed" lying uncovered and naked, displaying an unexpected appendage, she gave a little cry and fled. Lou, who was awake and witnessed her shock, was in stitches for days over the sighting.

The sparse setup at the hotel helped Lou focus singularly on *Coney Island Baby*. In between writing songs and recording, he met with his lawyers to discuss his three lawsuits against the Katz brothers. For entertainment, he listened to tapes of the comedian Richard Pryor and held court. In between Lou's raps, Rachel and assorted visitors whiled away the hours playing Monopoly. During his stay at the hotel, a friend brought a grateful Lou a copy of the manuscript of Lou's book of poems, *All the Pretty People*, that he wanted to get published. He had mislaid the collection during his recent move.

CONEY ISLAND BABY WAS FIRST RECORDED FROM OCTOBER 18 TO 25. RCA was very hopeful. "They said, you can do anything you want so long as it's not *Metal Machine Music*," Lou sneered. He entered the studio with Steve Katz again as coproducer and a full complement of new musicians.

It wasn't long, however, before Steve found Lou impossible to work with. And, stonewalled by Reed's amphetamine abuse, he quit. "There was no other way. Each day a new head trip. Finally I said to him, right in front of all the musicians who'd gone through this, 'I give up! If you're gonna play these games, I know you're gonna outwit me. I'm just your producer. I acknowledge that you're much smarter than I am—there's no point in playing these games.' " Asked "What's better than sex?" that week, Lou replied, "Facts!"

Steve recalled, "The drugs had taken over and things were completely crazy. I felt that Lou was, at the time, out of his mind. So I had to stop the sessions. I had someone in authority at RCA come to the studio and verify that I could not make an album with the artist—that was that."

During the recording of the album, Lou was so enmeshed in lawsuits with the Katz brothers it is amazing that he was able to concentrate on his work as well as he did. He thrived on conflict.

When Lester Bangs asked, "What do you think that the sense of guilt manifested in most of your songs has to do with being Jewish?" Lou snapped, "I don't know anyone Jewish." But he went out of his way to make anti-Semitic remarks about Dennis Katz, telling one astonished interviewer, "I've got that kike by the balls. If you ever wondered why they have noses like pigs, now you know. They're pigs. Whaddaya expect?" The lyrics to "Dirt" refer to someone who said shit tasted good for money. "I was specifically referring to my manager-lawyer at the time," Reed explained.

Reed and Katz sued each other for breach of contract. "There was a suit and a countersuit," Falk explained. "And by then, according to Dennis, it was black-and-white—Lou was a jerk and Lou was a . . . and don't even mention his name. This artiste he had extolled. And then Lou called me. He even asked me to manage him. I said, 'You don't want me to manage you.' I said, 'Lou, I will always tell the truth. I know that you feel hard done by, and in some ways you were, but I don't know if it was illegal. There may be things I don't know about. If you want to know anything, I'll tell you.' And I had a meeting with his lawyer at the time. And he was in my face with his finger and blah blah blah. I said, 'I'll be glad to tell you anything you want to know.' But he was trying to say that Lou was drugged-out half the time and didn't know what he was signing away and he was taken advantage of. But I said Lou was very bright and it was my impression that he was aware of what was going on."

Several years later, in an attempt to redeem himself before the eyes of the public, Lou published in *Punk* magazine the defendants' memorandum of laws concerning his suit with Steve Katz and Anxiety Productions. It read in part:

> *The relationship between an artist and his chosen producer is an intimate employer-employee relationship. The shocking bitterness and personal animosity with which Katz, the employee, regards Reed, the employer, is written in bold letters throughout Katz's Affidavit. For example, he calls Reed:*

> —confused, self-destructive and immersed in the drug culture
> (Katz Aff. p. 16)

> —an irresponsible drug-induced musical meanderer (p. 17)

> —financially irresponsible (p. 20)

Reed was convinced serious errors had been made. "I went over things with a microscope and found it so interesting. I've got three lawsuits going," he attested. "Everything from misrepresentation to fraud and back again. The management I had then had me in a cocoon in paranoia: when you're ripping somebody off that much, you don't want them outside talking to people."

"I was a bit erratic before," he admitted. "You get tired of fighting with people sometimes. And to avoid going through all of that, I mastered the art of recording known as 'capture the spontaneous moment and leave it at that.' Coney Island Baby is like that. You go into the studio with zero, write it on the spot, and make the lyrics up as the tape's running and that's it. What I wanna get on my records, since everyone else is so slick and dull, is that moment."

In October at the club of the moment, Ashley's, on lower Fifth Avenue, Lou met the man who would help bring Coney Island Baby to fruition. Godfrey Diamond, a talented young engineer in his early twenties, would become his next producer. Diamond admitted that he "really wasn't a huge fan of his up to that point. I guess I was too young. But I really loved the banana album and Transformer. 'Satellite of Love' was a work of art." Diamond returned to the Gramercy Park Hotel with Reed that night to listen to his new songs. "One thing that really impressed me is that he always goes for the tough edge, the risky stuff. I thought he was a real warrior, with such courage."

Around five o'clock on the morning of the day Reed and Godfrey finished Coney Island Baby, Lou took Diamond over to Danny Fields's apartment for an immediate judgment. Fields had become the critic and authority on the downtown music scene, and Lou regularly sought his opinion. As soon as they got there, they plugged in the record and took a seat in Fields's living room. To Diamond's dismay Danny pulled out a newspaper and appeared to be engrossed in it. Lou whispered to him that Danny always did this so you could not see the expression on his face while he listened to your record. After a tense (for Diamond) forty-five minutes, Fields snapped shut his paper and declared, "Great! Not one bad song." They stayed there until eight A.M. when Diamond had to go to work.

All that remained was for Mick Rock to do a photo session for the cover, and Lou had completed one of his finer solo recordings. RCA was as pleased with the results as he was.

As soon as Lou completed Coney Island Baby, like a musician on tour well oiled after playing six weeks of dates, he went straight into another project equally dear to his heart. Andy Warhol, who was in 1975 at the height of his game once again, had just published his best book, *The Philosophy of Andy Warhol.* It was full of advice about how to tackle the very problems that most beset Lou. Inscribing a photocopy of the proofs to his old disciple with "Honey, from Andy," Warhol seduced the prolific Reed into writing an album of songs based on the book for a projected Broadway show. It was a dry run of sorts for *Songs for Drella,* Reed's posthumous homage to Warhol, which he would release in 1990. According to Bob Jones, "Lou used to talk at great length about Andy and how Andy was somehow the ultimate figure of idealization. I remember Lou telling me that Andy was the strongest man that he'd ever met— physically. That he could leap over buildings in a single bound. He was absolutely crazed about it. He said Andy had arms like steel. For Lou, Andy was also, I remember him saying, like Aristotle. Like Aristotle and Leonardo and Andy. I remember a conversation in which I said surely you don't think Andy is as great as Leonardo. And Lou said, 'Absolutely, much greater than Leonardo, much more interesting and smarter.' "

"I see him all the time," Lou explained. "I've talked to him more than probably anyone I've ever talked to. He showed me how to save a lot of time."

Jones went to the Factory with Lou once when they were both speeding: "I remember sitting on the table and having Bob Colacello making fun of Lou in a catty way. And Fred Hughes coming around and Lou disappearing into the back with Andy. *Coney Island Baby* had just come out and he was bringing Andy a copy.

"Andy was a little bothered by him. They had had hard times together, had difficulties and arguments. Lou was pretending a greater closeness to Andy than those who were around Andy had so that Lou's attitude was, 'I'm closer to Andy than you would ever be, Bob or Fred.' And actually Bob and Fred resented that and were condescending about Lou. But Andy wanted to keep his distance from Lou."

Lou wrote his adaptation of Andy Warhol's *Philosophy* overnight. "I was so surprised," Warhol admitted. "He just came over the next day and had it all done." "I played the songs for Andy," Lou explained. "He was fascinated but horrified. I think they kind of scared him."

*   *   *

IN MANY WAYS, IN HIS ROCK-'N'-ROLL ANIMAL INCARNATION LOU WAS more completely the controlled self he wanted to be. During this period he reached his artistic maturity and was able to best collaborate with the differing selves he had picked up along the way. "Realism was the key, the records were letters, real letters from me to certain other people who had and still have basically no music, be it verbal or instrumental, to listen to," he wrote in the liner notes to *Metal Machine Music.*

Describing heavy-metal music, he wrote it was "diffuse, obtuse, weak, boring and ultimately an embarrassment." Responding to criticism about ethnic or racial slurs in his lyrics (he actually backed off from including "I Wanna Be Black" in the collection *Sally Can't Dance* for fear of a backlash), Reed snapped at one trembling interviewer, "What's wrong with cheap, dirty jokes? Fuck you, I never said I was tasteful. I am not tasteful."

AT THE BEGINNING OF 1976, LOU MADE A DEFINITIVE BREAK FROM HIS recent past. He no longer relied upon Katz to steer him through the twisted path to international superstardom. He no longer looked to Warhol for approbation and permission to be Lou Reed. Now, instead of hiring a new manager for the seventies, as so many of his peers were doing, he elected instead to hire a booking agent to oversee his increasingly profitable touring career, one Johnny Podell. Wrote Reed chronicler Peter Doggett: "Fast-talking, all skin and bone and at that time in his life very fond of cocaine, Podell was a man of the streets, and Lou adopted him as the latest in a succession of bosom buddies–comminglers, just as he had done Katz, Heller, Sesnick, and Warhol before him. At Ashley's, the music biz bar and restaurant on Fifth Avenue at Thirteenth Street where Lou and Podell hung out with their friends, the regulars quipped that their business relationship was 'a marriage made in the emergency ward!' "

Having, for all intents and purposes, rid himself of Dennis Katz— although their lawsuits would rage on for two years—Lou, in the enthusiasm of the moment, proceeded to talk up John Podell to the press. "I'm not unmanageable," he said. "Not true. It's just that I've never hit on the right people before. John Podell, my new man, is great. He got an MA in business psychology at twenty-one, and he's as good at practice as he is at theory. He doesn't handle my money, I've got all new people to do that, but he gets all the rest together. It's a whole new show now on that front. Anyone who was connected with me on a business level before is out. My accountants, lawyers, record-company manager, his brother quote producer—all out. With Johnny you've got a tiger by the tail. He's ready to go. The product is there. I like that. I'm the product and I call myself the product. Much better than being called an artist—that means they're fucking you, they think you don't know from shit. This time I'm doing it for real, because it seems that's what's supposed to happen."

Around the beginning of 1976, Lou's new status was made evident when he moved with Rachel and the new addition to their family, a dachshund named the Baron, into a furnished Upper East Side apartment building on Fifty-second Street a few doors down from the reclusive Greta Garbo. Although Lou did not make much of his famous neighbor, choosing to play the connection down, all his so-called two-bit friends were soon referring to Lou's new nest as "the Garbo apartment." "He lived for a time near Greta Garbo in an apartment in a high-rise with a doorman," recalled Bob Jones. "To me it seemed very glamorous—actually it was two rooms. But there was always the drug addict's lifestyle. There was nothing in the fridge except coffee ice cream. There were records in boxes and things, but that was it." The apartment fit the Lou Reed mold, furnished with electronic equipment, guitars, stacks of tapes, and a few personal items, such as the plastic plant that he insisted on watering.

"Lou was then wearing the A-head's uniform," Jones noted. "When you went out of the apartment, the uniform was quite set—it was a white T-shirt tucked into blue jeans worn with a belt. Boots or shoes, black. A cap of some sort. And very tight, a black leather jacket.

"Lou was getting into gay porn magazines. I remember having the same kind of interest in them as I did in the gory police stuff. It was not erotic to me but I was looking at another world. Because it was forbidden it was interesting—fascinating."

Lou's new dog, the Baron, bore a resemblance to Seymour. Lou, admitting that "underneath it all I'm just a sentimentalist," expressed the same kind of gentle, obsessive feelings toward him. "The Baron is a miniature dachshund with a forceful personality," noted a friend who visited Reed that January. "He justifies his name by his great ability to corner great chunks of the apartment in which he resides, and subjects all those who enter, including his co-inhabitants, to the random exhibition of his caprices. Mr. Reed, one of his co-inhabitants, is enamored of him. They have an excellent relationship based on Mr. Reed's acceptance of his menial role in the Baron's life."

Reed explained, "I'm here to feed him, walk him, act as chief thrower of chaseable objects and general dog's body—what an apt description! At first it was difficult, but now that I have learned the wisdom of the Baron's way, all is well. He's a total exhibitionist. This morning he displayed a full stem for us, the disgusting little beast."

When Lou wasn't in the studio, rehearsing for a tour, or voyaging around the city in search of characters or materials, he spent his time at home, writing songs, playing music, and receiving a stream of visitors ranging from his drug dealers through recording engineers and journalists to guitar players and assorted drug buddies. Ed Lister and Bob Jones would go around to see him and shoot speed. Lou was constantly worried that the police would come to his place looking for Lister—and on one occasion they did, because Lister had left a stolen car in Lou's parking space.

Through all the chaos Rachel looked on protectively, always making sure there was enough coffee ice cream and Marlboros. Rachel, to whom the title song on *Coney Island Baby* was dedicated, had proven more than dependable during the siege of the Gramercy Park Hotel. She was increasingly prominent in Lou's public life, appearing in photo spreads in rock magazines and constantly at his side whenever he went anywhere, affording Lou the silent admiration of a dog. An inscrutable, stone-faced Indian, she was undoubtedly the most comfortable of his live-in loves, largely perhaps because she offered him complete devotion with no strings attached, no demands other than the pleasure of his company—just like in a movie. With new resolve, Reed professed: "All the albums I put out after this are going to be things I want to put out. No more bullshit, no more dyed-hair, faggot-junkie trip. I mimic me better than anyone else, so if everyone else is making money ripping me off, I figure maybe I better get on it. Why not? I created Lou Reed. I have nothing even faintly in common with that guy, but I can play him well—really well."

Coney Island Baby's release in January 1976 brought Reed artistic acclaim and commercial success. Once the album was out, Reed was ready to return to the fray with what he considered his "strongest album, bar none," along with a newborn will to sustain his drive. "This time I'm gonna do it right," he said, "and everybody knows it. *Coney Island Baby* was a statement of renewal because it was my record. I didn't have much time, and I didn't have much money, but it was mine. Saying 'I'm a Coney Island baby' at the end of that song is like saying I haven't backed off an inch, and don't you forget it."

The reviews were overwhelmingly positive. "He meanders through his own solo twilight movie examining whatever catches his eye . . . [de-scribing] the aridity which T. S. Eliot recorded in *The Waste Land,*" wrote Mick Rock. "He has epitomized New York for fellow artists and media observers both in his lifestyle and in his art. Chronicler of the shadow world, the deviants, the drug limbo, the concrete jungle, he is the poet laureate of that city [New York]."

"New York is the most exciting, vibrant, vital . . . energy giver and energy taker," Lou rapped to a friend that year. "I mean, isn't it inter-esting the way New York is becoming *the* place all of a sudden? I'm from New York, I'm Jewish. Like Flo and Eddie once described me, 'Oh, Lou, you're just a typical fast-working little Jew guy from New York.' "

"Evoking Genet decadence . . . Warhol chic, European ennui . . . [his work] is expressed cinematically by Martin Scorsese and Sam Peck-inpah, novelistically by William Burroughs," wrote James Walcott in the *Village Voice*. He is "a master, narrator, short-story writer at heart," wrote Larry Sloman in *Rolling Stone*. "There's a little of lots of people in Lou . . . Jagger, Warhol, lots of Lenny Bruce," wrote Jack Garner.

"I have seen rock's future, and its name is Lou Reed," wrote Pat Ast, a Warhol superstar, in New York's *SoHo Weekly News*.

But to some Lou appeared to be veering away from the hard-core music he had been associated with. Peter Laughner, the lead singer of Pere Ubu, wrote a scathing review of *Coney Island Baby:* "The damn things starts out exactly like an Eagles record! And with the exception of 'Charlie's Girl,' which is mercifully short and to the point, it's a downhill slide.

"Finally there's 'Coney Island Baby,' just maudlin, dumb, self-pity: 'Can you believe I wann'd t'play football for th' coach? . . . ' Sure, Lou, when I was all uptight about being a fag in high school, I did too."

"As a Velvet, Reed was at once plaintive and biting, but gone solo he chose a monotone with a punk's lip and a snob's delivery," wrote Georgia

Christgau in the *Village Voice*. "Perhaps he was making an elaborate, five-record joke of his own mangled reputation (a dull fellow), or was hoping to cash in on his own great line, 'Of course you're a bore, but in that you're not charmless.' He didn't. Although his singing on *Baby* still drives the uninitiated from the room, I find an occasional inflection in the difference between a long-playing joke and a sincere effort, as I do his decision to take his hands away from his face and play guitar again. Maybe this boyfriend Rachel has been a good mirror.

"Since Reed is a self-professed liar who claims that a two-record set of feedback noise is his masterpiece, his work defies committed analysis, especially a Pollyanna analysis like this one. That he has become a lazy songwriter, repeating images like 'two-bit friends' and bottles of wine, I am sure. But even if he's replaced inventions with gimmicks (the chapel bells opening 'Crazy Feeling' are a bit much), it's comforting to know that Reed has been going on doo-wop runs ever since 'Candy Says,' in 1969. At least he's interested again. His ability to create mind-blowing rock songs is probably gone, but so what. Reed's been showing up at CBGB's a lot lately. In the audience."

This time, Lou Reed defended himself vigorously: "They're not what people think of as archetypal Lou Reed songs, but they forgot on the first Velvets album 'I'll Be Your Mirror,' 'Femme Fatale:' I've always liked that kind of stuff and now you're going to have a whole album full of it. *The Many Moods of Lou Reed*, just like Johnny Mathis, and if they don't like it, they can shove it."

Coney Island Baby came out the year gay liberation crossed into the mainstream. Once again, Lou's paean to a drag queen, the title song, became the sound track of the moment. It caught the gay spirit that was everywhere taking over the parade of New York City and offered redemption via love. But it was overshadowed by Dylan's *Desire*, which came out in the aftermath of the groundbreaking Rolling Thunder Review, and David Bowie's *Station to Station*, which won Bowie hundreds of thousands of votes in the "Who's more important, Bowie or Reed?" contest. Frank Zappa's *Apostrophe* and the Rolling Stones' *Black and Blue* were other gold records that year.

Coney Island Baby marked the end of Reed's commitment to RCA. It was Lou's most commercially successful post *Rock 'n' Roll Animal* venture until his *New York* album in 1989, reaching no. 41 on *Billboard*'s LP chart.

Yet, despite good record sales and Lou's success during the first four years of his solo career, he now reportedly found himself in debt to RCA to the tune of $700,000. Figuring that he would never make money as long as he remained with the label, he decided to shop for another record company.

"Then, I got a call from Clive Davis, the ex-president of Columbia Records now heading a new label, Arista, who had a reputation as a champion of the artist over the corporate man," Lou remembered. "He said, 'Hey, how ya doing? Haven't seen you for a while.' He knew how I was doing. He said, 'Why don't we have lunch?' I felt like saying, 'You mean you want to be seen with me in public?' If Clive could be seen with me, I had turned the corner. I grabbed Rachel and said, 'Do you know who just called?' "

Clive Davis had just begun his new Arista label, but he and Reed had known each other for some time. "Lou and I were friends prior to the business relationship," Davis recounted. "I remember touting Bruce Springsteen very strongly to Lou, and Lou had never seen Springsteen. We went down to the Bottom Line [in 1975 during Springsteen's famous summer run]. At the end of the performance I remember Lou saying, 'Look, he's good.' But he was not turned on, at the time, by what he felt was the rather tame imagery that was being evoked. I'll never forget that Lou took me on a tour of Manhattan the likes of which I've never had. It was an amazing experience. Seeing Lou Reed's world was a very revealing, very eye-opening situation. We were friends during this period when he was dissatisfied with his existing label. He called me and said, 'I see where you're going with Arista, I see what you're doing. Would you be interested in signing me?' The lawyers got together and we worked out a deal."

Declaring that he was now back in the saddle, Lou signed a contract with Davis. Asked by Lisa Robinson, "So what do you think Arista will do for you that RCA didn't?" Lou replied, "Sell records." Eager to follow up on the success of *Coney Island Baby*, and recharged by the relationship with Arista, Lou immediately went back into the studio to record his next album. Originally titled *Nomad*, it would be released as *Rock and Roll Heart*.

It looked as if all the factors were set up to create a successful record. Lou had a good band; Davis was fully behind him; his audience was growing; his relationship with Rachel was more stable than any other he had had since college. They were even talking about renting or buying a house in the country.

Clive Davis was well-known for taking a hands-on approach with his artists, particularly when it came to picking hit singles. He told Lou he could make him a million dollars if Lou would let him do a little work on the title song for *Rock and Roll Heart*. "He wanted to sweeten it up," recalled Reed, "horns or strings or something. [He argued] that the song had potential to really be radio-worthy if we just did that to it." Though he recognized Davis's talent, Lou turned his suggestion down flat. "I'm a control person," he repeated. "I fought so hard to get things to the point of having that control that I wouldn't relinquish it. He said, 'You'll be there. Nothing will be done without your approval.' 'Nah.' I'm like a brick wall sometimes."

Lou ended up writing most of the album in the studio: "I had a couple of songs before we went into the studio, but they changed. The rest I wrote in the studio. It's much more fun that way. No, it isn't expensive because I'm very quick. It took twenty-seven days to record that album, including mixing. It took as long to mix as it did to record. I just had the basic progressions, of two or three chords, but no lyrics."

Lou threw himself completely into the songs. To keyboardist Michael Fonfara, Lou's longest term musical collaborator during the 1970s, "it was like Method acting." Fonfara and the rest of the studio band soon discovered Reed's fresh determination during the recording sessions, where he turned out to be a rigid taskmaster. Lou would present each new song to the group once. Then Fonfara would rehearse the band until they knew the song and had the right arrangement for the vocal.

Feeling particularly comfortable and connected to the music, Lou picked up his guitar and played lead on the album for the first time since he broke up with the Velvets: "On other albums I let other people do what they liked; this time I got serious and played what I liked. Every track. There's lots of very dumb rock-and-roll songs on it, but then I like dumb rock and roll. It's very hard to find a dumb guitar player and a dumb piano player, everyone's so much into being technically together. But I fit the bill, because I play very stupid."

This gave him the distance to reflect objectively on his work while remaining a part of it: "This may sound perverse, but it helps keep me out of the way so whatever it is that people call creative talent can come through. It keeps the more esoteric aspects of my persona, if not exactly anchored down, at least available to anyone who wants to check them out. I don't have anything to do with it, I just have to let it have its own way. I think I've kept out of the way on this album more successfully than ever before. I know what I'm doing. I always look so crazy and disorganized, but I'm not.

"It's very hard to find someone who can play dumb on a nice rock-and-roll song. But I can play really dumb piano. And I write songs with only two chords in them. Like 'Banging on My Drum.' "

Beneath the surface buoyancy, however, all was not well. Throughout the summer of 1976, during an unexpected drought in the amphetamine market, Lou was scrambling to find a doctor to write a prescription for Desoxyn. The drought brought on depression, inactivity, and bone crushers.

After finishing the record, however, Lou managed to muster the energy to produce an album, called *Wild Angel,* by a friend of Lou's at Syracuse, Nelson Slater. "That was one of the best things I've ever done," Reed commented. "RCA released it to about three people, I think. So no one very much noticed it. I think we sold six copies." The critics who picked up on it singled out a track called "We" as a great showcase for Reed's production talents.

Lou was so broke at this time he rarely had $10 in his pocket. He was going to lectures on Warhol's films by Ondine and looking for speed connections. Part of his problem, he said, was his incipient honesty. "This is the worst period I've seen," he told one friend, "and it's not going to get better." A short reprieve came when he made a connection in July with a doctor who wrote him a prescription for Desoxyn. In the autumn, Lou and the band were gearing up to go back on the road in what he described as "that savage jungle called America. *Rock and Roll Heart* will be backed with a tour, a fully-fledged attack, a seething assault, I call it germ warfare." With drugs boiling on his stove, Lou rehearsed for the *Rock and Roll Heart* tour. Unfortunately, the prescription soon ran out and he found himself on the ropes once again.

The tour preparations were nearly as chaotic as being on the road. Mick Rock was on his way over to shoot the cover and design the stage and lights. Lister came round on several occasions. Lou's lawyers warned him that his lifestyle could be detrimental to his case against Katz. There was no way the lawyer could see it sitting well with the people in the halls of justice.

Rock and Roll Heart, released in October, was a disappointment. It received lukewarm reviews and sales. "Certainly don't bother with this record unless, that is, you're the kind of person that gets off on watching paint dry. Come to think of it, *Rock and Roll Heart* would make the perfect background music for that," wrote Nick Kent in *New Musical Express.* "*Rock and Roll Heart* is very well produced," Reed said in his defense. "I produced it. My records are for real. But that song—'I Believe in Love'—coming from Lou Reed is supposed to be a very strange statement. One kid said to me he really liked the lyrics on 'Banging on My Drum.' And I said, 'But there are no lyrics,' and he said, 'Frustration.' I thought I'd written a song about fun, fun, fun . . . But apparently not. *Rolling Stone* said that song was about masturbation, so that just goes to show."

RCA capitalized on the publicity by issuing a greatest-hits package, *Walk on the Wild Side,* notable for its cover Polaroids of Lou and Rachel. It included "Nowhere at All," a gritty outtake from the *Coney Island Baby* sessions, which sounded the way the Hunter-Wagner band would have if they had been let loose in the studio.

Lou was scheduled to tour the U.S. and Europe through December. Over the previous couple of years, Reed had assembled the most durable band of his career, the Everyman Band, led by the keyboard player Michael Fonfara, the lone survivor of the band that had cut *Sally Can't Dance* back in 1974, and saxist Marty Fogel, with Michael Suchorsky on drums. The bass player, Ellard Boles, aka the Moose, was a mountain of a man who became one of Lou's loyal companions through the end of the decade. "The other concerts don't count," Reed explained. "This is the first time I had total control. I'll be taking the same bunch of clowns I worked with on the album. I want to make some kind of a show of it. I didn't want the usual horseshit with opening acts and light shows and all that stuff. None of the dates will be played in very big halls; it's all three- or four-thousand seaters with hopefully a week of shows in New York City at a small theater. It'll be for those people who care. Hopefully the more bestial or vitriolic rock fans will be kept out. I'll be picking up from where I left off before I was so rudely interrupted; which spans a good degree of time.

"But this time I'll be coming in at a higher level with no dark glasses. It'll be as close to me as you'll ever get. As close to me as I've ever gotten. I want to junk a lot of that old stuff that people seem to get off on."

Bert van der Kamp interviewed Lou prior to his tour in Holland:

"I found him very sympathetic and a very sensitive guy, but I was very surprised that a year and a half later and he didn't seem to recognize me. I asked him and said we spent all these hours together and you showed me your poetry and all this, and he said to me, 'Well, I must have been in a good mood then.' He was acting like he had never seen me. This was in 1976. So I used a word to describe him that I had seen in print before. This was a word invented by Arthur Koestler, which he used to describe Bobby Fischer, who was sensitive as a mimosa towards his own feelings but towards other people's feelings he was like an elephant. So I used the word *mimophant,* and I started using that word for Lou. He was the sensitive guy who was easily hurt, but otherwise he would act like he was trying to hurt other guys."

He was accompanied by Rachel, who acted as a minder-cum-manager. "Rachel is very interesting," Lou said. "Doesn't react very much, but full of great quotes. The other day it was, 'If you're gonna be black be black, but don't give me no shades of gray.' Rachel has looked after the money and kept me in shape and watched over the road crew. At last there's someone hustling around for me that I can trust." She was a good supporter for Lou, loyal, reliable, and protective. What Rachel lacked, however, was the sharp eye that Lou needed to calm his paranoia. He complained to his friends that Rachel couldn't spot gangsters in crowds.

Despite poor sales for *Rock and Roll Heart,* Arista supported an extensive tour, which Lou kicked off in style. Performing in front of a band of forty-eight TV sets and accompanied by the surprise addition of Ornette Coleman's trumpet player, Don Cherry, Lou gave one of his most satisfying shows in years. Gone was the shambling rocker of 1975, replaced by the elegant jazz singer of 1976.

The Everyman Band perfected dynamics. They would sometimes quiet down to the point where the audience could hardly hear them at all, leaving Lou on his own, knowing that when he was ready, they could explode.

Lou had chosen a compelling new image with the care of a woman selecting an outfit for a night out. In place of the black look with leather and sunglasses, he appeared in tight blue jeans, high-heeled black boots and a long-sleeved sweater that covered his arms and hugged his ribs. His only prop was the occasional cigarette from behind which he threw baleful glances into the audience like darts.

"One realized what was missing only at the very end of the two-hour, fifteen-minute affair, when Mr. Reed deigned finally to pick up his guitar," John Rockwell noted in the *New York Times*. "The sound of a twanging electric guitar at long last lent the music—played previously by saxophone, keyboards, bass, and drums—a true rock aura."

Unfortunately, in December 1976 the tour ended in trauma when Rachel, who was suffering from an infected lung, was mugged in L.A. "He got kicked in the balls and had some internal bleeding," Reed explained. "That really had me strung out."

Chapter Fourteen

THE MASTER OF PSYCHOPATHIC INSOLENCE

1977–78

His credentials are unshakable.

—John Rockwell
The New York Times, March 13, 1978

"LOU REED'S ANGRY REACTION TO HIS GLITTER YEARS SERVES AS THE PER-fect dividing point between the early 1970s and the late part of the decade," Mark Edwards wrote in the *London Sunday Times*. "Annoyed at the travesty of his original self that he had become, he released *Metal Machine Music*. It's an hour of white noise. There is no music on it. Just distortion. Coming out in 1975, it neatly signaled the end of glam as a whole, while the emphasis of the record on nasty, angry, unmusical noise heralded the punk explosion that was to erupt the following year," Edwards concluded.

1975 was indeed a pivotal year in rock. The glitter scene died. Punk was born. Springsteen arrived. Dylan was reborn. Lou Reed was super-aware of the change. In fact, no single band and no single performer benefited from punk as much as the Velvet Underground and, in particular, Lou Reed.

When punk rock's New York headquarters, CBGB's on the Bowery, opened its doors at the end of 1973, the NY rock scene was mostly populated by touring superstars. The only remnants of the rock under-ground were the dying New York Dolls and the *Berlin*-era Lou Reed. Reed's raw reports from the underbelly of the city were an inspiration that helped open the way for punk rock. Fragments of, among others, the

Ramones, Blondie, Television, and Talking Heads began to coalesce as early as 1974. According to M. C. Kostek in the *VU Handbook*, "Brian Eno's quip about how not many people bought the *Velvet Underground and Nico* album but of those who did, everyone went out and formed a band, carried much truth. Many of the most creative people in rock music from the seventies—the Stooges, New York Dolls, Patti Smith, Television, Pere Ubu, Ramones, Richard Hell, Jonathan Richman, Roxy Music, David Bowie, Buzzcocks, Talking Heads, Wire, Cabaret Voltaire, and Eno himself strongly reflect and validate the Velvets' massive musical influence."

By the final months of 1975, however, while Lou was recording *Coney Island Baby*, two powerful streams of rock were surging forward, threatening to leave him in their wake. In the mainstream, Bob Dylan was going through a resurrection, touring with his Rolling Thunder Review and recording his next album, *Desire*, which would go to No. 1 around the world. David Bowie had, in collaboration with John Lennon, his first no. 1 American single, "Fame." The new boy, Bruce Springsteen, was simultaneously on the covers of *Time* and *Newsweek*. In left field, all the leading punk bands were poised to make the enormous impact they would soon have. *Coney Island Baby* and *Rock and Roll Heart* offered little competition to Springsteen's *Born to Run*, Patti Smith's *Horses*, or the Ramones' *The Ramones*. Where was Lou's place in all of this?

It wasn't until John Holmstrom's *Punk* magazine came along in New York in January 1976, pulling the disparate music of the punk groups together, showcasing them as if they were major stars, that punk could be looked upon as a movement. Holmstrom put Lou on the cover of *Punk*'s first issue. It was Holmstrom's view that Reed's independent spirit, enthusiasm, and dedication to passion made him the ultimate punk rocker. "If you were going to do a rock-and-roll time line, Lou's there for every decade," he pointed out. "From doo-wop to garage rock to psychedelic to glitter to disco to punk rock and beyond it later to alternative rock and to sober-rock." His cover portrait captured Lou's chemical-insect persona as perfectly as the cover of *Coney Island Baby*, released the same month, put across his chameleonlike MC role.

Everybody, it suddenly appeared, owed something to Lou Reed. Consequently, in the second half of the seventies when his career could well have taken the nosedive it was in the midst of, Lou was picked and held up by, in particular, Bangs, Meltzer, Holmstrom, Rockwell, Jon Savage, Charles Shaar Murray, Nick Kent, etc.

It was during a visit to CBGB's to see the Ramones just before Thanksgiving in November 1975 that Reed had the pivotal encounter that launched him onto the cover of *Punk*. Only twenty or thirty people were in attendance that night, but the rank, dark little room crackled with the exhilaration of rock in the making.

Sitting at a candlelit table with, of all people, Richard Robinson, Lou was approached by two raw, loony-looking Connecticut teenagers, Holmstrom and the magazine's resident punk, Legs McNeil, who would shortly become the Johnny Carson and Ed McMahon of the punk scene. "Hey, you!" they accosted him. "You're going to do an interview with us!" Lou, who was on one of this three-day cruises through the underbelly of the city, watching the parade of geeks and freaks pass before him, fell right into his part, giving one of his best interviews without thinking about it. Lou enjoyed talking to interviewers because they gave him a gloss on what was going on in the rock scene, but later claimed to have no recollection of this particular incident. Holmstrom commented, "He wasn't getting too many people to talk to him who liked *Metal Machine*. Danny Fields was there and Legs met Danny, and everybody went nuts because Lou Reed was there that night." To Legs McNeil, the Ramones' performance was the most moving thing he had ever seen in his life: "The Ramones came out in these black leather jackets. They looked so stunning. They counted off, then each one started playing a different song. Their self-hatred was just amazing, they were so pissed off." After taking in the Ramones' fifteen-minute set, Lou spent the next two hours sparring vigorously with the two punk kids and *Punk*'s British correspondent Mary Harron.

Lou apparently enjoyed the show.
Punk: Do you like the Ramones?
Lou Reed: Oh, they're fantastic!
Punk: Have you seen anyone else that you like?
Reed: Television. I like Television. I think Tom Verlaine's really nice.
Punk: Do you like Patti Smith?
Reed: Oh, yeah, yeah.
Punk: How about Bruce Springsteen?
Reed: Oh, I love him.

Punk: You do?

REED: He's one of us.

Punk: Thank you.

REED: He's a shit—what are you talking about, what kind of stupid question is that?

Punk: O.K.

REED: I mean, do I ask you what you like? Why does anyone give a fuck what I like?

Punk: Well, you're a rock star!

REED: Oh . . . I keep forgetting. Why, do you like Springsteen?

Punk: No, I think he's a piece of shit.

REED: He's great at what he does. . . . It's not to my taste, y'know, he's from New Jersey. . . . I'm very, y'know, partial to New York groups, y'know. . . . Springsteen's already finished, isn't he? I mean, isn't he a has-been?

Punk: I feel he's a has-been.

REED: Isn't Springsteen already over-the-hill? I mean—isn't everybody saying that they constructed him because they needed a rock star? . . . I mean . . . Already, like, groups are coming out and they're saying they're the new Bruce Springsteen, which is really . . . He was only popular for a week.

Holmstrom couldn't believe Lou was talking like this on tape. Legs, however, was not so easily won over. During a long discussion of *Metal Machine Music* and the record business, he started squirming in his seat like an impatient child. "I thought Lou was boring as hell," he remarked. "I was an eighteen-year-old guy, I didn't want to talk about art and the record company. I wanted to talk about cheeseburgers, that's all we had in common. I knew he was like so cool, and I was kind of like, we are not worthy, Lou. But, you knew whatever you did this guy was going to think you were an asshole. He was just too cool.

"Lou has this vibe of not being anyone. The guy just seems completely threatened by everything. But he's so good, you know, it's funny, because the punk way to appreciate people is to make fun of them. Like Tish and Snooky used to have a song and it was sung to the tune of 'Sweet Jane.' The refrain was 'Lou Reed' instead of 'Sweet Jane.' 'Lou Reed' . . . then they had all these funny lyrics. So I was paying tribute to him, but I didn't think Lou appreciated it."

Halfway through the interview Legs jumped in.

Legs: Did you ever hear the Dictators' lyrics—what they said about you?

REED: I hope it's nothing bad.

Punk: Yeah—"I think Lou Reed is a creep."

REED: That's funny—because when I ran into one of them, he was slobbering all over me saying, "Hey—I hope you don't mind what we say about you." And I just pat him on the head—y'know, nice doggie, nice doggie.

Mary Harron, mouth agape, sat through the sparring match with Holmstrom and McNeil. What impressed her most about the hysterically whacked-out interview is the extent to which Lou really looked down on them and how stupid he made them all feel. Out in the street after the interview, she recalled, "John was jumping up and down yelling, 'We got our cover! We got our cover!' But Legs flipped out, screaming, '*Who does fucking Lou Reed think he fucking is?*' " Legs felt as if his soul had been taken: "I felt that meeting with Lou, somehow we had been corrupted forever. You felt it in some emotional, stark way. I mean Lou always seemed like he wanted to go darker than sex, murder, mutilation, further. And you always got the feeling that you were definitely an idiot around him. I didn't want to sit at his feet that night. I didn't like him. He didn't seem like a nice guy. I mean, I wouldn't want to hang out with him."

Holmstrom, on the other hand, was in a trance, totally persuaded that putting Reed on the cover of their first issue was the most exciting choice possible. "I saw *Metal Machine Music* as the beginning of the punk-rock movement," he said. "It was the ultimate punk-rock album. It was the greatest punk statement ever made. It was fuck you to the record company and everyone who bought it. It was, 'This is what I want to do the way I want to do it.' How can you get more punk than that? It was more punk than the Sex Pistols, the Ramones, everything that came out afterward. I think he meant it that way, and we treated it that way."

Punk #1, containing the interview and a glowing review of *Metal Machine Music,* was published in January 1976, the same month *Coney Island Baby* came out. It had a terrific impact. Danny Fields praised Holmstrom in the *SoHo Weekly News* for "inventing a new interview form." "Instead of a photo, the cover was a wickedly accurate cartoon of

Reed as metal man: the feature inside was not typeset but told in *fumetti*,"
wrote the British rock historian Jon Savage. "The surrounding artwork is
as important as Reed's insults: when the interviewers follow Reed down
the block, there they are in cartoons. The effect was both immediate and
distanced, a formal innovation on a par with *Mad* magazine or the Ramones' own manipulations."

According to John Holmstrom, Lou was impressed. "He said, 'I barely
remember doing the interview and there I am on the cover of this thing.'
He thought it had the whole image thing perfect. I was just knocked out
because I was this twenty-year-old kid. And here was this guy who I'd pay
seven fifty to see live gushing over my magazine when he hated everything
in the world. It just blew me away." In retrospect, Holmstrom reflected,
"*Metal Machine Music* almost ended his career. He could have become
another forgotten Elton John kind of person if we hadn't put him on the
cover. Instead, he became the godfather of punk and it resurrected his
career."

"People who think I got something out of *Metal Machine*, monetarily
or otherwise, should have another think coming," countered Reed. "All
it accomplished was negative. It'll be that much harder for *Coney Island
Baby* to prove itself. A lot of people got turned off, and I am so happy to
lose the people who got turned off. You have no idea. It just clears the air.
That's the end of it. If anybody wanted *Coney Island Baby*, it was going to
be my way."

Rock-star ranks had swelled by the midseventies to such unmanageable
proportions that it was hard to know how to distinguish one from another. The cover of *Punk* picked Lou Reed out of the international swamp
and placed him squarely in the vanguard, as a heroic figurehead. The new
magazine brought Lou into the forefront of the punk world. Soon Lou was
pouring advice into the ears of Tom Verlaine of Television and David
Byrne of Talking Heads—mostly about getting a lawyer. But it was Lou's
presence more than anything else that turned everybody on. He went to
CBGB's in his uniform shades and black leather jacket with Rachel. They
sat at a table and listened to the music like everybody else. Lou didn't
grandstand and was obviously enjoying himself. When he saw Patti Smith
playing "Real Good Time Together" at CBGB's, he was genuinely
thrilled, clapping with glee and telling everybody at his table that he had
written the song. Johnny Ramone remembered how many of them really

began to feel something was happening when Lou started coming to the club.

James Walcott, writing in the *Village Voice,* had a particularly astute view of Lou's presence at CBGB's:

"Where Lou Reed used to stare death down (particularly in the black-blooded *Berlin*), he now christens random violence. Small wonder, then, that his conversation ripples with offhand brutality: though he probably couldn't open a package of Twinkies without his hands trembling, he enjoys babbling threats of violence. One night, when a girl at CBGB clapped loudly (and out of beat) to a Television song, Reed threatened to knock 'the cunt's head off'; she blithely ignored him, and he finally got up and left. No one takes his bluster seriously; I even know women who find his steely bitterness sexy.

"This walking crystallization of cankerous cynicism possesses such legendary anticharisma that there's something princely about him, something perversely impressive."

Cale scoffed at the comparisons between the punk bands and the VU: "Everybody's talking about this band the Velvet Underground influencing this and that. They're even saying Talking Heads are reminiscent of the Velvet Underground, which has absolutely nothing to do with what we sounded like. And many of these people making these assessments and writing these reviews never saw us live. All they've got to go by are live reissues by Lou Reed, that kind of narcissistic nepotism. He just regenerates the same material over and over again, in different form. Lou has his whole life sorted out now. He's become the Jewish businessman we always knew he was."

The parallels between Reed's and Cale's careers through the seventies reveal just how important image is in rock. As a body of work, John's solo albums are arguably superior to Lou's. As Lester Bangs pointed out, " 'Fear' and 'Gun' on John Cale's *Fear* are the kind of cuts Lou Reed could be writing now if his imagination had not short-circuited. Unlike much of Reed's recent work, the music of John Cale is never thin nor euphemized nor needlessly lurid. It is the kind of music that does the Velvet Underground tradition proud, and that's something to live up to." Cale's influence on punk—he produced among other notable works Patti Smith's first and greatest album, *Horses*—was arguably stronger than Reed's. Yet once they went solo, Lou's image was always stronger than John's.

But the direct influence of Lou Reed and the Velvet Underground on the punk-rock movement was exemplified by their prominent positions in record charts compiled in fanzines in Britain. Though these charts did not reflect the tastes of mainstream rock-and-roll audiences, they established Reed's and the Velvet Underground's popularity with the punk-rock audience. For example, the second issue of *Ripped And Torn* (January 1977), one of the most widely circulated British punk fanzines, gave "Foggy Notion" by the Velvet Underground the no. 5 position on its singles chart. The same fanzine's album chart listed six entries (including the no. 1 position) for Lou Reed and/or the Velvet Underground and included every Velvet Underground record.

ONE AND A HALF YEARS LATER, IN THE AUTUMN OF 1977, LOU PREPARED to record his godfather-of-punk album. Lou, who in his solo career had made an intense study of recording techniques and become something of an authority on the subject, had discovered a binaural recording process created in Germany by one Manfred Schunke. Schunke used computer-designed models of the average human head. The detail was as precise as possible down to the size, shape, and bone structure of the ear canal. Microphones fit in each ear so theoretically what they recorded would be exactly what a human being sitting in the position the head was placed in would actually hear.

"I had written these songs on the spot in Germany," Lou said. "I tried to teach them to the band really quick. The audience didn't understand a word of English—like most of my audience. They're fucked-up assholes, what difference does it make? Can they count from one to ten?"

Street Hassle was originally recorded at live shows in Munich, Wiesbaden, and Ludwigshafen, Germany. Lou brought the live tapes back to New York for overdubbing and mixing. In what looked like an extremely perverse move, he chose Richard Robinson as his producer. Several of the songs were dated. "Dirt" and "Leave Me Alone" came from the 1975 *Coney Island Baby* sessions. "Real Good Time Together" hailed from the Velvets final years. The title piece, one of the most riveting songs of Lou's solo career, was written in three parts, "Waltzing Matilda," "Street Hassle," and "Slip Away."

Needless to say, all was not copacetic in the studio. Lou's father-son relationship with Clive Davis would come to a head during the *Street Hassle* sessions.

After hearing an early version of the last section of "Street Hassle," Davis suggested Reed make the two-minute track longer. Although Lou accepted Clive's advice ("I wrote the lyrics for 'Street Hassle' out from beginning to end in about as long as it took to physically write it on paper"), he later complained of "being betrayed by all the evil people around me! The original producer [Richard Robinson] had walked out, I'd had to change studios because we had a fight there—and then Clive Davis came in and told me I should make a new record and throw this one away. But the record came out, and I wasn't crazy. They were just stupid. The head of Arista was stupid."

Making albums allowed Lou to be the Sylvester Stallone of rock, both directing and starring in the works. "Some people make movies of people who interest them," Reed was quoted in an Arista press release. "Andy Warhol has been doing it for years. . . . Actually, I do it with my songs."

Displaying what he had learned from Warhol, Raymond Chandler and Delmore Schwartz, Lou wrote a vivid story with short, neo-Céline-like sentences. The song, which ends the cycle about Rachel that began with "Coney Island Baby," laments the end of their relationship. As Bob Jones, who was also at the end of his relationship with Lou, said, "At a certain point the only way to be around Lou was to be secondary to Lou, and you either had to become an acolyte—which was a role that I don't think Lou would allow one to continue—or say good-bye. It would very much be part of the attitude of the time that one would say good-bye in a cynical way and be tough and rough about it."

One of the many nuggets in "Street Hassle" came from the unexpected contribution of Bruce Springsteen, who sang a few intense lines in the center of the piece. "He was in the studio below, and for that little passage I'd written I thought he'd be just perfect, because I tend to screw those things up," Reed recounted. "Like 'I Found a Reason,' it is my best recitation, but I just couldn't resist that 'Walking hand in hand with myself' part. I'm too much of a smart-ass. But I knew Bruce would do it seriously, because he really is of the street. Springsteen is all right, he gets my seal of approval. I think he's groovy."

The most striking thing about Lou's relationship with Rachel was how long it lasted, particularly considering that they spent virtually all of their time together. Unlike his relationships with previous girlfriends and his wife, Lou did not immediately try to push Rachel to an edge. Whether this was because he knew how much he needed her or because Rachel's personality was able to absorb Lou's blows without flinching, there's no question that from late 1974 through 1977, Rachel was a mainstay of Reed's life. And her personality permeates the albums from *Coney Island Baby,* a paean to Rachel that put Lou squarely on the map as the poet laureate of the gay world in New York in the seventies, to *Street Hassle,* which documents the sad conclusion to their affair.

The breakdown started somewhere in 1977. A friend visited Lou one afternoon that spring to find him alone and brooding over Rachel's disappearance. Speaking in the tone of a bereaved lover out of a broken-hearts novel, Lou was in despair and blaming himself for the break, crying plaintively that he would do anything to get her back. He was about to go on tour and remarked wistfully that they could have had such a ball together, but now everything was in doubt.

Two days later Lou got a phone call instructing him to go to a downtown bar where a surprise awaited him. Hastening to the specified location, Lou walked in to find Rachel sitting at the bar with open arms and a sweet smile. In such moments, Lou was the most romantic of men. He swept her off her feet again and they did have a ball on the subsequent tour. But in such intense relationships, once a crack like that appears, there is little chance of real recovery.

Although he clearly regretted it, by early 1978 Lou and Rachel were having a trial separation. Again, quite uncharacteristically, when Lou did break up with Rachel, rather than closing her out of his life with a slammed door, Reed admitted that he still had strong feelings about her and missed her. Ultimately, the relationship probably suffered more than anything else from writer's syndrome. When a writer makes use of his mate for his material, he risks losing the indefinable essence of their connection. Rachel should be remembered in the saga of Lou Reed as the muse who helped give birth to his finest work of the midseventies.

THE FIRST HALF OF THE SEVENTIES HAD BEEN A PROLIFIC TIME FOR LOU Reed. He produced six studio albums and completed a book of poems, *All the Pretty People.* "They have a certain progression," Lou explained. "From the start they got rougher and harder and tougher until it's just out and out vicious, doesn't rhyme, and has no punctuation, it's just vicious and vulgar." Largely through the auspices of Gerard Malanga, who remained Reed's astute connection to the poetry world despite Lou's rejection of his friendship and criticism of him in print for getting the poems published, several poems were published in literary magazines, ranging from the prestigious *Paris Review* through *Unmuzzled Ox* to underground publications like the *Coldspring Journal.* In late 1977, shortly after he finished work on *Street Hassle,* Lou won a prize for "The Slide" published in the *Coldspring Journal,* as one of the year's five best new poets from the American Literary Council of Little Magazines. He attended the ceremony at the Gotham Book Mart in New York and was given the award by Sen. Eugene McCarthy. Lou wondered if McCarthy read his poems about S&M, noting, "He was taller than he seemed on TV."

Street Hassle was released in February 1978 at the commercial height of the new wave and marketed as a grand statement from the man who invented punk. It received more press than anything Reed had done before, garnering reviews from *Time* to *Punk.* It took him to the pinnacle of his career as reviewers around the world praised it to the skies. "I'm right in step with the market," he said in *Creem* the week the album came out. "The album is enormously commercial."

An article in the *NME* in 1993 looked back at this period:

"Signs of his rejuvenation were most vividly apparent on his 1978 tour de force *Street Hassle,* an uncompromising howl of self-lacerating disgust and poisonous venom that against all odds turned out to be one of the major albums of the late seventies. The title track ranks with anything on the more celebrated *New York, Songs for Drella,* or *Magic and Loss.* In its final heartbreaking conclusion, Lou sounds exposed and vulnerable and hurt beyond words. 'Street Hassle' takes you to the edge and leaves you there—darkness below, no lights in heaven above."

"I keep hedging my bet, instead of saying that's really me, but that is me, as much as you can get on record," Reed elucidated. "I use my moods. I get into one of these dark, melancholy things and I just milk it for everything I can. I know I'll be out of it soon and I won't be looking at things the same way. For every dark mood, I also have a euphoric opposite.

Lou did a series of interviews, including an outstanding one with Allan

Jones for a British magazine, *Melody Maker*, in which he put himself in perspective:

"The Velvet Underground were banned from the radio. I'm still being banned. And for exactly the same reasons. Maybe they don't like Jewish faggots. . . . No. It's what they think I stand for they don't like. They don't want their kid sitting around masturbating to some rock-and-roll record—probably one of mine. They don't want their kid ever to know he can snort coke or get a blow job at school or fuck his sister up the ass. They never have. But how seriously can you take it? So they won't play me on the radio. What's the radio? Who's the radio run by? Who's it played for? With or without the radio I'm still dangerous to parents."

When another interviewer, the kid who had arranged Reed's first solo gig in the U.S. in 1972, Billy Altman, noted, "One thing that disturbs people about your music is its lack of what might be called a moral stance," Lou shrugged in disdain, saying, "They're not heterosexual concerns running through that song. I don't make a deal of it, but when I mention a pronoun, its gender is all-important. It's just that my gay people don't lisp. They're not any more affected than the straight world. They just are."

"*Street Hassle* is the best album I've done," he told another journalist. "*Coney Island Baby* was a good one, but I was under siege. *Berlin* was *Berlin*, *Rock and Roll Heart* is good compared to the rest of the shit that's going around. As opposed to *Street Hassle*, they're all babies. If you wanna make adult rock records, you gotta take care of all the people along the way. And it's not child's play. You're talking about managers, accountants, you're talking about the lowest level of human beings. *Street Hassle* is me on the line. And I'm talking to them one to one."

In the second half of March 1978, Reed played a five-night residency at the Bottom Line in New York with his favorite midseventies combo, the Everyman Band. Susan Shapiro described the shows in the *Village Voice*:

"Onstage he's puckish, like Chaplin, like the cover of *Coney Island Baby*, a live highlight. He moves like a go-go gymnast, awkwardly, authentically, uncorrupted by vanity. He's singing 'I Wanna Be Black,' but it's playful, a lie to tell the truth. 'Satellite of Love' and 'Lisa Says' top one another. The force is with him and he's maybe taking 'yes' for an answer. Wallace Stevens has nailed him, 'under every "no" lay a passion for "yes" that had never been broken.' Then he's given them the whammy, 'Dirt.' "

"People are always looking for a voice that works," noted Henry Edwards. "It took him years to find a strong performing voice. It was in him and he didn't let it out. Because he was so busy playing the faux junkie. I was amazed when I went to the Bottom Line in 1978 and he really was a rock-and-roller."

Andy Warhol wrote in his diary: "Lou was late coming out, but then he did and I was proud of him. For once, finally, he's himself, he's not copying anybody. Finally he's got his own style. Now everything he does works. It took years and Lou just kept on working. He's very good now, he's changed a lot."

"Andy always understood where I'm coming from," Reed responded. "He also said to me that work is the most important thing in a man's life and I believe him. My work is my yoga. It empties me out. Years ago he said I was to be to music what he was to visual arts. The man's amazing. You can't define it, but it's happening just the way he said it would."

The shows were recorded for a live album to be called *Take No Prisoners*. Reed noted, "We called it *Take No Prisoners* because we were doing a quite phenomenal booking in a tiny hotel in Quebec, where they'd normally have a little dance band. I dunno what we were doing there, but . . . All of a sudden this drunk guy sitting alone at the front shouts, '*Lou, take no prisoners, Lou!*' and then he took his head and smashed it as hard as he could to the drumbeat. We saw him doing it and we were taking bets that that man would never move again. But he got up and *bam bam* on the table! And that was only halfway through. What was gonna be the encore? He might cut his arm off!"

The fastest mouth in rock and roll combined his Method-acting, stream-of-consciousness spontaneity and Lenny Bruce–style wit to make a record unlike any other. The songs became background to the monologues—slapping down members of the audience, reeling off a succession of slick one-liners, throwing darts at Patti Smith or Andy Warhol, playing out every lyric for its full sexual innuendo.

As Reed recalled, "It is a comedy album. Lou Reed talks and talks and talks. Lou Reed, songwriter, is dried-up—ran out of inspiration. . . . Would you buy a used guitar from Peter Frampton?" Reed saved his most acidic bile for rock critics—notably John Rockwell of the *New York Times* and Robert Christgau of the *Village Voice*. "Who needs them to tell you what to think?" he railed before lecturing his audience.

Lou's outbursts on *Take No Prisoners* reveal a Lou Reed who is autonomous because he can talk back to himself. "What are you complaining about, asshole?" he asks himself, answering, "I just play the guitar." Later he quips, apropos of a literary reference, "for those who still read," then turns on himself, snapping, "What a snotty remark."

Despite the hatchet for a tongue with which he chopped Christgau and his ilk, Lou in fact continued to relate to journalists around the world as if they were his best—no, his only—friends. Bert van der Kamp recalled, "In 1978, at the end of the interview, he said to me, 'It's always nice to talk to you, you're such a good friend.' And I said to him, 'Why did you act like you didn't know me?' and he said, 'Well, I wanted to be sure it was you.' "

Lou kept in touch with *Punk*'s John Holmstrom, but Reed was a tough man to have as a fan. "I would run into him occasionally, but he was very down on the magazine after we did him," John recalled. "He'd say, 'Oh, you blew it, it's not as good as it used to be.' And he was right. He was always drifting away from us, then drifting towards us."

When *Punk* held its award ceremonies in October 1978, Reed was nominated for the Punk Rock Hall of Fame Award. Lou accepted the invitation to attend the ceremonies. As John recalled the night:

"We thought we were going out of business and we wanted to have a party and go out in style. A day or two before our party, Nancy Spungen was found dead. So New York went nuts. It was a crazy time and all the insanity focused on our event, because we were the punk event happening at the moment. TV crews came down and wanted to interview all the punk-rock stars about Sid and Nancy, and nobody wanted anything to do with this because people were shocked and horrified by what had happened.

"The media were always more interested in promoting those aspects of punk. They could have said, for example, that Lou was a great artist who expressed himself differently. But they had to focus on the ridiculous, shaving Iron Crosses in the side of his head. Which to us was not the point. Punk to us was more the attitude: you do what you want artistically and any other way, lifestyle-related, and screw you. Not that you have a tawdry or decadent lifestyle and get nasty about it. It was more like the ultimate individual against perversion."

What had been intended as a humorous ceremony deteriorated into a horror show owing to the hysterical intervention of the local press. The

----

audience started breaking the furniture and throwing it at the stage and booing.

Legs McNeil remembered "Lou laughing a lot. We gave him an award. I don't know what for. I'm sure it was really amateurish and stupid. It was the Punk Awards!" But Holmstrom saw a different reaction: "Lou accepted the Hall of Fame award. But he wouldn't come up onstage, he just took it and walked out. We had a big falling out over the awards ceremony. It was a disaster, it was horrible. Before the thing he had said, 'If you embarrass me, I'll never speak to you again.' And he was embarrassed. That was the last time he ever talked to me."

Chapter Fifteen

MISTER REED

1978—79

> I've probably had more of a chance to make an asshole out
> of myself than most people, and I realize that. But then
> not everybody gets a chance to live out their nightmares for
> the vicarious pleasures of the public.
>
> —Lou Reed

LOU COULD HARDLY HAVE PRESENTED HIS NEXT INCARNATION MORE DRA-
matically than with the infamous live album *Take No Prisoners*, released
in the U.S. that November 1978. A third of the double album was
devoted to Reed's Lenny Bruce–inspired running commentary. Disguising
his ravaged singing voice by either screeching and whining out lyrics, or,
more often, talking over the music, Reed filled the two albums with
anecdotes, jokes, and insults that reflected his state of mind. Meanwhile,
the band managed to keep up with Lou, drifting in and out of songs as
singing gave way to monologue. "It presents a portrait of Lou Reed more
authentic and vivid than any documentary or any amount of interviews
could possibly achieve," wrote Allan Jones, "and exploits more fully than
on any previous recording the full impact of his often pathologically
cruel—but incessantly hilarious—humor."

Although *Take No Prisoners* was more of a retrospective of Lou Reed
than of his music, he was as enthusiastic about the results as his fans. "I
think of it as a contemporary urban-blues album. After all, that's what I
write—tales of the city. And if I dropped dead tomorrow, this is the
record I'd choose for posterity. It's not only the smartest thing I've ever
done, it's also as close to Lou Reed as you're probably ever going to get,
for better or worse."

By November 1978, Lou was ready to go back to work. In a remarkable
confessional interview in *Creem* magazine, he announced a new level of

ambition: "My expectations are very high . . . to be the greatest writer that ever lived on God's earth. In other words I'm talking about Shakespeare, Dostoyevsky. I want to do that rock-and-roll thing that's on a level with *The Brothers Karamazov*. I'm starting to build up a body of work. I'm on the right track. I think I haven't done badly. But I think I really haven't scratched the surface. I think I'm just starting."

As the year neared its end, Lou had a feast of work on his plate. He was writing his next studio album, *The Bells*. For the first time since leaving the Velvets, Reed wrote songs in collaboration—composing tracks with the guitarist, singer, and songwriter Nils Lofgren, Don Cherry, and various members of his band. Interestingly, and perhaps uncharacteristically, he also shared credit for those tracks on the album sleeve. In addition to the new record, Lou was planning a spring and summer tour of the U.S. and Europe. The 1970s were the zenith of Reed's career in Europe; *Street Hassle* was popular and *Take No Prisoners* was soon to be released.

The same month *Take No Prisoners* came out, Lou added another guitarist to the band. Chuck Hammer, a twenty-four-year-old prodigy from Santa Barbara, felt that he had mastered the guitar to the point where he could approach his hero on the grounds of being a "qualified disciple."

"As a guitarist coming out of the seventies, you either work with Bowie or Reed," Hammer declared. "I also admired John Cale a lot."

Hammer wrote Lou, telling him that "I was what he needed" and was astonished when Lou responded with a call. Just as Doug Yule had done when asked to audition for the Velvets, Hammer dropped everything and excitedly rushed to New York. "I asked [Lou], 'Does anyone in your band know who you are?' 'Not really,' he replied. I said, 'I do, you're a genius. *Berlin* is a masterpiece, and I know the music.' "

Rehearsals were held at the old Star Sound studios where the band would work up material through the end of the year, convening daily for long, regimented practices. It turned out that Hammer was the antithesis of Reed: drug, alcohol, and even caffeine free, he was unprepared for the mind games he would face as a member of the band. The first track Hammer auditioned was "Sad Song." He had spent eighteen hours learning Bob Ezrin's string arrangement, and as he played it, Lou, with his collar up, silently glared at the young musician. Afterward, Hammer remembered, "Lou said softly, 'You're everything you said you were.' "

At the beginning of 1979 Lou recorded *The Bells* in Germany, working for the last time with the binaural process at Manfred Schunke's Delta Studios on a farm in Wilster, about sixty miles outside of Hamburg. Lou was ambivalent about recording in Germany: "I wasn't crazy about going to Germany in the first place. And the real reason was that I liked the binaural technique, but I didn't like the board. I don't like any of the sounds they got, across the board. Because they don't have good boards."

Don Cherry attended the sessions for their first studio collaboration. Though Cherry could play R&B riffs to order, his presence automatically tipped the balance toward avant-garde jazz, allowing Reed to make *The Bells* as much an exploration in sound as an exercise in lyrical composition.

"The Bells" itself is a perfect example of Lou's method of spontaneous composition. The song was inspired in equal parts by Edgar Allan Poe's poem "The Bells" and by Ornette Coleman. After listening to Cherry quote a musical line from Coleman's masterpiece "Lonely Woman," Lou stepped up to the microphone and recited the whole "Bells" lyric in one take, pouring the words into the wash of music. To this day he still wonders at their meaning, but the experience was so sublime that "The Bells" remains one of Lou's favorite tracks.

Unfortunately, there were few fans of the album at Arista. Clive Davis went so far as to write a lengthy critique, concluding that the record was only half-finished. Even the loyal Fonfara was never enamored of the work, agreeing that it needed more time. Naturally, this sort of response only made Lou more determined to release it the way he wanted.

With Lou in control, the record was released in April. And no sooner had it come out than he was up on his soapbox proclaiming that it surpassed *Take No Prisoners*, that it was the best record that he had ever made, that if he died tomorrow, etc. One can only imagine the bile he spewed forth on reading in Lisa Robinson's column how disappointed Arista's executives were with the new Lou Reed record. "I guess that's what happens," he snapped to the press, "when you don't respond to the suggestions of the president."

Though the album stalled at no. 130 on the *Billboard* charts, the critics were unusually kind to the flawed work. It was hailed as "powerfully cogent and authoritative, trenchantly universal," in the *Washington Post*. Christgau "hadn't found him so likable since the Velvet Underground."

Rockwell noted "a new intensity." Bangs outdid himself, pronouncing it "the only true jazz-rock fusion anybody's come up with since Miles Davis's *On the Corner* period."

In the wake of *The Bells*, Lou undertook one last, lengthy, booze-soaked tour that would take him to Britain, the West Coast of the U.S., back across America, and finally to Europe. The tour would be characterized by the conflict and violence that had greeted him on the Rock-'n'-Roll Animal tour of 1974. The three-month jaunt kicked off in the spring of 1979 with the British and West Coast legs of the tour.

Sterling Morrison, who hung out with Lou between shows in Texas, was saddened by the insularity that characterized Lou's progress: "The worship surrounding Lou was just awful. I love Lou. That's why it upset me that Lou is making rudeness and obnoxiousness part of his daily life. When he came to Austin, the only person he spoke to in the city was me. I said, 'Lou, what is the fun of going outside of your apartment if you're not going to talk to anybody? If you never meet a different person?' So we had all kinds of secret rendezvous all over the city, where I wasn't able to bring anybody. It was strange seeing him with a pickup band. Things were so different—a total sycophantic relationship with the band. Lou is the employer. It's not like an organic unity, it's like these touring mercenaries. People falling over backwards for him."

A reporter from *Rolling Stone* who saw several of the shows found Lou in a sedate albeit self-deprecating mood in his hotel room one night. Watching videos of the previous night's performance of "Street Hassle," he expressed a kind of healthy identity crisis:

" 'Look at that guy,' says Lou, pointing at himself on the screen. 'He sure is shameless about occupying his own life. Every time I'm doing that song, when it gets to that awful last line, I never know just how it's going to come across. "So the first thing they see that allows them to be, they follow it / You know what it's called?" And here comes that line and it should punch like a bullet: *"Bad Luck."* The point of view of the guy saying that is so awful. But it's so true. I only realize sometime afterwards what Lou Reed's talking about. I just try and stay out of the way.' "

Things moved from bad to worse as the tour progressed into its second leg, returning to Europe in the spring of 1979. A climax came in Germany where *Take No Prisoners* had just been released and audiences expected a crazed, ranting Lou Reed. One night when the band was playing a concert at a 2,500-seat gymnasium, a particularly rowdy audience of American soldiers and German kids started a riot.

Lou, who played best when he felt in control of his audience, walked offstage three times but he could not get them to calm down. Finally a girl leaped onstage and lunged toward him. Reflexively, Lou grabbed her and dragged her to the edge of the stage as security men and roadies fought to separate them. In the midst of the melee Lou, his adrenaline going full blast, grabbed his large Swedish roadie with one hand and lifted him off the ground. Screaming, "You're full of shit!" at the audience, he ordered the whole band offstage.

Pandemonium erupted in the hall. Meanwhile backstage, the police, who had been told Reed had attacked a female fan, came into the dressing room and arrested him.

According to Lou, "Some girl came up onstage and I didn't know who she was, some irate roadie or something, I hardly saw her, man, and there were all these drunk GIs too. They took me to jail alone. How would you like to get into a van with twelve goose-steppers saying they're going to test your blood? They took me to jail after the show. I slept in the cell overnight. I was tired. Then the next day they came to get me and I thought, oh, they're letting me out. But they came in and said, 'We want your blood.' The guy was sort of nervous because on the way he asked me for a light and his hands were shaking, but, you know, my German's good enough. I couldn't believe it, it was like I said to the guy, 'You must be an American or else all your life you wanted to be an American so you could have a great line like that. And now you said it.' They drove me to Frankfurt to have a blood test and urinology, to see if I had any drugs in my system, as they suspected I had. Of course . . . there was nothing."

No charges were pressed and Lou would later deny responsibility for the violence, claiming, "The problem was a bunch of American soldiers. They wanted to have a riot, and they had one."

A Swedish fan, Stellan Holm, who had seen Lou every time he had played in Stockholm, remembered the 1979 show as the most emotional. "He was crying on 'Men of Good Fortune' and saying, 'Look at the fortune, the fucking fortune.' And he was ranting. And he was really good. Most people hated it because it didn't sound like his songs. But for once he had charisma as a performer." After the show, Stellan and his best friend, Don, went to the bar of the Sheraton Hotel and got a table next to Lou, who was drinking with his bass player, the Moose. Stellan got a close-up glimpse of the noble savage:

"He just looked like some guy from Queens. He had big curly hair, jeans and maybe a leather vest. One of us was brave enough to walk over. So he invited us to come and sit with him, which we did. And he bought us drinks. I told him I had met Andy and he suddenly became very defensive. As if he had to live up to the role of Lou Reed. He was very, very obnoxious. He was rude. You'd say something and he'd say something bad back. Then the other guys got up for some reason and we were alone with him. Just me, Don, and Lou. And then he looked at us and said, 'I'm crazy, that's my problem.' Sort of like excusing his own behavior for being an asshole. But it was such a cheap way of trying to be interesting. He knew we really admired him enormously anyway. And he knew by talking to us that we were well-informed and we knew the records. He wasn't some old guy and he wasn't crazed on drugs. He was drinking, but he wasn't drunk. He was very together. He was just an extremely uptight and insecure person."

The denouement of what had deteriorated into a two-month international binge came after the last show in London when Lou and his entourage, featuring the giant, bodyguard-like Moose, dined with David Bowie, whose own career was going through a shaky period.

What began as an ebullient celebration soon disintegrated into an ugly exposure of the mad tension that had always existed between the two temperamental stars. Ever since Bowie had produced *Transformer*, he and Lou had flirted with the idea of collaborating again. That night, however, when Lou proposed that David produce his next album, Bowie demurred, commenting that Lou needed to do a lot of work on his songs and himself. Lou slapped David hard in the face. Both startled but quickly recovering, they made up, embracing across the table. Minutes later, Lou exploded again, screaming, "I told you to never say that to me!" as he belted Bowie a second time.

Before the two men could create superstar pandemonium, they were separated by the Moose, who, flinging one massive arm around his shoulder, led Lou out of the restaurant. Bowie cursed loudly as, one by one, he smashed the potted plants that lined the stairs from the restaurant to the street. When David showed up at Lou's hotel later that night looking for a rematch, Lou pretended to be asleep.

"Yes, I hit him," he admitted, "more than once. It was a private dispute. It had nothing to do with sex, politics, or rock and roll. I have a New York code of ethics. Speak unto others as you would have them speak unto you. In other words, watch your mouth."

The following morning Lou flew back to New York. Angie Bowie, who had dinner with Lou shortly thereafter, witnessed ominous mood swings: "I watched with growing concern as he swung through his changes and then went thataway: from real pleasure to see me, to a venomous but more or less rational attack on David, to a state of bugged-out, all-inclusive paranoia which struck me as truly insane. He was stoned, so his mood was affected by however his pharmaceutical cycles of choice were intersecting during that particular hour or two, but even so . . . You might get a better sense of Lou if I tell you something he told me during dinner. 'You have to get stoned in the city,' he said in absolute seriousness. 'It's a necessity. The atmosphere is so polluted that you have to put chemicals in your body to counteract it.' "

"He had a potbelly after touring," said Bob Jones. "I think that was because he quit speed. The speed scene ran out. There was no speed. Everyone got busted. Marty got busted. Turtle was sent away for five years. Lister . . . when I was arrested, they wanted Lister . . . they knew I was dealing with Lister and they wanted me to turn him in and I wouldn't."

"I met up with Lou again in 1979," recalled deejay Terry Noel, who had known Lou at Max's during the 1960s, "when he was blown up. Fat and waddling around the Village. That's when we started going down to Uncle Paul's, right off Christopher and Greenwich. He used to go in there to play the pinball machines. He seemed a lot more sedate and polite and receptive."

"I believe in all things in moderation—including moderation," Lou attested. "I did more than abuse my body in the past. I very often wounded it. I enjoy age. I was miserable when I was younger."

One night in June, he was playing a brief stint at the Bottom Line. Before the first show he was to have cocktails at the apartment of his longtime hero, the writer William Burroughs, whom he had never met. On his way to the party, he stopped in at the Bottom Line for a 5 P.M. sound check. There he discovered that his bosom buddy and bass player, the Moose, was nowhere to be found. Lou became increasingly upset as it emerged that no one had seen the big man since leaving him on a street corner at 2 A.M. the previous night. Soon Lou was convinced that the Moose had suffered grievous bodily harm and began blaming himself. At the same time he worried about the bass's absence from the upcoming show. Without a bass, there was no way the band could deliver. He decided that if the Moose could not be located by 7 P.M., the shows would have to be cancelled and the money returned.

Meanwhile, the time for Reed's meeting with Burroughs had come and gone. Then the door of the club flew open and the Moose came thundering in, guitar case in one meaty palm, eyes bugging out of his head like electric eightballs. He had overslept.

Reed went ballistic. Ordering everybody but the band out of the dressing room, he attacked the trembling giant in a tirade that could be heard out on the street. Then, storming out of the club with a final threat that if anything like this ever happened again, the Moose would instantly be fired, Lou, a bottle of Scotch in hand, accompanied by two band members, leapt into a limousine and motored over to Burroughs's apartment on the nearby Bowery.

He arrived forty-five minutes late at the home of the great writer, a punctilious gentleman of the old school who had cocktails at six and dinner at eight. Rather than apologizing for his tardy arrival, Lou cast a withering glance around the room, and abruptly asked if there was a chair or whether he was expected to sit on the floor. Provided a seat, he proceeded to take apart each of Burroughs's guests with deft one-liners that pinned their weakest points. Then, turning to Burroughs, he asked him if it was true that he had to have sex with publishers in order to get his books published. A few seconds later he asked the writer whether it was true that he had cut off his toe to get out of the draft. A lesser man than Burroughs might have got his back up against the wall at such an onslaught. However, as it turned out, the author was charmed by what turned into a hilarious exchange between the Martin and Lewis of the kingdom of junk about, among other things, how to shoot heroin with a safety pin.

After a whirlwind visit, Lou gathered up his entourage, left everybody in the room, except Burroughs, feeling as if they had been mentally raped, and swept back to the club where he was shortly due to perform. In the dressing room before the show he was so drunk he was regressing to a state of infantilism. Meanwhile, dripping with sweat, he looked like a punk version of the late-sixties belicose Jack Kerouac. However, when he hit the stage, he delivered a stunning set.

Beginning the revamped "Heroin," he greeted the audience's applause by calling out, "How do you think it feels when I hear you calling for a pop song called 'Heroin'? The evil of that drug—you don't know. When I say it's my wife and it's my life, do you think I'm kidding?" Reed's anger and frustration about his career was reaching a climax. Raging around in front of his audience, Reed smashed microphones against each other. When he spotted Clive Davis in the audience, Lou paused to give him the finger. "Here, this is for you, Clive," he said through the microphone. "Where's the money, Clive? How come I don't hear my album on the radio?" Reed kept his fans waiting twenty minutes for an encore. He received a standing ovation.

Later that week, Lou issued a press release through Arista: "I've always loved Clive," he said, "and he happens to be one of my best friends. I just felt like having a business discussion from the stage. Sometimes, out of frustration, you yell at those you love the most. I have a mouth that never sleeps, and I suppose that's why I make rock-and-roll records. Trying to read anything deeper into all this is pointless."

"Reed spent most of the seventies refining, amending, denying, and playing off his image," wrote Bill Flanagan. "He could be romantic ('Coney Island Baby'), funny ('The Power of Positive Drinking'), nasty (*Take No Prisoners*), almost incomprehensible (*Metal Machine Music*), and frightening ('Street Hassle'). But that is the mark of a good writer. That convention inclines the audience to believe that the singer/songwriter's work is autobiographical only added to Reed's power. His image was of a man outside society's conventions, a rebel."

"My attitude often gets to be, 'Screw you, and I'll screw your girlfriends just for spite,' " Reed told one interviewer. "Which is a terrible way to do things because it's not like I would enjoy it. Of course they would, it goes without saying.

" 'I Wanna Be Black' . . . it was transmogrified—that's a big word meaning Catholicism," he continued. "You want to know the real Lou Reed? Turn around. Now bend over."

In the same interview in which he had compared himself to Dostoyevsky and Shakespeare, Lou had, for the first time, come out of the closet publicly, insisting that he wanted his audience to know that when they looked at him they were looking at a gay man from head to foot. Clearly, a person as complex and multifaceted as Lou Reed cannot be confined to such statements, nor to a singular way of being. Since he went to college, he had been a practicing bisexual. However, friends who knew him well during the late seventies and early eighties, probably the most vulnerable period of his career vis-à-vis the public, were of the opinion that he was basically gay, but since he came from the 1950s world in which people despised queers, Lou also despised queers and hated being queer. Consequently, on and off over the decades he paid numerous psychiatrists to tell him that he wasn't.

IN THE FALL, LOU TOOK STOCK OF HIS SITUATION AND MADE PLANS TO SEE a therapist. This time, however, to bolster his decision he drew upon former advice from the towering figure of his college days, Delmore Schwartz. In times of emotional turmoil Lou often returned, mentally, to his college years, the time when he felt most open to change.

Lou recalled a conversation he had had with Delmore in his senior year at Syracuse when the drunken poet had given him an astute piece of advice. "He told me," Lou remembered, "that I should see an analyst, and it should be a female analyst, because I wouldn't listen to anybody else." Lou had always been adept at one of the cardinal rules of rock— being or finding the right person at the right time. Now, his powers of survival still intact, one of the great misogynists of the era went through a series of intense sessions with a woman therapist to whom he had been introduced by a mutual friend. As a result, he emerged claiming that he had never before been in such good shape.

"It's like I'm really healthy these days," he told John Holmstrom. "Physically and mentally. I went to a doctor, a lady psychiatrist, which I'm sure will turn every Lou Reed fan off and say, 'Oh, what a fag.' But, you know, in case there are people out there who might want to go see someone . . . I met this woman who is really fantastic. . . . I talked to her and she stayed with me practically like for hours every day during what was going on. And I was really in trouble. I mean, it's all the things that were going on but I wasn't coping with it. I was not handling it because of some things that were going on. It's like I had a problem, you know, so she solved the problem. Isn't that amazing? And ever since that day, literally a couple of months ago, my whole life has changed. And I'm totally different. You can probably tell. And I'm saying to you, isn't it amazing that if you try hard enough and if you have some friends who are okay and that, you know, I believe there's a God or something. I really do. Because there are things that go beyond coincidence. And I think a lot of it has to do with if you're a good person. I mean, if you've been honest on a certain level, and I think you get paid back for that in the oddest way, in ways you don't think of, and it's my honesty that let me meet her, for instance.

"I'm delighted," he concluded triumphantly, "because I think I've become an adult. I think I have a twenty-four-hour job I like, and I think I do it really good and everything. It's like I love being in a rock band. I mean, that's all I ever really wanted. And I got it."

He got a lot more than that. As Ellen Willis has written in one of her brilliant essays on Reed: "During the seventies virtually every significant development in rock and roll has borne Lou Reed's imprint."

Chapter Sixteen

LADYBUG

1978–83

I then thought, in a most delicious instant
That stands beyond all reflection,
Of dissolving you like a mint or
Crushing you . . .

—Lou Reed
"He Thought of Insects in the Lazy Darkness"
from *All the Pretty People*

THE END OF THE SEVENTIES SIGNALED A PERSONAL AS WELL AS PROFES-
sional rebirth for Lou. No sooner had he gotten his head straight about
being in a rock-and-roll band than he met the woman who was to become
his second wife and soul companion through the 1980s, Sylvia Morales.

An enchanting black-and-white photograph taken by David Godliis
perfectly captures the Sylvia that Lou met one night in 1978 while attending a meeting of the Eulenspiegel Society. Encased in a floral-print
white gown that hugs her voluptuous frame, she stands before the pock-
marked wall of some nightclub beside a series of signs that say, EXIT.
LADIES. EXIT. Framed by shiny, black, shoulder-length hair, Sylvia's high-
cheekboned face is illuminated by the flare of a match she holds to her
cigarette. She bears a remarkable resemblance to Rachel. Eyes hooded,
lips twisted around the fag, a black pocketbook clutched between elbow
and breast, she might have stepped off the page of some hard-boiled
Raymond Chandler thriller about the life and death of a harlot. Full of
the promise of the night, she wears the white shoes of a prom queen.

Sylvia, twenty-two, was a regular at CBGB's as the sidekick of her
striking roommate, the punk star Anya Phillips. A Chinese American
photographer, stripper, and underground spirit, Phillips was the most
erotic, powerful woman on the New York punk scene. Under Anya's

thumb, Sylvia joined her as a stripper and part-time dominatrix. However, according to a mutual friend, Terrence Sellers, "Sylvia was always
the butt of jokes and was always being teased and criticized by Anya—'I
hate your shoes' and 'Do this' and 'Dress up.' So she lived in Anya's
shadow. But I liked her. She was nice but very flat compared to Anya's
constant theatricals. Sylvia was kind of a coarser version of Anya. She
was pretty but she had a larger nose, darker skin—she looked more ethnic."

Though the half-Mexican Sylvia played lady-in-waiting to the regal
Anya, underneath her patina of punk glamour she was a much straighter,
steadier character than her flamboyant roommate. Her father was an
old-world Hispanic and lifetime military man. Army brats are often lost
souls, but Sylvia was grounded by the goals of the 1950s. Her aim in life
was to get behind a good man and devote herself to his success. Sylvia had
a strong ambitious streak. In between stripping and socializing at CBGB's,
she went to college to study writing. At two in the morning, while
everybody else was raving it up in the club, Sylvia could be found slumped
at the bar, her nose buried in a fat textbook as she waited patiently for
Anya to choose the next victim she was going to take home with her.
Glenn O'Brien remembered Sylvia as "a great presence at CBGB's. But I
also thought she really had a brain."

The few Syracuse friends Lou was still in touch with looked down on
Morales as a B-list girl for a man of his caliber. However, Shelley, who
had had one last meeting with Lou in 1978, understood that the relationship could work because Sylvia possessed two characteristics essential
for Lou: experience in New York's trashy underground world, plus a
down-to-earth, old-fashioned attitude to romantic relationships. And
Shelley believed it was the straight side of Sylvia that attracted Lou most.
When Shelley had seen him, Lou had been burnt to a crisp. First, it had
taken him a full day of drinking to get himself together to visit her. Then,
when he arrived, he had demanded a strong drink and spent their last
time together complaining about how lonely he was, and how success had
only made him lonelier. "Sylvia's a very fifties-type girl," Shelley remarked. "Lou's a very fifties-type guy. He's ultimately straight, I want my
woman to do what I want her to do, and I want her to take care of me,
cook that pound of bacon when I want it. He has the modus operandi of
the shark, always looking for a worthy opponent. It's wonderful if it could

be a woman. He really won't play with a guy who might literally punch him out or really is smart enough. As long as he keeps using this method on women, he's got a natural superiority."

Lou could not have been more titillated by Sylvia. Wasting no time with pleasantries, he whisked her away right under Anya's nose at the Eulenspiegel Society meeting. Terrence Sellers recalled Anya's rage that night when the specimen she considered to be her dowdy little slave went home with a prize as grand as Lou: "Lou just spirited her off, leaving Anya standing on the street corner ranting and raving and screaming. Sylvia did not come home for about a week and a half. When she and Lou got back, Anya was in such a rage she went completely crazy and Sylvia moved out." Sylvia moved to a building on East Twelfth Street that housed, among others, Allen Ginsberg and Richard Hell. One of Allen's friends, Rosebud, recalled seeing an unfailingly chivalrous Lou carrying Sylvia's garbage downstairs on more than one occasion. "And that was really the last we heard of Sylvia. She never came back to the scene. She never came back to the clubs and hung out. She just went off with him and that was it." John Holmstrom thought, "It was hilarious, it was nice, but I was shocked that Sylvia was going out with Lou, because Sylvia seemed like such a quiet person." Once he got hold of Sylvia, Lou would demand her total attention, cutting her off from her friends and family, just as he had done to Bettye and Shelley.

Despite the fact that he was still involved with Rachel—they were in the midst of a trial separation—Lou started going to Times Square to watch Sylvia strip at the Melody or the Madame Burlesque. Sylvia and the other girls were required to perform for twenty-five minutes, six times a day. A higher class of strip joint, more like theaters than bars, these venues didn't serve alcohol, and the dancers would go on in costume— though most of their clothes would quickly come off. The dancers performed onstage while, for the most part, the audiences sat and watched, but spectators could also approach the stage and deposit money in their garter belts and panties. That year, Sylvia also starred in an underground film by Beth and Scot B. Wearing a skimpy bustier that exposed her breasts, and brandishing a whip, she played a dominatrix torturing a nerdy customer who could have been a clone of Lou Reed.

One small fact that Sylvia neglected to mention to Lou up front when she met him was that she had recently spent a memorable night with John

Cale! Her liaison wasn't that coincidental considering how small the downtown music scene was, but just indicated once again that Lou and John shared similar tastes in women, adding another ironic chapter in their history of competition for women, going back to Nico. It is not clear exactly when Lou found out about Sylvia's relationship with John.

Seeing that Sylvia had embraced the S&M world, Lou must have been assured that he had chosen the real thing, that she wasn't a fake. However, a cooler head might have realized that in both stripping and S&M acting, Sylvia was just playing a part.

During the time Lou was falling in love with Sylvia, he was struggling through the breakup of his relationship with Rachel. When Lou had moved to Christopher Street, Rachel took a separate apartment. Lou's four years with Rachel had been emotionally charged on the deepest levels, and the loss of her doglike devotion left him at times despondent and cynical. Continuing to use quantities of amphetamine and alcohol, he found himself increasingly alone and desperate. During the remainder of 1978 Lou kept in touch with Rachel whilst privately nurturing a new partnership with Sylvia.

Whilst continuing to be a multiple-drug user through the end of the decade, by 1978 Lou was finding it harder to get speed. The Lister group was breaking up. Then, in a move typical of the hard-boiled drug culture, Lou's major dealer, Bob Jones, paid back a long-term debt. Back in '75, when Lou had introduced Bob to amphetamine, he'd sold him, for a considerable amount of money, a bunch of pills that turned out to be placebos. When Jones complained, Reed had snapped, "Welcome to the world of speed." Now, Jones, who had maneuvered himself into a position of considerable power within the group so that he could effectively block anybody else from supplying Lou, told him that he was sorry but he was fresh out of "chinamen" and did not expect to be receiving a fresh supply for some time. It was the perfect twist of the knife.

According to his own account, Lou tried to stop taking drugs by drinking alcohol, which led to such classic songs as "Waves of Fear" and "Underneath the Bottle," in which Lou lamented that he felt the same as he always did—so down he could not get any lower. Alcohol began to take a noticeable toll on the thirty-six-year-old Lou. One visitor to Christopher Street discovered a wasted Lou sprawled on the couch, whining at Sylvia just as he had carped at Shelley about Seymour: "You gotta take the dogs out so they can shit!" (By this time Baron had been joined by two other dachshunds, Duke and Count.) Lou often expressed the opinion that each of his dogs was worth one hundred times more than most human beings he had ever known.

APART FROM AMONG HER NEW DOMESTIC CHORE OF WALKING THE DOGS, Sylvia, who was close with her family, also attempted to bring Lou back to his family. She arranged for them to visit Freeport at Hanukkah for example. A friend pointed out how much Lou probably loved that "as long as he could say he didn't like it. As long as he could announce, 'I don't like being here, this was not my idea, I don't do this stuff, I'm much too hip, where's my present?' And, 'Why didn't you make what I like?' I bet his mother made his favorite meal. You bet he liked it. He's got to be clever enough to pick someone who's going to do that. It's perfectly safe."

Still, it was the consensus of opinion among Lou's friends that his obsessive misery came from his family. "His parents are totally dismissive of his achievements, and it's very irritating," observed one. "They could not relate to what he was doing at all. They couldn't accept anything about the reality of his life. They thought Sylvia was a nice girl."

Lou's parents were very straight people who were so insulated that, for example, they never traveled. On the one occasion the Reeds took the first real vacation of their lives, they made a trip to Hawaii that turned into an unmitigated disaster. As they had booked themselves into a hostelry in the most tawdry, commercial tourist section of town, Sylvia, who had spent a good part of her youth in Hawaii, urged them to switch their reservations to a more pleasant location. Flatly ignoring her advice, they took the grueling twelve-hour flight and checked in at their dismal lodgings, whereupon they found themselves unhappy with their surroundings and, more importantly, upset by the loss of their daily routine. The following day, despite having fully paid for a two-week stay, the Reeds returned to Freeport.

One can only imagine how well his parents' naive confusion about life beyond the hinterlands of Freeport must have gone down with Lou, as an adolescent and adult. In the mirror of his family Lou appeared to have changed little since he was a teenager. He trusted his mother. She was accessible and nonthreatening, and he knew she would always love him.

The problem was that she was never going to choose him over his father. Lou could not get around this fact. It seemed as if he wanted to be afraid of his father as a means of creating conflict. He didn't want to attack his father, but everything Lou did was a way of repudiating what Sid stood for. Lou had, for example, illustrated his refusal to take money seriously by losing whatever he made in the sixties and again in the seventies (even after Sidney had taken the trouble of going to Dennis Katz's office to sort out the financial paperwork). Then when Lou did have money, he squandered it in a blatant fashion designed to make an accountant sick. Living with Rachel had been another way of defying his father. Now in introducing Sylvia to his parents, he was raising the prospect of supplying them with grandchildren and a continuation of the Reed line. It was an effective trap that would soon supply Lou with another way to disappoint his long-suffering parents.

In 1979 the Reeds didn't understand Lou any better than they had twenty years earlier when they had dispatched him to Creedmore. Still, Lou's friends felt that he really loved his father and hoped the old man would live long enough to get some gratification, if Lou could ever open up to him. Lou undoubtedly adored his little sister, as he would make clear in a song with that title, but even Bunny had incurred the Reedian wrath when she married a man whom Lou portrayed in another family song as fat and brainless. Sylvia soon discovered that there was no discernible basis for an active relationship between Lou and his family. And there was no question that their blanket rejection of his incredible success bugged Lou to nightmarish proportions. The only people he appeared to be afraid of were his parents. On the rare occasion when they came by the dressing room after a concert or when he bumped into them by chance in New York, according to friends Lou would lose it, turning ashen and shaking all over. In the early 1980s, he told an interviewer, "I keep my distance from them so that I can get done what I have to get done."

IN 1978, LOU MADE A MOVE THAT SIGNALED ANOTHER FORM OF RETURN to his roots, buying a sizable property in the rural suburb of Blairstown, New Jersey. He used the place as a retreat from the city, where he and Sylvia still kept an apartment. In Blairstown he could fish on a man-made lake, shoot hoops in his backyard, and maintain his latest diet of fresh fruit and nuts. The move led so-called friends to smirk that Lou was safely "back in suburbia now," intimating that his adventurous exploration of the cultural underground had now ended and that in fact he had never felt comfortable with the denizens of the Lower East Side, but retained the soul of a suburban son. John Cale's reaction was typical: "We don't keep in touch. He's turned into a regular home bird, settled down on a nice farm out in Jersey. I don't see him. I don't even listen much to what he does." This sort of reaction made Lou's blood boil to such an extent that Sylvia soon took it upon herself to control which articles about him actually got through to Lou. Like so many men of distinction, he became increasingly isolated from the real world, surrounded, indulged, and, most significantly, informed by a praetorian guard of enablers.

The Blairstown property, some eighteen wooded acres approximately one and a half hours from New York by car, was beautifully situated, but the house itself was nothing more than a simple cabin dating back to the 1930s. Over the years Lou and Sylvia would add several haphazard extensions. Not ready to go completely back to nature, Lou installed a satellite dish and hooked up TVs and other electronic equipment, ranging from a jukebox and computer games to a pinball machine. Video equipment, amplifiers, and guitars were stashed everywhere. The master bedroom was cozy, and they had some big comfortable couches in the living room. In the garage, Lou kept a collection of vehicles ranging from motorcycles to snowmobiles.

To this cornucopia of country possessions Lou added one item that irritated Sylvia more than any motorbike, video machine, or other adolescent apparatus Lou might need. As soon as he got to the country, the paranoid Lou purchased a gun in case of any unlooked-for interruption into his privacy or person. Sylvia freaked. The last place on earth she wanted to be was alone in a secluded rural setting with an out-of-control drug addict and juicer like Lou Reed toting a gun! Yet, since she hadn't yet extended her power in the extremely unbalanced relationship, she relented, hoping, no doubt, that if push came to shove, the myopic Lou would shoot better than he could drive.

For the most part, however, Lou entertained himself with inanimate objects over which he had some control. When not composing songs, he spent his time tinkering with his bike, shooting hoops, working out, and trying biofeedback therapy. Meanwhile, fulfilling Lou's fantasy of living with his college sweetheart, Sylvia enrolled in writing classes at Sarah Lawrence College in a suburb north of New York City. Together they worked on video projects and took kung fu classes.

Sylvia's brother was also a help, introducing Lou to Wu-style tai chi chuan, or Chinese boxing, focusing on a powerful Chinese system of exercise organized, refined, and handed down from master to master since the time of the Yellow Emperor (2696–2598 B.C.). It evolved from the Taoists' search for a way to rejuvenate and heal the body and to increase internal strength and energy.

According to Master C. K. Chu: "Tai chi enables students to cultivate 'chi' [or 'qi']—the intrinsic energy or life force of the body. The circulation of the chi revitalizes the internal organs and all the biological systems. As an active meditation, tai chi promotes the integration of body, mind, and emotions. As a result, the student will find he or she is better able to deal with the internal contradictions and external stress."

Lou found it to be "a sport where the ritual of combat is as important as the outcome. It's an aesthetic and physical discipline that I find exquisite. The discipline is in the ability to relax. It's very beautiful to watch."

Spending long weekends out of the city with Sylvia and his dogs, Reed had plenty of time to think for the first time since his Freeport exile. "I really love it," he enthused. "It smells great. Even if you wanted to do something, there's nothing here. It's appalling how much sleep I get.

"I'm a happy person. And I would hope somebody like me would be. You *ought* to be happy. I'm happy I'm walking around alive. Which is not to say I'm happy about the state of the world. I'm just happy about my own personal situation. And from there I look out.

"I've always thought of myself as a writer. I work in a rock-and-roll format because I really like rock and roll and I really like playing the guitar and wouldn't it be great if I could combine these three things I really like. I'm just trying to get off like everybody else. And avoid working. If I can do something that I'd be doing *anyway*—and not have to have a job—well, that to me is really getting through this world pretty well. And if I could have a wife, too. . . . My God, who could ask for anything more?"

By early February 1980, Lou was back in New York making arrangements for his wedding to Sylvia. The event would herald the beginning of a new life for Lou. Then, just before the big day, the Sex Pistols' Sid Vicious, awaiting trial for murdering his girlfriend, died of a heroin overdose. Asked by a British journalist if Sid had died for Lou Reed's sins, the Pistols' Johnny Rotten replied, "Yes. Too many Lou Reed albums I blame it on. There was that horrible movement from New York to London, and they brought their dirty culture with them. Sid was so impressed by the decadence of it all. God! So dreary."

"If you meet the perfect woman," Lou said, "you should pick her up in your arms and dash off with her." On Valentine's Day, February 14, Lou Reed and Sylvia Morales, whom he described, invoking Poe, as his "child bride," got married in Reed's Christopher Street apartment. The vows, written by Lou, were taken from two poems by Delmore Schwartz: "I used, 'Would you perhaps consent to be my many branched little tree?' in my wedding ceremony," he said. "A lot of my ideas come from him. I just really adored him and his writing—that you could call up so much in so few words, in very simple language. It serves you well if you're trying to put a lyric in a song, where they go by so quick."

The formalities were overseen by New York Supreme Court justice Ernest Rosenberger and witnessed by the families of Sylvia and Lou, Lou's band members, his old Syracuse friend Garland Jeffreys, Sylvia's friends Roberta Bayley and Susan Springfield, who was a member of the punk band the Erasers, Lou's new manager-lawyer Eric Kronfeld, and RCA president Bob Summer and his wife.

The wedding marked a break from the past for both Lou and Sylvia. Her best friend, Anya, wasn't invited. "They had been best friends since they were like eleven—they were military brats together," observed one friend. "One can see Sylvia's point of view because Anya would probably have caused a big scene or done something to really get the attention of everything on her. Sylvia really did have this traditional, calm, sedate sort of wedding. But Anya was really bummed out." Much to his chagrin, Andy Warhol was not invited either. "I don't understand why I wasn't invited to the wedding," he complained in his diary. "They had a big reception and everything." And to friends he went even further, exclaiming, "What *is* a friend?" According to Glenn O'Brien, "Andy was totally sentimental about weddings. If Andy wasn't invited, it was real deliberate on Lou's part because in a way that's the only person that he wanted there, and Lou was trying to punish Andy. Maybe he felt he had to get revenge because Andy had forced him to fall in love with a transvestite. Lou had to break away in order to achieve that hetero bond."

In wedding photos taken by Roberta Bayley, Lou stood next to Sylvia and their parents wearing a suit and tie, coming across as a younger version of his father. Thirty-eight but looking nineteen, he appeared happy at last. Sylvia, twenty-four, wore her mother's satin and tulle wedding dress with gardenias in her hair. After the ceremony, everyone toasted the couple, then went off to a nearby restaurant on Barrow Street for wedding cake and champagne. Afterward Lou and Sylvia changed into casual attire and joined their friends. Piling into limos, they sped off to Times Square where they played pinball at the Broadway Arcade, whose proprietor, Steve Epstein, was a friend. "You know you won't be stabbed in Steve's place," commented Lou, who was an avid pinball player. "I got the highest score I've heard of on the Rolling Stones game," he boasted. "Twenty-nine million one hundred eighty thousand eight hundred and eighty. It's actually a pretty easy game, but I was there two hours getting my twenty-nine million."

The only ripple in an otherwise perfect wedding was the failure of Mick Rock, Lou's longtime friend and photographer, to attend and take pictures. Lou, who knew how to hold a grudge, was so furious he did not speak to Mick for the next ten years.

To Reed, the wedding marked another definitive attempt to take full control of his life. "I know now that certain things will get taken care of and looked out for on the home front, where you can get hurt a lot," he said soberly. "It's nice to have a trustworthy situation at home, a security situation. It's good to know that you're covered, and beyond just friendship. I'm a great one for commitment. I like to look at centuries past, when knighthood was in flower—I'm still a great one for that. I think I've found my flower, so it makes me feel more like a knight."

IN APRIL IN THE U.S. AND MAY ELSEWHERE, GROWING UP IN PUBLIC WAS released. The new album once again dealt with Reed's most personal problems. Despite, or perhaps because of, his difficulty in living with another human being and expressing his emotions, the marriage to Sylvia and the new straight life became the central themes of his work. "In his most recent albums, *The Bells* and *Growing Up in Public,* Reed has continued—as if he were picking a scab—to expose his/our need for love and stubborn defenses against it," wrote Ellen Willis. "He wants to believe in the most sentimental, romantic clichés and can't quite pull it off. The song that says it best, I think, is 'All through the Night.' "

Certainly the specifics chronicled in "Standing on Ceremony," or in "My Old Man" were not strictly autobiographical, but, as Lou suggested in interviews, the general tone and sentiment of the songs on the album were inspired by Lou Reed. "My mother's not dead, and my father never beat my mother—you've got to take it like I'm a writer. I'm not restricted to me. Whether my mother's dead or not really doesn't matter, it's the attitude I'm interested in. I want to express a view, so I manipulate the events to justify the view." One of the things old friends noticed on the cover of *Growing Up in Public* was that Lou looked like his father, a development he would later describe as "the final disappointment."

Despite Arista's ridiculous trailer for the album, "There are seven million stories in the city, *Growing Up in Public* is all of them," the album was not well received, and there was little company support for it. "Lou Reed is the smartest person regularly recording rock and roll," wrote Jeff Nesin in *Creem*. "But one of the great rock singers of the late sixties simply cannot sing anymore. Though he uses sharp rhythmic phrasing and some expressive dynamics to disguise the problem, he has no tonal pitch or control anymore and a drastically reduced overall range.

"I have witnessed Lou Reed in many strange incarnations over the years, but I never could have imagined him as a prattling, self-absorbed Central Park West analysand. No song is utterly without redeeming virtue, but all of them could stand considerable work. As a follow-up to *The Bells,* Reed's best recorded work since *Coney Island Baby, Growing Up in Public* is truly depressing, and I wish Lou would get off the couch and back into the streets."

When Lou flew to Detroit in May, a reporter from *Creem* was struck by a "new" Lou, or at least the twentieth new Lou: "Happily married to Sylvia Morales, Reed was healthy-looking, patient, pleased with his record company, and above all, cooperative. Lou's first words were, 'Where can you play pinball around here?' Upon being told where, he anxiously queried, 'Is it in a crummy part of town? Can you bring a lady there?' "

Defending the characters on the record, he said, "I don't see anything pitiful there. I think of the whole thing as being on a very up note. Like he's going ahead, like he's found the perfect lady with the incredible grace. I've had more of a chance to make an asshole out of myself than most people, and I realize that. But then not everybody gets to live out their nightmares for the vicarious pleasures of the public. But I'm certainly not restricted by me."

Meanwhile, praise for the Velvets was increasing. In the *New York Times*, Robert Palmer compared Reed's work with the Velvets to the beat writers of the fifties and sixties. Turning to Reed's latest work, Palmer was more guarded. "Lou Reed's latest album, *Growing Up in Public*, is reminiscent of some of Jack Kerouac's later books . . . and he runs the risk of veering too close to sentimentality."

"For the last few years," Reed said in defense of his music, "I was working with musicians who were into jazz and funk. I wasn't playing guitar on my records because I really couldn't play with those guys, being a simple rock-and-roll player. I thought it would be interesting to explore that direction, but there was a gap between me and them. You can hear it on the records. So I said, 'You've carried this experiment far enough. It's not working. The ideas are there and then they disappear, the music isn't consistent, you seem isolated, there's a certain confidence that's not there because you're not really in control.'

"I intend to keep playing for a while. I mean, I'm a long-term person, I prefer doing this to anything else. Period. I love making records and I love being in a band, performing."

June 1980 saw the kickoff of a brief European tour. Now, Lou's long-term strategy of slowly building a large European following was finally paying off when Lou found himself playing sixty-thousand-seat stadiums instead of theaters. For the first time, he made a lot of money touring Europe.

Drugs were off-limits on the tour, and though Lou continued to drink, he was toning it down. His moderate sobriety, however, had no positive effect on his collaborative skills. Relations between Lou and the band seemed to decline in direct proportion to the growth of his bond with Sylvia. Not only did Lou maintain tyrannical control of the band, con-

tinually criticizing their performance, but he refused to share with them
the highly lucrative profits. When they got back to the U.S., they played
some shows in California, but Lou was getting increasingly uncomfortable
with them.

Reed's bandmates found him almost impossible to deal with, while he
was incapable of acknowledging their gripes. Lou got particularly incensed when they began suggesting therapy programs. "I've had a decent
relationship with them and thought they were intelligent—the next thing
you know they're saying 'Lou' and finally confiding in you. They said,
'Lou, you know something, I've got something you'd really like,' " Reed
remembered being told. "And you always gotta be suspicious when somebody says that. I used to wear sunglasses to avoid that sort of thing—and
they're always good if you want to go to sleep too. So, I'm starting to get
wary now, and I say, 'Wha?' He says, 'Ya ever heart of est?' Now he was
the third person within a week to tell me that."

Reed repeatedly expressed the desire to produce records by other people, perhaps to demonstrate that he was better at it than Cale, but
something always went wrong. He had been negotiating with Jim Carroll
to produce his second album, after the success of Carroll's *Catholic Boy*.
The deal fell through when Lou started rewriting all of Carroll's lyrics,
telling him that he didn't know what he was doing, tried to persuade
Carroll's manager to make a record with him and forget Jim Carroll, and
then insisted that the whole thing be recorded in Berlin. As Carroll's
manager, Earl McGrath, observed, "Lou is a lovely person, and one of the
most charming people in the world—as long as you don't have to do
business with him."

The next candidate for the Lou Reed treatment was his acolyte Chuck
Hammer, who had eagerly accepted Lou's offer to produce his first solo
album. At first the arrangement seemed fine, and Arista was happy with
it. Lou and Chuck began meeting daily at Lou's apartment after Sylvia
had gone to school. Every morning as they walked his dogs, Lou would
tear apart a member of the Everyman Band, whom he had been with for
four years. Lou's serious case of *shpilkes* came to the fore. One by one
he fired every musician Hammer wanted to play with on Chuck's solo
album. When Hammer remonstrated that these were people who had
been with him for years, Lou said that he had no choice now but to tell
the record company that Chuck was too difficult to work with. The

project was abandoned, but there was a Reedian denouement. When they bumped into each other in the street several months later and shared a cab uptown, Lou forced Chuck to admit that he should have done everything Lou told him. According to a close friend, "Head games were Lou's true life's passion. He had an ability to manipulate other people that is unmatched, at least in my experience. He could not take the responsibility for his life and his mistakes, so he spent a lot of time making them the responsibility of other people. He needed a psychiatrist, but there isn't one in this world that's a match for him."

THE END OF 1980 BROUGHT THE RELEASE BY ARISTA OF *ROCK AND ROLL Diary*, a retrospective album that traced Reed's development from the Velvet Underground to the present. The album presented "the full span of impact of a seminal career," summed up *Time* magazine, listing Reed with the Clash, the Ramones, Smokey Robinson, and Bruce Springsteen among the best rockers of 1980.

Since the album was released by his old record company, which had the rights to the songs, and its cover was a series of Polaroids of him with Rachel, a relationship he was now denying (he would rip photographs of himself with Rachel out of magazines or books), Lou had little to do with the album's creation and chose to ignore its appearance. Then, after a Christmas, 1980, show at the Bottom Line in New York, he temporarily stopped performing.

Growing Up in Public sold poorly, and it is likely that on some level Reed blamed drugs for this. For years, along with Keith Richards, Lou Reed had been on everybody's list as "rock star most likely to die." Certainly the drugs and alcohol were now having a deleterious effect on Reed's appearance. Furthermore, in addition to erratic behavior on and off stage, he was experiencing problems with his writing and in retaining his ideas. "It's very difficult to retain things, to learn things and keep track of everything if it starts to get out of control, which it was," he said. "Then it got very out of control. So it was just obvious it had to stop. To really get a grip on my career and be true to the talent and everything, I have to have control."

At the beginning of 1981, Lou joined both Alcoholics and Narcotics Anonymous. "The last thing in the world I would be interested in is blowing it, on a personal-health level. I think drugs are the single most terrible thing, and if I thought there was anything I could do which I thought might be effective in stopping people dealing in drugs and taking them, I would do it. I just think it's the worst conceivable thing in the world. Before, I didn't care. Speaking for myself, I could not continue that way. When drugs and liquor turn on you, it becomes debilitating rather than energizing or making you more focused. Then it's just a terrible jumble. So I had to set about starting at square one again."

To accomplish his radical transformation, Lou needed a period of retreat. For this, his Blairstown estate was ideal. The home—replete with comforts and hobbies that gave Lou boyish delight—was the perfect substitute for his parents' house, just as Sylvia was an ideal replacement for Toby Reed.

For a while, struggling to remain sober and married was all he could concentrate on. "The Last Shot" and "Bottoming Out," two songs composed during his Blairstown retreat, described a Lou Reed desperate for a drink and reeling from emotional instability. The AA recruit's desire for alcohol represented the classic conflict between what Lou knew was good for him and what he craved for release and catharsis. And his resolve was undermined by the reckless, drug-dependent image his audience demanded. In light of this struggle, he now revealed a remarkable ability to open himself up in front of a different kind of audience: hundreds of other alcoholics and drug addicts. In AA meetings, recruits are expected to get up in front of the group to tell the story of how they became alcoholic, and what led them to stop drinking. Lou's speech was honest and unadorned. He admitted that while recently riding his motorbike he had spotted a bag of white powder on the side of the road and pulled over in the wild hope that it might be speed. On closer inspection he discovered that it was talcum powder, but ruefully admitted that had it been amphetamine, he would have been hard-pressed to leave it there. The anecdote received appreciative laughter and applause for its candor.

"Basically he said being sober was beyond his wildest dreams," recalled the member who witnessed his AA speech. "And to hear Lou Reed say that, a guy who achieved a lot, who was cool in everybody's eyes . . . He was very grateful, he was just very regular. He talked about how alcohol and drugs had affected his life and how it still made him stop." Another friend commented, "When I went to Narcotics Anonymous, Lou was there, I would see him and talk to him at the meetings, and he seemed perfectly normal. But he wouldn't hang out afterwards."

Outside of his contact with people at AA and NA meetings, Lou suspended or ended most of his personal relationships. "I ran into Lou one night at a movie theater and we had a very friendly fifteen-minute talk and vowed to get together, and I haven't seen him since," recalled his old Syracuse friend and Eldorados manager, Donald Schupak. "I guess he was sober, clean, straight, hetero, married, lifting weights, looking great. I think one of the rules laid down was no contact with your prior life—like an AA thing. Rather than differentiating between the good contacts and the bad contacts, it was like a cult, you've got to cut off everyone from your past life. It says something that he'd go along with that."

Discipline and control were the central themes in Lou's life, and he was characteristically unapologetic about his new lifestyle. "I'm not interested in any morality plays," he said of his attempts to clean up. "I'm not proselytizing, but as far as my early demise goes, I've made a lot of efforts in the other direction. Such things you might consider dull—working out, playing basketball, keeping my head together and all that. I find destructive people very, very boring, and I'd like to think that I'm not one of them."

Even though Lou had quit drinking and was attending AA, Sylvia continued to indulge. She didn't see herself as having a problem, claiming that she often went without a drink for days or even weeks without missing it. According to one friend, however, when she did get drunk, she could get crazy and out of control. In most respects, though, Sylvia was the epitome of the devoted wife, often submitting to Lou's wishes despite her own. Now, spending much of his time far from New York and strictly limiting all visitors, Lou could successfully isolate Sylvia, who had transformed from a downtown diva into a *Redbook*-style housewife. Where once she had said that if he ever broke up with her, she would sue him for palimony, the now domesticated Sylvia was happy to be with Lou and was flattered by the songs he wrote about her. "Sylvia is one hundred percent for Lou," noted Eric Kronfeld. "She's supportive. He relies on her a lot. He's certainly happy."

Sylvia was evidently just what Lou needed; he changed in ways that surprised his old friends. "Since he got married, he's been really happy," said Moe Tucker, "which makes me happy. Recently I dropped him a line to say we had a new baby. I didn't expect a reply—I mean, what does he care?—but I got a very sweet letter back." According to Lou, "Sylvia's very, very smart, so I have a realistic person I can ask about things: 'Hey, what do you think of this song?' She helped me so much in bringing things together and getting rid of certain things that were bad for me, certain people. I've got help, for the first time in my life [he had said the same thing about Bettye and Rachel]. I'm surrounded by good, caring, honest business people. In my life, that's a real change. I don't know what I would have done without her."

Sylvia also had a positive influence on his writing. "There's this real myth, as if by getting married you suddenly become old and senile and move to the suburbs and never do a meaningful piece of work again," Lou said. "I envision marriage as the romantic thing it is. How can you write about love when you don't believe in it?"

"He transferred to Sylvia, who had got him out of his alcoholic thing and his funk, those qualities that he would have to a mother, Mom says it's okay, I can do it," warned a close friend. "But the moment you give that to somebody, you hate them for it, and you have to separate from them or you're not going to grow up."

Lou defended himself against the charge that he had retired to the suburban married life and was no longer a relevant artistic force. "I've run up against resentment in the press about this. Getting married, if you're in rock and roll, seems to strike these people as if you'd been put out to pasture somewhere in the suburbs and stripped bare of your vital organs. Whereas another point of view might be that marriage could revitalize you. It could help you, make you stronger, more insightful, more percep-tive, give you even more ability to go about doing what you want to do in writing and all that. And make you a better person for it. I have a place in Jersey, so I read these things now: 'He's a suburbanite.' It's as though I donated my brain to science and I was now making rock and roll totally on a shallow field: 'memories of the dark underbelly of New York from before.' "

"I used to seek out extreme situations and live through them. Now I try to avoid them. I've discovered I'm a person who works best when there's no tension. I like to watch other people in extreme situations. I would have made the change all along if I could have."

The few friends Lou still saw were characterized by extreme loyalty and a belief in, or mirroring of, his new domestic situation. Most were married. He claimed not to understand why people would want to remain single. For Lou "happily married" was the preferred state of being, and friends who messed up their marriages found themselves persona non grata at his home. Even Andy Warhol, writing in his diary, commented that all Lou was interested in was his rural retreat. Ronnie Cutrone, who visited Lou in the country, told Warhol that Lou had "always just bought another motorcycle and another piece of land." Blairstown was great for Lou's writing, but, as he recalled, "the great breakthrough was the computer. My main thing is rewriting. I can edit in my head pretty well, but because of the handwriting and because I don't have the ability to contain one thought for very long, if I'm interrupted, that's it."

The change in the lyrical content of his songs was not the only by-product of his new life. Reed also toned down his image in an "average-guy" motif. "Some people like to think I'm just this black-leather-clad person in sunglasses, and there's certainly that side of me; I wouldn't want to deny my heritage. But I'm not saying I'm a primitive. I work really hard to make my songs sound like the way people really talk. My concerns are somewhat similar to what Sam Shepard and Martin Scorsese are doing, talking about things that people growing up in the city go through. I'm trying for a kind of urban elegance, set to a beat."

In his Blairstown retreat Lou found himself trying once again to reinvent the setup he'd had at Syracuse—going so far this time as to summon the ghost of Delmore Schwartz. One night at the cabin Schwartz put in an appearance via a Ouija board. The incident did inspire a song, "My House," in which Lou claimed Delmore Schwartz occupied a guest bedroom. "Something very strange happened," recalled Reed. "After a while we just had to stop, it was becoming too much for me to handle."

Chapter Seventeen

THE NEW, POSITIVE LOU (THE BLUE LOU)

1981–84

I think he loves his lives and I think he hates them.

—Robert Quine

LOU WAS MARRIED TO SYLVIA.

He had the ghost of Delmore Schwartz living in his house.

All he needed to complete the triangle he had thrived on since Shelley and Lincoln was a third person.

In 1981, Sylvia found that person in the guitar player Robert Quine.

Quine was from Akron, Ohio, where the deejay who gave rock and roll its name, Alan Freed, got his start. Though he had gone to law school and become a member of the Missouri bar, Quine had never practiced. Instead, in the early seventies he moved to New York to pursue his love affair with the guitar. A staunch Velvets fan who had devoured the band's San Francisco performances in 1969, Quine developed a slashing, tense style. "Lou Reed became such a big influence on my playing," he recounted. "He was a true innovator on the guitar who was never appreciated at the time. I completely absorbed his style. I've always liked those basic, simple rock-and-roll changes."

In the mid-seventies, Quine worked with Richard Hell, formed the Voidoids, and recorded their groundbreaking album, *Blank Generation*. Quine's spare, impeccably timed sonic assaults were in the vanguard of punk music. As Robert Palmer wrote in the *New York Times*, "Robert Quine's solos were like explosions of shredding metal and were over in thirty seconds or so." Unlike any other guitar superstar, Bob dressed conservatively and adopted a laconic, indifferent stance onstage and off. He could have passed for a retiring shoe salesman or pious cleric. His head was mostly bald. His tight facial features were shielded by the trademark black sunglasses he wore clamped over his sensitive eyes like a visor. A cigarette perennially dangled from his lip. The purest of musicians with the highest of standards, Quine let his music speak for him. As soon as he played a single, inimitable note on his guitar, there was no question that Mr. Quine was in control. If an artist's work can be judged by how quickly it is recognized, then Bob Quine was one of the all-time greats. By 1977, his playing was so inspired he had developed a cult following.

"Around October 1977 we were playing at CBGB's," Quine recalled, "and I didn't know Lou was there, but he was at the front table. We had done a pretty good set and I was walking by the table and he grabbed me and said, 'Man, you're a fucking great guitar player.' " Then he sat Quine down at the table and proceeded to lay into the band, snarling, "That is not a band you're playing with. I hope you know that. Music is about domination and power. You should just fucking dominate these people, they're not musicians. You should go over to the other guitar player and put him out of his misery." Somebody passed the table and Quine looked away for a second, at which point Lou said in a very low, serious voice, "When I'm talking, listen, goddamn it. When I'm talking to you, you look me in the eye, goddamn it, or I'll fucking smash you in the face, and I'm serious, I'm deadly serious."

It was not until four years later—by which time Lou had stopped drinking and married Sylvia—that Quine got his opportunity to play with his hero. Sylvia made the connection, calling Bob on the phone, inviting him to have lunch with Lou at some anonymous restaurant near Reed's flat. On the same cold March day in 1981 that President Reagan was shot, Quine met Reed for lunch at one of those glassed-in restaurants that decorate the lower expanse of Seventh Avenue in the Sheridan Square area. Lou was just checking Bob out to make sure he was not an asshole. "He was not interested in talking about old Velvet Underground days," Quine recalled. "We talked about guitars, this, that, and I guess he assured himself that I was an okay guy. Then we went back to his apartment on Christopher and he had some new guitars."

As Lou showed Bob his guitars, he discussed plans for his new band,

----

mentioning that he wanted to play more guitar himself. "That's absolutely great!" Quine exclaimed spontaneously. Before Bob left, Lou said he wanted Bob to be in the band. "He pretty much said, this is it and I could count on him. I was alarmed by the last album he had done, *Growing Up in Public*, which was my least favorite of his, but he said he didn't want to do anything like that again. He wanted a whole new band, he wanted to play guitar, he wanted a new record company."

To facilitate his fresh start, Reed elected to drop Arista in favor of RCA, the company he had left in 1976 in the wake of the infamous *Metal Machine Music*. His superstar success was enough to persuade them that, once again, Reed was a good investment.

A few months later, as Lou was getting ready to record the album, he sent Quine a cassette of himself playing the songs on acoustic guitar. A few days later he had Quine and the producer, Sean Fullan, ferried to Blairstown by limousine for a day-long visit. "That was a very nerve-wracking time for both of us," Quine explained. "We had never played together so we were both ill at ease. We're walking around kind of putting it off as long as possible, then we sat down to do it. I said, 'Well, maybe I think I can do this here.' I had a basic sound on 'Waves of Fear' down, and he was just surprised and happy. He pretty much liked everything I did."

Lou soon glommed on to Quine with invasive energy. A phone-aholic, Lou would call Quine fifteen times a day. Soon they were meeting for lunch regularly at a coffee shop on the corner where Lou lived. "I remember at the beginning of it I ran into them a couple of times just hanging out together, going out to eat Chinese food, stuff like that," said Robert Palmer. "Which is very unusual—I've never run into Lou sort of hanging around the Village the way you would run into Quine or somebody." Passionate, generous, vulnerable, Bob was the perfect and much needed musical foil for Lou. On top of that, he was as opinionated and articulate as Reed. For someone who was as easily bored as Lou, Quine's mind provided a big relief. They had endless discussions.

Lou needed receivers—people he could talk to endlessly through the day and night in person or on the phone—just as much as he needed musical collaborators. And Quine, who was, if anything, more articulate and opinionated than Lou, fit the mold almost too well for his own good. Lou loved to talk to Bob. "We hung out for about six months and we got to be pretty good friends," recalled Quine, adding, "which may have been a mistake in the long run. Who knows if you should become close friends with the people you work with. But we would go to see horror movies all the time; 3-D was making a comeback and we'd go see all the trashy 3-D horror movies. And he'd drag me to see the crappy kung fu movies in Chinatown. He'd want to watch ten in a row, but I couldn't absorb any more after three or four."

As they spent more and more time together, the friendship spilled over into other areas. Lou had suffered from insomnia for many years. Quine had discovered an over-the-counter pill, Unisom, which he turned Reed on to with positive results. Lou was gratified.

At first, their shared love for EC Comics bonded them as much as their love for the guitar playing of James Burton. When Quine showed Reed his collection of vintage horror and science-fiction comic books, in particular a patently gory and offensive series put out by EC Comics, "Lou really lit up. A typical comic would be a guy jealous of another team player on the baseball team would put poison on his spikes and spike the guy and he dies. So the other guys on the team find out about it and invite the guy to a midnight game, and the last few shots are these players playing baseball with this guy's body parts. His intestines are the baselines, his limbs are the bat, head the ball."

Quine also visited Lou and Sylvia out in Blairstown: "As a general rule we'd just hang around. It was sort of like a cabin, but a gigantic cabin with a second floor. Very rustic. It was very nice. But personally I like being close to the ocean, and being in the woods surrounded by ponds, it makes me claustrophobic. He had his motorcycle and in the winter he had his snowmobile. I was fairly terrified of the motorcycle. I took one ride with him and decided never again. His eyes aren't that good. We'd sit around and listen to records. I don't think we jammed too much, but he had some nice old ancient Fender amps and stuff out there. They must have been from when he was a kid. And he had a jukebox in his house with a lot of nice oldies on there. He had boxes of singles in the closet. Pinball. Pool. And he had those dogs."

Reed's comfortable relationship with his musicians made for sponta- neity and a raw vitality missing from some of his previous albums. A week before going into the studio Lou got together with Bob and ran through the songs once. Everybody knew the songs up to a point, but nothing was too structured. Quine remembered how liberating this approach was: "I was free to come up with whatever I came up with. Total freedom. We went in with no rehearsals."

In October 1981, they went to RCA's studio in New York, a gigantic barn of a room used by symphony orchestras playing live together, and recorded the tracks for *The Blue Mask* in one or two takes. Quine and Reed brought all the anxiety and fear they could muster to the sessions. The spark immediately ignited the band. Quine had never done a record like this before. "We went in and ran the songs down and started doing them. He was playing a lot of open chords in D, which was very nice, but to try and get a second guitar part to complement that was difficult. So I dropped my tuning a whole step. When he was playing an open D chord, I was playing an open E chord. That's partly the reason why that album sounds the way it does."

"I hadn't played guitar for a while," recounted Lou. "I started playing guitar again because of Bob Quine. Quine was real good about encouraging me to play guitar. I cannot play with just anybody. Ofttimes I would not play guitar rather than get involved in playing with people I'd clash with, where it just wouldn't work. I need somebody who really understands that little simple thing that I do and likes that stuff. And they're hard to come by. So when I ran into Quine, who understands that and plays that way, he really freed me up and gave me a lot of encouragement. He'd say, 'Lou, come on. You can take the solo.' With some other people, if I took a solo, they'd go, 'Oh my God,' and just hope it would end."

Quine knew he was working with a major talent: "There are people like David Bowie or Prince, people who have had millions of books written about them and are regarded widely as geniuses. I would admit that they are creative, intelligent people who have done some worthwhile things, but they are completely second-rate next to some of the things Lou's done. I don't even mention Bruce Springsteen, how could any intelligent person ever like him? But the other two at least could be regarded—still they're not even close to being in the same league as Lou Reed."

On *The Blue Mask*—whose revealing working title was *Heaven and Hell*—Lou regained the kind of control of his work that Warhol had handed him on a plate. He chose an engineer who would specifically "not fuck around with the shit." For the first time since 1978 and *Street Hassle*, Reed didn't share songwriting credits, and he controlled the mix: "I

couldn't stand working with these engineers, and they were always trying
to fuck around with me. At least you essentially got to hear what went
down before this guy fucks around with it and takes the fucking guts out
of it. I'd rather you heard it with the guts in than with a fucking pop sheen
to it. Going back to Andy Warhol, that was the worst of anything that
could happen as far as Andy was concerned, that it gets slicked up. I
believe that too. If you want to hear slick shit, my God, you could just
buy everybody else."

Lou and Bob played like jazz musicians listening and responding to
each other's music in kind. Lou had not had an experience this fine since
playing with Cale. His playing and singing became more confident. You
could see him pushing the music out like an action painter. To underscore
the music's spontaneity, Reed insisted on keeping the studio effects to a
minimum. "He was doing live vocals, which are crucial," said Quine,
"and we'd just do it. That's what's really cool about that record. People
are really intensely listening to each other, trying to cross barriers; they
did that magical jazz thing. Something special is happening and you can
hear it on the record. It still amazes me." Quine remembered the first
track they recorded was "My House." "There was such a sense of elation
and relief when he and Sylvia and I went out to dinner afterwards. We
knew we had it. I wish it had gone on longer on that kind of level."

Apparently Lou felt the same way. "Everything shifted around the time
of *The Blue Mask*. I was playing guitar with a *sympathetic* guitar player. A
monumental bass player, Fernando Saunders. And Doane Perry on drums.
Plus a good engineer. And I'd made some strides in the improvement of
the production. I do the writing, that's separate. But when you're working
out with the guys, doing the songs, playing, trying to bring it to life, it's
a mysterious process—recording. I'll tell you, all really good musicians—
forget about the notes they play—it's their tone that's important. They
have a certain tone and you're trying to capture it. They work quite hard
on it."

The way in which Reed used Quine's abilities to temper his own
provides a perfect example of Lou Reed at his best. Reed was an enormously seductive character, not just in a sexual sense but socially. To
really *be* with him, to play with him, was a joy for musicians of the caliber
of Cale, Chuck Hammer, and Bob Quine. And Quine, perhaps more
than the others, was such a perfect match for Lou because he knew how
to listen to both music and words.

Like Warhol, Lou could be warm, encouraging, even idolatrous of someone whose work he admired. Yet he could just as easily turn his praise to derision when he didn't get what he wanted or sensed a challenge to his authority. The fear of Lou's vituperative outbursts—or just plain abandonment—kept several of his musicians playing their best, close to the edge. Lou's exacting standards worked their effect on Quine, who already harbored a near pathological fear of mediocrity.

Quine worked from an encyclopedic knowledge of Reed's guitar playing. Within a short time he became the key musician in the creation of the new Lou Reed band. Quine bolstered Lou's faith in his own guitar playing. As a result, on *The Blue Mask*, for the first time since *White Light/White Heat*, Reed came in with some great guitar solos. Just as David Bowie had given a part of Lou back to himself ten years earlier, Quine urged Reed to take his guitar playing back to his subtle, insightful style. With Quine's help, Reed interpreted most of *The Blue Mask* as guitar songs, relearning much of what he had left behind with the breakup of the Velvets. "One imagines that major chunks of his being had to be rebuilt," commented one friend, "and that, to some degree, at least, he had to relearn how to write songs."

Backed by Quine and the excellent new band, Reed was once again on his own rock-and-roll turf. Gone were the experiments with funk and jazz, and the musicians with whom he couldn't play. Palmer would later write enthusiastically about the band. "The four musicians, especially Mr. Reed and Robert Quine on guitars, interact with a sort of empathy and lucidity one expects from a seasoned jazz combo, and the music always reaches out to invite the listener in, even at its most intensely personal level. There are no ego contests, no power plays. When he was asked why *The Blue Mask* succeeded so brilliantly where his other albums had been uneven, Reed said, 'It's mostly working with the right musicians.' "

"I had my share of fear and anxiety," recalled Quine. "I always bring that to the studio almost deliberately; you play better and it's a great relief and happiness. That's the only way I can put it. But I would work myself up into a state of fear every day for the next one because when really great stuff happens, you don't know exactly where it's coming from, and you don't have a lot of control over it, so how can it happen again? Every night I'd come home, my girlfriend would see me freaking out, and I'd be frantically trying to figure something out. 'Oh, no, this is fucked. I can't come up with anything decent on this song, I'm screwed,' and then it would just happen again.

"I remember the most specific thing he really ever said on that album, *The Blue Mask,* was on the song 'The Day John Kennedy Died.' He said, 'I'm gonna play the last chord on the song—don't play the last chord with me.' You could see he was getting more and more confident every day, and it was generally a good thing culminating in the end with one of the last songs we did, 'The Blue Mask,' where he went and took that amazing guitar solo. That was the turning point where he knew he had it."

Quine was happy with the results: "None of us had ever played together before, but it just clicked immediately. What you hear on the record is totally live. 'Waves of Fear' was one of the best things I ever did. I just let it go. The spontaneity was there. I said to Lou at the end of the song, 'I have an idea for a solo,' and he said, 'Just do it.' There are no overdubs, except one track . . . any mistakes that happened are on that record. If I take a solo, I stop playing rhythm. There's no rhythm-guitar fill going underneath. It's the way they used to do things in the fifties."

The method paid off especially well for Lou, who let go with his strongest guitar solos in years. "It was a turning point," continued Quine, "you can hear it on 'The Blue Mask' when Lou starts his guitar solo. He did it, and there it was as good as anything he had done ten years earlier. It was like a vindication.

"When he approached the end of *The Blue Mask,* I saw his confidence increasing day by day, and it was a great thing, even when it resulted in things like 'The Heroin,' which he did by himself. He got so exasperated with the band, he said, 'Screw it, I'm doing this myself.' The last few songs he took complete charge of. There was still spontaneity, but even then he saw what was possible. A song like 'Average Guy,' which was one of the last songs, he changed the whole chord structure and said, 'Do it this way.' "

"I spent a lot of time on the song order," Reed said. "These things are important. If you can get a feeling of continuity from the album, a feeling of somebody trying to speak to you, that's the difference between a good album and something that's finer. I'm not above appreciating my own work. And I don't think *The Blue Mask* is just a good album. It's way better than that."

The Blue Mask was released in February 1982. Lou dedicated it to

Delmore Schwartz. *Trouser Press* compared the album to John Lennon's *Double Fantasy*, commenting, "Precious few people in rock deserve the accolade of genius, but Lou Reed is surely one of them." "The intuitive responsiveness between Lou Reed and Robert Quine is a quiet summit of guitarists' interplay," Tom Carson wrote in *Rolling Stone*. "The notes and noise soar and dive, scudding almost formlessly until they're suddenly caught up in the focus of the rhythm. . . . With *The Blue Mask*, Lou Reed has done what even John Lennon couldn't do—he's put his *Plastic Ono Band* and his *Double Fantasy* on the same record, and made us feel that, at long last, these two paths in him are joined." Although a commercial disappointment—*The Blue Mask* reached only No. 169 on the *Billboard* chart in early March—Robert Palmer in the *New York Times* called *The Blue Mask* Lou's best in years, and the first rock masterpiece of 1982.

"The thing about Lou's guitar playing," he said, "is he's able to use all of these nonmusical elements, really screeching feedback, and integrate them into something musical. But, he does tend to ramble. I love what he plays, but sometimes it doesn't have a beginning, middle, and an end, it doesn't build. On *The Blue Mask*, Lou's playing is as concise as Quine's. There's a certain kind of real raging going on within it, yet it's all very directed towards the song.

"There's one other aspect of vocal influence on Lou that I remember him bringing up, which was his real and intense love of doo-wop. He pointed out one or two songs on *The Blue Mask* that were very influenced by fifties doo-wop records. You would never hear it just listening to the records because it's set in the middle of this raging guitar noise. But when he pointed it out to me, like on 'Heavenly Arms' . . . That's been a really important source for him all the way through."

"I suspect, and Lou admitted as much, he has a certain inferiority complex about his guitar playing. Because it is, from one point of view, very basic. But from another point of view it's very cool because of the fact that he plays so hard and so intensely and sort of transcends his instrumental limitations: conceptually he's got the ability to go over the top and then beyond that.

"The thing about *The Blue Mask* that's so impressive in that respect is that he really escaped his own clichés. He was in danger before *The Blue Mask* of becoming a total parody of himself, and he was very well aware of it. He was playing the rock-and-roll animal as a role and then the role swallowed him up, I think there was a definite sense of liberation in *The Blue Mask*—of having escaped from that. It was a very impressive thing to do—especially at that stage in such a long career."

The American critic Ellen Willis wrote in an RCA press release, "For those of us who are always confronting our own history through rock and roll, this album is more than the summation of one artist's career; it is the spiritual record of a decade in the life."

BETWEEN THE RELEASE OF *THE BLUE MASK* IN FEBRUARY 1982 AND THE commencement of work on *Legendary Hearts*, in the summer, the relationship between Quine and Reed was put to the test. On one occasion, said Quine, "when we were doing *Legendary Hearts*, he was doing the vocals for 'Pow Pow' in the vocal booth. He wasn't sure what approach to take so he started going through his catalog of voices. He said, 'I think I'll do my *Transformer* voice on this one.' It was amazing. He did his voice from *Transformer*, and then he said, 'Nah, I think I'll do my—voice,' and he did three or four. He certainly has a handle on it, but it's a conflict."

The first cracks appeared when Lou noted that in the reviews Quine was receiving as much attention as he was. Ever since Lou had fired Cale from the VU, it had been clear that he could not stand sharing credit. Quine, not restricted by the desire to be a star, singularly focused on the music, was not at first aware of the problem.

By the early summer of 1982, Lou began working up material for the next album. However, with his confidence soaring, Lou depended less on his collaborators and often got angry when they didn't perform as he wished. "I think of the word *uptight*," said Quine. "The working title for *Legendary Hearts* was *The Argument*."

"There started to be a slight strain in our friendship. He's a strong and intimidating personality, but this didn't keep me from being outspoken at various times. I have a couple of theories about *Legendary Hearts*. It's more of a subdued record."

Before the album was completed, Lou resorted to an old tried-and-true trick. Going back into the studio without informing anyone on the record, he remixed the entire album so that his voice and his playing stood out. Some of Quine's best playing was either mixed down so as to be barely distinguishable or cut altogether. On receiving his copy of the album,

Quine smashed the cassette to smithereens with a hammer. "I got very upset when I heard the mix of that album," he admitted. "I ended up working with him for two more years, but things were never the same after that. After I got *Legendary Hearts* I didn't return any of his calls for weeks. I went out to Ohio to visit my parents. When they drove up the driveway, they saw me with a hammer smashing this cassette into a million pieces.

"Lou calls my house in Ohio, and my mother picks up the phone. He says, 'Hello, is Quine there?' And she says, 'Which Quine would you like to speak to?' He told her which one. 'It's Lou!' So I took that call, and we just took it from there. I never talked about it. I'm sure he understood."

"I was always dissatisfied with the mix on *Legendary Hearts*," said Robert Palmer. "Both on the album and live it seemed like Quine was not quite loud enough. And I think the songs are stronger on *The Blue Mask*. It's more focused and it's got a sharper sense of cutting. Having made that breakthrough with Quine on *The Blue Mask*, it seems like Lou then started being a little self-conscious. When he gets self-conscious, he starts exercising control. It seemed like there was more and more of him exercising control and less of the music itself controlling it, which you got the impression happened on *The Blue Mask*."

NINETEEN EIGHTY-THREE BROUGHT NEW ALBUMS FROM THE POLICE, DAVID Bowie, Talking Heads, and a $28-million contract to the Rolling Stones. In February, Lou returned to the road. The tour started at the Bottom Line in New York. There were no drugs or alcohol allowed in the dressing rooms. One night's show was filmed for video release as *A Night with Lou Reed*. (Another Quine-era video, entitled *Coney Island Baby*, recorded at the Capitol Theater in New Jersey, was issued in 1987.)

The shows sold out and got an overwhelming positive response from critics and audience alike. The *New York Times* review gushed: "The new Lou Reed quartet is one of the most distinctive and powerful bands in all of rock." Once again, Lou was upset by reviews that singled out Quine for the same amount of praise as Lou got. In collaborating, Lou was good at sharing the work, but never the praise.

"The music was just ferocious," Palmer recalled. "And you'd look at Quine standing there with a bemused expression on his face ripping the stuff out of the guitar and Lou too. There was definitely a sense of Quine pushing Lou as a guitar player, and they were really digging that, I felt. I didn't really feel anything competitive between them."

What was surprising, however, was that much of the material was reworked Velvets and Lou Reed hits. The set included sixties favorites like "Sunday Morning," "New Age," and a closing medley of "Sister Ray" and "Rock & Roll." There were also a few improvements, and perhaps an attempt to disguise his commercial turn. Andy Warhol, in the audience the first night, wrote, "Lou's lyrics you can understand now, and the music was really loud. He did a lot of familiar songs, but you didn't recognize them, they sounded different."

Legendary Hearts was released in March 1983 to mixed reaction. At best, the press embraced the virtues of a new Lou Reed. "Much of the tension that has made his records and songs compelling, and often un-settling, derived from the apparent dichotomy between his more or less conventional roots and the succession of bizarre roles he has chosen to play," wrote Robert Palmer in the *New York Times*. "But recently the two Lou Reeds, one a literate craftsman, the other a self-styled 'monster,' have been coming together."

At their worst, the reviews accused Reed of being exactly what he was: over forty, married, contrived, sober—all unacceptable states by rock-and-roll standards. "Lou ended up doing album after album of reissues of the same song," said John Cale. And Chris Bohn, writing in the *NME* saw a more subtle desperation in Reed's latest attempts: "You can always tell a bad Lou Reed song by the level of urgency he imparts it with." *Melody Maker* dismissed Reed's work altogether for being "so out of touch and unreal that it's shocking. . . . The most insulting appalling release in years by any major artist." *Legendary Heart*'s sales were pallid.

After the resounding success at the Bottom Line, and coaxed by an RCA record offer, Lou decided to take the show to a few cities in Europe where he could fill stadiums. In September 1983, Reed, Quine, Saunders, and Maher flew to Italy, where the local RCA Records branch was to tape the shows for a double album—*Live in Italy*—to be released in Europe in early 1984. The album material was taken from dates at the Verona arena and Rome Circus Maximus, where the band played in front of thousands of screaming fans.

Live in Italy wasn't the finest achievement of the Reed-Quine partner-ship, though it was still a powerful, if slightly monotonous, double live

----

album. Reed fired up "Kill Your Sons" as if the scars of the past would never disappear, while Quine helped create a storm of guitar noise on a memorable fifteen-minute melody of "Some Kinda Love" and "Sister Ray." In effect, Reed was presenting a greatest-hits show—half-Velvets, half-solo—performed with enough grace to give the concerts a craftsman-like air.

The British critic Matt Snow wrote: "Lou's going on forty-two, and *Live in Italy* documents how he regards his history as of September 1983, just as *Take No Prisoners* did in '79, *Rock 'n' Roll Animal* and *Lou Reed Live* five years before that. And when I say history, I mean that seven out of fifteen tracks are the Velvet Underground's greatest hits, and two others are 'Walk on the Wild Side' and 'Satellite of Love.' Of the rest, only two come from his latest pair of LPs, *The Blue Mask* and *Legendary Hearts*, the latter providing the lineup of musicians who play here. Lou and Quine mesh in an empathetic steel-and-glass grid, aluminum sound which spirals into jaggedly lyrical solos, even psychedelic as on a stunning 'Kill Your Sons'; Tom Verlaine and Richard Lloyd of Television, spring to mind: rhythms are crisp and slightly jazzy."

By now, the tension Reed created between him and Quine became detrimental to the results. "Unfortunately they didn't present that band at its best," recalled Quine. "We were very tense at the first concert, we did not play as well as we could. Only the encore. We had a guitar roadie who would consistently put our guitars out of tune. And the result was almost none of the ballads could be used. We had great arrangements to 'Sunday Morning,' 'I'll Be Your Mirror,' 'Femme Fatale.'

"Another highlight was 'Heroin' at the Rome concert. We were teargassed at that one and we were playing Circus Maximus—an outdoor place. Apparently a crowd had gathered outside the fence before the concert, and the police dispersed them using teargas the moment before we came out. When we came onstage, the wind blew the teargas directly on us. So during the first forty-five minutes of the show I could not see a thing. I could not even see the little dots on the neck of my guitar. And there was snot running down my face and they were throwing wine bottles full of piss on the stage. People said we were really brave to stay onstage, but we had to. There would have been a riot. There were God knows how many of them. And it was a pretty emotional performance."

Reed had not had a collaboration on the level with Quine since work-

ing with Cale. Quine and Cale were both high-strung and had an ability
to share their own light with others. These qualities made them particularly vulnerable to Lou Reed, whose reptilian mind loved nothing more
than to attack such creatures.

An incident on the return flight from Italy to the States illustrated
Lou's hang-up. According to Quine, "We were coming back on the plane
from the *Live in Italy* thing. We were fried, we were wasted, we all got sick
from the food we'd had in this horrible hotel we were staying in. . . . I
was sitting next to Fred Maher on the plane, and Lou came over and gave
me cassettes of the two shows we had had recorded to put on an album.
He said, 'Well, Quine, here's what I want you to do. Make a list of the
songs you did at the Verona show and the Rome show, and then check
off the version that's best.' I said, 'You know, you can just use your own
judgment really. I think we'll agree. If you're really stuck, just call me up.'

"I knew from the beginning that it was probably pretty obvious which
version was best, since one version would always be better than the other,
but he wouldn't let up. 'No, you can do this, can you just . . . ,' and after
he insisted about five times, I snapped. I said, 'Look, why should I humor
you by doing this? You've done this before and you end up totally ignoring
my opinions. There's no point in this, and I'm not going to insult your
intelligence by humoring you. It's just pointless. It's a waste of my time
and it's a waste of your time.' And he turned several colors and he said in
a very low, menacing voice, 'Quine, you're going to be very sorry you did
this.' "

"Quine hated every minute of playing with Lou after *Legendary
Hearts,*" recounted one close friend. "He thought that Lou was losing it.
Their falling out had to do with Lou's megalomania, with stealing credit.
Lou would enjoy humiliating Quine. There were real problems in the
music. Although he adored Quine and was using Quine, it was obvious he
was jealous of him as a guitar player. If Quine would come up with
something great, Lou was jealous. I mean, he was a jealous person. The
impression I got was that he was really fucked-up, vindictive, sick . . .

"*Miserable* was his favorite word for Lou. Not just once, not just twice,
many, many, many times. Lou Reed was the incarnation of misery. For
many people misery is an attractive, seductive subject. Teenagers identify
with suffering, basically. The thing that's intriguing about a lot of Lou's
music is that it makes suffering happy. He celebrates it. And the music

itself is catchy, it's dancey, and so it's embracing the suffering, making it lovable. But in embracing it, you're not trying to change it, you're just dressing it up, you're recognizing it and you're wallowing in it. Lou wallows in it, and he makes sure everybody else is wallowing in it. Maybe he got stuck in it because it became his subject matter. It's a self-fulfilling prophecy. That's what misery's about, it's about obsessiveness. The nature of being a miserable person requires that you obsess about it. And you do this over and over and over, and you absorb things and turn them in on yourself."

Reed recorded his next album, *New Sensations*, December 1983 through February 1984. Quine was fired from the band two days before they were supposed to record *New Sensations*.

"A couple of days before doing *New Sensations*," Quine recalled, "we were checking out the studio, and I was still allegedly going to be on it. I did not want to be on the record because I knew I was going to put all this effort into coming up with parts and getting a good sound and he was just going to mix me off the fucking thing again, and it's nothing I can ask him point-blank about, and I realized I was just dragging my feet every way I could. A couple of days before the recording I demanded more money from Eric Kronfeld, something that was pointless to do since I was already being paid well. Then I was meeting the producer, John Janson, for the first time, and he, Lou, and I had lunch together. When we went over to the studio, John was very enthusiastic. He said, 'You know, I think of myself as the fifth member of the band. I'd like to contribute arrangements and be a fifth member of the band,' and you know that was never going to happen. I had to open my mouth and say, 'Well, you know, that's really not necessary. We have enough problems between the four of us on arrangements.' It was a pointless thing to say; it was stupid. And looking back ten years later, I realize exactly why I was doing it. I did not want to be on that record.

"There was some really strange disagreement that he precipitated, and I said, well, you know, I don't think this is going to work out. Lou said I should call him back about it later, and I did call him back the next day. Then the next day after that I received a call from his manager saying that Lou planned to do the guitar by himself." Reed told the press Quine wasn't available for the sessions because he was recording his own solo album, *Basic*.

Lou's inability to continue the fruitful collaboration with Quine had negative results comparable to those following his firing of Cale. In dumping Quine, Lou came across to friends as a cutthroat Machiavelli. "With Quine it was a little too even for Lou," said one friend. "Bob is a really smart guy, a little bit too equal. So that had to go." Another friend recalled, "Bob gave Lou a lot of musical credibility and really good musical direction, and then Lou just fucked up the friendship. Lou really couldn't handle having a friend. Lou doesn't have any friends, he just wants a guy to sit around and listen to him discussing equipment, guitars, recording, and just go, 'Really, really, really . . .' "

NEW SENSATIONS WAS RELEASED IN APRIL. THE ALBUM'S SINGLE, "I LOVE You, Suzanne," was released with "Vicious" as a B side. "I Love You, Suzanne" captured significant radio airtime and MTV video play. A second video, "My Red Joystick," boosted sales of Lou Reed albums present and past. Where sales of *The Blue Mask* and *Legendary Hearts* were disappointing, the two reaching only 169 and 159 on *Billboard*'s LP chart respectively, *New Sensations* peaked at 56, his best showing since *Coney Island Baby* eight years earlier. *New Sensations* was also no. 9 in the *Village Voice* albums-of-the-year poll.

Hand in hand with the Reeds' move toward a more commercial career came a physical move from downtown Christopher Street to a high-rise on the Upper West Side, at Eighty-first Street and West End Avenue. The new home was not, however, to provide him and Sylvia with the harmony they had experienced on Christopher Street.

"*The Blue Mask*, *Legendary Hearts*, and *New Sensations* explored marriage not as happiness ever after, but as a convention that imbues familiar emotions (love and jealousy, optimism and anger) with new intensity," summed up Bill Flanagan. "What emerged from those albums was a rock-and-roll romanticism with illusion. In 'High in the City' (*New Sensations*) Reed, the quintessential New Yorker, praised the pleasures of Manhattan while warning to arm against attackers. In 'My Friend George' (*New Sensations*) the grown-up street kid ran into an old pal and recognized him for the first time as a dangerous bully. Reed writes of husbands and wives at each other's side and at each other's throat."

Meanwhile, despite the fact that Reed had dropped Quine from the

----

New Sensations album, he brought him back to play for the New Sensations world tour of 1984, restoring the band to the five man lineup that had given the 1979 tours their high pitch. "He called me to go out on tour in early '84," recalled Quine, who said he signed for the money. "I thought it was fairly curious to be asked to go out and support this record. And his manager, Eric Kronfeld, was shocked and amused that I accepted." The keyboardist Peter Wood signed on for the tour along with Fernando Saunders and Fred Maher.

Quine got a pretty good view of his role in the new band during rehearsals: "We would be working on arrangements to songs we hadn't done yet and Lou would say, 'Well, I wonder how many times we should do the bridge here,' or 'How long should the solo be? What do you think, Fred? Well, Fernando, what do you think?' as if I wasn't there. I mean, not too subtle, and it wasn't meant to be. Finally, because of that attitude, after the little brief tour in July and before the long tour I actually called up in a calmer moment and, you know, tried gently to say I might be better off leaving the group. He said, 'What are you talking about?' and I said, 'Well, I'm really not contributing anything.' We ended up having one of those long, better conversations where I approached it, you know, not on a confrontational level saying that I really felt like there was no place for me, and he convinced me that I was important. The next day he bought me a very expensive amplifier with the premium speakers, the premium road case, the whole thing."

After the July tour, Fred Maher, who had another booking, was replaced on drums by Lenny Ferrari. Ferrari gave an amusing account of his first meeting with Lou: "I go to the session and I walk in and it's the first day and there's Robert Quine, Fernando Saunders, Lou, and myself. The first thing Lou says to me is, 'The last thing I want to do is audition a drummer.' And I looked at him and said, 'But you called me!'

"We didn't know each other yet. I could see he was annoyed he had to audition somebody. So after I get to meet everybody he says, 'Okay—I usually like to start out with "Sweet Jane." ' I said, 'Excuse my ignorance here, but "Sweet Jane," what's that?' Robert Quine sort of held his hand over his mouth, and Fernando Saunders sort of knew what I was saying because he's an R-and-B player too. Lou looked startled that I had said this—like it was the Bible or something, and I later found out it was. So I said, 'Hey, Lou, never mind, just hum a few bars and I'll fake it.' Robert

Quine falls over laughing and Fernando said, 'I can't believe you just said this to Lou.'

"So Lou counted it off and I sort of figured it out that this was my first song with him and they're gonna try and mess me up and see if I'm gonna hold the beat, which, as a drummer, is your main job. So I just locked into the beat and they tried to pull the rhythm against me and I felt it but I just held strong. After he does this, Lou stopped and said, 'Gee, we were trying to mess you up and you didn't move, so I was wondering if you'd like to do a world tour with us starting in two weeks?' It was sort of serious and hilarious at the same time. We did eight days of rehearsal."

"I saw Quine shortly before he went on the tour," recounted a close friend. "He was anxietized. He agreed to go on the tour, but had made a lot of demands on Lou. Quine was a passionate person, deeply and profoundly emotional. He loved Lou's music. He gave him back himself. He was very bitter about the fact that Lou did not give him credit for that and in fact went in the other direction to put him down. The only good thing about the trip was the playing part. The before and after he hated. Lou was a sick person. A mean person. I had a sense that he derived great pleasure out of hurting people. Not just any old people, though, people who threatened something in his own sense of self. For example, if Quine had too much integrity, he would make Lou face his own lack of it. Quine would be a reminder to him of certain things about himself that he couldn't face, so he would lash out at Quine and try to hurt him. And because Quine was such a lovely person, such a polite person, he was an easy target."

"We did America in the first two months," recalled Lenny Ferrari. "Lou was moody and it was a crucial point in his life. At the beginning of the tour he pissed Quine off by saying, 'No sunglasses on this tour.' "

"The basic thing behind that was the new, positive Lou Reed," recounted Quine. "Lou had T-shirts made up with a big smiling Lou Reed on them. When we were rehearsing for the seven-month tour, Lou interrupted 'Waves of Fear' saying, 'Look, you know, when I wrote this song, I was in a completely different head. I don't feel this way anymore. I want to do a happy arrangement.' "

Quine was dumbfounded. "I said, 'Well, Lou, you know that the name of the song is called "Waves of Fear," . . .' He said, 'Yeah, but can't we play it a little happier?' I said, 'The happier we play it it's gonna come out even more grotesque.' I tried to accommodate the no sunglasses. I really couldn't do it. Everyone had been enthusiastic about the video for 'Women' on *The Blue Mask,* but more than one executive came up to me and said, 'Yes, great album. We hope the next one will be more upbeat.' You can see that was happening on *Legendary Hearts* to an extent. By *New Sensations,* it was the new, positive Lou."

"Every day he was a different person," Ferrari continued. "He was being Mr. Clean. We weren't allowed to do anything, we couldn't have a drink, actually we couldn't have any fun, so we renamed it the No Sensations tour. The whole band was not having a good time together. Quine also called it the No Sensations tour. Lou didn't want the temptation back in his life. Nobody was drinking. Except the manager was sneaking it, and the bodyguards. And the crew members were having fun. We had about sixty dates around the world. There were sixty parties scheduled, but he canceled fifty-eight of them so we only had a party in New York and L.A. We were not allowed to have any fun so it was a business thing, which was okay with me."

"It would be a drag sometimes because we would be so isolated, there would be nowhere to go and nothing to do," said Quine. "We'd be in the airport Hilton in Rome with no car. I'd be looking out the window at Rome—I hadn't seen it in thirty years."

"We'd get back to the hotel and talk about the show," recalled Ferrari. "It was business. There wasn't any passion. Lou's a square. A week before I got the call from Lou I had decided to quit smoking grass, which was about the extent of my drug taking, and maybe a glass of wine. But after four months, five months, man, we were crying—you're crying for some fun."

Aside from being forbidden drugs, alcohol, and after-concert partying, the band members felt Lou's nervousness in other ways. To prepare for a show Lou would hang out with Sylvia in the dressing room, smoke a few cigarettes, and do some tai chi to calm down. But onstage, he would often lash out at various band members, leaving them humiliated and angry. For the first part of the tour he took out his frustration on the new kid, Ferrari. "He acted like a dick so many times onstage," Ferrzi recalled. "He felt he was under pressure and he released it on me, the new kid."

Lou had a conflict with each of his musicians primarily, it would seem, as a way of keeping the hate that fueled his music. Ferrari, for example, had been excellent in rehearsal, but when they got out on the road, he frequently could not hold the beat. Lou would often turn to him in the midst of a song and scream at the top of his lungs, "Asshole!"

Then he switched to Wood and Saunders and, finally, Quine, who recalled:

"Another one of his major power plays: Every night, week by week, whoever he was picking on, just to make clear to everyone who that person was, at the end of the show he would say, for example, if it was me, as it got near the end of the show, he would say, 'Okay, ladies and gentlemen, I want to introduce the members of the band. On bass we have the magnificent, incredible, the virtuosic and dedicated Fernando Saunders. Please give him a hand. On keyboards we have the blah, blah, blah.' He would go on and on. And then, 'On guitar, Robert Quine,' mumbling the name; not too subtle.

"Another example of his contempt of me as this negative person: Coming into the New Sensations tour, I couldn't say anything; even the most sensitive suggestion ended up setting him off. We were having a sound check in Paris once, and it was horrendous—one of those echoey places, like a gym, where there's this endless Grand Canyon echo, and he said, 'Well, what do you think of the sound check; think we have pretty good sound?' Well, I lied and said, 'Yes, it's pretty good. I just hope that once the audience is here, there'll be a little less of that echo.' He just snorted, he turned another color, and he stalked off because of this, you know, terribly negative thing that I had said."

But such incidents were more than offset by the good pay and per diem expenses for his band members. Moreover, the group was housed in the finest hotels, fed in the finest restaurants, and transported by limousines.

Still, Lou's mania for maintaining complete control over his environment got on their nerves. "Everything was Lou's way," said Ferrari. "I knew Sylvia from the TV party days before she met Lou. And she liked the way I dressed and would be saying, 'Lou, look at that suit he's got on.' And Lou would start getting a little uptight, 'cause he was like in a leather jacket and it looked like I was in a different band, and I didn't want that to be the case. So I was trying to dress down. I would wear just a cravat instead of a tie. But I just didn't want to wear blue jeans. I wore blue jeans in Vietnam, I didn't want to wear blue jeans in civilian life.

"He gave me *ageda*. That's an Italian term for an upset stomach. I have to say Lou was a strange bird. He would never pump up the band members. Eric Kronfeld told me, we were in L.A. and *Entertainment Tonight* was interviewing him after a show and they said, 'Who's your tremendous drummer?' and Lou told them to scratch that from the tape.

"When we played the Beacon Theater in New York on what was Lou's biggest tour of the time, the Beacon was sold out three or four days. We were given two names each per night on the guest list. So the first night I had Andy [Warhol] and Jean-Michel Basquiat, and when I put the names down, Eric Kronfeld made sure Lou didn't see Andy's name down there or I would have been on the shit list.

Despite the friction within the band and Lou's new bid for sobriety, the tour managed some Olympian moments. " 'Am I glad to see you,' said a lean and clean Lou Reed to last week's crowd at the Beacon Theater in New York before launching into 'Waiting for the Man,' " wrote one reviewer. "The feeling was mutual. But the show's real centerpiece was Reed's brilliant orange guitar. He couldn't keep his hands off the instrument, only shifting it to his back to hitchhike his way through 'Walk on the Wild Side,' soloing seraphically in 'Legendary Hearts' and 'New Sensations,' and goading Saunders and especially Quine to increasingly dazzling flights. Indeed, Quine's playing was practically an illegal stimulant, sending the band rushing back into a song after every solo."

But other critics felt Lou had lost a lot of his former edge. A reviewer for the *Washington Post* noted that "Lou Reed has no stage moves and not much of a voice," while adding that Lou managed to transfix the crowd anyway. Ferrari had also noticed Reed's awkward stage presence and joked that when he tried to clap his hands, Lou looked like the comedian Jerry Lewis.

Lou's long-term obsession with Bob Dylan reached a crucial turning point in November 1984. Lou was in L.A. doing a TV show on the New Sensations tour. The band was poised on stage waiting for the cameras to roll when Lou looked down to see Bob staring up at him. For a split second their gazes locked, and they grunted in mutual acknowledgement. Plunking himself in a seat next to Sylvia, Bob watched intently as Lou launched into "Doing The Things That We Want To." Halfway through the song Bob turned to Lou's wife and intoned, "Man, that's a great song. I wish *I* had written that song." After the show, no sooner had Lou been informed of this statement than he grabbed his roadie and charged him to leave the theater immediately and not return until he had acquired every Dylan album available. From that moment on, Lou, who had previously never had a decent word to say about Bob, became a dyed-in-the-wool Dylan fan—a fact he would broadcast almost ten years later when he gave one of the few outstanding performances at Dylan's fiftieth birthday concert at Madison Square Garden in 1992.

Ferrari, who went from resenting Lou to feeling that he wanted to give him a hug when he saw him, realized Lou was extremely ambivalent in his feelings about other people, swinging from hot to cold and from kindness to cruelty in a matter of seconds. "It's interesting that he wrote the bible on hip but personally he was not hip," the drummer remembered. "He was just intelligent enough to know what was hip. I think that's what led to his longevity in the music industry.

"Lou tried not to get close to anyone. He said to me, 'I already have enough friends, I don't need any more.' It was stressful, because the only thing he'd say to me is, he'd turn around and say, 'Play harder!' and I was playing harder than you can imagine. I was breaking everything and I broke two snare-drum stands, which is unusual because I've never broke them in my life. One time in Germany my roadie comes out and was saving the day by holding the snare drum. His ears in there without earplugs, and the band is playing loud and the snare drum is ear-piercing, so I'm worried about his ears, and Lou knows this fact and Lou turned around and said, 'Play harder!' If I wasn't such a professional, I would have put my sticks down and walked offstage because that was just inhumane. He didn't respect that roadie who was saving the show that night in Düsseldorf."

But Ferrari also remembered times when Lou could relax and enjoy his company: "There were many funny moments onstage when Lou was very honest with the audience. We were playing some college, a music school somewhere, and Lou said, 'You probably figured it out, I'm playing the same song over and over and changing the lyrics.' Another funny thing was, Lou would say to me, 'I couldn't believe it, I'm singing an older song and I'm making up the lyrics 'cause I can't remember them, and then the audience is singing the right lyrics and I'm reading their lips.'

"Then we went to Australia. We were in Perth; Perth is lovely, it was warm. And Lou just looked at me one day while we were at the beach and said, 'They really have it down, here.' There was always moments like that—when he was really with you.

"Lou and I went out and had a bite to eat a few times. It was very amicable—Sylvia was there. And as usual, Lou [just like his father] would divide the check up, he would never pick the check up. I used to say, 'Give me the check, I'll take it.' Lou wanted to hang out with us, but we didn't want to hang out with him. Peter Wood had his wife, so now it's the honeymoon tour, Peter and his wife and Lou and Sylvia. They were always doing things together to the point that we were a little ill about it. And they wanted us to go to the zoo with them, to a petting farm, as a band, to pet the koala bears or something. I just couldn't bring myself to suffer that much. We passed it up. But when they came back, they were sure to tell us about it.

"It was a passionate, intellectual group of people. The music was simple, but the personalities were complex. Nobody was mean to each other, but it was the underlying thing with Robert Quine and Lou, we knew that was there. They were headed for a big breakup, and it was that tour that did it. Quine and Reed were like the odd couple. It was a love-hate relationship. Mostly the love was coming from Lou. And Quine hated to go on tour. He's a funny guy, he's a sleeper and he acts like he's not on top of things completely. The thing that held Lou and Bob together was Quine's infatuation with Jim Burton. He was Quine's favorite guitarist and ended up becoming Lou's favorite guitarist, and whenever we would have a tour bus to take us to the hotel from the airport or something, it was all that was played on the bus. I felt like Lou was into it to brownnose Quine. Lou really wanted to get tight with Quine, but Quine wasn't letting it happen. No matter what. Still, to this day I'll run into Quine and he'll have something not nice to say about Reed. I don't even want to tell you what Quine was saying.

"Lou was starting to get off on playing the guitar solos a bit more. Quine was a master of the obscure notes, and Lou was catching the groove and at times it was very good. When it was good, I would let him know. And then Lou would tell Quine, 'I'm gonna take this solo in this song again.' And then he was torturing Quine to the point where Quine said, 'Well, what do you want from an ex-junkie homo?' [Quine denies saying this.] The way Quine delivers a line, he's so cold-faced and so intellectually witty that you start to pee your pants because he's so funny.

"A big fight in Australia [in December 1984] ended it. That's when Quine was coming off the stage getting really upset because Lou was stepping on Quine's turf. Lou was taking all the solos. And then Lou canceled Japan."

"There was a definitive break right at the end of the tour," Quine confirmed. "He has his version and I have mine, but it was a major falling-out. Allegedly over musical problems. It's nothing that didn't happen with other members of the band, but I wouldn't stand for it. I will not take shit from anyone. Whether he had his reasons for being annoyed with me—I'm hardly a saint, but I did deliver the goods. By the second concert in Australia I called my wife and said I'm certainly never playing with him again, ever. I like to think I stoically endured it, but he was not a moron, he probably saw my attitude. Some stupid little incidents happened. The last thing we did was a concert in New Zealand. We were doing 'Sunday Morning.' It was pretty much just the two of us—the bass and drums and keyboards were just so subdued. And I was looking out into the crowd thinking, 'This is a total drag. I'm never going to play this song with him ever again.' "

Everybody scattered at the end of the New Sensations tour. Quine explained, "We were in Auckland, New Zealand, after our last concert, and I think Lou and Sylvia were going to take a little vacation in Hawaii. I'll never forget it. This tour was a long tour—seven months—and everybody was in the lobby. A lot of people were drinking [not Lou]. It was a celebration; I had to be there. I just remember sitting there, and I went up to Lou and shook his hand and told him to have a nice trip. And that's the end of the story."

THE COMMERCIAL, POLITICAL LOU

1984—86

I think he would do a situation comedy at this point if they paid him enough money. Doesn't Lou Reed think he's Delmore Schwartz? Absolutely!

—Glenn Branca

AFTER THEIR HAWAIIAN VACATION, LOU AND SYLVIA RETURNED TO NEW York and entered a period of their "great adventure" defined more by commercials than music. In early 1985, Sylvia launched a new campaign for increased media exposure and revenue. Lou signed an advertising contract with Honda motor scooters. With "Walk on the Wild Side" playing in the background, the quick-cut heavy TV ad, directed by Steve Horn, showed a leather-clad Lou wearing shades perched on a scooter in a variety of Manhattan locations. The official line, "Take a walk on the wild side," came from a Mr. Neil Leventhal, Honda's motor-scooter manager, who proclaimed, "Reed is an innovator—one of the pioneers of new music. His music is unique and experimental—much like scooters."

In May 1985, Lou signed a contract with American Express to advertise credit cards. Appearing beneath the tag line "How to buy a jacket" in print ads aimed at the college audience he had been cultivating with his MTV appearances, Reed posed casually in trademark leather jacket and shades.

When they appeared in June, the Honda commercials were widely reviewed and became one of the most acclaimed ads filmed in New York. "Rock singer Lou Reed flings off his sunglasses, unbuttons his jacket, and with a cool stare declares, 'Don't settle for walking!' " read one. "Posed astride a red, two-passenger scooter in front of New York City music club the Bottom Line, Reed is the latest in a string of unusual celebrities [like Miles Davis and Devo] Honda has chosen to advertise its scooters." In addition to the TV spots, Honda ran in several prominent magazines a full-page color ad of Lou astride the bike by Manhattan's Hudson River docks. Honda reported the commercials helped sell as many as sixty thousand scooters. This kind of exposure was a surer sign of commercial success in the United States than anything Reed had done before.

In the mid-1980s, Lou also accepted assignments to write songs for other projects that had little in common with his own work. Lou claimed to enjoy the work, declaring, "I really love it if someone wants me to contribute a performance or a song and they give me a subject." Taking a line from a 1975 book that had particularly influenced him, *The Philosophy of Andy Warhol*, he added, "And it's even better if they tell me what kind of attitude they want. I can divorce myself from it completely."

During the mid-1980s, apart from commercials, Sylvia booked Lou into a string of interviews, TV spots, films, public appearances, celebrity concert tours, and assorted publicity outings, culminating in hundreds of mentions of Lou and his work in every media venue available. The campaign helped sell Reed's latest product and renewed interest in his large back catalog.

In 1980 Lou had played a small role as a record executive in a movie written by and starring Paul Simon called *One-Trick Pony*. Despite claiming that he had not enjoyed the experience at all, in the mideighties Lou did a slew of film work. In 1983, Lou contributed "Little Sister" to the film *Get Crazy* and made a playful comment about aging rock stars by appearing in his first scene covered in cobwebs in the famous Bob Dylan pose on the cover of *Bringing It All Back Home*. Despite the film's failure the song was well received, particularly by his little sister, who was proud to be the final and only member of his family to receive good press in a Lou Reed song. Late in the year, Lou contributed a song to a rock cartoon, *Rock and Rule*. The sound track also included songs from Debbie Harry, Iggy Pop, and other punk performers. In 1985 he wrote a zany, three-chord dance track reminiscent of his 1964 Pickwick compositions, "Hot Hips," for the film *Perfect*, starring John Travolta and Jamie Lee Curtis. The same year he came up with a disco number, "My Love Is Chemical," for the film *White Nights*, starring Mikhail Baryshnikov.

"When they're alone in the dance studio, you expect him to put on Mozart and instead he puts on Lou Reed," noted director Taylor Hackford, who felt Reed's song gave depth to Baryshnikov's character. In 1988 Lou contributed "Something Happened" to the film *Permanent Record.*

Lou's most famous quote about rock and politics had been made from the stage at the Bottom Line in 1977 when he'd snapped, "Give me an issue, I'll give you a tissue, wipe my ass with it." And on another occasion he had been quoted saying, "Nixon was beautiful, if he had bombed Montana and gotten away with it, I would have loved him. I have no fear . . . of anything." He had not been recruited into any political party in the 1970s, being, if anything, a political liability. He made a tentative entry into the political arena in 1984, singing backup vocals on Carly Simon's theme song for the disastrous Democratic National Convention that summer, "Turn the Tide," alongside Shirley MacLaine, Mia Farrow, Dick Cavett, Mary Travers, and Phoebe Snow. When Bob Dylan invited Reed to play his Farm Aid benefit on September 22, 1985, he jumped at the opportunity.

On the country-musician-heavy bill next to Johnny Cash and Willie Nelson, and lined up for performance between George Jones and Loretta Lynn, Lou's presence sparked humorous speculation as to whether he and John Denver might team up for a duet on "Rocky Mountain High." However, Lou told David Fricke of *Rolling Stone* that he had overcome his city-dweller attitude and could appreciate the problems the farmers were having. "I'd show up out there in Blairstown and go, 'What the fuck is going on? It's raining here. What is this, another weekend with rain?' Finally they sat me down to tell me the facts of life, such as there are farmers out there and they're getting killed by the drought. I became aware of what weather means, besides New Yorkers going away for the weekend." Lou delivered a blistering set, but there were more than a few cynics who questioned his use of a charity event to gain publicity. "How do people in New York perceive Farm Aid?" asked one cynical journalist who appeared surprised to see Lou in Champaign, Illinois. "I don't know how the people in New York perceive anything," Lou riposted. "We're like snowflakes, we're all different." On the two occasions that Lou played a show at Bob's request—Farm Aid and Dylan's fiftieth birthday—he made sure he gave an outstanding performance. The reviews of his Farm Aid show were unanimous in describing Reed's set as a blistering rock 'n' roll show. And Lou's shit-eating grin at both events indicated his own satisfaction. Backstage, however, he had a different experience. Lou's bodyguard, Big John Miller, was accompanying Lou and Sylvia across a field backstage at Farm Aid when they spotted Bob some two-hundred feet away. On seeing them Dylan lit up like a Christmas tree and started running toward them, his arms spread wide open. Lou stopped in his tracks, returning the gesture with a big smile of his own. But the euphoria of recognition was to be short-lived when Dylan hurtled past Reed to throw himself into the arms of Big John, leaving Lou staring at his feet as he turned eighty-five different shades of red. Farm Aid eventually generated $50 million to help save 2.3 million American farmers from over $212 billion of debts.

Once Lou got going in a new direction, he was, like his mentor Warhol, relentless. No sooner had he done Farm Aid than he volunteered to take part in the Artists United Against Apartheid Sun City project. The Panamanian superstar Ruben Blades, whose lyrics were on a par with Reed's, had suggested that Lou take part in the effort. "I couldn't not be vocal about apartheid," Lou explained. He sang one line on the record "Ain't Gonna Play Sun City," a multiracial effort headed by "Little" Steven Van Zandt, who had left Springsteen's E Street Band the previous year. The Sun City gang comprised artists from a variety of musical disciplines and included Dylan, Springsteen, Jackson Browne, Bono of U2, Jimmy Cliff, Kurtis Blow, Run-D.M.C., and Afrika Bambaataa. The organization got more than they bargained for when Lou came to the studio and started advising them on how to produce the record. The *Los Angeles Times* called the song "a refreshing attack on the practice of isolating musicians by category." Lou appeared in the video of the song and was also in several scenes of the documentary, *The Making of Sun City*. Besides the record and the video, the Sun City project released a book and eventually undertook a concert campaign to force the release of the South African nationalist leader Nelson Mandela.

Lou benefited from the exposure all these do-good benefits gave him. But he found the experiences less than satisfying personally, largely because he could not handle it when so many lesser mortals than he appeared more prominently in the spotlight. One character who Lou particularly despised was "Little" Steven Van Zant, who organized the Sun City benefit.

To help put Lou's segue from commercial songwriting into political songwriting into perspective, in the early summer of 1985 he joined another star-studded project, including Sting, Tom Waits, and Marianne Faithfull, recording Kurt Weill's "September Song" for a tribute to the German composer most famously associated with Bertolt Brecht. It was a project he felt particularly close to. "I want to be a rock-and-roll Kurt Weill," said Lou. "My interest—all the way back with the Velvets—has been one really simple guiding-light idea: take rock and roll, the pop format, and make it for adults. With subject matter written for adults so adults, like myself, could listen to it." The 1985 release of his recording of the Kurt Weill song on the album *Lost in the Stars* coincided with another strong resurgence of interest in the VU, largely perhaps because culturally the first half of the eighties was a rerun of the first half of the sixties.

On November 13, 1985, Bob Dylan attended an exclusive party honoring his achievements at New York's Whitney Museum. His guest list featured dozens of rock-and-rollers, including Lou Reed, Pete Townshend, Billy Joel, Little Steven, Dave Stewart, Ian Hunter, David Bowie, Roy Orbison, Yoko Ono, Judy Collins, and members of the E Street Band, as well as the writer Kurt Vonnegut Jr., artists Andy Warhol and Keith Haring, the filmmakers Brian De Palma, and Martin Scorsese, and actors Mary Beth Hurt, Robert De Niro, and Griffin Dunne. "There's no way you can be a pop artist today or do anything in contemporary music without being influenced by Bob Dylan," said Billy Joel. Dylan was photographed with an uncomfortable-looking Reed on the steps of the museum.

In public Lou was now vocal in his praise of Dylan, and Dylan, whose whole career carried more weight than Lou's, was vocal back, not only singling out Lou as one of the very few current artists he could listen to, but publicly thanking him on the back of one of his albums. However, in private Lou could still not control his *shpilkes*. Why was Bob always getting these awards and special editions when he, Lou recalled, received virtually nothing in the way of honors. You could see his point. The Velvet Underground are generally now considered to be the second most influential rock band of the 1960s. Lou had always been an artist on the same level as John Lennon, Keith Richards, and Bob Dylan, but, until the 1990s, without anything like the recognition afforded his peers.

At the beginning of 1986, as if refreshed by the excursions into other worlds, Lou recorded his next solo album, *Mistrial*. The album, released in April 1986, was designed to follow up on the pop vein originally tapped into by *New Sensations*. RCA released a promo tape called *He's Got a Rock and Roll Heart* based on an MTV interview and a number of remixes and special editions of his songs. In addition to Reed's customary print interviews, on May 19 he was on the *Late Night with David Letterman* talk show, along with the basketball player Michael Jordan and the actor Alan Alda, promoting *Mistrial* and its single, "Video Violence."

Mistrial, artistically the lowest rung of Lou's mideighties trilogy commencing with *Legendary Hearts*, received bored reviews and ran into several problems. The video for its second single, "No Money Down," was cut from the MTV playlist for being too violent. In it, a Lou Reed look-alike robot has its face torn apart, which Lou thought was hysterically funny. "My wife didn't," he reported. "My mother felt the same way. She looked at it and said, 'What can I say, Lou? I'm sure it's very clever, but I don't like seeing that happen.' "

After four albums with RCA he once again became dissatisfied with their handling of his work and determined to find another label. It was also the last record he would make with Fernando Saunders—although they would play the Grammies together in 1988. *Mistrial* marked the end of another period in Reed's career.

What it came down to: "I think the album is a very up album. I think somebody in my situation should be positive. At this stage of the game it would be, possibly, disappointing to other people as well as to myself had it not been a positive album. I mean, after all, I'm getting paid to do something I would want to do anyway. I don't have to work for a living. I don't have to go through a whole bunch of things I couldn't bear. I just think I'm very lucky and that attitude is reflected on the record I think. I want everyone watching to forget everything else and just listen to the music, and to have lots of positive energy and emotional moments. I think this is all *any* singer can hope for."

IN THE SUMMER OF 1986, LOU MADE HIS STRONGEST ALTRUISTIC COMMITment when he joined a tour celebrating the twenty-fifth anniversary of Amnesty International, the human rights organization that seeks the release of prisoners of conscience throughout the world.

Perhaps because he often saw himself as a persecuted artist, he could sympathize with others who suffered for their convictions. "I had never been a member of a group besides a rock band," he said. "But I've joined Amnesty International. In a country where Reagan is president, it is very easy to be cynical. But I'm really fascinated about why people are arrested and what happens to them in jail. I mean, for the rock-and-roll records I've made, I'd be dead ten times over if I was over there." By the time the Conspiracy of Hope tour kicked off June 4 at the Cow Palace in San Francisco in front of thirteen thousand fans, the permanent lineup included Lou Reed, U2, Sting, Bryan Adams, Peter Gabriel, Joan Baez, and the Neville Brothers. Guests who popped up along the way included Bob Dylan, Tom Petty, Jackson Browne, Bob Geldorf, Dave Stewart, and the comedian Robin Williams. During the tour, Lou would be called a great guitar player by some of the greatest guitar players ever. At the Amnesty concerts, he was introduced as "the legendary Lou Reed." Lou's continuing work with the program grew not only in time but also in intensity. Along the way, barnstorming across the country in the tour's Boeing 707, he composed a song for the Amnesty cause called "Voices of Freedom."

Bonded by the cause, mutual respect, as well as "fun" (a word he used to counteract criticism of his intentions), the musicians developed a strong sense of camaraderie. On the road Lou cemented his friendship with Bono, whom he had met on the Sun City project, urging him to read "a really great short story," Delmore Schwartz's "In Dreams Begin Responsibilities." According to U2's biographer, Eamon Dunphy, "There was a part of Bono that could have lived where Reed had lived, in the drug-induced twilight of New York City. Reed understood what U2's music was trying to say, the difference between freedom and responsibility."

When the Amnesty tour arrived in Atlanta, Georgia, they celebrated at the Ramada Renaissance Bar. When the house band finished their set, a number of the Amnesty musicians jumped onstage. "Bono, high on the absurdity of the night, got up to sing. He started Lou Reed's 'Sweet Jane' and sang it to a raunchy young lady posing at the bar," wrote Dunphy. "They jammed the night away, Baez, Gabriel, Adams, the Neville Brothers, Larry, Adam, and Bono. When they heard about it the next day, Lou Reed and Edge were sorry to have missed it. 'If you ever do that again, be sure to wake me,' Reed chastised Bono. 'Okay, we'll do it again tonight,' Bono replied. Only this time it was contrived. The magic was missing on

Tuesday night. But not the pleasure. Reed was one of Bono's heroes. Bono had been no great record collector when he was young, but one of the few good records he had was of the Velvet Underground. . . . Bono called on Lou to play the next night at the Ramada. Reed, after much persuasion, shyly consented, offering rare renditions of 'Sweet Jane' and 'Vicious.' "

Ironically, despite Lou's heartfelt involvement, several members of the press were even more cynical about his involvement with this venture than they had been about Farm Aid or Sun City, openly questioning his motives for enlisting. "Lou Reed is a washed-up ex-rocker who couldn't fill my garage with paying fans," commented one particularly riled journalist. "Somehow he managed to cash in on a Honda scooter commercial, and now he's turned up on television and the Amnesty tour with his latest product, *Mistrial*, in tow." And another scowled, "The Amnesty lineup consisted of such superstars as Sting, U2, Peter Gabriel, the Neville Brothers, and other has-beens such as Lou Reed, Jackson Browne, and Joan Baez also attempting to rekindle their flagging careers." Even positive reviews were tinged with similar sentiments, as in the *New York Times*: "These concerts also helped seasoned, consistently creative artists like Mr. Gabriel and Mr. Reed reach the wider audience their work has long merited."

On June 15, after two weeks of sold-out touring across the country, the concert's core performers mustered their combined efforts and enthusiasm for a grand finale. From noon until midnight MTV presented, live from Giants Stadium in East Rutherford, New Jersey, the last show in the Conspiracy of Hope tour. Lou, who had done his set earlier, returned to the stage during U2's set to join Bono and the rest of the band in the antiapartheid song "Sun City."

At the end of the month, Reed was back on the road, touring behind the *Mistrial* effort. "The most surprising thing about Lou Reed's Tuesday-night August 19 concert at the Universal Amphitheater was that the hall was only half-filled," commented one reviewer. "Those who attended, however, saw what amounts to Lou Reed's Rock and Roll Survivor Traveling Roadshow—nearly two hours' worth of two-chord rockers, third-person story-songs, and seven tunes off his latest album, *Mistrial*."

In the autumn of 1986, Lou was recruited into RAD, a series of MTV Rock Against Drugs public-service announcements, joining the ranks of

ex-drug-addict rock stars behind slogans such as "Drugs suck." Although
eager to participate, Reed was concerned about being hypocritical: "I had
a lot of problems with that spot. When all these rock people make these
announcements—'I did it, you shouldn't'—my attitude when I was out on
the street was, now he's had his fucking fun, and he's going to turn around
and say, 'Don't have any fun because I tell you it's not worth it.' Who the
fuck are you to tell me anything? I was prefacing it, saying, 'I don't want
to tell you what to do, but speaking for myself, da, da, da . . .' And the
director said, 'Lou, no offense, but this is aimed at eight-year-olds. You do
that and they'll go to sleep.' So I thought about it, and that's when I came
up with what I said: 'I did drugs. . . . Don't you.' "

As 1986 DREW TO A CLOSE, THE SPORADIC MISTRIAL PUBLICITY WAS ON
hiatus, as were the Amnesty tours. To keep his schedule full, Lou concentrated on more collaborations. Tipping his hat to an early influence,
he joined his friend the bass player Rob Wasserman on a version of Frank
Sinatra's "One for My Baby," which wound up on Wasserman's *Duets*
album. Lou also worked through early 1987 with Ruben Blades on the
latter's first English-language record, *Nothing but the Truth.* "Lou and I
finished a draft for a song about a son coming back to a painful reunion
with his parents," Blades recounted. While Blades sat in the library of
Reed's New Jersey home, in the music room above, Lou played the
melody to the song on his guitar. The tune prompted Blades to write some
lyrics, and from this partnership came "The Calm Before the Storm."
"We were both emotionally exhausted," Blades recalled. "I almost had an
anxiety attack that night."

On December 22, in Japan at the close of a two-day U.N. International Year of Peace Conference, Lou joined rockers from the Soviet
Union, the United States, Europe, Africa, and Japan at the Japanese
Jingu Baseball Stadium before some thirty-two thousand listeners in a
benefit concert the performers called Hurricane Irene after the name of a
Greek peace goddess. Hurricane Irene's aim was to raise public awareness
as well as money to establish a computer-based information network at
the University for Peace in Costa Rica.

At the beginning of 1987 Reed flew to London to play the yearly
Amnesty International benefit, the Secret Policeman's Third Ball, with

Peter Gabriel, Duran Duran, Mark Knopfler, Jackson Browne, and many others at the London Palladium.

By May, Lou was back on the road in the U.S., promoting *Mistrial* again. That summer his tour met up with U2 in Europe. This was the first time Lou had ever worked as a support act at a commercial concert.

In October, as a mark of his new, positive image, *Rolling Stone* magazine's twentieth anniversary issue came out carrying long interviews with Mick Jagger, Paul McCartney, and, among twenty other major rock stars of the sixties through the eighties, Lou Reed. The same month a local Syracuse paper published an interview with a Scottish punk rocker who had visited the city and demanded to know where there was "a monument to Lou Reed at Syracuse University." One of Lou's favorite teachers, the poet Phillip Booth, recalled earlier that year discovering a tribute in the English-department men's room where some wiseass had scrawled LOU REED SHAT HERE above the toilet.

In December, Reed played a benefit concert for homeless children in New York. The event, held at Madison Square Garden, was organized by Paul Simon. The first of a number of celebrity surprise appearances came when Debbie Harry and Grace Jones introduced Lou Reed and sang backup on "Tell It to Your Heart," "New Sensations," and "Walk on the Wild Side." Reed, in turn, introduced Dion, who sang "The Wanderer" and "Runaround Sue." Then, Dion was joined onstage by Reed, Paul Simon, Ruben Blades, James Taylor, Billy Joel, and Bruce Springsteen, calling themselves—after Dion's legendary group—the Belmonts. As they sang Dion's "Lonely Teenager," the crowd leapt to its feet. "These guys all loved being Belmonts," marveled Dion, adding, "Lou Reed, it was like, he knew the part."

IN LOU'S TRAGIC, MAJESTIC WORLD THERE WAS A FEELING THAT AN END OF something was being reached. Another beginning was necessary. Lou and Sylvia had recently clashed over his refusal to have children. When things were going well with Lou, Sylvia did not communicate with her old friends Susan Springfield, Roberta Bayley, and Risé (John Cale's wife!), but when things started going badly with Lou, she got back in touch.

His least interesting albums are arguably *New Sensations* and *Mistrial*.

He was beginning to lose fans who had been with him since the Velvet days. And one man who was in Lou's AA group became fairly disenchanted with his work and him in the middle of the 1980s. When a member of their group who had been a close friend of Lou's for twenty years went nuts and Lou was called upon to help him out, he expressed total indifference to his "friend's" plight, exclaiming, "Who gives a fuck about him!" He really did not give a shit, and maybe that, acquaintances increasingly thought, was what really made him tick. "He doesn't care for anyone except himself," opined one.

"Maybe he has concerns for the masses. I mean maybe that's what like Stalin was like, maybe he had no friends but really loved people! I always liked Sylvia. I used to hear a lot of dirt. I think they had some bad moments."

In rock, the decades ruthlessly winnowed out the losers. As the eighties entered their second half and the clarion call of the century's final decade could be heard in the distance, more voices from the sixties and seventies fell silent. Dylan was still being heard. Neil Young was still out there.

"How long do you try to do it [make that grand comeback]?" challenged avant-garde guitarist-composer Glenn Branca. "At some point you have to actually start doing it. He hasn't been trying to start doing anything as far as I can see."

Chapter Nineteen

IMITATION OF ANDY

THE BATTLE OF THE LOU REEDS:

1987—89

Even today he looks unhappy, like a walking disaster.
What's wrong with him? He married a man, he married a
woman . . .

—Paul Morrissey

THEN ON FEBRUARY 22, 1987, SHOCKING THE WORLD AND IN PARTICULAR those like Lou whose lives had been so irrevocably tied up with his, Andy Warhol died in New York Hospital following a routine gallbladder operation. Warhol's sudden exit forced Reed to confront not only his sense of grief, but the sense of himself he had gained through his association with the pop artist and his entourage at the Factory. "Andy had a great effect on my formative years. His way of looking at things I miss. I owe him that. His whole aesthetic. I still wonder, if I look at something new and interesting, oh, I wonder how Andy'd think about that." Andy had thought of Lou as a friend and was hurt. He suspected it had something to do with Lou's marriage, suggesting that maybe Lou "didn't want to see peculiar people." Still hurting from Reed's refusal to hand over the money due him from their early collaboration, and envious of Reed's newfound commercial success, Warhol had stepped up his critical remarks and cold-shouldering of his former protégé. According to a Factory acolyte, "Lou totally idolized Andy and Andy rejected Lou very deliberately so that Lou was aware of it. And so Lou always had to be the kind of prodigal son, who was trying to prove himself to Andy. If Andy liked you, he rejected

---

you in that way. And then he would go and put everybody down to everybody else, so he would say, 'What's wrong with Lou, he's so talented, it's such a waste.' I don't think Lou ever outgrew Andy." People in Warhol's entourage recalled Andy treating Lou "very, very badly" on several occasions when Reed had visited the Factory in the 1970s, which, considering how mean Andy could be when he put his mind to it, is a chilling image.

According to Lou, the final break came in 1981 when he and Sylvia were riding in a car with Warhol. "It was snowing out and the driver was speeding. I asked him to slow down. Andy turned to me and in a fey, arch, whiny voice said, 'You wouldn't have said that a few years ago.' He was being so evil I never spoke to him again. He stirred me up and he did it on purpose. He got me very mad that he did it. You see, Andy had to be the leader.

"The Factory was a really strange place. People came and went, got used up, then moved on. One particular person became dominant there for a while and I just didn't like what was happening there and stopped going. Andy would moan at me, but I really couldn't face it. Things build up between people, but basically—and this is going to sound strange—he just wanted me to call him. On the phone. I'd see him around, but I wouldn't call him.

"We had a very major falling out. I was in touch, but not close. I didn't want the things I said regurgitated into the diaries I knew he was going to put together. I wanted to have a normal personal conversation with Andy and that wasn't possible. He used to tape-record everything, every conversation he ever had, and I didn't want our talk to end up in some publication, which is what would have happened. He would only talk to me on his terms. Everything always had to be on Andy's terms."

Indeed, Warhol had been recording entries in his diaries for years. In several of them Lou figured prominently. But, the latest in September 1986 read starkly: "I hate Lou Reed more and more, I really do, because he's not giving us any video work."

By the time Lou went to Warhol's memorial service at St. Patrick's Cathedral in New York on April 1, 1987, he realized just how much he missed Andy's vision and humor. Later, at the postservice luncheon, as his recorded voice sang VU songs over the chattering mob, Lou suddenly found himself standing on one side of Billy Name with John Cale standing on the other. Not knowing that they had hardly spoken in years, Billy drew them both into the orbit of his conversation. Lou and John talked, and John immediately felt that the tension between them had eased.

At the same lunch the painter Julian Schnabel told Cale that he should write a memorial for Warhol. Cale spent several months working on an instrumental piece, but found writing about Warhol difficult. He was such a mercurial, dominant figure it was hard to capture him in conventional ways, and those who appreciated him feared their work would not measure up.

RETREATING TO BLAIRSTOWN, REED THREW HIMSELF INTO A PRO-tracted writing binge. Memories of Warhol and the Factory came flooding back to him. Like a man freed from a long, vague sleep, he eagerly awoke at 5 A.M. to hunch over his word processor day after day. "I suffer from insomnia, I only sleep about three hours a night," he explained. "So that's when I write. I get up, no one else is around, it's relatively quiet. That's when you can tag in. I'm not getting it from out there, I'm getting it from in here. Everything else doesn't exist." A shape began to coalesce in Lou's mind. The album would be a musical sketch of his New York.

Writing about the landscape of the city he loved, Lou looked back to the fabulous, gay Halloween parade, and friends who had died of AIDS, finding beauty, humor, and compassion amid despair and decay.

A year later, in May 1988, when John had finished a first run-through of his memorial for Warhol, he asked Lou to listen to the piece and tell John what he thought. They got together and talked about Andy, filling in gaps in each other's knowledge. Cale, for example, "was stunned that Lou fired Andy, I thought Andy left."

"We were both keen because, after talking at length about Andy, there seemed to be a great need for us to put the record straight," Reed recalled. "The things I was disturbed about with Drella were these evil books presenting Andy Warhol as just a piece of fluff. I wanted to show the Andy I knew. John Cale and I got together in a little rehearsal place to see how it felt to play and to have some fun. John had already written an instrumental piece for Andy, a mass of sorts, but then the opportunity arose to do the bigger thing."

Reed and Cale quickly discovered that the musical chemistry was still there. In ten days they composed fourteen chronologically arranged biographical songs. Lou handled the majority of the lyrics while John focused on the music.

"John and I just rented out a rehearsal studio for three weeks and locked ourselves in," Reed said. "I wouldn't call it working through emotions. My disposition improves immeasurably when I know I can make that guitar do what I want and not just what I hear in my head, and when I'm writing with the discipline and focus to have it come out the best it could, not almost as good as it could. There's a craft to all this—it's not just spewing out emotions. It's very ordered and very specific work."

"I was really excited by the amount of power just two people could get without needing drums," said Cale, "because what we have there is such a strong core idea that the simpler the better. I wanted to see if the power was still there between us, and I found out that it was, very quickly. Working with Lou again is enthralling. We're still tiptoeing around, but in all the sessions that we've worked together, the results have been very exciting."

"It was done by osmosis," Cale explained. "When we first sat down and started playing, there was this amazing energy—it was aggressive. We sat down and talked about all these memories we had, and then Reed shut himself in with a tape recorder running and showed up later with a kind of summation of what had happened. We sat there and bandied them around. It's difficult for him to collaborate on that level—it's difficult for him to collaborate period. And he admits it."

"I very much like playing with John," said Reed. "He's a very exciting musician. It's fun playing with him. We play very well together."

They called the collection *Songs for Drella.*

The collaboration was fraught with problems from the onset. Cale and Reed worked in noncomplementary manners. When Lou went into the studio, he worked from a series of lists composed by Sylvia and had everything scheduled to the second. Cale was accustomed to coming into the studio, reading through six newspapers, making a number of international phone calls, then launching himself at the work with ferocity.

"In order for things like that to happen again between Lou and me, we had to go through that same sort of process; we had to play these things over and over just like we had in the past," said Cale. "And we did that.

But this time we kind of knew what the landscape would look like, and we were prepared for those things that we needed to be aware of—the distractions and stuff."

"Things would be a thousand times better without that tension," Lou said. *Drella* was "an excruciating son of a bitch to write. I did it on my word processor—what a tool!—and had to do rewrite after rewrite. And all the time I was finding out more about what I really felt about Andy and trying to put that into the right words."

Just as Lou and John were in the middle of the album, they received the news that Nico had died as unexpectedly as Andy on July 18, 1988, in a bicycle accident on the Spanish island of Ibiza. She was forty-nine.

JUST AS HE FINISHED WRITING THE LYRICS TO SONGS FOR DRELLA, LOU WENT into the studio to record his next solo album, *New York*.

Lou recorded *New York* in the second half of 1988, working with a new guitar partner, Mike Rathke, who was married to Sylvia's sister. Rob Wasserman was on bass; Fred Maher and Moe Tucker alternated in the drummer's seat. Lou worked hard at getting the words, the music, and the sound right, taking longer with this record than anything else he had ever recorded.

To emphasize another new beginning, Lou chose this moment to leave RCA and sign with Sire Records, an arm of Warner Brothers that had played a major role in the punk-rock explosion ten years earlier, putting out records by, among others, the Ramones and the Talking Heads. Sire was run by Seymour Stein, generally considered to have the most sensitive and intelligent ears in the industry, and certainly someone who knew and understood Lou Reed. A younger version of Clive Davis, Stein was more on Lou's wavelength than any other record-company president he had ever worked with. Their relationship would usher in the most creative and commercially successful period of Lou's career.

New York was released in January 1989 and pitched Lou back into the center of the rock world, very near the top, bringing him legions of new fans and returning to him some who hadn't bought a Lou Reed record for more than a decade. The *New York Times* suggested that it was finally time to "think about taking him seriously."

New York was his best-selling album since *Sally Can't Dance*, reaching

No. 1 on *Rolling Stone* magazine's college chart, and getting into *Bill-board*'s top fifty. The reviews were, for the most part, excellent. One of America's leading rock critics, Jonathan Cott, wrote, "This record provides the perfect musical medium for Reed's highly charged depiction of and verbal onslaught against an AIDS-stricken New York in which friends are continually 'disappearing'—a city of abused children and battered wives; of child police-killers, teenage bigots, and racist preachers; and of thousands of homeless people panhandling, rummaging for food in trash baskets, and sleeping in streets, alleys, and doorways. It is a world of hypocrisy, greed, ugliness, selfishness, and degradation—in comparison, Bob Dylan's 'Desolation Row' is like a weekend outing to the Hamptons."

When Cott commented to Lou that the *New York* album was nihilistic and contained not one love song, Reed pointed out the redemption written into "Dime Store Mystery," which he saw as a love song, "dedicated to Andy Warhol, whom I really miss and had the privilege to have known."

"I spent almost three months writing those words, and I tried to find a way to surround them properly to get the rhythm of the words working in the right way against the beat, and get the nuances in the vocals so that the listeners could hear the words—that was the raison d'être of this record. This is my vision of what a rock-and-roll album can be. Put it this way. I'm writing for an educated or self-educated person who has reached a certain level. I'm not aiming *New York* at fourteen-year-olds.

"Supposedly when you get older, you get something from all of it before, or you drop dead and that's the end of it," Reed mused. "I think I know about certain things better than other people. And I'll fight for it. And I don't think that's being difficult. I mean, it sounds tacky, but it's like being true to your vision.

"In *New York*, the Lou Reed image doesn't exist as far as I'm concerned. This is me speaking as directly as I can to whoever wants to listen to it."

In the *New Musical Express*, Sean O'Hagen wrote the best review in the British press, describing the album as "one of the hardest, strongest, most cohesive, and perfectly realized rock statements of 1989. 'New York is like this huge person that's shaped me as much as genetics,' Lou Reed tells me in that same deadpan drawl that is his consistent signature. 'This album is a result of a convergence, if you like, of everything that went before.' That means all the learning, all the mistakes, all the twisted fuck-ups from a legendary life. Like his friend Keith Richards, Lou Reed is an individual for whom the term *survivor* is an understatement. Personal survival is measured against impending social and global collapse with AIDS, pollution, and the death of the American dream at the top of the agenda. In this doom-laden context, you keep asking yourself why *New York* is such a, at times, hilarious record. 'Good, good, I'm glad you got to that. People who say, "Oh, Lou is just bitching on and depressin' everybody," they're missin' the point. I mean, it ain't about moral admonishment. Shit, I walk away fast from all that stuff. It's funny and urgent.' "

"People don't talk enough about Lou's wit," said Penn Jillette of the magician duo Penn and Teller. "Like the tension in a horror movie, there's tremendous proper use of wit."

The album was popular for a while. Four months after its release, *Rolling Stone* put Lou Reed on the cover of their May 4 issue. The *New York Times* published the lyrics to "Hold On" from *New York* on the op-ed page on May 10.

While most of the reviews for *New York* were positive, a few cutting ones slipped into the press. "Unfortunately, the product (as record companies call their output) at hand displays just how unsubtle and fuzzy the new Lou Reed's social awareness is," commented the *Nation*'s music critic. "There's 'Common Ground,' a muddled anti-anti-Semite attack on Kurt Waldheim, the Pope, and Jesse Jackson. Vet homilies of 'Xmas in February'; and the jejune pseudomyth called 'Last Great American Whale.' " *Rolling Stone* and *Daily News* video critic Jim Farber said, "The 9 million printed raves try to excuse his indefensibly clunky lyrics with some of the most ornate rationalizations in rock-critic history. Apparently, critics feel the need to take this record as seriously as it takes itself."

"Bon Jovi did New Jersey and Lou Reed does New York," sniped the innovative guitarist Glenn Branca. "Gimme a break! Lou Reed has been dead for at least ten years. This is a simulacrum; this is not a real person!"

Lou was greatly buoyed by the success of the album, but he played it cool, speaking down to the audience in interviews as if he had been planning this all along. Unfortunately, this spectacular success was hobbled when, near the beginning of the international tour in support of the record, Lou slipped and fell coming offstage after a sound check, broke his ankle. He was in a cast for six weeks, and the tour was cancelled.

Despite being stopped in his tracks by the accident, Lou had much to occupy himself with through the remainder of 1989. A major retrospective boxed set of his solo career was in the works, and he turned his attention to it. At the same time, Walt Disney's publishing arm, Hyperion, approached him about releasing a book of his lyrics and poems, and Lou felt that in conjunction with the boxed set this was finally the right time to put out a book he had been thinking about for thirty years.

THE SAME MONTH *NEW YORK* WAS RELEASED, JANUARY 1989, REED AND Cale staged two workshop performances of their Warhol suite at St. Ann's Church in Brooklyn under the auspices of the church and the Brooklyn Academy of Music. "*Songs for Drella* is a brief musical look at the life of Andy Warhol," ran the program notes for the initial performances, "and is entirely fictitious." In the small church they created the most enlightened of memorial services for Andy Warhol. They played the fourteen songs in chronological order, gradually building up a prayer-service atmosphere that was perfect for the moment and the setting. Backstage after the show, Billy Name held court once again, finally introducing Lou to his other guru, La Monte Young, whom Reed, incredibly, had never met.

In the spring, just as John and Lou were putting the finishing touches on *Songs for Drella*, Warhol's *Diaries* were published. Despite the caution he had taken in not talking to Andy, Lou was mentioned some fifteen times in caustically negative entries from the 1980s. Asked if it bothered him to read "I hate Lou more and more," Reed replied, "Not at all. I know Andy; he's like a child. He would have said that in the way a child says, 'I really hate you!' It's not meant like real hate."

Although both Lou and John thought the diaries were an unfitting epitaph to Warhol, they realized how much they captured the artist's quirky personality and decided to use them in an added song. What they came up with was an imagined diary entry, "A Dream," in which Cale employs the same storytelling voice he used in "The Gift." "It was John's idea," said Reed. "He had said, 'Why don't we do a short story like "The Gift"?' But then he went away to Europe, saying, 'Hey, Lou, go write a short story.' But I thought, no, not a short story, let's make it a dream. That way we can have Andy do anything we want. Let me tell you, man, it was really hard to do. But once I got into Andy's tone of voice, I was able to write for a long time that way. I got to the point where I was able to, you know, just zip-zip-zip away—just because I really liked that tone so much. It's certainly not my tone of voice at all. I really don't talk that way. I had to make myself get into that way of talking."

"A Dream" was essentially a cut-up of quotes from the Warhol diaries.

"When John was doing the reading, I kept telling him that when we get to that line, 'I hate Lou,' you gotta say it like a kid," said Reed. "It's not like, 'I fucking hate Lou Reed, I really hate that son of a bitch.' It's more like, 'Oh, I hate Lou; oh, oh, I really do.' It's all in the nuance, and that's why the production both during the performances and on the record was so critical—especially on that cut."

In November 1989, Lou and John performed the completed *Songs for Drella* to a larger audience at BAM.

The BAM shows got excellent reviews and set people thinking about a VU reunion again. However, Moe thought Lou still wasn't interested because "he's worked so hard to get his own career going, and especially with the success of his latest album, I really don't think he'd want to plunge in and have everybody talking about the Velvets again." Cale saw it differently. "For the time being I'm really happy with the results; now that we've accomplished that and shown that we can do it, we can move ahead to something more challenging. Collaboratively, I think Lou and I could come up with something very imaginative that would be more in the form of a dramatic situation. We're really efficient, and I think we could do anything. I don't think there's a limit."

Songs for Drella were released in April 1990. Reed and Cale shared songwriting credits and split the money fifty-fifty.

Cale realized the deep significance of the work for Lou. "I think *Drella* was a way of healing that for Lou, and he had to do it right or be seen to be guilty of opportunism. But recording *Drella* with Lou was very difficult. There was a lot of banging heads. It was exhilarating, and working with Lou is never dull, but I wouldn't want to go through it again. I'm much more interested in the spontaneity of playing live.

"Lou felt that I didn't appreciate how much effort he had put into the words. He never actually said this to me . . . personally. The comment

was made to a lot of other people. That was a shocker; it's very difficult
to fight with, or argue. If someone thinks that you don't really appreciate
what they're doing, well, then what can you say? It's just a very sad and
disappointing turn of events. I mean—and whether you actually base it
on anything substantial or not—it's just the clincher."

In the liner notes to the album, however, Cale wrote, "*Songs for Drella*
is a collaboration, the second Lou and I have completed since 1965, and
I must say that although I think he did most of the work, he has allowed
me to keep a position of dignity in the process."

Although after completing *Songs for Drella* Lou swore that he would
never, ever work with John again, the album would eventually lead to the
reformation of the Velvet Underground.

Chapter Twenty

DEATH MAKES THREE

1990—92

> I think the most important thing in life is art. It's art that I
> turn to for sustenance. It's art that elevates things to the
> finest level where you can go for examples of greatness,
> and that's what I want to try and impart on this record
> Magic and Loss. Not the Lou Reed character who at this
> point is rather amorphous, unless you want to think of it
> as a literate sensibility tempered by compassion.
>
> —Lou Reed

ANY CONCERN REED HAD ABOUT LOSING HIMSELF IN THE ASSOCIATION
with Warhol or Cale were assuaged by a great climax of Lou's career that
followed fast on the heels of the release of *Songs for Drella*.

In the spring of 1990, Lou was invited to sing in front of 72,000 people
at Wembley Stadium in London in a benefit for the South African political hero Nelson Mandela, recently released from prison after twenty-
seven years. Returning to the folk roots of his college days, Lou, playing
an acoustic guitar, performed two songs from the *New York* album. Unlike
other acts performing that day, Lou made no attempts to meet Mandela
or make any statements of his views about the momentous occasion.
Instead, he watched Mandela's speech from backstage on a TV monitor.

From London he traveled on to Prague to interview Czechoslovakia's
new president, the writer and former dissident Václav Havel, for *Rolling
Stone*. Havel was a big fan of the Velvet Underground and had agreed to
do the interview as a tribute to Lou.

On the way to the interview, an uptight Lou worried about his tape recorder malfunctioning, his mind going blank, failing at the task of interviewing he had so often belittled as work fit for a moron. "We passed a bust of Kafka on a street but were told not to bother to see his apartment," he recalled. "We ate some dumplings in the oldest restaurant in Prague and then gathered ourselves to go to the castle to meet Václav Havel."

The opening exchange should go down in the history of the interview as a classic example of the bald-faced arrogance of a journalist. Lou embarked on the taped discussion with a description of how he was sure the waiters who had served him breakfast at the hotel were members of the secret police:

Havel: The State Security was liquidated in our country, but these people work in spite of this fact. I think they are interested more in me than in you, these people.

Reed: I don't think so, I don't think so.

When Havel interrupted Lou's lengthy account of how he, a rock star, had reduced himself to a mere interviewer, saying, "I think I have some message work for this magazine, and I would like to tell it to you in this interview, but we must begin immediately because unfortunately I have a lot of work," Lou barreled on regardless, pressing upon the chief executive a copy of *Songs for Drella*. When he finally let Havel get a word in, the famous writer and revolutionary launched a spiel about the influence of the VU on the "velvet revolution" of 1968 and the relevance of rock music in general. Lou, however, seemed famously unable to listen, throwing in abstract comments like "Joan Baez says hello" and "I admire you so much." The remainder of the interview, which could have been written by Samuel Beckett, was dominated by Lou's explanation of why he could not and would not play for Havel: "You see, I'm a very private person; when I came here, I didn't want any photographers at the airport because I don't like my picture taken. I don't like being interviewed—and, er, I like controlled situations—as opposed to just a lot of people. It would be a privilege to play for these people under the right circumstances, but I'm not aware of the circumstances, and it's difficult for me to walk into—"

Little wonder that *Rolling Stone* turned down the manuscript. Lou wasn't Andy Warhol. He thought anybody could do an interview. He was wrong.

It turned out that, as one man who interviewed him pointed out, the man who was legendary for his antipathy toward being interviewed was even more uptight about being on the other side of the tape recorder: "The only reason I did it was that I really wanted to meet him, and here was a chance to meet him and ask him things that I was really interested in. But it's just really hard work."

Reed later said he was "dumbstruck" when Havel presented him with one of the two hundred hand-printed editions of his lyrics ("from the Velvet Underground straight through") that had circulated among Czech dissidents in pre-glasnost Prague.

"He was amazing—the whole thing was amazing!—and I found out how much the Velvet Underground meant to those people in Eastern Europe all those years ago. They were out listening to us, only we just didn't know it." Not since Delmore Schwartz and Andy Warhol had Lou been recognized by such a heavyweight character.

At the end of the interview, Lou grudgingly agreed to play in a small club in Prague for Havel, his friends, and associates that night. "I did a few songs from my *New York* album. I started to leave and Kocar [his guide] asked me if the local band [Pulnoc] could join me. They did and we blazed through some old VU numbers. Any song I called, they knew. It was as if Moe, John, and Sterl were right there behind me, and it was a glorious feeling."

REED'S NEXT SOLO ALBUM, *MAGIC AND LOSS*, FOCUSED ON A SUBJECT that had always been at the core of his writing, the value of lost friendship. The album commemorated the deaths of two close friends in the early 1990s. One was the songwriter Jerome "Doc" Pomus, whom Reed had befriended in 1988. Pomus had penned a stack of hits in the 1950s and 1960s for, among others, Dion and the Belmonts, Elvis Presley, and the Drifters. The other friend, Rita, was unknown. "Within a short period, two of the most important people in my life died from cancer," said Lou, "so the piece is about friendship and how does it transform things. These were people who were inspiring me right through to the last minute. These were people I was lucky to have known all the way through.

"Though I only got to know him in the last couple of years, I really loved Doc. He was an amazing creature. A mutual friend said we should meet, and I only lived two blocks away from him so I started traipsing round. I went to his writers' workshop and it was a real thrill for these people to have their songs edited by him. I went over to talk, but not as much as I wished. It's really sad not being able to call Doc Pomus up right to this day, because he was like the sun. He was just one of those people that you feel good when you're around them. You could be feeling bad, and you go visit them and they say two words and you feel good. But it would have been even worse not to have known him at all. That's part of the whole *Magic and Loss* deal.

"It's inspiring to see how a real man and a real woman face death. I could visit Doc while he was going through these extreme medical processes, and I still felt great when I was around him. Both of them made jokes straight through. Unbelievable. I had said there's this great wide-screen color TV I could get for you, and I'll hook up all the wiring for you, you don't have to worry about any of that. And he said, 'Lou, this is not the time for long-term investments.' "

Though the album focused on the deaths of Pomus and Rita, it also gave Lou the opportunity to touch on other losses he had recently experienced. In February 1990, his closest friend from Syracuse, Lincoln Swados, was found dead in his East Fourth Street storefront slum apartment. This caused a small sensation and local press coverage because of the suggestion that his death was hastened by a greedy landlord who was forcing Lincoln to abandon the premises so he could renovate. Lou, who had turned his back on Lincoln in the midsixties, incurring the wrath of Swados's sister, Elizabeth, made no comment at the time, but would later react in the way he knew best.

Reed wrote two songs, "Home of the Brave" from *Legendary Hearts* and "My Friend George" on *New Sensations*, about Swados. And now "Harry's Circumcision" on *Magic and Loss* was also about Lincoln. Zooming back to 1962 when Lincoln was more famous than he was, Lou reflected that "Lincoln Swados will become a celebrity for this. Lincoln had jumped in front of a train, and lived to tell the tale. Albeit, missing an arm and a leg on the same side. That's the closest thing I could think of that resonated with 'Harry.'

"This album is not particularly about Lincoln. It was just that thing—I did know someone who did that, literally. He was a very talented guy. He was just insane. I always thought he made the people at the Factory pale by comparison. Nothing I saw there was anything compared to what I saw him do."

Reed and Rathke spent "incalculable hours" in research and refinement. "I practically studied with some technical people who really helped me out. Because there's millions of choices out there, and even if you had a zillion dollars and bought all these machines to try them, it'd take forever. So you really need someone knowledgeable and talented to guide you. Even down to the kind of tape you record on. I find the sound on this album awe-inspiring."

Lou's development as a writer mirrored his increasing technical proficiency. "I know more about writing now than when I was a lunatic," he explained. "I'm very respectful of it now and I try to do everything in my power not to impede the process. I've been around a long time, and I know things that do impede it: drugs impede it; getting in a fight with a friend impedes it; tension impedes it. I'm not a person that works well from tension. In fact, for me, calm is absolutely the essential thing or what I write will be way off-base or be for a purpose that's incorrect."

Lou finished writing and recording *Magic and Loss* between January and April 1991, then for marketing reasons waited until January 1992 for its release.

While finishing *Magic and Loss*, Reed also completed his selected lyrics and poems, *Between Thought and Expression*, published in the summer of 1991 by Disney's Hyperion Press. "I took those songs that satisfied two criteria," said Lou. "One, that, as most of the lyrics are supposed to do, they did not need the music. They could survive on the printed page. Two, they helped rhythmically advance a narrative, following someone through New York over three decades—the sixties, the seventies, and the eighties.

"The book is arranged and annotated to give you a sense of movement from the sixties to the nineties. I just love all of it. From day one, it was adult-oriented material, avoiding slang that would date. In the sixties I didn't want to use slang terms like *dig it* and then be faced with it twenty years later. The most you get is a couple of *hey, mans*. In 'Heroin' I made up my own slang—'Jim-Jims'—so that the song wouldn't be tied to a particular time period.

"It isn't a rock star's compilation. There's no picture of my house or of the band. I didn't bring in some Belgian to paint the cover. It was serious. A lot of the lyrics only existed on record. I don't have drawers full of 'em and I've thrown away the notebooks. I couldn't read the handwriting anyway. The songs are like my diary. If I want to know where I was, the book gives me a good idea.

"Well, I'm thrilled that the collection is out. I always wanted to do it, but just never had the opportunity. Put it this way: when people approached me regarding books, it was always a rock-star book they were talking about. That is to say, 'Here's where he was born, this is his first guitar, and, look, here's a drawing too.' Illustrated stories. But this book is very straightforward. Lyrics that can stand alone."

There were also two poems first published in 1976 ("The Slide," "Since Half the World Is H$_2$O"), and interviews with Václav Havel and a writer Lou greatly admired, Hubert Selby Jr.

"The collection vividly traces how he swam up and out of his original bookish gloom so cherished by a vanished dropout demimonde," wrote Milo Miles in the *Voice*.

To publicize the book's release, Lou gave two readings in New York, one at Central Park's Summer Stage in July, the second at the NY Center for Ethnic Studies in November. They were both as successful as his 1971 reading at St. Mark's Church had been and harkened back to it also in marking another beginning of sorts. At the Summer Stage Lou held a crowd of several thousand spellbound on a hot night as his acrid voice recited some of his most famous lyrics devoid of music. He ended both performances with an impassioned reading of material from the as yet unreleased *Magic and Loss*, none of which appeared in the book.

"These shocking lyrics tangled the feelings of loss and guilt, gallows humor, and dark despair," reported Bobby Surf in the *NME*. "The standing ovation that greeted this unnerving finale was more genuine and heartfelt than anyone connected to this bald promotional stunt could have dared wish for. Here was an audience who recognized an artist at the height of his powers nearly twenty-five years after they were first saluted."

On the release of the single most significant piece of work he had so far handed down to the public, Lou made a revealing gesture that no reviewer or interviewer picked up on. He dedicated the book to his parents, sister, and wife: "For Sid, Toby, Bunny and most of all for Sylvia."

Reed's audience had grown steadily over the years. Many of the early bohemian fans of the Velvets and the gay fans of *Transformer* had stayed with him. They were joined later by supporters of punk rock in the 1970s and of political and vintage rock in the 1980s and 1990s—particularly on college campuses.

In November 1991, Lou made a triumphant visit to London where he was presented with the *Q* Magazine Award of Merit for his outstanding contribution to rock music. Reed was introduced to the audience as a man who "still says, on occasion, that there's nothing to beat two guitars, bass, and drums—but his work has broadened our vision of rock's possibilities, forming it into something more real, more literate, and more grown-up than we'd probably have settled for otherwise. Scores of musicians will readily admit their debt to this man's influence, and any that won't are probably lying."

In December, RCA Records released Reed's solo boxed set, also titled *Between Thought and Expression*. Reed, who had worked hard on compiling the collection in collaboration with Rob Bowman, had discovered among other surprises that the master tapes for some of his albums, such as *The Bells*, had either been lost or stored so carelessly that they had oxidized or disintegrated. Reed had agreed to take part only if he had control of the sound. For example he had bought an unopened copy of *The Bells*, which was no longer available, for $50 and put it through a process called Sonic Solution, which created, by the time they had finished, a clearer sound than the original. Lou had every reason to be proud of the results. The only criticism was that, as with the book, he had virtually denied the whole period of his relationship with Rachel. Otherwise, the excellent reviews were well-deserved.

"Bruce Springsteen may be more user-friendly, and Neil Young may own the territory west of the Mississippi, but Lou Reed's loud works of art speak with the same extralarge authority, and burn with the same enduring dedication to authentic feeling and hard answers," wrote a reviewer in the *New Yorker*. "His new greatest-hits boxed set, *Between Thought and Expression*, is an utterly convincing document made up of equal parts of nastiness, tenderness, and sorrow, and it is astonishingly mature from start to finish. When he's playing those songs live, this man is the King of New York."

With the widespread international recognition accorded Reed's book and boxed set, the release of *Magic and Loss* in January 1992 could not

----

have come at a better time. "If a song cycle about a friend's death from cancer seems to be the stuff hits are made of, well . . . it's not," commented one reviewer. "But what *Magic and Loss* lacks in pop appeal is more than made up by emotional impact. With arrangements so skeletal they're barely noticeable, the album stakes everything on its songs. Reed makes them work with sly melodic twists and a well-framed narrative, assuring that we not only understand his emotional turmoil, but share in it. Which, in the end, makes this a perfect modern blues: heartbreaking, thought-provoking, involving as life." *Newsweek* called it "the most grown-up rock record ever made."

The album received some of the best reviews he had ever had around the world, but there were, as always, some dissenting voices. Adam Sweeting commented: "Reed has suggested a link between *Magic and Loss* and 1973's *Berlin*, but the telling difference is that the latter mediated its harrowing subject matter through powerful, vivid music. Though *Magic and Loss* touches upon a range of styles, Reed is so immersed in the minutiae of suffering that his musical ideas remain undeveloped, while the subject matter has squeezed out the sardonic wit and throwaway cynicism of his best writing. What's left is a slim volume of morbid verse, set to half-finished music."

Lou now saw himself, and rightfully so, as a warrior king more than a rock-and-roll animal. "This isn't a bleak record," he claimed. "I'm not the only person in the world who's experienced loss—especially these days with what AIDS and other diseases are doing. These are complex emotions. There's a song, 'The Warrior King,' which is about the anger that the narrator of the record feels about what the disease is doing to his friends. Of course, he's impotent; there's nothing he can really do about it. You have the best doctors in the fucking world sitting there—they're going to try new techniques, they're going to put isotopes the size of a nickel inside you. The cure is to try and kill the cancer, but, unfortunately, in the process, they're killing healthy cells—you. It's whichever gives out first.

"We're talking about people with indomitable spirit. Nonetheless, nonetheless, they do not survive the process. This puts the narrator in a rage and he pictures the disease as a person and himself as the warrior king. The warrior king seems like the only character powerful enough to beat something as all-powerful as this enemy.

"You can't walk around with anger in your heart. It causes very negative things," Lou said of "Harry's Circumcision," "a suicide fantasy worthy of William Burroughs," wrote Stephen Holden in the *New York Times*, "in which a man who is unhappy about the fact that he is growing to resemble his parents cuts off his own nose, then slits his own throat but is saved from dying."

"The beauty, however dark, of *Magic and Loss* is in the asking," wrote David Fricke in *Rolling Stone*, "in the subtle elegiac lift in Reed's stony sing-speak, the sepulchral resonance of his and Mike Rathke's guitars, and the Spartan grace of the storytelling. On *Magic and Loss*, Ol' Poker Face looks straight into the face of the Big Inevitable—and flinches."

"By the eerie closing title track, Reed has reached some kind of reconciliation," wrote Simon Reynolds in the *London Observer*. "There's even a suggestion, in the line 'there's a door up ahead, not a wall,' that he's come to believe in the hereafter."

"You can call it a spiritual awakening," Reed admitted. "The song resolves the whole album. You don't want to come to the end of that experience still feeling splintered. You have to reconcile yourself to it. It's inspiring to see real people facing death.

"There's a process going on in the record—it has a beginning, middle, and end. There's a song—that's repeated, but the song is transformed when it's repeated. At the beginning of the record, the song is defining the situation and the illness from the outside—you loved the life that others throw away nightly. Towards the end of the record, the song reappears, but this time it's upbeat, not melancholy, and it's approached proudly. The album is about how that transformation takes place."

"You notice it's not *Magic and Death*, it's *Magic and Loss*," Lou told critic Jim Derogatis. "I can't emphasize enough, it's about loss. Warhol said that it's too bad in school they don't have a course about love, like practical stuff. Or maybe one on loss, like what do you do with yourself, who do you ask, where do you turn.

"For instance, with the Warhol thing, *Songs for Drella*, I thought, 'Jesus Christ, we could call this a new category: biorock.' And here's a chance for black rappers to do their constituents a great service. They could make just like what I did trying to introduce you to Malcolm X or Langston Hughes or James Baldwin. Has it happened? No. Should it happen? I think yeah. Don't you? Think of what an educational tool that

----

would be for inner-city kids. They have computers and they have CDs. Then you could put graphics on the CDs and illustrate it with music and everything. I can't imagine this isn't going to happen. It's so obvious. What a quick way to get kids to learn.

"Of course you need someone to write it. Suppose Hammer did a thing about James Baldwin. Isn't that possible? Certainly schools might order them by the batch. What an educational tool. And if it got on the radio, why not? I think Hammer should think about it. Michael Jackson should think about it. All they have to do is look at *Songs for Drella,* my Warhol album, this is how it's done. It's easy. It's the writing that's hard. You're talking about sustained thought, which in America right now is not easy."

In 1992, Reed was informed that the French government had decided to make him a knight of the order of arts and letters. On February 18, he flew to Paris for the investiture ceremony, conducted by the French minister of culture, Jack Lang. "Some have seen you as a star of malaise, perhaps even of evil," Lang told the rocker. "I prefer to see in you a great poet of our anguish and, perhaps, of our hopes."

"I'm deeply touched and moved," Reed responded. "In a world of many negative capabilities, it is wonderful to live long enough to experience something so directly opposite and pristine, something so unilateral, which looked at from my age remains thrilling and challenging. I'll tell you what it really is. I think the most important thing in life is art. It's art that I turn to for sustenance. It's the art that elevates things to the finest level where you can go for examples of greatness, and that's what I want to try and impart."

Before him lay a world tour on which he would share the emotional transformation of *Magic and Loss.* "Death is one of the great themes," he began to tell interviewers. "There's a lot of what you might call violent or vicious songs in my work, but I feel compassion for the characters in them. Because I know what it's like to be outside. I know what it's like to have an unhappy childhood. And I delineate these people because either I identify with them or I think they deserve their moment in the sun."

Still, for all its promise of transformation and redemption, *Magic and Loss* was a doeful album that dredged up feelings a lot of people would rather forget. It was the kind of album that people owned but rarely played. And the album's promotional concert tour in the spring and summer of 1992, though impressive in its dignity and careful detail, left Lou's fans and critics feeling distinctly uncomfortable. According to Lou's dictates, audiences were instructed to listen in stony silence. No one was to smoke, eat, drink, take photographs, talk, or react in any way that would break Lou's concentration. If the ticket holders obeyed, Lou rewarded them with an uptight, controlled act, more like a recital than a rock-and-roll performance. It lacked both passion and spontaneity, except in his penultimate performance of "The Dream" from *Songs for Drella.*

Even Reed's hard-core European fans had a hard time adjusting to this new rock-and-roll regimen. "At the Hammersmith Odeon in London, Lou wanted respect," wrote Adam Sweeting. "It was announced that petulant Dame Louis would leave the stage if people shouted requests at him. Amusingly, Reed would sing, 'Does anyone need another self-righteous rock and roll song?' during 'Strawman,' in the show's second half, but sadly it wasn't self-mockery. By the end of the concert the crowd's enthusiasm had thawed Reed, who returned for some nostalgic encores—'Sweet Jane,' 'Rock 'n' Roll,' 'Satellite of Love,' even 'Walk on the Wild Side.' It would be a pity if the man who wrote those ended up drowned in his own pomposity."

"The whole evening felt more like watching a play or being at a poetry reading," commented another reviewer. "By the time his Louness strides on the stage the audience is practically cowed into submission."

"I'm trying to move the audience in a certain direction; I do want to take them with me," Reed explained. "But I also must do for myself. It's not a matter of choice, it's just the way it has to be. And I'm willing to lose part of the audience if that's what it takes. Although I certainly hope they come along on this little trek. Because this is where my ambitions lie."

American reviewers were blunt. "I love Lou Reed. I hate Lou Reed. I want to invite him to dinner to meet my family and then kick him out the door," wrote Dan Aquilante in the *New York Post* that May. "At Radio City Music Hall Tuesday night, the man barely kept me awake. Then he made me sit up and listen. It was one of the best and worst concerts I've seen."

To the members of the new generation of Lou Reed fans who complained that an album about death and loss was bound to be depressing, Reed argued, "Look, this piece isn't called *Loss,* it's called *Magic and Loss.* I think the record is a perfect example of transforming a difficult situation into something more positive. People who like to listen to music where the lyric and music engage them intellectually, emotionally, and spiritually will get something from the music." However, during his live shows he did seem more interested in challenging than entertaining his audience.

"The problem is, you feel more like a voyeur than a spectator, and we're never really involved with what's going on," wrote Neil Gowans. *"Magic and Loss* may well work beautifully in the comfort of your own home, but in a live setting it just doesn't cut it. Uncle Lou just seems altogether too impressed with himself, and apart from the odd flash of humor, such as 'Harry's Circumcision,' the whole thing is just too deadly serious for my taste."

Andrew Mueller, reviewing the concert video, had a similar reaction. *"Magic and Loss* is indeed a fine album, a brutally detailed examination of death and grief, but there are limits, and they fall well before this grim muso workout."

During the tour Lou picked up his relationship with U2 and their singer Bono. In July he joined them onstage at Giants Stadium in New York, performing an oddly touching version of "Satellite of Love" in which he came across as dignified but fragile. In Reed's face you could see the horrifying price he had had to pay for his success, existing, as the German film director Rainer Fassbinder had pointed out about Warhol, "as a shell. Destroyed by his own work."

Two images of Lou in October and November 1992 perfectly summed up his conundrum vis-à-vis the public. In October, Lou played at Bob Dylan's thirtieth anniversary concert at Madison Square Garden. Publicly, he was now a great Dylan fan. Privately, he muttered that he didn't understand why Bob always got these kinds of honors and he didn't.

Lou chose to perform "Foot of Pride" from *The Bootleg Series* box set. "I chose 'Foot of Pride' because I just got back from an eight-month tour," he said. "Once a day I would listen to it and just fall down laughing. I always go out and get the latest Dylan album. Bob Dylan can turn a phrase man. Like the album *Down In the Groove,* his choice of songs. 'Going Ninety Miles an Hour Down a Dead End Street'—I'd give anything if I could have written that. Or that other one—'Rank Strangers to Me'. The key word there is 'Rank'. "

The concert consisted of some thirty superstars singing Dylan songs. The challenge was to make the song yours. Lou was arguably the only one who succeeded.

"Looooo," the audience bayed at Reed, who looked onstage more than ever as if he should be staring down at them from the side of Mount Rushmore. He broke into an astonishing version of "Foot of Pride." Reed ended with a burst of feedback and then stood onstage for a moment grinning as if he knew he had just played an original version of the song. No one dared rush him off. "It proved at a stroke that the old sod's still got rock-and-roll balls," confirmed one observer.

"That was as much fun as I could ever have," Lou, who spent the day blissfully bonding with his fellow performers, enthused backstage. "As much fun as anyone could legally have."

Backstage, the atmosphere was friendly and surprisingly low-key and amusing, even with a procession of notables that included Martin Scorsese, John McEnroe, Tatum O'Neal, Penny Marshall, Billy Idol, Cyndi Lauper, Shirley MacLaine, Lenny Kravitz, Sean Lennon Ono, Jakob Dylan, Carly Simon, Sinead O'Connor, and Neil Young. The entrepreneur Donald Trump forced his way into a conversation between Tom Petty and Lou Reed; he left them bemused by his hearty endorsement of their "jamming."

However, the event was somewhat marred for Lou by two incidents. The audience booed Sinead O'Connor when instead of performing her allotted Dylan song, she recited a passionate statement about war by Bob Marley. Lou thought the crowd's behavior was absolutely reprehensible. "You'd think that if any audience would be responsive to protest music, it would be Bob Dylan's. She's a real artist, and now they say Madonna's attacking her, which is totally ridiculous." An interviewer from the Howard Stern radio program, Stuttering John, who made a point of asking celebrities embarrassing questions, approached Lou backstage.

Stuttering John: Can I ask you a question for ninety-two point three KRock?

Reed: Yeah.

Stuttering John: Do you still masturbate?

Lou turned away, then turned back and grabbed Stuttering John by the throat. Shocked, John did not resist. Lou held John's throat tight for several seconds, then let go. Meanwhile, an MTV girl dashed up, crying at the hapless radio geek, "You insulted him!"

"He looks at me," John recounted the story the following day on Stern's show, "looks the other way. Looks at me and grabs my neck. He woulda punched me. He was choking me!"

Stern snapped, "He's such a jerk. This is the guy who's gone downhill since 'Heroin.' He was horrible, right? He's been horrible for years."

For the most part, however, Lou was granted the attention due his work and accepted the responsibility that came with it. In November he accepted an invitation to be a keynote speaker at the CMJ Music Convention in Manhattan opposite Jesse Jackson, whom Lou had attacked on the *New York* album. Black and Jewish tempers in New York City had recently become frayed by the accidental killing of a black child by a Hasidic Jew and violent reprisals in which a Jewish man had been killed by a black mob. A hushed audience hung on Lou's every word. He rapidly veered from defending Sinead O'Connor's recent attack on the pope to a protest of the not-guilty verdict in the Crown Heights murder of Yankel Rosenbaum, reserving his venom for black leaders who refused to condemn the anti-Semitism. "I wish my tax dollars didn't go to support anti-Semitic rantings," he thundered. "Where is the Rainbow Coalition?"

A *Village Voice* writer gave him Rockbeat's "Light's On but Nobody's Home" award, explaining, "Reed departed from the topic of censorship to denounce Leonard Jeffries and fault black leaders for not standing up to 'hatred.' Hewing to passion not reason, he invoked his elderly cousin Shirley ('Much to my disbelief, she contributes monthly to the NAACP') and cited the *New York Post*'s Mike McAlary's comparison of the Crown Heights verdict to the Rodney King trial. Reed then issued a challenge to Jesse Jackson: 'Before Shirley writes another check, and I'm sure she will, I'd like to know how very much elation black leadership feels for this occasion . . . of murder by mob, murder by trial, murder by jury. . . . Or is it really time to light the torch that sets the flames that brings Brooklyn sizzling to the ground? Because as we've all heard, the Jew is smart—he won't burn down his own house.' "

On March 2, 1992, Lou Reed had celebrated his fiftieth birthday. As each decade passed, he honed and focused his vision. In the sixties a defiant Lou was ready to try for the kingdom. In the seventies he went to hell and came back. In the eighties he studied his reactions to society's madness. Throughout all three decades he worked on his writing skills. In the nineties he established a comfortable but engaged identity. He had achieved his original ambition to be the Kurt Weill of rock and roll and produced a canon of work that few rock musicians could rival. If rock had a Mount Rushmore, surely Lou Reed's face would glare down from its craggy heights next to the heads of Bob Dylan, Neil Young, and Paul Simon.

In 1992 Reed's record-label bio read: "Just as there is only one Marlon Brando, one William Burroughs, one Miles Davis, and one Tennessee Williams, there is only one Lou Reed."

Much as Lou had transformed himself professionally, he remained stuck in the same groove personally. Just like everyone else who had taken on the onerous task of being his manager, Sylvia, despite all her hard work and great success, fell afoul of Lou's temper, increasingly drawing his resentment and wrath. Sylvia, in turn, harbored her own resentment, which, as she exercised the power of her position, she was increasingly willing to show. In the midst of all the rock and roll, Lou and Sylvia started reeling from the blows their psyches had been delivering to each other. The competition between them reached an impasse over the question of having children. As Sylvia approached thirty, she told Lou the time had come for them to have children, characterizing it as a great adventure. Lou, however, saw the question of children through realistic eyes. Though admitting that it might be fun to have a small version of himself to kick around, he rejected the proposition. Sylvia was not pleased, and consequently Lou, perhaps fearing an accidental pregnancy, stopped sleeping with her.

Stated one friend, "There's no way Lou would ever have children, he's the archetypal classic constant child. At least he can admit that it would be a big disaster if he had children. So at least it's better that he's aware of it.

"During 1992, Sylvia was very, very insecure, and Lou is *the* person who hones in on every insecurity, attempting to undermine you in every possible way. It's so sick. She's insecure and overcompensating for it in a lot of ways, so it's strenuous to be around her sometimes because she'll be flaunting her money around. They're really getting in the bucks now.

"Sylvia had gained a whole bunch of weight during the marriage. Then she lost a lot of it on the summer of 1992 European tour as a result of nervous exhaustion. She was really overworked and overstressed because of everything that was going on with Lou. In one way she was just coming to the realization that it was all going to be over, because the likelihood of their having an amicable break was slim. It's like John and Yoko. Yoko wanted to get divorced from John at the end, but then realized that John couldn't let her manage his business if she wasn't married to him."

During their final years on the Upper West Side they had separate bedrooms. Sylvia professed to be stunned by the development, telling friends that Lou used to like her and she couldn't understand why he did not seem attracted to her anymore. They started to live separate lives, going out with friends rather than each other. Despite the deep fracture, Sylvia continued to play, if anything, a stronger role in Lou's business affairs.

Worse than the lack of sexual intimacy was Lou's growing tendency to use Sylvia as a psychic punching bag. A comparison of photographs of her in 1978, the year they met, and 1992, the year Lou reached his great climax, are starkly revealing. The sultry, sexy girl he had picked up at his S&M society had turned into a rumpled, overweight hausfrau who looked as if she had spent years being beaten mentally, spiritually, to a pulp.

Now that Lou had Sylvia more trapped than he had ever had a woman before, he could torture her all the more for it. After ten years of being Mrs. Reed, with all the glamour, power, and wealth that went with the title, she had nowhere to turn. Not allowed to make any friends during their marriage, she had also alienated most of the people she dealt with in business matters by becoming rude and aggressive. It was a tendency that would grow worse over the coming years.

According to one close friend of the blighted couple, Sylvia "obviously still does feel this great loyalty to Lou, she obviously still does find him attractive. She definitely thinks he's Mr. Big Musical Genius. Almost all great artists are complete jerks as people when it comes to how they treat other people. Their primary concern is their work. They're married to their work; anybody else emotionally involved with them has to play the role of, at best, a cherished assistant."

Lou, meanwhile, continued to manifest the arrested emotional development that is often the bane of rock stars. Though he could be a most charming person at social functions so long as he was the center of attention, he became a petulant eight-year-old when the spotlight faded, often insisting on leaving precipitately when the conversation turned away from him.

With his cleaned-up image so celebrated—and remunerated—Lou underwent a period of denial about his past. Many friends reported that, as far as Lou was concerned, he had never been a drug addict or a homosexual. He was straight, he said, and always had been. He didn't take drugs or drink and never had. And anybody who brought up the subject in his presence was thrown out of the room. Since she couldn't bring herself to leave Lou, Sylvia had no choice but to go along with his make-believe. In Lou's world one lived by Lou's rules or perished. Sylvia never seemed to accept, for example, that Lou had ever been gay, referring to Rachel, if at all, as simply another girlfriend. During this period of denial their friends found it increasingly difficult to be around either of them. As the decade drew to an end, Lou cut off his long-term friendships with the poet Jim Carroll and the painter Ronnie Cutrone, ostensibly because the two men had left their wives. Lou chose instead to surround himself with yes-men like Sylvia's brother-in-law, Mike Rathke, who massaged his ego with their attentiveness and praise.

Ironically, the impending collapse of Lou's marriage did not do him any harm on the professional front. In fact, the worse things got for the Reeds, the more Lou appeared to bask in the across-the-board success he had always craved.

By the time Lou completed work on *Magic and Loss,* he and Sylvia had begun to talk about getting a divorce and consulted their respective lawyers.

Sylvia went through a particularly difficult period as she faced the facts. She knew she was going to be comfortable financially—Lou's financial situation had changed dramatically since they had joined forces and even he openly credited Sylvia for this—but the realization that she was going to lose the glamour and drama of being Mrs. Lou Reed weighed heavily upon her. Meanwhile, her lawyer advised her not to move out of their Upper West Side apartment because that would put her in the weakened position of desertion. She told friends that she was waiting for Lou to move out, but the consensus of opinion was that Lou was not going to move out, that he had her exactly where he wanted her and could torture her to his heart's content.

Lou, meanwhile, was totally denying his past. "Couldn't he just be out there like a John Lennon type saying, 'Yeah, I did all that wacky stuff, but now I don't do that stuff?' " remonstrated one witness to the tangled web of Lou and Sylvia's affairs. "No. He's just been acting like it never happened, and if anybody should bring that up, they're bodily thrown out of there. 'That didn't happen. I'm straight, I've always been straight.' " Friends found it increasingly difficult to contend with Sylvia's blanket acceptance of Lou's denial, which she appeared to have bought lock, stock, and barrel. "They could never say to her, 'But what about Rachel?' She spoke about Rachel as if she was an ex-girlfriend." "I've never heard her accept the fact that Lou was gay," recalled another observer. "The only thing she comes out with is, 'We don't have sex anymore,' which, after being married for twelve years, is to me no shocking revelation."

At the beginning of 1993, Lou moved back downtown—to the same block of Christopher Street he had lived on between 1978 and 1983. Shortly thereafter, Sylvia rented an apartment on nearby Tenth Street.

Sylvia had been turned into a mother figure whom Lou could order around. Indeed, it now fell to her to take primary care of her dog, Champion Mr. Sox. But anytime Lou felt the need for the mutt's company, usually somewhere around three or four in the morning, all he had to do was pick up the phone and Sylvia would come scurrying over with the hapless hound in tow.

"He's got an image to keep up," said a friend. "Beyond the fact that he's thinking, 'God, I'm alone, I've got to find somebody else.' I'm sure in the middle of the night, that's the reason he calls Sylvia, because that's when it hits him—'Oh my God, I'm by myself.' That picture of him on the cover of *Vox* [in May 1993] was so awful. He looks like a ghoul. You heard this thing about his liver. I'm surprised he's still alive."

Whether out of fear of loneliness or of losing a lot of money, Lou suddenly pulled an about-face with Sylvia, deciding he didn't want to proceed with the divorce. There was no plan to resume living or even spending time together. Rumors that Lou was having a relationship with a man persisted alongside other gossip that he was going out with the androgynous artist Laurie Anderson. Caught once again in a delicate transition between image and album, Lou, aged fifty, could not proceed unprotected. As a tough and dedicated manager, an intelligent sounding board, a submissive wife, and somebody to bounce anything off, Sylvia had remained remarkably resilient. Even the self-destructive side of Reed must have realized he would, at this stage of the game, be insane to cut himself loose from her.

In a major summation of Neil Young's career, *Neil Young and the Haphazard Highway That Leads to Unconditional Love,* Nick Kent wrote that at the dawning of the last decade of the twentieth century "it became increasingly clear that Dylan, Reed, and Young were now well and truly the three leading lights out of their aged but unbroken generation of mythic rockers."

Still, though isolated and in control, Lou had himself to contend with—and in his own judgment he shit on himself because his self wasn't good enough. That constant torture outweighed any criticism that could have been inflicted on his work. In *Magic and Loss,* he had summed up his existential situation. He was stuck with himself and a rage that could hurt him. It was the same feeling he had had at Syracuse when he was reading Kierkegaard. What stretched before him but fear and nothing?

Chapter Twenty-One

IN WHICH LOU REED CANNOT PUT ON THE VELVET UNDERWEAR

1990–93

> *Just say that John Cale was the easygoing one and Lou*
> *Reed was the prick.*
>
> —Lou Reed

THROUGHOUT LOU'S SOLO CAREER, HE HAD BEEN HAUNTED BY THE VEL-vet Underground and had repeatedly toyed with the idea of reforming the band. But his attitude toward John Cale made that impossible. During the first half of the eighties, as Lou's star rose and John's fell, their relation-ship languished. As Mary Harron pointed out, "John Cale, who was as brilliant as Lou Reed, has been more consistent [than Lou], but through-out his solo career he has not simply avoided success, but tried to throttle it with both hands." After Lou married Sylvia in 1980, the door that slammed shut on Lou's past closed Cale out.

However, in 1978 a typical young VU enthusiast, Phillip Milstein, started publishing *What Goes On, the Velvet Underground Appreciation Society Magazine*, in Cambridge, Massachusetts. By the second half of the 1970s so many VU-influenced bands were on the scene that Sterling Morrison commented, "I didn't really think about my years with the Velvets much until recently, when the climate seemed the same again. With new wave, the music went back to the people who were kind of screwing around on records, who knew they couldn't possibly achieve mass appeal, and didn't care. I was looking at all these little punk bands and thinking, 'Well, there goes us again.' " Even Moe Tucker felt the effect of this proliferation: "Stuck out here [Tucson, Arizona] in the middle of nowhere, the only friends we have are my husband's from work. But quite a few of them have heard of the Velvets, and they're impressed." By 1983, Britain's leading music publisher, Omnibus Press, had published the illustrated history of the group, *Uptight: The Velvet Underground Story,* by Victor Bockris and Gerard Malanga, which went on to gain an impressive readership, being published in, apart from the U.K., Japan, Germany, Spain, Czechoslovakia, and the U.S. Meanwhile, on college campuses a new generation of rock-and-roll fans discovered the Velvets albums. In *The 1983 Rolling Stone Record Guide,* another longtime fan, Billy Altman, wrote, "The Velvets' influence hovers over all current music seeking to do more than entertain. Reed's songwriting rang with an honesty and compassion that few songwriters ever reach." By 1985, there were so many bands proud to be indebted to the VU, and so many Lou Reed clones, a radio station in Los Angeles ran a popular program called the *Battle of the Lou Reeds,* and a radio station in Austin, Texas, had a "Sweet Jane" contest. Many new, postpunk, and experimental bands, previously relegated to college and alternative charts, began to break into the mainstream.

By 1985, British bands ranging from the Smiths, Echo and the Bunnymen, Lloyd Cole and the Commotions, and Simple Minds to a host of other chart-toppers paid tribute to Reed and the Velvets. Morrissey, then lead singer of the Smiths, for example, was called a "reasonable postliberation version of the early Lou Reed." The Scotsman Lloyd Cole owed a large debt to Lou Reed, as his singing voice evoked Reed and his material was redolent of what the *Los Angeles Times* called the "sparse, beat-ear expressionism of the Velvet Underground." Jim Kerr, Simple Minds' lead singer, claimed Reed as one of his greatest influences.

Similarly, quite a few American bands had, by the mideighties, brought the Velvets' work a degree of fame. Ric Ocasek of the Cars was often compared to Reed in voice and delivery, and the singer also claimed many of the same beat-generation roots as Reed. Georgia's R.E.M. with Michael Stipe also drew Velvet comparisons and often performed such Velvets material as "Femme Fatale" and "Pale Blue Eyes." The Violent Femmes'

Lou Reed–derived vocal style put them on top of the college charts in 1986. More cutting-edge eighties rockers were bands like Scotland's Jesus and Mary Chain, who developed the Velvets' love of feedback and drone. Contemporary groups like Nirvana, Jane's Addiction, the Cowboy Junkies, and Sonic Youth would bring the Velvet influence into the 1990s.

This new attention to Reed's work helped sell his back catalog, and placed him in the company of the greatest rock legends. In an article about artists as visionaries, Robert Palmer wrote in the *New York Times*, "The best artists—such as John Lennon of the Beatles, Lou Reed of the Velvet Underground, and Bob Dylan—broke down the barriers, creatively reimagined present-day conditions, and future possibilities, and redefined themselves with almost every record release."

Meanwhile, material the Velvet Underground had recorded while under contract to M.G.M. was discovered in Polydor's vaults and was remixed and released with the title *VU* by the company's new owner, Polygram Records, in February 1985. "The Velvet Underground were so far ahead of their time," wrote Lynden Barber in *Melody Maker*, "that hearing them now it seems scarcely believable that they're not a contemporary group." "These guys were a great rock-and-roll band," commented *Stereo Review* in 1985, "and it's good to hear from them again, even fifteen years after the fact." Cale, Morrison, Nico, and Tucker also agreed to be filmed for the English-television *South Bank Show*, which was doing a special on the band's history (aired in 1986), but Reed refused to be interviewed. A brief interview with Lou in front of a graffiti-covered building on the street in New York, wearing leather and sunglasses, was purchased from another source. In September 1986, a second compilation of Velvets tracks, *Another View*, was released. "Yet another surprisingly upbeat, energetic brace of previously unreleased material from this seminal New York band, circa 1969," wrote a critic in *Playboy*. "And believe it or not, Lou Reed actually sounds as if he's enjoying himself here."

VU and *Another View* created a flurry of rumors of a reunion. Lou flatly refused to take part, snapping, "It'll never happen." However, Lou's business entanglements with his former partners multiplied as sales of the VU catalog increased internationally. While the publishing royalties poured into Lou's coffers, the other band members threatened a lawsuit.

Cale's New York–based British lawyer, Christopher Whent, who brought to his profession a sharp legal mind wedded to a love of music, made it his goal to straighten out the VU's tangled legal affairs. He took on representing Maureen and Sterling as well as John. Lou admitted that the distribution of VU royalties had been unfairly biased in his favor, and was willing to share some of what was legally his with the others. This gesture opened channels of communication with Morrison that had been closed for years. "The band went into the black with the record company in about '83," said Whent. By 1986, he delivered renegotiated contracts to his clients, and they started to receive royalty payments, which considerably improved the lots of Morrison and Tucker. "It's not a bad chunk of change. Not enough to live on. But a comfortable settlement."

Still, Lou displayed an ambivalent attitude to the VU, cutting off every interviewer who asked, "Will there be a reunion?" with answers like "I don't believe in high school reunions." John thought Lou would never come around: "I don't really know what that sixties period means to Lou. He's spent so much time saying it was a time of sophomoric activity."

IN THE AFTERMATH OF ANDY WARHOL'S DEATH, THE ARTIST'S STOCK HAD risen tremendously. Between 1989 and 1990, a retrospective of his work traveled to museums around the world. In June 1990, the original members of the Velvet Underground, along with Factory manager and photographer Billy Name, the Warhol superstar Ultra Violet, and the prominent art historian David Bourdon, were invited by the Cartier Foundation to Jouy-en-Josas, a small French town twenty miles southwest of Paris, for the inauguration of the Andy Warhol Exposition, at which Lou and John were to perform *Songs for Drella*.

When he arrived at the festival site, Lou was so overwhelmed by what he had seen, though he insisted to the last minute that a reunion was impossible, he realized that it would be churlish not to respond in kind to the efforts of the organizers. And so it was that Reed, Cale, Morrison, and Tucker occupied the same stage for the first time since the late summer of 1968.

The band's first reformation was, Nick Kent wrote, totally unexpected. "Everyone ate separately on their first day together, while Lou Reed announced flatly at a press conference during the same afternoon, 'You'll never get the four of us together on one stage again . . . *ever*. The Velvet Underground is history.' At the same event, however, John Cale showed himself more open to such a possibility. 'So many ideas were left unfinished in the Velvet Underground. If it's possible to do it again, I think we should really take the bull by the horns. . . . I think we have a lot left to give.' "

Sterling Morrison found himself in an awkward position. The French journalist Christian Fevret, who had met him in his Paris hotel the evening before the opening, recounted, "He was tired, anxious, and suddenly became very agitated. He wanted to know what Reed and Cale were playing the next day. 'What a blow for me! What am I supposed to do? Stand at the back of the stage and watch them play—paralyzed by bitterness and rage?

" 'And what are people going to think? That I can't play guitar anymore?'

"It's another stab in the back, the most cruel yet, for somebody who thinks that his role in the band has been horribly underestimated by history. On the most important day, he is put to one side and humiliated."

Still, he wanted it on record that "he held nothing against Lou Reed," added Nick Kent. "He just wanted to play with the Velvet Underground once again. He even brought his guitar over. Only Lou Reed didn't want to play with them.

"Lou Reed quite rightly has his own slew of bitterness regarding the Velvet Underground; only he more than anyone else was openly nursing them pretty much up to the last minute. Whatever, he was clearly overtaken by something approximating the spirit of glasnost at midday on Friday; for, as some two or three hundred guests were arriving, Reed broke a ten-year silence with Morrison, inviting him, Cale, and Tucker all to have lunch together."

Fevret, with an appropriately fine sensibility, set the scene: "11:30. On the balcony of a private house, isolated at the back of the park, three silhouettes were chatting. The vision of Cale, Morrison, and Tucker together was already a bit of an event for those who managed to see it. Three minutes later a pair of dark glasses, curly hair, and a leather jacket came forward timidly. He shook Sterling Morrison's hand nervously, even a little reluctantly. The four of them sat down at a balcony table and didn't leave until lunch was over.

"3:30. Lou and his wife, Sylvia, drove a few hundred meters across to an open-air stage. Cale and Reed were supposed to be playing in ten minutes. 'I think it would be nice to ask Sterling and Moe to come up onstage for a while,' said Lou. There was an astonished silence in the car. Even Sylvia Reed was choking. 'And what about doing "Pale Blue Eyes"?' he reckoned, before someone discreetly mentioned that John Cale hadn't been around when they recorded that one. It would be 'Heroin' then."

Noted another observer: "In the late afternoon of June 15, 1990, two musicians strolled onto an open-air stage in Jouy-en-Josas. One clutched an electric guitar; the other took up position behind a simple display of electronic keyboards. Lou Reed, clad in his uniform shades, leather jacket, and blue jeans, nodded curtly to his companion; and John Cale, hair shaved severely above his ears, fringe flopping decadently over his eyebrows, began to play their canny evocation of Andy Warhol." After a few songs from *Drella*, Reed announced, "We have a little surprise for you. I'd like to introduce Sterling Morrison and Maureen Tucker." There was a moment of stunned silence before the Warhol audience knew that they were about to see something that, according to Lou Reed, was never to happen: a reunion of the original Velvet Underground.

They then proceeded to play a seventeen-minute version of "Heroin" to an audience of some one hundred and fifty handpicked journalists and art people. Since it was in the open air, in the daytime, they had not rehearsed and Sterling had been reduced to borrowing a guitar, it had more impact as history than music. The most important thing that happened was that, like people who had once had great sex and suddenly realized they could again, they were stunned by playing together.

"That was one of the most amazing experiences I've ever had in my few years on Earth!" Lou, who was reportedly moved to tears, exclaimed to Maureen. "That was extraordinary! To have those drums behind me, that viola on one side, and that guitar on the other again, you have no idea how powerful that felt. I moved up into the pocket between you, John, and Sterl and . . . *holy shit!"*

THAT NIGHT THE BAND AND BILLY NAME HAD DINNER TOGETHER—AND the night after that, and the night after that. They even visited the Louvre together. John and Lou were considering playing some *Drella* concerts in the U.S. and Europe. The band talked of getting together to play in a club in Paris, although nothing came of it. However, the French reunion would not die, and throughout 1990 to 1992 Lou was plagued by the question, "Is there any chance of something like that happening again?"

He answered emphatically, "It will never happen. It was purely a moment in time. Again, a tribute to Andy. Once in a while these things happen. It was a wonderful, joyous occasion, but no, because I wouldn't want to give people the impression that there's any chance ever that the Velvet Underground could exist again. It won't. Or play again in public, which it won't, because I won't be there."

Asked, "Why?" he responded, "You must remember, I wrote, what, ninety-seven percent of the material for the Velvet Underground. So these are things I've gone through on my way to making *Magic and Loss*. So I don't want to—and I don't, not in real life—look back, you know, dwell over my shoulder. There's nothing to be gained from it. I believe that. You're trying to grow and go forward, and the people you were with then are not where you are now. So it's not a fair matchup."

In August 1990, Lou toured Japan with Maureen Tucker's band as his opening act at several shows. During the tour Lou and John played what may have been the last *Drella* show in Tokyo.

By this time, both *Songs for Drella* and *New York* had come to represent to the public a reborn Lou Reed—a Lou Reed seemingly unafraid of recognizing the vast influences of Warhol and the Velvet Underground.

The spring of 1992 brought Lou together again with Moe and Sterling. Lou was touring Europe with *Magic and Loss* at the same time Moe was touring behind her latest album with Sterling on guitar. The three of them ran into each other in Paris; Lou played at one of their shows. Sylvia hung out with Sterling and Moe, threatening to move in with them if Lou screamed at her one more time.

Sterling got the feeling that Lou might be open to a reunion. He clearly saw that Lou wasn't enjoying himself onstage anymore because he had become such a control freak. When Lou admitted that he had had fun playing with Moe and Sterling in Paris, Sterling replied, "Well, see, Lou, if you'd only consider . . ."

Polygram had started work on a boxed set of VU music. This led to a meeting in New York in December 1992. "It was really a great meeting, because we were all friends again," Moe Tucker recalled. "We were fooling around, when Lou suggested that we get back together to play

Madison Square Garden for a million dollars. It was just a joke, but it was the first time any of us had said anything like that in front of the other three. After a lot of thought, we all decided, 'Yeah, a Velvets reunion is a really cool idea.' "

On December 5, Cale played a concert at New York University accompanied by Sterling. Lou joined them onstage for two songs. "The evening's biggest treat came when Lou Reed strode onstage in suburban casuals, guitar strapped to his chest," wrote Ann Powers in the *New York Times*. "Mr. Cale, Mr. Reed, and Mr. Morrison launched into "Style It Takes," from *Songs for Drella*. Only the crucial absence of drummer Maureen Tucker kept this from being a Velvet Underground reunion. Mr. Reed's aggressive playing dominated the proceedings, but the three men did listen to one another, building a fractured reflection of the foundational Velvet sound."

After that night, Lou started talking eagerly about a reunion. Sylvia began investigating the possibility of the Velvet Underground doing some shows in Europe in 1993. Shortly thereafter, Cale went on the *Tonight* show and told Jay Leno that they were planning to get back together ("for the money!").

In February 1993, "we all got back together in New York for a rehearsal," Tucker recounted. "We played music together for five or six hours. Everybody was feeling a bit nervous at first. We really didn't know what was going to happen. None of us had any idea how the others would react. But, in the end, we were all extremely happy with the result."

They agreed to do a short tour of Europe that summer. In retrospect, though Lou insisted that it was just a whimsical notion based upon having fun, this was a brilliant career move for Reed, engineered by Sylvia.

As soon as word of the agreement was out, the businesspeople—spearheaded by Sylvia, who would also become the VU's road manager—set up the dates and worked out the contracts for a three-week tour, followed by a live album and video to be recorded in Paris. It was left to the band to carry out a series of rigorous rehearsals not unlike the rehearsals of 1965 that had bolted the musicians to their sound. They were conducted, fittingly, in a former factory on West Twenty-sixth Street in Manhattan.

Although glad to get back together, they were not without apprehensions. It was not possible to simply erase the years of bitterness between the rest of the band and Reed. Even now, he held the whip over them because he owned the publishing rights to the vast majority of the VU's material. According to the proprietor of the Mudd Club, Steve Mass, who had many conversations with Cale in the early 1980s, "John would say to me—he would crow—that he wanted to extract the Velvet Underground, the history, the culture, from Lou Reed. Reed wanted to kill the Velvet Underground and Cale was the carrier of the virus. The way Cale would express it to me was in terms of the financial elements, the lawyers and the accountants, and Lou Reed just controlled it. He had the legal power and had it all tied up."

At first Cale emerged as their spokesman, telling Richard Williams, in a piece for the *Independent on Sunday* magazine, "Nothing would have gotten done without Lou thinking it was a good idea. There was nothing happening for him this year, so he decided to try it. We had two days of playing to see if it was fun, and it turned out to be fantastic. All the original enthusiasm was there.

"It's good that Lou has about twenty thousand guitars, or he'd be spending hours retuning between every number. That's what we used to do, and it drove people crazy. But Lou is being Lou Reed again—he's turning up his guitar and wailing. Which is how most of those songs work anyway: turn it up and crank it out."

In another interview with Allan Jones for *Melody Maker* earlier that year in Paris, Cale had reflected upon their motives for performing: "As far as I'm concerned, this is an opportunity to take care of some unfinished business. The business we started when we first put the VU together. We never saw it through."

He seemed hopeful about the possibilities of doing new work: "I've got three pieces I've almost finished that I've already talked to Lou about, and he wants to do them. I don't really think he's interested in doing something that'll come out as just another Lou Reed solo album. From what he's said, he sees this very definitely as a group thing."

When Jones remarked "that sounds uncommonly democratic of him," Cale snapped, "Lou, democratic? Let's not go too far. Let's put it this way: if he thinks I'm going to turn up to play 'Walk on the Wild Side,' he's going to be very disappointed."

Once they had found their groove and felt as comfortable with each other as they ever would, the band agreed to receive a series of European journalists whose publications were willing to treat their reformation as a cover story. Matt Snow from *Q* came away with a sharply etched image of the four veterans: "The first is small, late forties, dressed in black with a paradoxically mumsy face. The second wears jeans, T-shirt, and a pair of hexagonal glasses, giving him the aspect of an intimidatingly intelligent monkey. The third sports a Gothic profile, gray-edged chestnut Eton crop. The fourth, like the previous two an alarmingly well-preserved fiftyish, has the ranginess, acne-scarred complexion, and graying, slightly receding Prince Valiant haircut of a perpetual student. They are Maureen 'Moe' Tucker, Lou Reed, John Cale, and Sterling Morrison, the names as hallowed to the alternative-rock fan as John, Paul, George, and Ringo are to everyone else."

Every journalist who interviewed the band emerged with some colorful images. Despite his repeated insistence that they were there primarily to have "fun," Lou Reed's uncomfortable presence dominated the sessions. Max Bell, writing in *Vox*, described Lou as alternately staring at Sterling "like one of the Gorgons" and speaking "in a voice that creaks like the cellar door at Frankenstein's castle." Bell thought that the band and everyone involved in the project were living in "Lou's world."

Reed was undoubtedly calling the shots. It was he, for example, who made their much debated decision to open for U2 on several dates in Europe following their own tour. And it was he, not Cale, who conducted the rehearsals. Despite his often dour mien, Lou attempted to present their position in as light a vein as possible. He repeated over and over again like a mantra, "The only raison d'être for this is fun. Fun. To play for fun. This is not about money. I like playing with them; we had fun in France; we had fun sitting in with one another. And so long as money doesn't get in the way of anything and you can afford to do it just for fun and not lose any money and it doesn't become a career—that is, it's in essence pure, driven only by the instinct to make something nice—that's a nice, pure thing to do."

Ever since they had started meeting in late 1992, Sterling and Lou had appeared to old friends to have fallen in love, giving each other messages of appreciation as strong as valentines. Consequently, Sterling was shocked and hurt when Lou started screaming at him one Friday during rehearsals. Morrison told friends that if he had had a day like that at the beginning of the rehearsals, he could have saved everyone the trouble of going through with them. But then, much to everyone's surprise, at the end of the day Lou actually called up Sterling and apologized. Lou's handlers put the tantrum down to his nervousness about the fast-approaching shows, pointing out that he was as nervous now about performing as he had been when he was fifteen.

Reed, Cale, and Morrison all suffered from paranoia, taking a conspiratorial view of the world. The difference between 1968 and 1993 was that Sterling and John were able to see Lou with enough detachment to feel sorry for him. With a little help from their handlers, they were able to see that Lou was trapped inside this paranoia like a mastodon in an arctic ice cap, that he was not to be condemned for his brattish mouth, but rather pitied for the pain his every waking minute contained.

By then, though, they were all suffering from some of the anxiety that goes hand in hand with any international rock tour in the 1990s. The sheer financial logistics were terrifying, as was their vulnerability before the rock press. Veteran rock writers were warning that the Velvets had more to lose than any other band in rock history if they blew even one gig on the three-week tour. The consensus of opinion was that agreeing to open for U2 had already put their reputation in jeopardy. "Wouldn't that be like Jimi Hendrix opening for the Monkees?" queried one fan in a letter to *Rolling Stone*. Meanwhile, despite another letter published in the magazine that stated simply, "The Velvet Underground are back. There is a God," other fans voiced their opinions that they should never have threatened the VU myth in the first place. To make matters more uncomfortable, the band was criticized for the outrageously high ticket prices—as much as $75 in London and Amsterdam.

For the most part, the positive chemistry of the foursome overcame their collective fear, and Sterling and Moe worked as a buffer between Lou and John. In fact, the reunion might have been a great success, and perhaps even a long-lasting one, if it hadn't been for the added pressure of Sylvia, whose ego had ballooned out of proportion to her job. According to several people involved with the shows, Sylvia made no secret of her contempt for the other members of the outfit, particularly John, whom she called stupid and untalented. John was convinced that she had learned everything she knew in this department from Lou, but others were not so sure. After lasting through twelve hard, embattled years with Lou, Sylvia had developed a tough shell and an instinct for self-preservation that led her to lash out at others. Sylvia seemed more intent than ever on shoring up Lou's image and, by extension, her own.

She virtually showered contempt on Cale, going so far at one point as to make the curious remark that as he had grown older John had become exceedingly ugly while Lou had grown more and more handsome. Sterling and Moe were also subjected to foulmouthed put-downs. Sylvia seemed to think that the "lesser" band members should feel grateful to Lou for stooping to their level to help them.

Being tough and highly self-confident themselves, the band members could have shrugged off Sylvia's cutting remarks, had she not been their road manager. Worse still, Lou put Sylvia between himself and the band. Despite living with Lou for over a decade, Sylvia did not appear to understand the chemistry of collaboration in creative rock music. She had no conception of how important Cale was to Reed. In the long run, observers noted that it was Sylvia's separation of Lou from the band that would do the most damage.

In the opinion of one observer, Lou was simply reverting to the adolescent pattern he had never grown out of. "Mother is going to take care of this for Lou," she said. "I mean, there are people who don't grow up. I think as an adolescent Lou probably went through the same thing that all kids do, which would tell you something about his intelligence. He isn't smart. Sometimes very simple propositions take an incredible amount of time to explain to him. I mean, he doesn't understand simple things about deal-making, like if you want to get a higher royalty rate, you'd better have something to trade off for it. A simple rule of life. If you give me something, I'm going to have to give you something. Most people have a sense of this. Lou doesn't. Lou thinks the way you're going to get a higher royalty rate is just go and ask for it. Which I suppose is like an eight-year-old."

Even though Lou managed to place a certain amount of distance between himself and the band, it wasn't long before the rivalry surfaced between Lou and John, just as it had twenty-five years earlier. The dispute that emerged centered around who was going to produce the live recordings of their reunion tour. Each man thought he was the only one capable of pulling it off. Soon, they were both preparing for a pitched battle. Lou told everybody when the tour started, "Catch it while you can, it's probably not going to last that long."

"Somebody said Lou Reed wouldn't have existed if it hadn't been for John Cale," commented one friend. "Lou recognized that and that was one of his biggest problems. The sad thing about it was that John didn't recognize this. John represented everything that Lou wanted to be. In terms of the musical reputation and the other intellectual things. John is probably the most highly trained musician ever to play rock and roll. Cale was very insecure about what he wrote, but he was not stuck in the sense that Reed was—stuck in adolescence."

WITH LOU PREDICTING ITS EARLY DEMISE, THE TOUR KICKED OFF IN Edinburgh on June 1. The first show did not live up to the expectations of an audience geared up for an exciting set composed at least in part of the VU's new material. After waiting for the five-minute standing ovation to quiet down, Lou yelled, "One-two-three . . . ," and the band launched into "We're Gonna Have a Real Good Time Together." Much of the ensuing material, however, failed to make good on the band's promise to premiere new songs and improvise on the classics, leading one attention-seeking Caledonian to shout, "This is the most boring load of shit I've ever seen." Chris Whent heard other things being shouted that night that were highly positive. "I thought it was like a lovefest. I have never felt such a warmth of emotion. And the sound was different than anything I'd ever heard before. The entire evening sounded utterly and remarkably like the Velvet Underground."

By other accounts the band was tense on the first night. "The first thing you notice as the Velvet Underground stutter and stumble through their first few numbers is the inappropriate rude health of Lou Reed," wrote Pat Kane in the *Guardian*. "He bulges out of his black T-shirt and blue denims like a cross between Bryan Adams and Nosferatu; the pebble glasses make him look more like a pop professor than real pop professors do."

" 'I Can't Stand It' ends the set," wrote one critic. "But everyone knows they'll be back, and the cheers are just turning to impatient boos when Lou leads them back out for two encores: a tense, neurotic, and inevitable 'Waiting for the Man,' and a spellbinding trip through 'Heroin.' At the end they line up like chorus girls or the cast of *The Mousetrap*. Cale puts his arm around Lou. Lou jumps. You get the feeling that the last time Cale touched him, his fists were probably clenched. There's still a lot of history between these two. Lou smiles, puts his arm around Maureen. Sterling taps her on the head."

The following night's show was far superior. "The revelation on Thursday, though, was the diminutive Ms. Tucker's drumming," wrote John Rockwell in the *New York Times*. "Standing at her kit and whacking away, she makes a tom-toms of doom sound that inspired straight-ahead punk drumming for a generation. The effect is not quirky or amateurish; it is rock like in the granitic sense of that word, the foundation on which the band could build a creative future to match its potently nostalgic past."

From Ediburgh they traveled down to London for two shows on June 5 and 6. The first was at a 1,200-capacity club, the Forum. David Fricke wrote in *Rolling Stone*: "You could definitely feel the invisible lightning flashing between Reed and Cale as they faced off during the extended guitar-viola jousting in 'Mr. Rain.' Reed lancing Cale's agitated Arabic droning with paint-peeling feedback."

From England they went to Holland for shows in Amsterdam and Rotterdam. Back in 1988 a poll of Dutch journalists had voted the first VU album the best record of all time. Since then Lou had received the Dutch equivalent of a Grammy—the Edison Award—for the *New York* album. The tour was turning into a triumphal procession.

The Paris shows at the Olympia Theater were recorded on June 15 to 17. Asked by a member of the audience if he could repeat the name of the single new composition, "Coyote," Lou replied, "Of course. We're the Velvet Underground. We can do anything."

"I slowly made my way out of the Olympia thinking about Reed," wrote an American critic, Ira Kaplan, in *Spin*. "Why had he, with a thriving solo career, made this dive into his past? Now fifty-one, he's used his two most recent records, *Songs for Drella* and *Magic and Loss*, to consider mortality. The flip side of the bitterness that Morrison expressed (though he denied the term 'bitter,' preferring 'cold') is a past yet unreconciled. And while you obviously can't change the past, by reuniting the band gets a chance to change the ending. The Velvet Underground reunion provides an opportunity—not just for Reed, of course—for closure, for vindication. I hope that when his fists rose at the end of their show, it meant he's found it."

From Paris they traveled to Berlin for two final shows. As soon as the tour was over, the Velvets joined U2 in Italy for four stadium concerts in front of audiences of up to sixty thousand. After these concerts they returned to the U.K. to play a short set at the Glastonbury festival.

Though press reaction to the tour was soberly positive, criticism came from purists, who objected to the fact that Lou allowed "Venus in Furs" to be used for a Dunlop tire commercial in the U.K. Others viewed the VU's opening for U2 as a further sellout.

According to tour insiders, the group got along reasonably well until the U2 dates in Italy, when friendly relations soured. The band members had grown tired of Lou's screaming at them onstage with a live mike in front of him. "I've never seen him be so uptight on stage," Cale later commented. "And giving the fascist salute during 'Heroin' in Italy . . ." "I'm always nervous," Lou responded. "I'm nervous about life. I'm calmer onstage, I have my guitar. Offstage, that's something else." Morrison too was upset by Lou's nasty gibes. By the time they left England, he was already wishing he had never agreed to tour in the first place. Lou's behavior was not his only beef. He was also put off by Lou's prima donna posturing for the press and record executives. Sterling complained later, for instance, that during the tour nobody from Sire Records ever said a single word to anybody in the band except Lou.

Making matters worse for Morrison, Cale, and Tucker was the overbearing presence of Lou's surrogate, Sylvia. One observer opined that Lou and Sylvia had lasted so long together because she was not a nice person, that she mirrored his nastiness and encouraged that side of him, that she recharged his unpleasantness and gave it back to him. In other words, they deserved each other. Or, as one friend put it: "They were fucking each other's brains."

By the time the Velvet Underground returned to the States their camaraderie had dissipated. Once home they scattered—Moe to Georgia, Sterling to his tugboat on the Gulf of Mexico, Lou and John to their separate camps in Manhattan. On the positive side, they had received a massive amount of good publicity, and both Sterling and Moe, who would each end up with something like $75,000–100,000 when the smoke cleared, had been rescued from penurious conditions.

No sooner had Lou safely retreated from face-to-face contact with the band members than he initiated an all-out fax war. Previously a phoneaholic, Lou had now become a fax maniac, spending hours composing messages and then keening over the machine in anticipation of a snappy reply. It was the perfect mode of communication for the hermetic Reed. He began with a four-page fax to John, explaining in formidable detail that though John was a very good friend of his, Lou never wanted to play on the same stage with him again. He then proceeded to delineate all the things that John had done wrong throughout the brief tour.

Cale, who had maintained a called-for reserve and dignity throughout the entire episode, replied, "I can understand what you're saying, but we just got back, we're too close to it all happening, we're exhausted, and we shouldn't be dealing with this now." There was too much at stake for him to take Lou's fax seriously. Not only was the band anticipating the release of its upcoming live album and a video of the Paris shows, but Polygram was working on the VU box set. Moreover, MTV had invited them to record an "unplugged" acoustic concert. Most importantly, a fall tour of the U.S. would reap considerable profits for all involved. Warner Brothers, whose Sire label was due to release the live album in October, was urging the band to seize the moment.

Despite the bright commercial prospects of his continuing involvement with the band, Lou drove a spoke into the wheel of the whole project. Perhaps his rekindled animosity toward the band had to do with intensifying problems on the home front. For one thing, Sylvia had rented her own apartment on East Tenth Street. At her housewarming party in August, Lou made it obvious he was pissed off. Accompanied by Mike Rathke, who was in the process of divorcing Sylvia's sister, Lou turned up a couple of hours late. He entered the flat without a word or glance to anybody and sequestered himself in the kitchen, feeding on the assorted food and glaring ferociously at anybody who dared enter the room. A short while later he departed without saying a word.

Perhaps the most telling response to Lou's antisocial behavior came from the ever loyal and loving Moe, who was becoming increasingly alarmed by Lou's salvos in the fax war. Even though reports were circulating in the media that the band was definitely scheduled to tour in October and November, the fax battle heated up through the end of September. Lou demanded that he be given complete control of producing any records the reunited band released, with particular emphasis on

the MTV unplugged album. Sterling was sequestered on his faxless tugboat, leaving John and Moe to take the brunt of the attack.

It wasn't long before Lou took the game one step too far. He sent Moe
a nasty note, charging her with being ungrateful for all he had done for
her. Although Moe was a tough alley cat who did not need to be defended, when Lou sent the fax chastising her for being ungrateful, so far
as the others were concerned, that was it. The time had come to unplug
the channels of communication as if—fuck you—forever. The scales finally fell from Moe's eyes, and she decided to stand up for the band. On
listening to the live album, mixed adequately by Lou's man Rathke, and
studying the video, she realized where the weakness lay in the group and
why Lou was so insistent on controlling the production. Lou's failing
ability to sing and his less than inspirational guitar playing had not been
completely covered up in the live record and video. She figured that Lou's
need to produce any VU product came in part from a desire to protect
himself from the discovery of his musical shortcomings. Realizing that she
would rather get the music right than cover it up, Moe sided with John
in issuing a definitive negative to Lou's demand. As Cale pointed out in
one of the many reply faxes he sent to Reed, their communication had
from the outset revolved around a series of ultimatums from Reed to the
band. They had to draw the line somewhere, otherwise they simply dissolved into Reed's backing band and a third-rate rock group.

In the midst of all this, as a sure sign of his schizophrenia, Lou spent
a weekend at Cale's Long Island place as if nothing out of the ordinary
was going on and their friendship was unaffected. Later, in the first week
in October, Lou attempted a reconciliation, sending John a fax saying
how much the group meant to him and that that was a reason why he had
been so insistent about producing the MTV unplugged album. John replied, "Lou, I didn't realize how much it meant to you, let's cut the crap
and start playing." The next day a fax came back from Sylvia, the thrust
of which was: It's a good thing you've seen the sense, and, of course, Lou
will have to get the producer's fee. When Cale simply refused to go along,
he received a final cold-blooded fax saying, "Good luck in your future
career," signed, Sylvia and Lou.

While Lou had been manning the fax machine, Sylvia had been working behind the scenes booking and unbooking the tour, designing a cover
for the live album, and worrying about her financial settlement with Lou.

However, in light of the conflict with John, Sterling, and Moe, the three people to whom he had been referring back in June as among his few real friends, there were those in the VU camp who seriously worried that Lou was finally going over the edge. He seemed, they mused, to have little sense of how much harm he had done to himself with his record company by blocking the potentially lucrative VU tour. They also wondered how his U.S. fans would respond to the return of the solo Lou, and indeed what he could possibly do to follow up *Magic and Loss* that could stand up to what he might have done with the Velvets.

Meanwhile, with the release of the live album, *MCMXCIII*, in late October, the searchlights of the press were once more turned upon him. "Following a quarter century's hiatus, the reunited Velvets are less concerned with re-creating what was than with exploring what could have been and what might still be," wrote a reviewer in *Rolling Stone*. "With the exception of Neil Young, there isn't a rocker who understands as well as Reed does that stylistic extremes have more in common than either edge shares with a safer middle ground. Reed's streetwise eye for detail and ear for everyday poetry find common spirit—and frequent challenge—in Cale's conservatory-trained experiments with dissonance, decibels, and repetition, while the jittery precision of Maureen Tucker's garage-band drumming is as crucial to the Velvets as Charlie Watts's is to the Rolling Stones. After the professorial tone of Reed's recent tours and the elegiac turn of his nineties albums, the physical rush of this music has him sounding like a man possessed."

In public Lou put on a good face, appearing in Manhattan at a party for the live album and video that Sire Records threw at Nell's on November 3. Looking healthy and rested, he maintained a definitive distance between himself and everybody else except a male companion and bodyguard.

Reviews for the video were not so favorable. "Four chronologically advanced musicians performing basic, broody adolescent rock songs with about as much passion as a quartet of railway announcers," wrote Roger Morton in the *NME*, "makes for a strange spectacle. Sawing away at his violin, the curatelike Cale deports himself with bizarre solemnity. Morrison just stands there and follows the notes. Maureen Tucker whacks out the mono-beat with at least some commitment. And Reed croaks on, seemingly viewing it all with detached amusement. The whole thing has the deadening atmosphere of an angst-pop masterclass."

On November 11, Lisa Robinson reported in her *New York Post* column that the VU would once again disband. "We won't continue because John Cale and I and other members of the band can't agree on certain things," Reed told her. Phoning Lisa from Buenos Aires where he was on a brief tour, Cale countered, "He's a control freak. I wanted to try and create new music—more songs like 'Venus in Furs,' 'All Tomorrow's Parties.' I don't want to just go in and become some third-rate rock-and-roll band. We didn't contribute anything to ourselves on this tour; we didn't step outside ourselves again and reach for that extra bit." As far as John was concerned, the saddest thing about the whole "reunion" was that, despite stated intentions to the contrary, Lou had never really rejoined the band, comporting himself throughout as Lou Reed, never a member of the Velvet Underground.

Reed's reply: "I didn't want to get involved in writing any more songs unless I knew that I would be involved in the production of anything that came out of it. I am a control freak, I'm a perfectionist when it comes to music and writing, and I want it to exist on the level I know I can deliver, and I won't settle for anything less."

It soon became apparent though that, despite Lou's apparent determination to slay his dragon once and for all, history would in fact simply repeat itself—only this time on a much larger scale than in 1970. Whereas twenty-three years earlier, when Lou had first left the group in a dispute over control of the sound (Reed and Sesnick were mixing and remixing, and remixing, *Loaded* at the time), the band retained a tight coterie of die-hard fans, they now maintained a much higher profile and a gigantic international following. In the interval they had also come to be judged as the second most influential band of the 1960s. And maybe, as Dimitri Ehrlich wrote in *Mademoiselle*, "of the seventies, eighties, and nineties too." In that magazine's survey of other musicians' interest in the upcoming VU boxed set, Billy Idol, who had recently released a cover of "Heroin," exclaimed, "I like the stark perverted vision of the Velvet Underground. It was the most shocking music I ever heard." Gordon Gano of Violent Femmes said, "Their music hit me like an electric current. They have both an expression of vulnerability and also an incredible swagger." And Margot Timmins of the Cowboy Junkies (whose cover of "Sweet Jane" dominated the sound track of Oliver Stone's masterpiece *Natural Born Killers* in the summer of 1994) concluded, "I think we have the same mood as the Velvets. Their approach was to get the groove and not worry about making everything perfect." On first seeing *Uptight: The Velvet Underground Story*, Andy Warhol had chuckled, "It makes it look so clean, and it was *so dirty.*" In truth, the dirty realism of 1966 has given way to the magazine glamour of 1995, which has turned the band into a part of history—i.e., an imagination of the past. In the last five years of the twentieth century, that imagination will undoubtedly be allowed to expand. Each country conceives the band in a reflection of its own history. To Florian of Kraftwerk they had a heavy German Dada influence from the twenties and thirties. In France, where they had significantly chosen to record their live album, they were looked upon as romantic saints. In Japan they were seen as science fiction monsters. In Italy they were communists. In Czechoslovakia they were dissident revolutionaries. In Scotland, etc.

And just as Lou had profited most in the aftermath of the original breakup, so would he undoubtedly profit in these reflections. From Lou's point of view, breaking the band up again was just as strong a career move as getting them back together. Like all the so-called "great artists" of his era he was a selfish bastard, but—to paraphrase Bill Graham on Mick Jagger—that cunt could sure write some motherfucking beautiful songs, which in fact, whether one likes it or not, transcended any concerns a sensitive fan might have had about the effect of the fallout of all this bullshit on John, Sterling, and Moe, who could obviously have had their lives dramatically changed had Lou chosen to soldier on with them. In time, all that will be remembered are the *sounds* and *words*. Lou's life, or wife, notwithstanding.

Chapter Twenty-Two

QUEEN OF SCARS

1993—94

*It always worries me that people actually think there's
something wrong with me and what I'm doing. What is
this thing that they want me to correct?*

—Lou Reed

LOU MAINTAINED A HIGH PROFILE AT THE END OF 1993 AND INTO EARLY
1994. He had started having an affair with the coolest performance artist
in the world, Laurie Anderson, who bore a resemblance to the young
Shelley Albin. They met at an arts and music festival in Munich. Lou
invited Laurie to sing "A Dream" from *Songs for Drella*. "I was astounded
when she did it exactly the way I would do it rhythmically, with just the
right pauses," he recalled. Back in New York, both Lou and Laurie, who
were normally reticent about their personal lives, were outspoken to
friends in praise of their relationship. For Laurie it was, she said, "wonderful." They were both great storytellers who enjoyed listening as much
as talking on the rare occasion they found the right person. As writers,
they shared a fascination with computers as the tool of their trade. Lou
was the funniest person Laurie had ever met. As for Lou, he pulled out all
the stops saying that Laurie was the kindest person he'd ever met, as well
as being "incredibly sexy, vibrant and beautiful." They were spotted
smooching in the back of limousines and in restaurants.

At first, Sylvia welcomed the affair since it helped quell rumors that
Lou had dumped her for an older black guy, a guard at the Natural History
Museum, with whom he regularly had breakfast at a local café. In November, Lou and Laurie went to the premiere of *The Black Rider*, an opera
by Robert Wilson, William Burroughs, and Tom Waits, and smiled for
the cameras at the dinner party after it.

He was rehearsing uptown at the Guggenheim Museum for a benefit performance for the opening of the Robert Mapplethorpe Gallery. On the night of the show, November 8, playing acoustic guitar with electronic pickup, accompanied by a single guitarist and a stand-up bass, he complained acidly about the acoustics, but seemed otherwise to enjoy himself with the band. Wearing tight blue jeans and a skintight black leather T-shirt zipped up the side, he played folk versions of "Satellite of Love," "Walk on the Wild Side," and "Sweet Jane." The audience, though enthusiastic, was not attentive. Many people maintained conversations during the show, a practice outlawed by Lou in concert halls. His craggy face suggested a cross between his father and Delmore Schwartz.

In December, the German director Wim Wenders's film *Faraway, So close!* starring Willem Dafoe, Nastassja Kinski, and Peter Falk, with a cameo by Lou singing a new composition, "Why Can't I Be Good?" opened in New York. Lou performed the song at a party after the premiere, telling the press, "It's always a privilege and an honor to be involved with Wim Wenders."

On February 2, 1994, Lou was not so complimentary to Kris Kristofferson when they performed at a songwriters' night at the Bottom Line. According to a reporter for the *New York Observer*'s Transom column: "Kris Kristofferson seemed eager to jam with Lou Reed at a concert that also featured Suzanne Vega and Victoria Williams. When Mr. Reed began a solo version of his classic 'Sweet Jane,' Mr. Kristofferson tried to accompany the former Velvet Underground member on harmonica. But Mr. Reed did not seem to want his spare song cluttered. 'No harmonica, Kris,' said Mr. Reed, interrupting his singing. Mr. Kristofferson stopped, but later tried to pick up his acoustic guitar along to Mr. Reed's electric one. Again, Mr. Reed broke off his singing. 'Shhh,' he said. Mr. Kristofferson, looking a bit like a reprimanded child, obeyed."

IN THE AFTERMATH OF THE VELVET UNDERGROUND'S UNPLEASANT PUBlic breakup debacle, Lou was thrust into just the kind of position he had particularly thrived on throughout his career—a 100 percent shift in the public's view of him. Suddenly, a lot of the same people who had been praising *Magic and Loss* as if it were a play by Samuel Beckett started to joke—grimly—that nobody was going to be interested in Lou's divorce album. Only a year earlier at the end of 1992, Lou had stood at the pinnacle of his long, hard diamond-in-the-rough career. As he surveyed all that was his and looked forward to the Velvet Underground reunion European tour—sure to be one of the great events in rock history—he was a man who had, somewhat like Elvis, dreamed all his childhood dreams ten times over. He was more successful than Delmore Schwartz had ever been. He was more successful than Andy Warhol could ever have expected him to be. He was worth several million dollars. And he had truly done it his way and meant every word he had ever written.

Now, at the end of the troubled, trembling 1993, he had plummeted from being one of the—if not *the*—most venerated, for all of the right reasons, figures in his field to coming across like a small-minded wart. What else can be said about a man who threw away the proferred lifelong collaboration of Cale, Tucker, Morrison, and Morales as if they were used napkins. Who could not summon the psychic strength to tour America with the Velvet Underground because it was his ball. Who was still a boring adolescent.

The question that hung most on every Lou Reed fan's lips was, what kind of music was the old bugger going to play now? What was he going to come up with? Lou Reed had upset all the fans in the U.S. who had looked forward to seeing the Velvet Underground. His last trilogy of solo albums had left off with the depressing *Magic and Loss*. Where could he go from there? He claimed to be working on a novel. Allegedly, he approached Warner Brothers with the desire to make a covers album. Warner Brothers had been fully informed of Lou's behavior during the collapse of the VU reunion and cannot have been particularly pleased with how he had undermined the commercial potential of the live album by refusing to tour with the band. Their response was negative. How could he have the effrontery to go on the *Tonight* show, bumping the VU, who had been scheduled to play the gig, then do his own lame version of "Waiting for the Man" with his band of bozos who made rock-and-roll musicians look like uninteresting carnival freaks, when he could have stood next to John Cale, whom he had known for thirty years? His "Waiting for the Man" was less exciting than Cale's on the album. After the performance Lou looked distinctly vulnerable.

If he went out and played a bunch of VU stuff, he might get crucified. On the other hand, what period of his life would he be best to choose from? Maybe he should do a bunch of old Pickwick covers to remind people where he had come from.

That wasn't a bad guess actually, because Lou did a fairly similar thing, which turned out to be—no big surprise—very interesting indeed. In 1994, Lou Reed started singing cover versions of songs by people—like Elvis, Dylan, Smokey Robinson, etc.—who had such distinct phrasing that it was almost impossible to make any of their songs your own. Lou had found it easy to imagine Frank Sinatra laying down "Heroin" at the Sands in front of the Nelson Riddle Orchestra. It is hard to imagine Lou Reed laying down "Like a Rolling Stone" at Madison Square Garden and even getting away with it.

Later in February Lou flew to Los Angeles and appeared at an Artists' Rights Foundation benefit with Los Lobos and Chris Isaak. According to Tom Chao in the *Los Angeles Reader:* "His crack four-piece touring unit really locked into its huge monolithic sound with a fiery reading of Bob Dylan's 'Foot of Pride,' and Reed also interpreted works by Pete Townshend, Victoria Williams, and Elvis(!). His recasting of the Kurt Weill–Maxwell Anderson classic 'September Song' as a slow soul number was hypnotic; and who would have guessed that Reed could make 'Tracks of My Tears' indisputably his own."

According to Erik Hasen in *LA Village View*, "He proceeded to perform a hauntingly stark version of Elvis Presley's 'Mystery Train.' Considering Lou Reed's appearance was much awaited by the crowd, it was strange to see hordes of people exit during his set."

From Los Angeles, Lou jetted back to New York, where he appeared at a tribute to Pete Townshend at Carnegie Hall. Singing "Now and Then" from Townshend's recent album *Psychoderelict,* with the same phrasing as "Sweet Jane," he made the song his own. On March 26, Lou played at a group concert at the Beacon Theater in New York to mark the release of Rob Wasserman's album *Trio.* "A sardonic Lou Reed growling iconoclastic versions of 'The Tracks of My Tears' and 'One for My Baby' was the high point of the nearly three-hour benefit concert," wrote Stephen Holden in the *New York Times.* "Intoning these classic songs in an impassioned monotone, Mr. Reed demolished and reconstituted them in his own image. Lovelorn ballads became minimalist rock anthems whose tearful emotions were transmitted into a more generalized, barely suppressed rage."

• • •

ON LOU'S FIFTY-SECOND BIRTHDAY, MARCH 2, THE *NEW YORK POST* RAN his photograph above a horoscope that read, "Although no one can really question your motives or undermine your confidence, a marvelous aspect between Venus and Neptune on your anniversary signifies that it might be wise to make an adjustment, especially when dealing with projects which involve a large number of people."

At the same time that he was fighting with John, Moe, and Sterl, Lou was brawling with Sylvia over getting divorced or not getting divorced. Having decided not to get divorced, he started considering the financial settlement. Many people who knew Lou were sure that Sylvia could not last much longer. Not only did Sylvia take it for granted that she would continue to manage Lou, she started thinking about managing other stars too. When Kurt Cobain overdosed in his Rome hotel during the first week of March 1994, Sylvia rang Lou suggesting they should send flowers and a note. No, Lou replied, he wanted to talk about their financial settlement. She should come over.

When Sylvia got there, she was met by a barrage of figures. Lou would pay her a salary of $150,000 per year, but no percentages. Since Lou earned approximately $1 million a year, and a standard managerial contract gave the manager 20 percent, and since Sylvia had been instrumental in bringing Lou to this level of income, she reacted negatively. She threatened to send appraisers to his apartment to assess how much of their money he had spent having his new place fixed up. It was more than $100,000, and she knew Lou had recently taken Laurie Anderson to Antigua for a week's vacation, on which he spent $25,000.

On the following day Lou fired Sylvia as his manager, canceling her credit cards, car service, and other accounts. Now she had no choice but to sue him for a divorce. However, one friend noted, "I wouldn't be surprised if he and Sylvia went back and forth on this for years. Now Sylvia has left him for whatever reason, but whether he said, 'Get out,' whether he stomps on her, kicks her out, throws her out, beats her up, she's not supposed to get out. She's supposed to say, 'No, I'm coming back.' "

Meanwhile, Reed's lawyer, the venerable Alan Stein, dismissed Reed as a client. "Don't underestimate the fact that Lou was fired by his attorney," one observer pointed out. "Alan Stein is in his seventies and he has been one of the top entertainment lawyers for years. He began to represent Lou because one of his close friends is Lou's accountant, David Gotterer from Mason and Co., whom Lou has used for many years and who seems to be one of the few people whom he trusts. Alan is a class act. Alan represents Seymour Stein and has done for many years. So this was a heavy rejection."

LOU REED HAS SAID THAT HE HOPED HIS MUSIC WOULD LIFT CHILDREN OUT of their confusion. "If you play my albums all in a row, one of the things that I think is fun about me is that if you follow me, in each and every way from day one up till now, you're following a person. A real person I've tried to make really exist for you—Lou Reed.

"If you line the songs up and play them, you should be able to re-late and not feel alone—I think it's important that people don't feel alone."

Changing his life by rejecting whole groups of people had been Lou's recurring tactic, but the consensus of opinion among Lou's acquaintances was that he was scared of spending the rest of his life alone. "When you hit fifty, there are a lot of frightening changes," noted one. "A lot of doors close, new possibilities no longer open up. You suddenly realize that that's it." Lou knew, for example, that closing the door on Sylvia was dangerous. Laurie Anderson was not going to become his mommy, man-ager, and protector. She had as healthy a career as he did and as strong and ambitious a personality. "He may fantasize that he's going to replace Sylvia with Laurie Anderson," his friend continued, "but he's going to make a horrible discovery. You may be a fucking rock star, but if you're fifty-two years old, you're an old fart."

Some observers thought Lou might escape by blaming everything on Sylvia. During the VU negotiations she had drawn hostility even from the kindhearted Moe. "At the very least Lou must have seen she made him vulnerable," one go-between commented. Sylvia responded to com-plaints by saying, "If it hadn't been for me, this whole Velvet Under-ground reunion would never have happened. You don't understand how hard it is to deal with Lou."

"Lou may be particularly mean now because I would believe that he is twice as scared," stated one long-term friend. "I would think he must be pretty crazy right now. Lou can stand in front of the world and say I'm rich and famous and pearls of wisdom drop from my teeth. Yet I think what he really still is the little boy who wants all his mother's attention. If I wake up at four in the morning and I want you to cook me a pound of bacon and two hot dogs, of course you're going to do that, or I'm going to smack you, or I'm going to be real cold and withdrawn—that's the way an artist does it. To punish her. And he watches himself as all writers do, he stands back and restructures the scene a little and edits.

"Lou's pretty crazy about Sylvia, as I understand, so for him not to be happy is the most dismaying thing, because more than anybody else he's such a romantic. And I think in some ways that Lou is bewildered, lost in the way that a young kid in love might be. Here he is rejected, and how can you reject someone who's so smart and good? That's what really makes him tick."

In 1994, Lou Reed often sat alone in his Christopher Street penthouse playing his guitar with an array of machines he controlled with his foot. His solitude ended however that fall when Laurie moved in. Anderson was working with Brian Eno on her first studio album in five years, *Bright Red.* Lou collaborated on one song, "In Our Sleep." They wrote, sang, and recorded it together. As Stephen Holden noted in a profile of Anderson in *The New York Times,* "A repetitive chant that goes "In our sleep as we speak/Listen to the drums beat," finds a comfortable space between their minimalist styles and can be read as a deadpan love song evoking the depths of a relationship that both describe in glowingly romantic terms."

Lou had a high opinion of Laurie as a musician and engineer. In an intriguing collaboration that harkened back in more ways than one to Lou's meeting with Cale back in 1964, they began considering an album of duets on which Anderson would accompany Reed's guitar with her electrified violin. Lou described the style of the songs as "Lou and Laurie music."

The majority of Lou's acquaintances—he had few friends—predicted that based on Lou's track record the relationship simply could not last. However, Reed has made a career of finding rebirth through collaboration, which is essentially a marriage that begins when the collaboration begins and ends when it ends. The proof of it is its child: the work. In the long term it is the work one remembers.

The twin talents that made Lou Reed stand out are as a writer and a collaborator. That a man of his complexity could in his early fifties find another writer with whom he could make love and work is an engaging introduction to the second half of his life.

APPENDIX

EXTRACT FROM AN INTERVIEW WITH LOU REED, THE SINATRA OF THE 70S.

By Victor Bockris, New York, 1974.

VB: Are you interested in Frank Sinatra at all?

LR: Oh, Sinatra's fantastic! Somebody really gave him a really good song, with real lyrics, coming from him, and at this point he certainly could do it, you know. I mean shit, Frank. Tell us what you know, come on, Frank. You know, and I'll bet he could lay something coherent down.

VB: Well, why doesn't he?

LR: I don't know, why don't you ask him?

VB: He does actually, 'cause he was gonna get that guy who had to hire two bodyguards and stuff.

LR: See, like he did that song, "I was seventeen . . ." That one. That was like scratching the surface, but imagine if he got a little deeper than that.

VB: So, does he just need a good song, or does he have to change his head around? I mean, he won't do anything.

LR: He . . . you know . . . I'm just saying, wouldn't it be fantastic, Frank Sinatra, in *his* style, with *his* type of music, for *his* audience, everything the same except the lyrics.

VB: Well, is politics part of it?

LR: I don't see why.

VB: Would you like to work with him?

LR: Sinatra. Oh, sure.

VB: Like the two of you onstage together, doing a number?

LR: Oh, no. I'd like to write for him. I would love to put some lyrics to, you know, get to know him, then put the lyrics in his mouth, then all he'd have to do would be to sing them, wouldn't matter if he understood 'em.

VB: Well, are you at all confused by this friendship he has with Agnew, in relation to you? Obviously, a friend of yours is not George Wallace, or something. Do you think you look like Frank Sinatra, a bit?

LR: Don't say that to Frank Sinatra. I mean, he's really so good.

VB: You do, you look quite a bit like Frank.

LR: It'd really be fantastic, I mean, can you imagine him, with his audience, at the Sands, laying down a song, with Nelson Riddle conducting and all that shit, can you imagine if he laid down "Heroin"?

VB: Yeah!

LR: And got very serious with them for a minute, what might happen? But the thing is, that wouldn't be him. See, the way you'd have to do it with him is make it real.

VB: Yeah, his lyrics and his style are not really serious.

LR: Written by somebody else, but sounding like him. So, in other words, it'd be interesting to write that kind of style, that kind of song, you know, his Sinatra singing. Can you imagine that in Las Vegas?

VB: You could write that song, right?

LR: In about two minutes.

LOU REED MEETS WILLIAM BURROUGHS

by Victor Bockris

I had always wanted to witness a meeting between William Burroughs and Lou Reed, for although they come from different eras, they live on the same edges, having both survived long, sometimes torturous journeys to bring their useful visions back to a large public. Indeed, there are many parallels in their careers. To start with, Reed's most famous song is still "Heroin" (1966), Burroughs's most famous book, *Naked Lunch* (1959).

In the fall of 1979, we managed to squeeze the twenty-eight minute meeting in between their equally busy schedules. At sixty-five and thirty-seven respectively, Burroughs and Reed were at a peak of their careers. The writer was leaving for Zurich the next day on the first leg of a month-long reading tour of Europe, the singer was passing through New

York, playing four shows at the Bottom Line on a three-month international tour. We (Reed, half his band, Sylvia, and I) arrived at Burroughs's headquarters, otherwise known as the Bunker, on downtown Manhattan's notorious Bowery at 7:15 P.M. on a Monday evening, forty-five minutes late due to a problem at the sound check. Burroughs was having a drink with four friends. I was a little tense when I introduced them.

Lou Reed: (*Entering Burroughs's apartment, bottle of whiskey in hand*) Well . . . what's happening here?

Victor Bockris: Lou Reed—William Burroughs. (*Burroughs stands up. They shake hands across the broad table.*)

LR: Well, shall we get some more chairs or are we all going to sit on the floor?

VB: (*Following Burroughs over to the fridge*) Shall I help you with the drinks?

William Burroughs: (*Pulling an almost empty bottle of vodka out of the fridge*) Well, that's all there is, man.

VB: Well, Bill, is there a store nearby where I can get some more vodka?

WB: Well, yes, there is if you turn left and go straight up the street a way.

LR: Victor, you can't go; you have to moderate this.

VB: (*After a long silence in which Burroughs and his entourage stare across the table at Reed and his entourage*) So, what happened to you in Germany?

LR: (*Deprecating gesture with hand and mouth*) Nothing.

VB: We heard you were put in jail!

LR: Oh, that was just, yeah, they put me . . . after some girl came up onstage and I didn't know who she was, some irate roadie or something; I hardly *saw* her, man, and there were all these drunk GIs too. But yeah, the cops came.

VB: And they arrested *you*?

LR: Just me, yeah. They took me to jail after the show. I slept in the cell overnight, I was tired. Then the next day they came to get me and I thought, "Oh, they're letting me out." But they came in and they said, "We want your blood!" I couldn't believe it, it was like I said to the guy, "You must be an American or else all your life you've wanted to be an American so you could have a great

line like that, and now you said it." They drove me to Frankfurt
to have blood tests and a urinology, to see if I had any drugs in
my system, as they suspected I had. Of course . . . there was
nothing. The guy was sort of nervous because on the way there he
asked me for a light and his hands were shaking, but, you know,
my German's good enough.

VB: Did you play Italy this time? (*Last time Reed played Italy he was
attacked onstage.*)

LR: We played Germany instead.

VB: No, but I mean I hear they want rock again in Italy now.

LR: Yeah, I hear that too. We played Basel, Switzerland, one night
though and all the people from Italy drove up to see us there. They
got there and there were no tickets, so they broke every door and
window in the place and came in through any hole they could find.
And they really looked weird, too, they had these hoods on, and I
thought "Uh-oh, here we go all over again," but they were the
sweetest, greatest audience. The place was jammed full and they just
sat there quietly and listened.

VB: William's going to Basel tomorrow.

WB: Zurich. I'm going to Zurich.

LR: Mr. Burroughs, I read somewhere recently, I think it was in a review
of a book about the beat generation by Aram Saroyan, where the
reviewer said the guy didn't know anything about the beat generation, but anyway there was a quote where someone said about you
that you are the only person they ever met who they felt was capable
of murder and that you were a very cold person. Is that true?

WB: (*Short silence*) I neither deny nor confirm these kinds of rumors. It
doesn't do any good to deny them anyway. Last week a visitor told
me a story about when I was walking with Beckett in Paris discussing
random and vicarious murder, and Beckett said, "If it's random it's
not murder." I said, "Sam," as I suppose I would address him if I
were walking along the banks of the Seine with Beckett—never
having walked *anywhere* with him, I don't know—"this is not correct at all and I will prove it to you," at which point I am supposed
to have pulled out a pistol and shot a passing Paris clochard, throwing her body in the water. Then "Sam" and I walked on.

LR: Wasn't Beckett James Joyce's secretary?

WB: He was for a while, yes. In fact it is obvious that this is what *WATT* (*a novel by Samuel Beckett*) is all about is his apprenticeship to Joyce. It was an apprenticeship more than anything else, the master telling the pupil how to do it, but he had to handle a good deal of typing and secretarial work too.

LR: Can a pupil ever do better work than his teacher?

WB: In this case, I believe so.

LR: Really? Ah, you see . . . Really!

WB: I think the whole body of Beckett's work is wider in scope than Joyce's.

LR: Well, you wrote a book called *Junkie*, which I read and really liked very much, and in it you had a scene where a guy is shooting up with a safety pin, right?

WB: Ah, that is correct, yes.

LR: How is that done?

WB: Look, man, see a lot of old junkies used to do this. You make a hole with the pin and then you put the dropper over the hole and the stuff is supposed to run in.

LR: Oh, you put the dropper *over* the hole. 'Cause I thought in, see, 'cause I thought eugh . . .

WB: Well, no, right, *over* the hole. It usually works. Sometimes you lose it though.

LR: (*Mutual laughter*) Well, Mr. Burroughs, let me ask you, which one of your books is your favorite? I mean there must be one.

WB: Well, authors are notoriously bad judges of their own work, so I don't really know . . .

LR: You published . . . you published . . . let's see what was that book I was . . . what am I thinking of . . .

VB: *Naked Lunch?*

LR: Right. *Naked Lunch.* Now when that book came out, man, I went right out and bought it, because there was *nothing* like that happening. So I wanted to ask you what you thought about two books like *City of Night* by John Rechy and *Last Exit to Brooklyn* by Hubert Selby. Now, like, these two books, for example, couldn't have been written without what you'd done. Do you know if these guys read what you . . .

WB: Well, I admire *Last Exit to Brooklyn* very much. You can see the amount of time that went into the making of that book. It took seven years to write. And I like Rechy's work very much too. We met him out in L.A. Very pleasant man, I thought, we only saw him for about half an hour.

LR: Did you know whether he'd read your work?

WB: Well, I didn't ask him, no.

LR: Why did you use the pen name Bill Lee on *Junkie*?

WB: *William* Lee.

LR: Oh, yeah. But why?

WB: Because my parents were still alive and I didn't want them to be embarrassed.

LR: But did they read it?

WB: Well, they might have.

LR: See, I know you wrote a lot of other books, but I think *Junkie* is the most important because of the way it says something that hadn't been said before so straightforwardly. . . . Is this boring you?

WB: (*Staring blankly at the table*) Wha . . . ?

LR: Okay. Another thing I heard I wanted to ask you about, I also heard you cut your toe off to avoid the draft. Is this true?

WB: (*Chuckling*) I would prefer to neither deny nor confirm any of these statements.

LR: Well, I wanted to ask you. . . . I read this great piece you wrote in *High Times* about Jack Kerouac, and it was really so great, you were right there with that. Why don't you write more like that?

WB: Well, I write quite a lot.

LR: But have you ever written any more books with a really straight narrative line, like *Junkie*?

WB: Certainly. Certainly. *The Last Words of Dutch Schultz,* for example. And my new novel *Cities of the Red Night* has a fairly straight narrative line.

LR: (*I hand Lou a copy of* The Last Words of Dutch Schultz) Oh, this is really great, the last words, yeah; what is this, some kind of opera?

WB: No, man, no. Well, you don't know about *The Last Words of Dutch Schultz*? You obviously don't know. They had a stenographer taking down everything he said. He was dying at the police station after he was shot, and these cops are all sitting around asking him questions. He's saying things like, "A boy has never wept nor dashed a thousand kin," and the cops are saying, "C'mon, don't give us that. Who shot ya?" It's incredible, man, the whole thing. . . . Gertrude Stein said he outdid her. Gertrude really liked Dutch Schultz.

LR: Is this the only copy you've got?

VB: You can get it in the store, Lou.

LR: I *know* that Victor. I can get anything in the store. Can you imagine what would happen if intelligence got confused with your mouth? (*William gets up to fix himself a vodka; Lou whispers*) I wanted him to give it to me. Listen, you ask him to give it to me.

VB: Okay, I will. I will.

LR: When are you going to do it?

VB: Before you leave.

LR: Oh, okay. No! I want you to do it now. (*Raising his voice*) Mr. Burroughs! Mr. Burroughs! I asked you if this was the only copy you had because I wanted to ask you to sign it and give it to me.

WB: (*Bemused, but then amused*) Well . . . I can always get another copy. . . . I suppose. Of course I will. I'd be delighted.

LR: (*Watching Burroughs take off his glasses*) Oh! You have to take off your glasses to see?

WB: No, man, it's just like, I put my glasses *on* to see anything (*putting them on*) distant (*looking across the table at Lou*), but if I'm going to read (*taking them off firmly*), I gotta take them off.

LR: See, because I wear contact lenses now like you can't . . . you don't ever take them out.

WB: Ever?

LR: Well, once a month to wash them or something, but they're new. But I wanted to ask you . . . (*Bill hands the signed book across the table*) Oh, thanks. God, that's really great. Thank you so much.

WB: Not at all. Not at all.

LR: About Kerouac: How could a guy that was so good-looking and romantic and writing that myth for generations end up a fat, dumb asshole—if you don't mind my being crude—sitting in front of television in a T-shirt drinking beer with his mother? What happened to make him change?

WB: He didn't change that much, Lou. He was always like that. First there was a young guy sitting in front of television in a T-shirt drinking beer with his mother, then there was an older, fatter person sitting in front of television in a T-shirt drinking beer with his mother.

LR: What do you think of what Patti Smith's doing, if you don't mind my asking.

WB: Well, yes. I've always liked what Patti does. I last saw her I think it was out in New Jersey. Have you ever listened to any joujouka music?

LR: My sole experience with joujouka is the Ornette Coleman record, which I have and play. The Ornette Coleman band with Don Cherry was the first band I followed around when I came to New York, so, you know, now when I'm playing with Don Cherry, that's really something.

VB: Bill was with Ornette Coleman during those sessions in Morocco.

LR: Wait a minute, wait a minute. Is it Bill or William? 'Cause, see, a lot of people call me Lewis, even though my professional name is Lou, but my mother calls me Lou. Is that the way it is with Mr. Burroughs?

VB: No, well, some people call him Bill, others William.

LR: Well, Mr. Burroughs, let me ask you this. Did Kerouac get a lot of his books published because he slept with his publisher? I mean, is there a lot of that in the literary world? Sleeping with editors and publishers in order to get published?

WB: Not nearly as much as in painting. No, thank God, it is not very often that a writer will have to actually make it with his publisher in order to get published, but there are a lot of cases of a young artist who will have to sleep with an older woman gallery owner or something to get their first show, or get a grant. I can definitely assure you that *I* have never had sex with *any* of my publishers. Thank God, it has not been necessary.

LR: And you're both really relieved. . . . Do you know my work at all? Have you ever listened to any of my records?

WB: Yeah, I was listening to it this afternoon.

LR: Which one? Which one?

WB: The latest one, of course.

LR: Oh, *The Bells, The Bells.*

WB: Yes.

LR: Do you like it? I hope you don't mind my asking, but I'm sure you wouldn't mind telling me if you didn't like it.

WB: Yes. I like it very much.

LR: I can't get over the fact that I believed . . . somebody told me, I don't know who, maybe it was Dorothy Dean . . . do you know Dorothy?

WB: Yes.

LR: She loves you. "Oh, he's *great*," she says. "But cold." No, no, I just added that myself. I can't get over the fact that somebody made me believe you cut your toe off to get out of the draft! I mean, can you imagine why I would believe that?

WB: I have no idea at all. (*Burroughs is missing the top half of the small finger on his right hand, blown off in a chemical explosion when he was fourteen.*)

LR: (*Looking at his watch*) Well, we who play cannot stay. We have to get back to do the gig. Listen, I really enjoyed meeting you, it was a great pleasure for me and I want to thank you very much.

WB: Well, it was my pleasure.

LR: Do you mind if I have your phone number?

WB: No. Sure.

LR: Could we get together sometime and just have dinner together without all this . . .

WB: Certainly. I'd be delighted.

VB: That's a good idea. We should do that.

LR: Who included you? What's this *we* all of a sudden? I just want to have a quiet dinner and talk.

SOURCE NOTES

I really like people.

—Lou Reed

THE PRIMARY SOURCE FOR TRANSFORMER: THE LOU REED STORY IS INFORmation that the author gathered from interviews with Cathleen Aiken, Penny Arcade, Jessica Berens, Gretchen Berg, Phillip Booth, Chris Charlesworth, Jim Condon, Tony Conrad, David Dalton, Henry Edwards, Lenny Ferrari, Mick Farren, Mark Francis, Bernie Gelb, Larry Goldstein, Mary Harron, Clinton Hevlin, John Holmstrom, Allen Hyman, Andy Hyman, Jim Jacobs, Alan Jones, Bert van der Kamp, Gary Luke, Gerard Malanga, Steve Mass, Earl McGrath, Legs McNeil, Miles, Phil Millstein, Richard Mishkin, Glenn O'Brien, Robert Palmer, Bob Quine, Matt Snow, Chris Stein, Andy Warhol, Michael Watts, John Wilcox, Barbara Wilkinson, Carol Wood, Mary Woronov, Doug Yule, and Tony Zanetta.

Other interviews and articles drawn on in this book come from work by Bobby Abrams, Billy Altman, Katrine Ames, Thomas Anderson, Dan Aquilante, Al Aronowitz, Lester Bangs, Bill Barol, Steve Beard, David Belcher, Max Bell, Peter Blauner, Michael Bonner, Glenn Branca, Allen Brown, Peter Buck, Keith Cameron, Cath Carroll, Paul Carroll, Tom Carson, Chris Carter, David Cavanaugh, Robert Christgau, Jay Cocks, Scott Cohen, Mark Coleman, Jim Condon, J. D. Considine, Mark Cooper, Jonathan Cott, Richard Cromelin, Giovanni Dadomo, Stephen Dalton, Jim Derogatis, Dave DiMartino, Peter Doggett, Dan Durchholz, Ben Edmonds, Richard Fantina, Christian Fevret, Bill Flannagan, Emma Forrest, David Fricke, Stephen Gaines, Mikal Gilmore, Tony Glover, Danny Goldberg, Robert Greenfield, Paul Grein, Richard Guilliatt, John Harris, Richard Hattington, Martin Hayman, Gary Hill, Geoffrey Himes, David Hinkley, Brian Hogg, Stephen Holden, Scott Isler, Waldemar Januszczak, Betsey Johnson, Allan Jones, Cliff Jones, Nick Jones, Pat Kane,

Lenny Kaye, Mark Kemp, Nick Kent, Jim Koch, Marek Kohn, M. C. Kostek, Wayne Kramer, Jon Levin, Kurt Loder, Andrew Lycett, Jim Macnie, Jessie Mangaliman, Greil Marcus, Dave Marsh, Kenny Mathieson, Annalena McAfee, Ed McCormak, Adam McGovern, Wayne McGuire, Helen Mead, Lisa Mehlman, Milo Miles, Jim Miller, Phillip Milstein, Mike Nicholls, Jeff Nisin, Richard Nusser, Sean O'Hagan, Robert Palmer, Anastasia Pantsios, John Pareles, Sandy Pearlman, John Peel, John Piccarella, Steve Pond, Edwin Pouncey, Ann Powers, Lou Reed, Simon Reynolds, Allan Richards, Jonathan Richman, Lisa Robinson, Mick Rock, John Rockwell, Alex Ross, Robert Sandall, Ed Sanders, Mark Satlof, Jon Savage, Karen Schoemer, Robin Smith, Matt Snow, Jean Stein, Zan Stewart, John Strausbaugh, Caroline Sullivan, Barry Taylor, Ben Thompson, Nigel Trevena, James Walcott, Richard Walls, Peter Watrous, Michael Watts, Chris Welch, Kevin Westenberg, Daivd Wild, Jane Wilkes, Richard Williams, Simon Williams, Ellen Willis, Emma Willis, Tom Wilson, and Carlo Wolff.

They were published in *Advertising Age, Aquarian, Arena, Aspen, Bob, Chicago Sun-Times, Circus, Cover, Crawdaddy, Creem, Details, Entertainment Weekly, Esquire, Evening Standard, Evergreen Review, Forced Exposures, Freeport Leader, Fusion, GQ, Guardian, Guitar, Guitar World, High Times, Hit Parader, Independent, Interview, Jazz and Pop, Life, Little Caesar, Lonely Woman Quarterly, Los Angeles Free Press, Los Angeles Times, Ludd's Mill, Melody Maker, Mojo Penthouse, Musician, New Musical Express, Newsweek, New York, New York Newsday, New York Post, New York Rocker, New York Times, New York Times Magazine, New Yorker, Observer, Option, Partisan Review, People, Phonograph Record, Playboy, Pulse, Punch, Q, Rapid Eye, Record, Record Collector, Record Mirror, Reuters, Riverfront Times, Rock, Rolling Stone, Scene, Select, Smart, Sounds, Spin, Sunday Correspondent, Sunday Times, Tatler, Time, Time Out, Times, Trouser Press, USA Today, Utne Reader, Vanity Fair, Vibrations, Village Voice, VOX, Washington Post, Weekend Guardian, What Goes On: The Velvet Underground Appreciation Society Newsletter,* and *Wire.*

BIBLIOGRAPHY

INDISPENSABLE WERE THE NUMEROUS BOOKS ABOUT LOU REED, PARTICU-larly, *Between Thought and Expression: Selected Lyrics of Lou Reed* by Lou Reed (New York, Hyperion, 1991), *Beyond the Velvet Underground* by Dave Thompson (London, Omnibus Press, 1989), *Uptight: The Velvet Underground Story* by Victor Bockris and Gerard Malanga (London, Omnibus Press, 1983), *The Velvet Underground Handbook* by M. C. Kostek (London, Black Spring, 1992), *Lou Reed & the Velvet Underground* by Diana Clapton (London, Bobcat Books, 1987), and *Growing Up In Public* by Peter Doggett (London, Omnibus, 1991).

Other books include:

Abate, Anna, *Lou Reed: The Life, the Poems, and the Music of a Hero of American Rock*, Milan, Savelli Editori, 1980.

Albertoli, Carlo, *The Velvet Underground*, Rome, Redazione, 1993.

Alexander, Franz G. M. D., and Sheldon T. Selesnick, *The History of Psychiatry*, New York, Harper & Row, 1966.

Algren, Nelson, *A Walk on the Wild Side*, New York, Fawcett World Library, 1957.

Aquila, Richard, *That Old Time Rock and Roll: 1954–1963*, New York, Schirmer Books, 1989.

Artaud, Antonin, *The Theater and Its Double*, New York, Grove Press, 1958.

Atlas, James, *Delmore Schwartz: The Life of an American Poet*, New York, HBJ, 1977.

Bangs, Lester, *Psychotic Reactions and Carburetor Dung*, New York, Vintage Books, 1988.

Barkentin, Marjorie, *James Joyce's Ulysses in Nighttown*, New York, Modern Library, 1958.

Bellow, Saul, *Humbolt's Gift*, New York, Viking, 1973.

Bergerot, Frank, and Arnaud Merlin, *The Story of Jazz: Bop and Beyond*, New York, Harry N. Abrams, 1991.

Bockris, Victor, *The Life and Death of Andy Warhol*, London, Hutchinson, 1989.

Bockris, Victor, and William Burroughs, *With William Burroughs: A Report From the Bunker*, New York, Seaver Books, 1981.

Botts, Linda, *Loose Talk: The Book of Quotes From the Pages of Rolling Stone Magazine*, New York, Quick Fox Press, 1980.

Bourdon, David, *Andy Warhol*, New York, Harry Abrams, 1989.

Bowie, Angela, with Patrick Carr, *Backstage Passes: Life on the Wild Side with David Bowie*, New York, Putnam, 1993.

Bowman, Rob, and Jim Campbell, *Between Thought and Expression* (booklet to the Lou Reed Anthology Box Set), New York, BMG/RCA, 1993.

Broadman, Evan, *Social Guide to New York Bars*, New York, Collier, 1973.

Bruce, Lenny, *How to Talk Dirty and Influence People*, Chicago, Playboy Press, 1963.

Carducci, Joe, *Rock and the Pop Narcotic*, Chicago, Redoubt, 1990.

Carroll, Jim, *Forced Entries: The Downtown Diaries, 1971–1973*, New York, Penguin Books, 1987.

Chandler, Raymond, *The Lady in the Lake*, New York, Vintage, 1976.

Chandler, Raymond, *The Simple Art of Murder*, New York, Ballantine, 1972.

Chaplin, J. P., *Rumor, Fear and the Madness of Crowds*, New York, Ballantine Books, 1959.

Chapple, Steve, and Reebee Garofalo, *Rock 'n' Roll Is Here to Stay: The History and Politics of the Music Industry*, Chicago, Nelson Hall, 1977.

Charters, Ann, *The Portable Beat Reader*, New York, Viking, 1992.

Christgau, Robert, *Rock Albums of the Seventies*, New York, Da Capo, 1981.

Cohen, Harvey, *The Amphetamine Manifesto*, New York, Olympia Press, 1972.

Cohen, Stanley, *Dodgers! The First 100 Years*, New York, Carol Publishing, 1990.

Colacello, Bob, *Holy Terror: Andy Warhol Close Up*, New York, Harper Collins, 1990.

Coleridge, Samuel Taylor, *The Rime of the Ancient Mariner*, Van Goor Zonen Den Haag, 1965.

Crane, Paul, *Gays and the Law*, London, Pluto Press, 1982.

Davis, Clive, with James Willwerth, *Clive: Inside the Music Business*, New York, William Morrow, 1975.

Davis, Stephen, *Hammer of the Gods: The Led Zeppelin Saga*, New York, Ballantine, 1985.

de Grazia, Edward, *Girls Lean Back Everywhere: The Law of Obscenity and the Assault on Genius*, New York, Random House, 1992.

Denselow, Robert, *When the Music's Over: The Story of Political Pop*, London, Faber & Faber, 1989.

Diamant, Anita, and Howard Cooper, *Living a Jewish Life*, New York, Harper Perennial, 1991.

Dickson, Morris, *Gates of Eden: American Culture in the Sixties*, New York, Basic Books, 1967.

DiMucci, Dion, with Davin Seay, *The Wanderer: Dion's Story*, New York, William Morrow, 1988.

Duberman, Martin Bauml, *About Time: Exploring the Gay Past*, New York, Sea Horse, 1986.

Dunphy, Eamon, *Unforgettable Fire: The Story of U2*, London, Penguin, 1987.

Edelstein, Andrew J., and Kevin McDonough, *The Seventies: From Hot Pants to Hot Tubs*, New York, Dutton, 1990.

Edmiston, Susan, and Linda D. Cirino, *Literary New York: A History and Guide*, New York, Gibbs/Smith, 1991.

Ehret, Arnold, *Arnold Ehret's Rational Fasting*, New York, Benedict Lust Publications, 1971.

Ferlinghetti, Lawrence, *A Coney Island of the Mind*, New York, New Directions, 1958.

Finkelstein, Nat, *Andy Warhol: The Factory Years, 1964–1967*, New York, St. Martin's Press, 1989.

Flanagan, Bill, *Written in My Soul: Conversations with Rock's Great Songwriters*, Chicago, Contemporary Books, 1987.

Freeman, Gillian, *The Undergrowth of Literature*, London, Panther Books, 1968.

Frommer, Arthur, *New York: A Practical Guide to . . .* , New York, Frommer/ Pasmantier, 1964.

Goldman, Albert, *Ladies and Gentlemen, Lenny Bruce!* New York, 1974.

Goldman, Albert, *Sound Bites*, New York, Turtle Bay, 1992.

Goldman, Eric F., *The Crucial Decade and After: America, 1945–1960*, New York, Vintage, 1956.

Goldstein, Richard, *Goldstein's Greatest Hits: A Book Mostly about Rock and Roll*, New York, Tower Books, 1966.

Goldstein, Richard, *The Poetry of Rock*, New York, Bantam Books, 1969.

Gooch, Brad, *City Poet: The Life and Times of Frank O'Hara*, New York, Knopf, 1993.

Hadleigh, Boze, and Leonard Bernstein, *The Vinyl Closet: Gays in the Music World*, San Diego, Los Hombres Press, 1991.

Hardin, Evamaria, *Syracuse Landmarks*, Syracuse, Syracuse University Press, 1993.

Hemphill, Paul, *The Nashville Sound: Bright Lights and Country Music*, New York, Pocket Books, 1971.

Henry, Tricia, *Break All Rules! Punk Rock and the Making of a Style*, Ann Arbor, UMI Research Press, 1989.

Herman, Gary, *Rock and Roll Babylon*, London, Plexus, 1982.

Hester, John, *Soho Is My Parish*, London, Lutterworth Press, 1970.

Hewison, Robert, *Too Much: Art and Society in the Sixties, 1960–1975*, New York, Oxford University Press, 1987.

Heylin, Clinton, *From the Velvets to the Voidoids: A Pre-Punk History for a Post-Punk World*, London, Penguin, 1992.

Heylin, Clinton, ed., *The Penguin Book of Rock and Roll Writing*, New York, Viking, 1992.

Hopkins, Jerry, *Bowie*, New York, Macmillan, 1985.

Hutchinson, Larry, *Rock and Roll Songwriter's Handbook*, New York, Scholastic, 1972.

Joyce, James, *Ulysses*, New York, Random House, 1990.

Kavan, Anna, *Asylum Piece*, New York, Michael Kesend Publishing, 1981.

Kavan, Anna, *Julia and the Bazooka*, London, P. Owen, 1970.

Kelly, Kitty, *His Way: The Unauthorized Biography of Frank Sinatra*, New York, Bantam Books, 1986.

Kessey, Ken, *One Flew Over the Cuckoo's Nest*, New York, New American Library, 1962.

Knight, G. Wilson, *The Wheel of Fire: Interpretations of Shakespearean Tragedy*, Oxford, Oxford University Press, 1930.

Koch, Stephen, *Stargazer: The Life, World and Films of Andy Warhol*, New York, Marion Boyars, 1973.

Koestenbaum, Wayne, *Double Talk: The Erotics of Male Literary Collaboration*, New York, Routledge, 1989.

Kostelanetz, Richard, *The Theatre of Mixed Means*, New York, Dial Press, 1968.

Krassner, Paul, *Confessions of a Raving Unconfined Nut and Misadventures in the Counter-Culture*, New York, Simon & Schuster, 1993.

Lait, Jack, and Lee Mortimer, *New York: Confidential*, New York, Dell, 1951.

Lazell, Barry, *Rock Movers and Shakers*, New York, Billboard Publications, 1989.

Lehmann, John, *Three Literary Friendships*, New York, Quarter Books, 1983.

Leigh, Michael, *The Velvet Underground*, New York, McFadden, 1963.

Lindesmith, Alfred R., *The Addict and the Law*, New York, Vintage Books, 1965.

Litweiler, John, *Ornette Coleman: A Harmolodic Life*, New York, William Morrow, 1992.

Loder, Kurt, *Bat Chain Puller: Rock and Roll in the Age of Celebrity*, New York, St. Martin's Press, 1990.

MacInnes, Colin, *Loving Them Both: A Study of Bisexuality and Bisexuals*, London, Martin Brian & Okeeffe, 1973.

Malina, Judith, *The Diaries of Judith Malina: 1947–1957*, New York, Grove Press, 1984.

Margolis, Dr. Isadr, And Rabbi Sidney L. Markowitz, *Jewish Holidays and Festivals*, New York, Citadel, 1990.

Marsh, Dave, *Rock & Roll Confidential*, New York, Pantheon, 1985.

Matlock, Glen, with Pete Silverton, *I Was a Teenage Sex Pistol*, London, Faber & Faber, 1990.

McLuhan, Marshal, and Quentin Fiore, *The Medium Is the Massage: An Inventory of Effects*, New York, Bantam Books, 1967.

McShine, Kynaston, *Andy Warhol: A Retrospective*, New York, Museum of Modern Art, 1989.

Meltzer, Richard, *Gulcher: Post-Rock Cultural Pluralism in America 1964–1993*, New York, Citadel Press, 1993.

Miles, *David Bowie: Black Book*, London, Omnibus Press, 1980.

Miles, Barry, *Words & Music—Lou Reed*, London, Wise Publications, 1980.

Miller, Alice, *The Drama of the Gifted Child*, New York, Basic Books, 1981.

Mottram, Eric, *Blood on the Nash Ambassador*, London, Hutchinson Radius, 1983.

Murray, Charles Shaar, *Shots from the Hip*, London, Penguin Books, 1991.

Nietzsche, Friedrich, *Twilight of the Idols/The Anti-Christ*, New York, Penguin, 1978.

Peelaert, Guy, and Nik Cohn, *Rock Dream: Rock and Roll for Your Eyes*, New York, R&B, 1982.

Perelman, S. J., *The Last Laugh*, New York, Simon & Schuster, 1981.

Platt, John, Chris Dreja, and Jim McCarthy, *Yardbirds*, London, Sidgwick & Jackson, 1983.

Poe, Edgar Allan, *Selected Stories and Poems*, New York, Airmont, 1962.

Pynchon, Thomas, *The Crying of Lot 49*, London, Picador, 1966.

Ragni, Gerome, and James Rado, *Hair*, New York, Pocket Books, 1969.

Reed, Lou, *Lou Reed: Words and Music*, New York, Warner Publications, 1991.

Reed, Lou, *Velvet Underground: Lyrics*, Milan, Arcana Editrice, 1982.

Research Inc., *Incredibly Strange Music*, San Francisco, Research Publications, 1993.

Ribowsky, Mark, *He's a Rebel: The Truth About Phil Spector—Rock and Roll's Legendary Madman*, New York, Dutton, 1989.

Rinzler, Alan, *The New York Spy*, New York, David White, 1967.

Rivelli, Pauline, and Robert Levin, *Giants of Rock Music*, New York, Da Capo, 1981.

Rock, Mick, *Ziggy Stardust: Bowie 1972/1973*, New York, St. Martin's Press, 1984.

Rolling Stone, *The Rolling Stone Illustrated History of Rock and Roll*, New York, Rolling Stone Press, 1976.

Rolling Stone, *The Rolling Stone Rock Almanac*, New York, Collier Books, 1983.

Roszak, Theodore, *The Making of a Counter Culture*, New York, Anchor Books, 1969.

Santoli, Al, *Everything We Had: An Oral History of the Viet Nam War . . .* , New York, Ballantine, 1981.

Savage, Jon, *England's Dreaming*, New York, St. Martin's Press, 1992.

Schwartz, Delmore, *In Dreams Begin Responsibilities and Other Stories*, New York, New Directions, 1978.

Schwartz, Delmore, *Summer Knowledge: Selected Poems (1938–1958)*, New York, New Directions, 1967.

Selby Jr., Hubert, *Last Exit to Brooklyn*, New York, Grove Press, 1957.

Shakespeare, William, *Hamlet*, New York, Washington Square Press, 1957.

Smith, Joe, *Off the Record: An Oral History of Popular Music*, New York, Warner, 1988.

Smith, Patrick S., *Andy Warhol's Art and Films*, Ann Arbor, UMI, 1986.

Smith, Patrick S., *Warhol: Conversations About the Artist*, Ann Arbor, UMI, 1988.

Smith, Patrick S., "Art in Extremis: Andy Warhol and His Art," 3 vols., Ph.D. dissertation, Northwestern University, Evanston, Illinois, 1982. (A shortened version was published in 1986 by UMI Research Press, Michigan, as *Andy Warhol's Art and Films*.)

Somma, Robert, *No One Waved Goodbye: A Casualty Report on Rock and Roll*, London, Charisma Books, 1973.

Spoto, Donald, *Lenya: A Life*, Boston, Little, Brown, 1989.

Stallings, Penny, *Rock and Roll Confidential*, Boston, Little, Brown, 1984.

Stein, Jean, edited with George Plimpton, *Edie: An American Biography*, New York, Alfred A. Knopf, 1982.

Stevenson, Ray, *The Sex Pistols File*, London, Omnibus, 1978.

Swados, Elizabeth, *The Four of Us*, New York, Plume, 1993.

Symons, Julian, *The Tell-Tale Heart: The Life and Works of Edgar Allan Poe*, London, Faber & Faber, 1978.

Szatmary, David P., *Rockin' in Time: A Social History of Rock and Roll*, New York, Prentice Hall, 1991.

Thomas, Donald, *The Marquis De Sade: A New Biography*, New York, Citadel, 1993.

Thompson, Hunter S., *Fear and Loathing in Las Vegas*, New York, Popular Library, 1971.

Time, Inc., *Time Capsule/1968*, New York, Time Life Books, 1968.

Tosches, Nick, *Hellfire: The Jerry Lee Lewis Story*, New York, Delacorte, 1982.

Tosches, Nick, *Unsung Heroes of Rock and Roll*, New York, Scribner's, 1984.

Tracy, Jack, with Jim Berkey, *Subcutaneously, My Dear Watson*, Bloomington, James A. Rock, 1978.

Tynan, Kenneth, *Oh! Calcutta!* New York, Grove Press, 1969.

Violet, Ultra, *Famous for Fifteen Minutes—My Years With Andy Warhol*, New York, HBJ, 1988.

Viva, *Superstar*, New York, Putnam, 1970.

Warhol, Andy, A., New York, Grove Press, 1968.

Warhol, Andy, edited by Pat Hackett, *The Andy Warhol Diaries*, New York, Warner Books, 1989.

Warhol, Andy, *Andy Warhol's Index Book*, New York, Random House, 1967.

Warhol, Andy, *The Philosophy of Andy Warhol*, New York, HBJ, 1975.

Warhol, Andy, and Pat Hackett, *Popism: The Warhol 60s*, New York, HBJ, 1980.

White, E. B., *Here Is New York*, New York, Harper & Brothers, 1949.

White, Theodore H., *The Making of the President: 1964*, New York, Signet, 1965.

Wilcock, John, with a Cast of Thousands, *The Autobiography & Sex Life of Andy Warhol*, New York, Other Scenes, Inc., 1971.

Wilson, Colin, *The Occult: A History*, New York, Random House, 1971.

Witts, Richard, *Nico: The Life and Lies of an Icon*, London, Virgin Publications, 1993.

Woodlawn, Holly, with Jeff Copeland, *A Low Life in High Heels: The Holly Woodlawn Story*, New York, St. Martin's Press, 1991.

Wrenn, Mike, *Andy Warhol in His Own Words*, London, Omnibus Press, 1991.

Young, James, *Songs They Never Play on the Radio: Nico, the Last Bohemian*, London, Bloomsbury, 1993.

Zappa, Frank, with Peter Occhiogrosso, *The Real Frank Zappa Book*, New York, Poseidon Press, 1989.

Every attempt has been made to track down the original sources of this book. If anybody whose work is quoted herein is not mentioned above, the author apologizes and would be glad to rectify the mistake.

INDEX
